Costa Rica

FOR

DUMMIES

1ST EDITION

by Eliot Greenspan

Brad —
Have a wonderful trip.

Be Safe !

Love
Mom
2016

WILEY

Wiley Publishing, Inc.

Costa Rica For Dummies®, 1st Edition
Published by
Wiley Publishing, Inc.
111 River St.
Hoboken, NJ 07030-5774
www.wiley.com

WILEY

About the Author

Eliot Greenspan is a poet, journalist, and travel writer who took his backpack and typewriter the length of Mesoamerica before settling in Costa Rica in 1992. Since then, he has worked steadily as a travel writer, freelance journalist, and translator, and continued his travels in the region. This is Eliot's first *For Dummies* title. He is also the author of *Frommer's Costa Rica, Frommer's Belize, Frommer's Cuba,* and *The Tico Times Restaurant Guide to Costa Rica,* as well as the chapter on Venezuela in *Frommer's South America.*

Dedication

I'd like to dedicate this book to Allen Ginsberg, Fielding Dawson, and Jane Faigao — three dear friends and teachers whom I treasure and miss.

Author's Acknowledgments

Here's to all the industry insiders, longtime locals, and everyday tourists, whose thoughts and impressions add immeasurably to my own wanderings, adventures, test runs, and site inspections. I'd also like to thank my editor Jennifer Reilly.

Publisher's Acknowledgments

We're proud of this book; please send us your comments through our Dummies online registration form located at www.dummies.com/register/.

Note: Swimming with dolphins has its critics and supporters. You may want to visit the Whale and Dolphins Conservation Society's website at www.wdcs.org. For more information about responsible travel in general, check out these websites: Tread Lightly (www.treadlightly.org) and the International Ecotourism Society (www.ecotourism.org).

Some of the people who helped bring this book to market include the following:

Editorial

Editors: Elizabeth Kuball, Project Editor; Jennifer Reilly, Development Editor; and M. Faunette Johnston, Production Editor

Copy Editor: Elizabeth Kuball

Cartographer: Antony Crane

Editorial Manager: Michelle Hacker

Editorial Coordinator: Carmen Krikorian

Editorial Assistant: Nadine Bell

Senior Photo Editor: Richard Fox

Cover Photos: Front Cover Photo: © Monteverde Clamer/Getty Images; Back Cover Photo: © Gary Neil Corbett/SuperStock, Inc.

Cartoons: Rich Tennant (www.the5thwave.com)

Composition Services

Project Coordinator: Kristie Rees

Layout and Graphics: Lauren Goddard, Barbara Moore, Heather Ryan, Julie Trippetti

Proofreaders: Leeann Harney, Jessica Kramer, TECHBOOKS Production Services

Indexer: TECHBOOKS Production Services

Publishing and Editorial for Consumer Dummies

Diane Graves Steele, Vice President and Publisher, Consumer Dummies

Joyce Pepple, Acquisitions Director, Consumer Dummies

Kristin A. Cocks, Product Development Director, Consumer Dummies

Michael Spring, Vice President and Publisher, Travel

Kelly Regan, Editorial Director, Travel

Publishing for Technology Dummies

Andy Cummings, Vice President and Publisher, Dummies Technology/General User

Composition Services

Gerry Fahey, Vice President of Production Services

Debbie Stailey, Director of Composition Services

Contents at a Glance

Maps at a Glance

Table of Contents

Chapter 21: Chilling on Costa Rica's Caribbean Coast...322

Introduction

● ●

Costa Rica is hot. And I'm not just talking about its sun-drenched beaches and steamy jungles. Costa Rica is the hottest new vacation destination in the Americas.

It's easy to see why. Aside from those sun-drenched beaches and steamy jungles, Costa Rica has a wealth of attractions and adventures to please a wide range of travelers. Whether you're a family looking for something new, a snow bunny seeking a winter break, or an avid naturalist itching to delve into the wonderful world of the tropical rain forest, there's a Costa Rican vacation waiting just for you.

This book makes planning that vacation easy. Instead of an endless list with encyclopedic entries, this book focuses on the best that Costa Rica has to offer.

About This Book

Costa Rica For Dummies is a concise and precise guide to the top vacation options in Costa Rica. I've done the legwork for you and weeded out the unnecessary and overrated. I've tried to anticipate your every question, without bogging you down with superfluous details.

This book gives honest and accurate descriptions of Costa Rica's various hotels, restaurants, and attractions. I'm not afraid to take a stand to help you decide what to include in your Costa Rican vacation — and, even more important, what *not* to include.

There's no one single answer, or one single vacation, for everybody. This book, however, helps you narrow your choices, no matter what your budget or interests.

Feel free to skip around or skip certain sections altogether. Use the indexes and table of contents — and the brief intro that I include here — to zero in and find the information most important to help you plan and enjoy a perfect vacation.

Please be advised that travel information is subject to change at any time — and this is especially true of prices. You may want to write or call ahead for confirmation when making your travel plans.

Dummies Post-it® Flags

As you're reading this book, you'll find information that you'll want to reference as you plan or enjoy your trip — whether it be a new hotel, a must-see attraction, or a must-try walking tour. Mark these pages with the handy Post-it® Flags included in this book to help make your trip planning easier!

Conventions Used in This Book

In this book, hotels and restaurants are listed alphabetically with actual prices and frank evaluations. I include lists of hotels, restaurants, and attractions. As I describe each one, I often include abbreviations for commonly accepted credit cards. Take a look at the following list for an explanation of each card:

AE: American Express

DC: Diners Club

MC: MasterCard

V: Visa

I also include some general pricing information to help you as you decide where to unpack your bags or dine on the local cuisine. I've used a system of dollar signs to show a range of costs for one night in a hotel (double occupancy) or a full meal for one at a restaurant (included in the cost of each meal is soup or salad, an entree, a dessert, and a nonalcoholic drink). Check out the following table to decipher the dollar signs:

Cost	Hotel	Restaurant
$	Less than $75	Less than $10
$$	$75–$125	$10–$20
$$$	$126–$200	$21–$30
$$$$	$201–$350	$31–$45
$$$$$	More than $350	More than $45

The dollar-sign ratings allow you to make quick comparisons of the costs of various establishments. However, I also list specific and detailed pricing information in every listing.

Throughout this book I use the exchange rate of 470 colones to the U.S. dollar. However, the Costa Rican colón is in a steady rate of devaluation. To check the very latest exchange rates before you leave home, point your browser to www.xe.com/ucc.

For those hotels, restaurants, and attractions that are plotted on a map, a page reference is provided in the listing information. If a hotel, restaurant, or attraction is outside the city limits or in an out-of-the-way area, it may not be mapped.

Foolish Assumptions

As I wrote this book, I made some assumptions about you and what your needs as a traveler may be. Here's what I assumed about you:

✔ You may be an experienced traveler who hasn't had much time to explore Costa Rica and wants expert advice when you finally do get a chance to enjoy the country.

✔ You may be an inexperienced traveler looking for guidance when determining whether to take a trip to Costa Rica and how to plan for it.

✔ You're not looking for a book that provides all the information available about Costa Rica or that lists every hotel, restaurant, or attraction available to you. Instead, you're looking for a book that focuses on the places that will give you the best or most unique experiences in Costa Rica.

If you fit any of these criteria, then *Costa Rica For Dummies* gives you the information you're looking for!

How This Book Is Organized

Costa Rica For Dummies contains eight parts. Parts I and II provide the nuts-and-bolts information to help you choose where and when to go and plan your trip. Parts III, IV, V, VI, and VII give detailed information on the best hotels, restaurants, and attractions to be found at the various destinations across Costa Rica. Part VIII provides some quick and clear final recommendations and important facts.

Part I: Introducing Costa Rica

This first part gives you an overview of what Costa Rica is all about, so you can get psyched about all the fun that lies ahead. It includes a general overview of the various destinations and attractions and helps you decide what spots you can skip and what spots you should just not miss. This part includes

✔ An easy-to-scan list of the very best of the best — my personal picks of Costa Rica's top hotels, nature lodges, restaurants, beaches, adventures, and more

✔ A quick look into Costa Rica's history, culture, and cuisine

- An introduction to the different regions and destinations in Costa Rica

- Straightforward advice on how to budget your time and decide where to visit

- The scoop on the seasons and when to go

- Five detailed itineraries to help you envision and begin planning your own perfect vacation

Part II: Planning Your Trip to Costa Rica

In this part, I get down to the serious trip preparation, including:

- How much you can expect your trip to cost and how to save on costs no matter what your budget is

- The pros and cons of planning your trip on your own, using a travel agent, and buying an all-inclusive package deal

- The real deal on how to get to Costa Rica and how to get around the country after you arrive

- Special considerations for families, seniors, travelers with disabilities, and gay and lesbian travelers

- Detailed information for couples who want a perfect tropical wedding

Part III: San José and the Central Valley

This part covers Costa Rica's capital city, San José, and its environs. A vast majority of visitors to Costa Rica spend some time in San José, whether as a transportation hub or as an initial base for their trip. This part tells you all you need to know about settling in and dining in style in San José and the surrounding Central Valley. It also includes advice on must-see attractions and exciting day trips.

Part IV: Guanacaste and Environs

This part primarily deals with Costa Rica's "Gold Coast," the beaches of the northwestern province of Guanacaste. This part delves into a variety of beach towns and destinations, with recommendations for everything from small boutique hotels to large, full-scale resorts. It also describes the many tour and adventure options available in Guanacaste, including side trips to the inland Rincón de la Vieja National Park.

Part V: Manuel Antonio and Environs

This part explores Costa Rica's most popular ecotourism destination, the lovely Manuel Antonio National Park. It also covers the surrounding Central Pacific coast, both north and south of Manuel Antonio, touching on the beach destinations of playas Jacó, Herradura, and Hermosa, as well as Dominical.

Part VI: Monteverde and Environs

Monteverde, with its misty cloud forests, and Arenal, with its active volcano, are Costa Rica's principal inland attractions. This part covers both
of these major attractions, while also introducing you to the area surrounding Lake Arenal. You'll find ample information about nature hikes,
rafting trips, volcano viewing, hot springs, and more in this rich region.

Part VII: Touring the Rest of Costa Rica

In this part, I cover some of the farther flung and less visited — although
no less spectacular or interesting — Costa Rican destinations. This part
features information, recommendations, and planning advice for trips
to the remote beach destinations of the southern Nicoya peninsula,
the lush rain forests of southern Costa Rica, and the country's unique
Caribbean coast.

Part VIII: The Part of Tens

Every *For Dummies* book has a Part of Tens. These three fun and pithy
chapters are a little gift to you. Chapter 22 dispels some common myths
and misconceptions about Costa Rica. Chapter 23 provides a concise list
of some of the top experiences, attractions, and activities to be had in
this beautiful country.

In back of this book I've included an appendix — your Quick Concierge —
containing lots of handy information you may need when traveling in
Costa Rica. This one-stop reference section includes important phone
numbers and Web addresses, as well as the inside scoop on issues
running from safety to water quality. Check out this appendix when
searching for answers to lots of little questions that may come up as
you plan or travel. You can find the Quick Concierge easily because it's
printed on yellow paper.

Icons Used in This Book

Think of the following icons as signposts. I use them to highlight especially useful advice, to draw your attention to things you won't want to
miss, and to introduce a variety of topics.

 Keep an eye out for the Bargain Alert icon as you seek out money-saving
tips and/or great deals.

 The Best of the Best icon highlights the best the destination has to offer
in all categories — hotels, restaurants, attractions, activities, shopping,
and nightlife.

 Watch for the Heads Up icon to identify annoying or potentially dangerous situations such as tourist traps, unsafe neighborhoods, budgetary
rip-offs, and other things to beware.

Find out useful advice on things to do and ways to schedule your time when you see the Tip icon.

Look to the Kid Friendly icon for attractions, hotels, restaurants, and activities that are particularly hospitable to children or people traveling with kids.

This icon points out secret little finds or useful resources that are worth the extra bit of effort to get to or track down.

Where to Go from Here

A Costa Rican vacation can be many things to many people. Options range from bird-watching and rain-forest hiking, to high-octane adventuring, to simply settling into a chaise lounge on a quiet beach and sipping cool cocktails.

Don't think of choosing your Costa Rican destinations and solidifying the details as a burden or bore. Let this book help make the process an exciting time of discovery and opportunity. Enjoy and savor the planning. And then, have a great trip!

Part I
Introducing Costa Rica

The 5th Wave   By Rich Tennant

"He said this was the first thing he wanted to do when he got to Costa Rica."

In this part . . .

So you want to begin finding out about Costa Rica? In this part you'll find all the basic information you need to start planning a perfect vacation particularly suited to your needs and interests.

Chapter 1 tells you briefly about the best places, experiences, and attractions in Costa Rica. You'll find much more information and detailed descriptions later on, but this is the place to come to for a condensed listing of the highlights. If you want some historical background, cultural insight, or local language tips, Chapter 2 offers that up, and more.

Chapter 3 describes the various regions and destinations to help you choose where to go. In addition, this is the place to go to find out about the local weather patterns and seasons, and some interesting Costa Rican holidays, celebrations, and events. Finally, Chapter 4 lays out several potential itineraries that you can either follow to the letter, or use as a rough draft in designing your perfect trip to Costa Rica.

Chapter 1

Discovering the Best of Costa Rica

In This Chapter

▶ Scoping out Costa Rica's top accommodations

▶ Finding the finest restaurants

▶ Exploring the best beaches, adventures, and attractions

*F*or such a small country, Costa Rica is a rich and varied destination. You can visit rain forests, cloud forests, and active volcanoes. You can walk along miles of beautiful beaches on either the Pacific or the Caribbean coast. And, you can stay at luxurious large resorts or romantic boutique getaways.

Adventure hounds will have their fill choosing from an exciting array of activities, and those just looking for some rest and relaxation can grab a chaise lounge and a good book.

 This chapter is designed as an at-a-glance reference to the absolute "best of the best" that Costa Rica has to offer. These attractions are highlighted by — what else — a Best of the Best icon when they appear elsewhere in this book.

The Best High-End Hotels and Luxury Resorts

As recently as five years ago, finding anything to fit in this category was difficult. Not any longer. Costa Rica now boasts quite a few top-notch luxury properties ranging from isolated and unique boutique hotels to large beach resorts. The following are the best of the best:

✔ **Costa Rica Marriott (San José):** The Marriott is hands down the best of the large resort and business class hotels in the San José area. Everything is in great shape, the service is bend-over-backward, the restaurants are excellent, and the hotel features all the facilities and amenities you could want, save a golf course. See Chapter 11.

✔ **Peace Lodge (north of Varablanca):** The rooms here abound in beautiful design touches, and the bathrooms in the deluxe units are the most spectacular in the country. Each room comes with at least one custom-tiled Jacuzzi on a private balcony. The hotel adjoins the popular La Paz Waterfall Gardens. See Chapter 11.

✔ **Four Seasons Resort (Papagayo Peninsula):** This is the first major resort to really address the ultra-high-end luxury market in Costa Rica. Within its first month of operation, both Madonna and Michael Jordan were notable guests. A beautiful setting, wonderful installations, world-class golf course, and stellar service make this the current king of the hill in the upscale market. See Chapter 13.

✔ **Paradisus Playa Conchal (Playa Conchal):** This large and luxurious all-inclusive resort has all the trappings, including an 18-hole Robert Trent Jones golf course. As a bonus, it's located on the beautiful seashell-strewn wonder of Playa Conchal. See Chapter 13.

✔ **Makanda by the Sea (Manuel Antonio):** The large and luxurious villas here are superbly decorated and set on a forested hillside with wonderful views out to the sea. The overall vibe here is intimate and romantic, and the service and food are excellent. See Chapter 15.

✔ **Villa Caletas (north of Jacó):** Spread out over a steep hillside, high above the Pacific Ocean, these large and luxurious individual villas have a Mediterranean feel. The "infinity pool" here was one of the first in Costa Rica and is still my favorite. Sitting in a lounge chair at the pool's edge, you'll swear that it joins the sea. See Chapter 16.

✔ **Hotel Punta Islita (Nicoya Peninsula):** Perched on a high, flat bluff overlooking the Pacific Ocean, Punta Islita is very popular with honeymooners, and rightly so. The rooms are large and luxurious, the food is excellent, and the setting is stunning. If you venture beyond your room and the hotel's inviting hillside pool, there's a long, almost always deserted beach for you to explore, as well as a wealth of activities for the more adventurous. See Chapter 19.

✔ **Flor Blanca Resort (Playa Santa Teresa):** The individual villas at this boutique resort are some of the largest and most beautiful in the country. The service and food are outstanding, and the location is breathtaking, spread over a lushly planted hillside just steps off Playa Santa Teresa. See Chapter 19.

The Best Accommodations Values

Not looking to spend a fortune? No problem. Costa Rica is chock-full of excellent hotel and lodging values. Get the most for your accommodations dollar by booking into one of these fine establishments:

✔ **Hotel Grano de Oro (San José):** San José boasts dozens of old homes that have been converted into hotels, but few offer the luxurious accommodations or professional service that can be found at the Grano de Oro. See Chapter 11.

✔ **Hotel Le Bergerac (San José):** This classy little hotel has been pleasing diplomats, dignitaries, and other discerning travelers for years. Ask for one of the garden rooms, or get the old master bedroom with its small private balcony. See Chapter 11.

✔ **Villas Nicolás (Manuel Antonio):** Most of the spacious, separate units here feature large, private balconies or terraces with classic views over the rain forest to the sea at a fraction of the cost of most other Manuel Antonio hotels offering similar views. See Chapter 15.

✔ **Villa del Sueño Hotel (Playa Hermosa):** It's not right on the beach (you'll have to walk about 90m/295 ft.), but everything else about this place is right on the money, including clean, comfortable rooms; an inviting refreshing pool; and an excellent restaurant. You can't find a better deal in Playa Hermosa. See Chapter 13.

✔ **Hotel El Sapo Dorado (Monteverde):** Roomy wooden cabins with fireplaces and private porches are spread across an open hillside planted with fruit trees and tropical flowers. The hotel has an excellent restaurant and is a great place to enjoy some of the best sunsets in town. See Chapter 17.

✔ **Amor de Mar (Montezuma):** The rooms here are simple, but they are also clean, comfortable, and well-maintained. And the setting is superb. A long grassy lawn leads down to the rocky coast, where you'll find a swimming-pool-sized tide pool carved into a coral rock outcropping. See Chapter 19.

✔ **Azania Bungalows (Playa Cocles):** This place features large and lovely private wooden bungalows spread around lush grounds. Just 90m (295 ft.) or so away, however, are the warm waves of the Caribbean Sea. See Chapter 21.

The Best Ecolodges

Costa Rica is a major ecotourism destination, and you'll find a wealth of wonderfully run ecolodges and nature resorts. Some of them, including several listed here, make a strong case for being listed among the top luxury hotels in the country.

✔ **Arenal Observatory Lodge (La Fortuna):** Originally a rustic research facility, this lodge has upgraded quite a bit over the years and now features comfortable rooms with impressive views of the Arenal volcano. There are also excellent trails to nearby lava flows and a beautiful waterfall. Toucans frequent the trees near the lodge, and howler monkeys provide the wake-up calls. See Chapter 18.

✔ **La Paloma Lodge (Drake Bay):** If your idea of the perfect nature lodge is one where your front porch provides some prime-time viewing of flora and fauna, this place is for you. If you decide to leave the comfort of your porch, the Osa Peninsula's lowland rain forests are just outside your door. See Chapter 20.

✔ **Bosque del Cabo Rainforest Lodge (Osa Peninsula):** Large and comfortable private cabins perched on the edge of a cliff overlooking the Pacific Ocean and surrounded by lush rain forest make this one of my favorite spots in the country. There's plenty to do, and there are always great guides here. See Chapter 20.

✔ **Lapa Rios (Osa Peninsula):** Costa Rica's first upscale ecolodge has aged well. The duplex bungalow rooms all have spectacular views and are set into a lush forest. A number of tours are available for guests, and the guides are often local residents who are intimately familiar with the environment. See Chapter 20.

✔ **Corcovado Lodge Tent Camp (Osa Peninsula):** Located right on the border of Corcovado National Park, the accommodations here are in spacious individual tents set within walking distance of the crashing surf. The whole operation is run by the very dependable and experienced Costa Rica Expeditions. See Chapter 20.

✔ **Playa Nicuesa Rainforest Lodge (Golfo Dulce):** This new lodge is by far the best option on the Golfo Dulce. Set in deep forest, the individual bungalows here are a beguiling blend of rusticity and luxury. See Chapter 20.

✔ **Selva Bananito Lodge (inland from the Caribbean coast):** This is one of the few lodges providing direct access to the southern Caribbean lowland rain forests. There's no electricity here, but that doesn't mean it's not plush. Hike along a riverbed, ride horses through the rain forest, climb 30m (100 ft.) up a ceiba tree, or rappel down a jungle waterfall. See Chapter 21.

The Best Restaurants

Although Costa Rica is not known for its fine food, you'll have no trouble dining well. The following restaurants run the gamut in terms of cuisine and ambience, from local fresh seafood served on plastic lawn chairs set in the sand to top-notch Pacific-Rim fusion served in an elegant and refined setting. If your travels take you near any of these, don't pass up the chance for a meal:

✔ **Bakea (San José):** The creative and varied décor of this rambling old colonial home, coupled with the excellent fusion cuisine coming out of the kitchen, makes this one of the top restaurants in the city. See Chapter 11.

✔ **Grano de Oro Restaurant (San José):** This elegant little hotel has a similarly elegant restaurant serving delicious Continental dishes and decadent desserts. The open-air seating in the lushly planted central courtyard is delightful, especially for lunch. See Chapter 11.

✔ **Camarón Dorado (Playa Brasilito):** Simple, fresh seafood served on plastic lawn furniture set in the sand just steps from the crashing waves makes this place a wonderful spot. The attentive, semiformal service makes it even better. See Chapter 13.

✔ **La Laguna del Cocodrillo (Tamarindo):** The newest high-end fusion restaurant to hit the scene in Tamarindo is so far the best. The atmosphere is casually elegant, and the dishes are downright delicious. See Chapter 13.

✔ **Sunspot Bar & Grill (Manuel Antonio):** The menu changes regularly at this elegant restaurant housed under canvas tents poolside at one of Manuel Antonio's top hotels. There are precious few tables here, so be sure to reserve in advance. See Chapter 15.

✔ **Ginger (Playa Hermosa):** Serving an eclectic mix of traditional and Pan-Asian-influenced tapas, this sophisticated little joint is taking this part of Guanacaste by storm. Ginger even has a list of creative cocktails to match the inventive dishes. See Chapter 13.

✔ **Sophia (Monteverde):** This new place serves excellent Latin fusion fare in an intimate setting about halfway along the rough dirt road between Santa Elena and the Monteverde Cloud Forest Preserve. See Chapter 17.

✔ **Nectar (at Flor Blanca Resort, Santa Teresa):** Guanacaste's best boutique resort also has one of its best restaurants. The menu changes nightly but always has a heavy Pan-Asian fusion flavor to it. The setting is romantic and subdued in an open-air space just steps from the sand. See Chapter 19.

✔ **La Pecora Nera (Puerto Viejo):** I'm not sure that a tiny surfer town on the remote Caribbean coast deserves such fine Italian food, but it's got it. Your best bet here is to allow yourself to be taken on a culinary roller-coaster ride with a mixed feast of the chef's nightly specials and suggestions. See Chapter 21.

The Best Beaches

With more than 1,200km (750 miles) of shoreline on its Pacific and Caribbean coasts, Costa Rica offers beachgoers an embarrassment of riches.

✔ **Playa Tamarindo:** Although it's on the verge of becoming a little too overdeveloped, crowded, and chaotic, Tamarindo is still one of Costa Rica's best beaches. Tamarindo has ample lodgings to suit every budget, as well as excellent restaurants at almost every turn. The beach here is long and broad, with sections calm enough for swimmers and others just right for surfers. Located about midway along the beaches of Guanacaste province, Tamarindo also has one of the liveliest nightlife scenes on this coast. See Chapters 13 and 14.

✔ **Playa Nacascolo:** This narrow band of soft white sand is a rare treasure on this coast, which is typified by coarser, darker sand beaches. Although it's within the grounds of the massive Four Seasons Resort, it's public property and open to all. See Chapter 14.

✔ **Playa Manuel Antonio:** Costa Rica's original rain-forest-meets-beach destination retains its charms despite burgeoning crowds and mushrooming hotels. The beaches inside the national park are idyllic, and the views from the hills outside the park are enchanting. This is one of the few remaining habitats for the endangered squirrel monkey. See Chapter 15.

✔ **Playa Montezuma:** This little beach town at the southern tip of the Nicoya Peninsula has weathered fame and infamy and yet retains a funky sense of individuality. The nearby waterfalls are what set it apart from the competition, but the beach stretches for miles, with plenty of isolated spots to plop down your towel or mat. Also nearby are the Cabo Blanco and Curu wildlife preserves. See Chapter 19.

✔ **Malpaís:** If you're looking to visit Costa Rica's newest hot spot before the throngs discover it, head out to Malpaís. Here you'll find miles of nearly deserted beaches, great surf, and just a smattering of lodges, surf camps, and simple *cabinas*. If Malpaís is too crowded for you, head farther on down the road to Santa Teresa, Playa Hermosa, or Manzanillo. See Chapter 19.

✔ **Punta Uva and Manzanillo:** Below Puerto Viejo, the beaches of Costa Rica's eastern coast take on true Caribbean splendor, with turquoise waters, coral reefs, and palm-lined stretches of nearly deserted white-sand beach. Punta Uva and Manzanillo are the two most sparkling gems of this coastline. Tall coconut palms line the shore, providing shady respite for those who like to spend a full day on the sand, and the water is usually quite calm and good for swimming. See Chapter 21.

The Best Adventures and Activities

Costa Rica is a top-notch destination for adventure travel. The options and activities are many. Here are some of the best activities and adventures awaiting you:

✔ **Rafting the Pacuare River (near Turrialba):** This class III and IV river passes through primary and secondary forests and a beautiful steep gorge that, sadly, might be dammed soon. Get there quick! **Ríos Tropicales** can take you on this river. See Chapter 12.

✔ **Surfing Guanacaste Province:** This northwestern province has dozens of respectable beach and reef breaks, from Witch's Rock up near the Nicaraguan border to Playa Nosara more than 100km

(62 miles) away. In addition to these two prime spots, try a turn at **Playa Grande** and **playas Negra** and **Avellanas.** Or, find your own secret spot. Rent a 4-x-4 with a roof rack, pile on the boards, and explore. If you want to learn, most of the popular surf beaches up here have surf schools. See Chapter 14.

✔ **Battling a billfish off the Pacific coast:** Billfish are plentiful all along Costa Rica's Pacific coast, and boats operate from most coastal beach and port towns. Go to **Quepos** (just outside Manuel Antonio) for the best fish scene, or head down to **Drake Bay,** the **Osa Peninsula,** or **Golfo Dulce,** if you want some isolation. See Chapters 15 and 20.

✔ **Swinging through the treetops on a canopy tour:** This unique adventure is becoming quite the rage. In most cases, after a strenuous climb using ascenders, you strap on a harness and zip from treetop to treetop while dangling from a cable. There are canopy tours all around Costa Rica. **The Original Canopy Tours** runs several operations in locations around the country. See Chapter 17.

✔ **Mountain-biking the back roads of Costa Rica:** The lack of paved roads that most folks bemoan is a huge boon for mountain bikers. There are endless back roads and cattle paths to explore. Tours of differing lengths and all difficulty levels are available. The area around Lake Arenal and the Arenal volcano is a perfect place to ride some fat-track bikes. Contact **Bike Arenal.** See Chapter 18.

✔ **Kayaking around the Golfo Dulce:** Slipping through the waters of the Golfo Dulce by kayak gets you intimately in touch with the raw beauty of this underdeveloped region. In addition to the open gulf waters where dolphins often frolick, **Escondido Trex** takes folks on trips into mangrove swamps and into river estuaries. See Chapter 20.

The Best Family Spots

Costa Rica's rugged reputation should not discourage family travel. Here are a few of the ample attractions and activities available to please tourists of all ages, as well as some of the hotels, resorts, and destinations perfectly suited to family travel:

✔ **La Paz Waterfall Gardens:** This multifaceted attraction features paths and suspended walkways alongside a series of impressive jungle waterfalls. Kids love the variety of natural attractions, from the immense butterfly garden to the hummingbird garden. The rooms at the **Peace Lodge** here are some of the best in the country. See Chapter 12.

✔ **Playa Tamarindo:** This lively surf town has a bit of something for everyone. This is a great spot for teens to learn how to surf or boogie-board, and there are a host of tours and activities to please the entire family. **Hotel Capitán Suizo** has an excellent location on a calm section of beach, spacious rooms, and a great pool for kids and adults alike. See Chapters 13 and 14.

✔ **Manuel Antonio:** Manuel Antonio has a little bit of everything: miles of gorgeous beaches, tons of wildlife (with almost guaranteed monkey sightings), and plenty of active tour options. Numerous lodging options are available, but **Hotel Sí Como No** with its large suites, two pools, water slide, and nightly movies, is probably your best bet. See Chapter 15.

✔ **Playa Hermosa:** The broad stretch of sand and protected waters of this Pacific beach make it a family favorite. However, just because the waters are calm doesn't mean it's boring here. Check in at **Aqua Sport** where you can rent sea kayaks, sailboards, paddleboats, beach umbrellas, and bicycles. See Chapter 16.

✔ **Allegro Papagayo Resort:** This large all-inclusive resort probably has the most extensive facilities, widest array of tours and activities, and best-run children's program in the country so far. The hotel is located on a very calm section of Bahía Culebra, and it even has a separate "Fun Club" on a beautiful nearby white-sand beach. See Chapter 13.

✔ **Monteverde:** Monteverde not only boasts the country's most famous cloud forest, but it also sports a wide variety of related attractions and activities. After hiking through the reserve, you should be able to keep most kids happy and occupied riding horses; squirming at the local serpentarium; or visiting the butterfly farm, frog pond, and hummingbird gallery. More-adventurous families can take one of the local zip-line canopy tours. See Chapter 17.

The Best Nightlife

Costa Rica has plenty of places to dance the night away — many of my favorites are set right on the water's edge. Here is a sampling of what you'll find:

✔ **El Cuartel de la Boca del Monte (San José):** This is where San José's young, restless, and beautiful congregate. From Wednesday to Saturday, the place is jam-packed. Originally a gay and bohemian hangout, it's now decidedly mixed and leaning toward yuppie. There's frequently live music here. See Chapter 12.

✔ **Terra U (San José):** At night, the streets of San José's university district are filled with students strolling among a variety of bars and cafes. The Calle de Amargura, or "Street of Bitterness," is the heart and soul of this district, and Terra U, a bustling bar, sits smack-dab in the center of this street. See Chapter 12.

✔ **Mar y Sombra (Manuel Antonio):** Located on the beach a couple hundred meters from the national park entrance, this is the hottest spot in the Manuel Antonio area. There's a large, open-air dance floor and plenty of tables set in the sand. If the dancing gets too intense, you can always cool your feet in the ocean. See Chapter 15.

✔ **Night Tours (countrywide):** Most Neotropical forest dwellers are nocturnal. Animal and insect calls fill the air, and the rustling on the ground all around takes on new meanings. Night tours are offered at most rain- and cloud-forest destinations throughout the country. Many use high-powered flashlights to catch glimpses of various animals. Some even have high-tech night-vision goggles. Some of the better spots for night tours are **Monteverde,** the **Osa Peninsula,** and **Tortuguero.** Volcano viewing in **Arenal** is another not-to-miss nighttime activity. See Chapters 17, 18, 20, and 21.

✔ **El Bambú (Puerto Viejo):** The tiny beach town of Puerto Viejo has one of the most active after-dark scenes in the country. The small, open-air waterfront bar El Bambu is my favorite of the bunch. This place is packed every Monday and Friday for Reggae Night. If the dance floor gets too hot and sweaty, you can always grab a table in the sand. See Chapter 21.

Chapter 2

Digging Deeper into Costa Rica

*T*his chapter will give you some handy background information and a glimpse into *Tico* (Costa Rican, culture, cuisine, and idiomatic idiosyncrasies), so you can take better advantage of your time in this beautiful country. I also recommend a list of excellent books, if you want to delve deeper into Costa Rica.

History 101: The Main Events

Costa Rica enjoyed thousands of years of human occupation before it was "discovered" by Christopher Columbus in 1502. Its history includes a civil war, the abolition of its standing army, and the building of a banana-exporting empire.

Costa Rica history timeline

13,000 B.C.	Earliest record of human inhabitants in Costa Rica.
1000 B.C.	Olmec people from Mexico arrive in Costa Rica searching for rare blue jade.
1000 B.C.–A.D. 1400	City of Guayabo is inhabited by as many as 10,000 people.
1502	Columbus "discovers" Costa Rica in September, anchoring off what is now Limón.
1519–1561	The Spanish explore and colonize Costa Rica.
1563	City of Cartago is founded in the Central Valley.

1737	San José is founded.
Late 1700s	Coffee is introduced as a cash crop.
1821	On September 15, Costa Rica, with the rest of Central America, gains independence from Spain.
1823	San José is named the capital. The decision is disputed and isn't officially settled until 1835.
1848	Costa Rica is proclaimed an independent republic.
1856	The Battle of Santa Rosa: Costa Ricans defeat the United States, which backed proslavery advocate William Walker.
1870s	First banana plantations are established.
1889	First election is won by an opposition party, establishing democratic process in Costa Rica.
1890	Inauguration of the railroad connecting San José with the Caribbean coast.
1899	The United Fruit Company is founded by railroad builder Minor Keith.
1941	Costa Rica's social security and health system is instituted by President Rafael Angel Calderón.
1948	After an aborted revolution and short civil war, the Costa Rican army is abolished.
1949	Women and blacks are given the right to vote.
1956	Costa Rica's population tops 1 million.
1963	Cabo Blanco Reserve becomes Costa Rica's first national park.
1987	President Oscar Arias Sánchez is awarded the Nobel Peace Prize for orchestrating the Central American Peace Plan.
2002	For the first time in history, the presidential elections are forced into a second-round runoff. Abel Pacheco of the Social Christian Unity Party (PUSC) emerges as the winner.
2004	An aggressive public prosecutor and national press expose massive governmental scandals, landing two former presidents in jail and leaving another on the lam.

The early years

Little is known of Costa Rica's history before its colonization by Spanish settlers. The pre-Columbian Indians who made their home in this region of Central America never developed the large cities or advanced culture that flowered to the north and south. Still, ancient artifacts demonstrating a strong sense of aesthetics have been found at excavations around the country, primarily in the northwest. Beautiful gold and jade jewelry, intricately carved grinding stones, and artistically painted terra-cotta objects point to a small but highly skilled population.

Colonizing Costa Rica

On his fourth and final voyage to the New World, in 1502, Christopher Columbus anchored just offshore from present-day Limón. Whether he actually gave the country its name is open to discussion, but it wasn't long before the moniker took hold.

The early Spanish settlers found that, unlike the Indians farther north, the native population of Costa Rica was unwilling to submit to slavery. Despite their small numbers, scattered villages, and tribal differences, they fought back against the Spanish until they were overcome by superior firepower and European diseases. When the fighting was finished, however, very few Indians were left for the settlers to force into servitude. The few settlers who braved this outpost were often forced to till their own lands, a situation unheard of in other parts of Central America. Costa Rica was nearly forgotten, as the Spanish crown looked elsewhere for riches to plunder and souls to convert.

It didn't take long for Costa Rica's few Spanish settlers to head for the hills, where they found rich volcanic soil and a climate that was less oppressive than in the lowlands. Cartago, the colony's first capital, was founded in 1563, but it was not until the 1700s that additional cities were established in this agriculturally rich region. In the late 18th century, the first coffee plants were introduced. These plants thrived in the highlands, and Costa Rica had its first and foremost cash crop.

Staking out independence

In 1821, Spain granted independence to its colonies in Central America. Costa Rica joined with its neighbors to form the Central American Federation, but in 1838, it withdrew to form a new nation and pursue its own interests. By the mid-1800s, coffee was the country's main export. Free land was given to anyone willing to plant coffee on it, and plantation owners soon grew wealthy and powerful, creating Costa Rica's first elite class. Coffee plantation owners were powerful enough to elect their own representatives to the presidency.

This was a stormy period in Costa Rican history. In 1856, the country was invaded by William Walker, an ambitious Tennessee mercenary who, with the backing of U.S. President James Buchanan and prominent early industrialists, was attempting to fulfill his grandiose dreams of presiding over a slave state in Central America (before his invasion of Costa Rica, he had invaded Nicaragua and Baja California). The people of Costa Rica, led by their own president, Juan Rafael Mora, rose up against Walker and chased him back to Nicaragua. In 1860, was defeated and captured for the last time in Honduras, where he was promptly executed.

In the 1870s, Costa Rica began construction of a railway from San José to the Caribbean coast, in order to facilitate the transport of coffee to European markets. It took nearly 20 years and cost more than 4,000 workers their lives constructing the railway. Partway through the project, as funds were dwindling, the second chief engineer, Minor Keith, proposed an idea that not only enhanced his fortunes but also changed the course of Central American history. Banana plantations would be developed along the railway right-of-way (land on either side of the tracks). The export of this crop would help to finance the railway, and, in exchange, Keith would get a 99-year lease on the land with a 20-year tax deferment. The Costa Rican government gave its consent, and in 1878, the first bananas were shipped from the country. In 1899, Keith and a partner formed the United Fruit Company, a business that eventually became the largest landholder in Central America and was the cause of political disputes and wars throughout the region.

Growing democracy in Central America

In 1889, Costa Rica held what is considered the first free election in Central American history. The opposition candidate won the election, and the control of the government passed from the hands of one political party to those of another without bloodshed or hostilities. This pattern of peaceful democracy continued for the next 60 years.

In 1948, however, Rafael Angel Calderón, who had served as the country's president from 1940 to 1944, refused to concede the country's leadership to the rightfully elected president, Otillio Ulate. Civil war ensued. Calderón was defeated by forces led by José "Pepe" Figueres. Following the civil war, a new constitution was drafted; among other changes, it abolished Costa Rica's army, so that such a revolution could never happen again.

In 1994, history seemed to repeat itself — peacefully this time — when José María Figueres took the reins of government from the son of his father's adversary, Rafael Angel Calderón.

In 2001, the new Citizen's Action Party (PAC) forced the presidential elections into a second round, opening a crack in a two-party system that had become seemingly entrenched for good. The traditional two-party system was further threatened in 2004, when major corruption scandals became public.

As this book goes to press, two former presidents, Miguel Angel Rodriguez and Rafael Angel Calderón, are in jail, and another, José Maria Figueres, is in Switzerland refusing a legislative call to return and testify, as well as avoiding an Interpol warrant for his capture and arrest. All are implicated, as well as a long list of other high-level government employees and deputies, in various financial scandals or bribery cases. Even the sitting president, Abel Pacheco is under investigation for accepting illegal campaign contributions. The far-reaching effects of these corruption scandals are hard to predict.

However, despite these scandals, more than a century of nearly uninter-
rupted democracy has helped make Costa Rica the most stable country
in Central America. This stability, adherence to the democratic process,
and the country's staunch position of neutrality are a source of great
pride to Costa Ricans, who like to think of their country as the
"Switzerland of Central America."

Building Blocks: Local Architecture

Costa Rica lacks the grand cities and distinctive Spanish-influenced
architecture of other former Spanish colonial cities. You can still find
some old examples of adobe buildings with high doorways and large
windows, all topped with red tile roofs, especially in Liberia and some
of the other smaller cities.

Modern Costa Rica is being overrun with strip malls and commercial
centers and nondescript housing built of concrete block and other
modern materials. Perhaps the most noticeable and striking architec-
tural feature you'll find almost universally across the country is the use
of metal grating over all exterior windows and doors. Unfortunately,
though occasionally ornate, this metal grating is a direct response to
rampant petty crime and theft.

A Taste of Costa Rica: Local Cuisine

Simply put, Costa Rican cuisine is unspectacular. Rice and beans are
standard Tico fare and are often served at all three meals a day. Mixed
together, they're called *gallo pinto*. Either as *gallo pinto,* or served separately, rice and beans are an integral part of most Costa Rican meals.

If you're looking for typical (and cheap) eats, you'll find them in little
restaurants known as *sodas,* which are the equivalent of diners in the
United States. Your best bet at a *soda* is a *casado* (which translates as
"married" and is the name for the local version of a blue-plate special).
A *casado* usually consists of cabbage-and-tomato salad, fried plantains,
and a chicken, fish, or meat dish of some sort. *Casados* also often come
with a hard-boiled egg and/or slab of fresh cheese.

Costa Rica has two coasts, and, as you'd expect, plenty of seafood is
available everywhere in the country. Corvina (sea bass) is the most
commonly served fish. You'll also come across *pargo* (red snapper),
dorado (mahimahi), and tuna on most menus, especially along the
coasts. Although Costa Rica is a major exporter of shrimp and lobster,
both are less common and more expensive than you might expect.

Corvina is one of my least favorite fish options. Costa Rican corvina is
a distant cousin to the cold-water Chilean and other sea basses served
in restaurants across the United States and Europe. In many cheaper
restaurants, particularly in San José, shark meat is sometimes even sold

as corvina. I highly recommend sticking with dorado, red snapper, and tuna, whenever possible.

Costa Rica is a major producer and exporter of beef. Unfortunately, quantity doesn't mean quality. Unless you go to one of the better restaurants or steakhouses, you'll probably be served rather tough steaks, cut rather thin.

Still, all is not lost. With the increase in international tourism and the need to please a more sophisticated palate, local chefs have begun to create a "nouvelle Costa Rican cuisine," updating timeworn recipes and using traditional ingredients in creative ways. At many of the better hotels and local restaurants you'll find chefs doing interesting and tasty things with the local fruits and vegetables and fresh seafood, meats, and poultry.

You can also get good international cuisine at a host of Italian, Peruvian, Mexican, Pan-Asian, and other restaurants across the country.

Getting the most out of eating in Costa Rica: Bocas and fresh fruit

Appetizers, known as *bocas,* are served with drinks in most bars. Often the *bocas* are free, but even if they aren't, they're very inexpensive. Popular *bocas* include *gallos* (tortillas piled with meat, chicken, cheese, or beans), ceviche (a marinated seafood salad), tamales (stuffed cornmeal patties wrapped and steamed inside banana leaves), *patacones* (fried green plantain chips), and fried yuca. Tacos, tamales, and empanadas (turnovers) also are quite common. Making an evening and full meal out of a long list of bocas is easy and enjoyable.

Costa Rica has a wealth of delicious tropical fruits. The most common are mangoes (the season begins in May), papayas, pineapples, melons, and bananas. Other fruits include the *marañón,* which is the fruit of the cashew tree and has orange or yellow glossy skin; the *granadilla,* or *maracuyá* (passion fruit); the *mamón chino,* which Asian travelers will immediately recognize as the rambutan; and the *carambola* (star fruit).

All of these fruits are readily available in markets across the country and are sold at roadside stands on most major highways and thoroughfares.

Fresh fruits are also served in drinks made in a blender either with water *(en agua)* or with milk *(con leche).* Named either *frescos, refrescos,* or *jugos naturales,* these are my favorite drinks in Costa Rica. Among the more common fruits used are mangoes, papayas, blackberries *(mora),* and pineapples *(piña).* You'll also come across maracuyá and carambola.

Enjoying a cup of joe

If you're a coffee drinker, you may be surprisingly disappointed in Costa Rica. Most of the best coffee has traditionally been saved for export, and

Ticos tend to prefer their coffee weak and sugary. The better hotels and restaurants cater to gringo and European tastes and serve up superior blends.

If you want black coffee, ask for *café negro;* if you want it with milk, order *café con leche.* Most restaurants serve the milk warmed and in a separate container. If you want to ensure your milk comes separately, ask for *con leche aparte.* See Chapter 22 for more tips on Costa Rican coffee.

If you want to try something different for your morning beverage, ask for *agua dulce,* a warm drink made from melted sugar cane and served either with milk or lemon, or straight.

A Word to the Wise: The Local Language

Spanish is the official language of Costa Rica. Most hotel and restaurant staff have some functional knowledge of English, and all guides and higher-level tourism workers speak respectable English.

Costa Rican Spanish is neither the easiest nor the most difficult dialect to understand. Costa Ricans speak at a relatively relaxed speed and tend to enunciate clearly, without dropping too many final consonants. The *y* and *ll* sounds are very subtly pronounced, almost inaudible. Perhaps the most defining idiosyncrasy of Costa Rican Spanish is the way Ticos have of overemphasizing, almost chewing, their *r*'s.

For a glossary of Costa Rican terms, see the Cheat Sheet in the front of this book, or check out *Spanish For Dummies* (Wiley Publishing, Inc.).

Throughout the book you'll see the term *Tico.* This is the common local slang for a Costa Rican, and by inference all things Costa Rican. The name comes from the Costa Rican habit of adding a diminutive suffix to the end of many words and phrases. *Poquito* becomes *poquitico. Chicito* becomes *chicitico.* A Costa Rican woman is a *Tica.* Never use the term *Tican,* though; it's just wrong.

Background Check: Recommended Books and Movies

If you're looking to find out more on Costa Rica, a wealth of excellent resources is available. In this section, I list some of my favorite books, as well as a couple of films you should check out to round out your understanding of Costa Rica.

Costa Rica on paper

Some of the books mentioned in this section may be difficult to track down in U.S. bookstores, but you'll find them all in abundance in Costa

Rica. A good place to check for most of these titles is **Seventh Street Books,** on Calle 7 between avenidas 1 and Central (☎ **256-8251**).

For a readable look into Costa Rican society, check out *The Ticos: Culture and Social Change,* by Richard, Karen, and Mavis Biesanz (Lynne Rienner Publishers), an examination of the country's politics and culture, by the authors of the out-of-print *The Costa Ricans.*

To find out more about the life and culture of Costa Rica's Talamanca coast, an area populated by Afro-Caribbean people whose forebears emigrated from Caribbean islands in the early 19th century, pick up a copy of *What Happen: A Folk-History of Costa Rica's Talamanca Coast,* by Paula Palmer. This book is a collection of oral histories taken from a wide range of local characters. A new and improved edition was slated to be published in early 2005 by Distruibuidores Zona Tropical.

If you're looking for literature, *Costa Rica: A Traveler's Literary Companion,* edited by Barbara Ras, with a foreword by Oscar Arias Sánchez (Whereabouts Press), is a collection of short stories by Costa Rican writers, organized by country regions. If you're lucky, you may find and pick up a copy of *Stories of Tatamundo,* by Fabian Dobles (University of Costa Rica Press). This collection of short stories is based on the character Tata Mundo, a rural peasant, who has come to embody and represent much of Costa Rica's national identity, or at least the idealized version of that identity — simple, kind, open, joyful, and wise.

Young adults will enjoy Aileen Kilgore Henderson's *The Monkey Thief* (Milkweed Editions) and Kristin Joy Pratt's *A Walk in the Rainforest* (Dawn Publications). David Norman publishes a series of coloring books with short descriptive texts, including *Let's Help Costa Rica's Endangered Animals* (WWF) and *Costa Rican Wildlife* (WWF).

I personally that think everyone coming to Costa Rica should read *Tropical Nature,* by Adrian Forsyth and Ken Miyata (Touchstone Books). My all-time favorite book on tropical biology, this is a wonderfully written and lively collection of tales and adventures by two Neotropical biologists who spent quite some time in the forests of Costa Rica.

Costa Rica on film

Be forewarned, even though it is set in Costa Rica, *Jurassic Park* was not filmed here. For a glimpse of Costa Rica on film you can check out Ridley Scott's *1492,* which was filmed here, but is set in Hispaniola.

For films in which Costa Rica plays a more prominent role, you can look for the small independent films *Tropix* and *Caribe,* both of which were written, set, and shot in the country. The former is in English, while the latter is in Spanish.

Chapter 3

Deciding Where and When to Go

In This Chapter
- ▶ Figuring out where to go
- ▶ Decoding the secrets of the travel seasons and climate
- ▶ Zeroing in on special events you may want to catch

Although not an especially large country, Costa Rica offers a wealth of destinations. Understanding a bit about the geography and the different attractions will help you choose where to go and how much to try to fit into your time here. In addition to giving you the lowdown on Costa Rican life during the distinct wet and dry seasons (which coincide nearly exactly with high and low tourism seasons), this chapter includes a calendar of events if you'd like to plan your visit around a particular activity.

Going Everywhere You Want to Be

Visitors to Costa Rica come for a variety of reasons. Some come to just crash on a beautiful beach and unwind, others want to experience the wonders of the tropical rain and cloud forests, and some come to partake in an adventure or two. If you want, it's easy to combine one or more of these options into a perfect and personalized vacation.

But first you'll want to know a little something about the country's geography and what each destination has to offer.

Seeking the center: San José and the Central Valley

Unless you're flying in and out of Liberia, San José will serve as a default hub or transfer point. In many ways and for most visitors, San José is little more than a rough-and-tumble, overcrowded Central American metropolis. The downtown area is a congested mess — for pedestrians and drivers alike. Sidewalks are poorly maintained and claustrophobic, and street crime is a problem. Most visitors quickly seek the sanctuary of their hotel rooms and the first chance to escape the city.

Still, San José is the most cosmopolitan city in Central America, with several decent museums, some very good restaurants, and a handful of excellent hotel options.

San José also makes a great base for a variety of day trips and excursions. Within an hour or two, you can climb a volcano, go white-water rafting, hike through a cloud forest, and stroll through a butterfly garden — among many, many other activities.

San José sits in the center of the Central Valley, or *Valle Central*. The climate is mild and spring-like year-round, and this is Costa Rica's primary agricultural region, with coffee farms making up the majority of landholdings. However, the Central Valley is also densely populated, containing three of the country's largest cities, San José, Alajuela, and Heredia.

The rolling green hills and peaks that form the rim of this valley rise to heights between 900m and 1,200m (2,952–3,936 ft.) above sea level Several of these are volcanoes, including Poás and Irazú, which are both active.

Going for gold in Guanacaste

Guanacaste province occupies the northwestern corner of Costa Rica. It is home to many of the country's sunniest and most popular beaches and has earned its reputation as Costa Rica's "Gold Coast."

With about 65 inches of rain a year, this region is by far the driest in the country and has been likened to west Texas, with better beaches. Guanacaste province borders Nicaragua and is named after the shady trees that still shelter the herds of cattle that roam the dusty savanna here. In addition to the beaches and cattle ranches, Guanacaste boasts several volcanoes and one of the last remnants of tropical dry forest left in Central America.

Guanacaste is the only place in Costa Rica where you'll find several large-scale resort hotels. However, you'll also find scores of excellent smaller beach resorts and hotels, and I list the best of each category in the chapters that follow. Guanacaste currently boasts three championship golf courses, and more are allegedly in the works.

 Guanacaste also has the country's only international airport, aside from San José. The number of direct flights and charters arriving here is increasing every year. If you want to spend your entire vacation in this area, be sure to book a direct flight into and out of Liberia.

Enjoying magnificent Manuel Antonio

Manuel Antonio is the name of a coastal national park, as well as the resort area that surrounds it. Many first-time visitors to Costa Rica plan their vacation around a visit here. The hills just outside the national park are still covered in thick rain forest. The whole thing seems to gently tumble down to the sea. The views from these hills are spectacular, and the beaches are beautiful.

There's no real town of Manuel Antonio. The closest thing is the small port city of Quepos. Between Quepos and the national park entrance runs a 7km (4⅓-mile) stretch of narrow road that winds through the forested green hills here. Along this road, and in Quepos, you'll find all of the area's hotels, restaurants, and shops.

However, Manuel Antonio's popularity has brought with it more crowds and a growing sense of overdevelopment. On weekends, the beaches are filled with people, and the disco near the park entrance blares its music until early morning.

Living the luxe life on the central Pacific coast

Costa Rica's central Pacific coast lies relatively close to San José and is much less developed than the northern province of Guanacaste. The beaches here are long, wide, and often nearly deserted. Most are backed by densely forested hills and mountains.

Although Manuel Antonio is the crown jewel of Costa Rica's Central Pacific coast, the nearby beaches to the north and south are beginning to come into their own.

To the north of Manuel Antonio, the beach towns of Jacó and Playa Herradura are some of the closest to San José. Jacó is a bustling surf town popular with itinerant surfers, foreign snowbirds, and young Ticos and Costa Rican families looking for a close and inexpensive getaway.

Playa Herradura is home to a large and luxurious Marriott resort, featuring the area's only 18-hole golf course. On the hills above Playa Herradura sits Villa Caletas, one of the country's top boutique hotels.

Meanwhile, toward the southern end of this coast lies the funky little surfer town of Dominical, which is the gateway to Ballena National Marine Park and several barely discovered beautiful beaches.

Visiting the cloud forests of Monteverde

Monteverde sits high on the mountainous spine that runs down the center of Costa Rica. *Monteverde* translates as "green mountain," and this is an area of lush and luxurious rain and cloud forests.

Cloud forests are a unique phenomenon. The mountaintops and forests of Monteverde are blanketed almost daily in dense clouds. For reasons that I explain in more detail in Chapter 17, this unique climatic phenomenon forms an ecosystem that is incredibly rich in biodiversity. Within this small area are more than 2,500 species of plants, including 400 types of orchids, 400 species of birds (including the spectacular Resplendent Quetzal), and 100 different species of mammals.

The tiny villages of Santa Elena and Monteverde are gateways to the Monteverde Cloud Forest Reserve. You won't find any large resorts in Santa Elena or Monteverde. What you will find here are scores of small mountain lodges and ecolodges that run the gamut from decidedly rustic to nearly luxurious.

In addition to hiking and visiting the cloud forest, a host of activities are offered in the area, including horseback riding, canopy tours, ATV outings, and canyoning.

Watching the lava flow from Arenal volcano

Rising to a near-perfect cone, Arenal volcano is Costa Rica's most consistently active and pyrotechnically impressive volcano. Volcano viewing is the major attraction and activity here, although there's plenty more to do.

La Fortuna is a small rural town set at the foot of the volcano. La Fortuna has several hotels and is the base for most of the area's tour and adventure companies. From here a road skirts along the edge of the base of the volcano heading toward Lake Arenal. You'll find the best hotels and restaurants along this stretch of road.

Lake Arenal sits below the volcano and is the country's largest body of fresh water. It's a great spot for fishing and canoeing. During the winter months, it's also a world-class and world-renowned windsurfing destination.

Also near the foot of the volcano are several beautiful and soothing hot springs, as well as the impressive La Fortuna waterfall. All around the lake and volcano are large expanses of rain and cloud forest, with ample opportunities for myriad tours and activities.

Because they're both located in the north-central part of the country, combining a couple of days each at Monteverde and Arenal is easy and common.

Seeking solitude on the Nicoya Peninsula

South of Guanacaste lies the Nicoya Peninsula. Although this area is similar in terms of geography and climate, and has nearly as many beautiful beaches, it's much less developed and populated.

This place is great for solitude and a true sense of getting away from it all. You'll find some very lovely boutique hotels along the southern coasts of the Nicoya Peninsula.

The two main beach towns and vacation destinations in this area are Montezuma and Malpaís. Between them lies the Cabo Blanco Absolute Nature Reserve, Costa Rica's oldest official nature reserve.

Montezuma is a longstanding beach destination popular with backpackers and adventurous travelers. Montezuma sits just on the inside of the Golfo de Nicoya (Nicoya Gulf), and its beaches are relatively calm and protected. It also features two lovely waterfalls.

Malpaís and neighboring Playa Santa Teresa are Costa Rica's next hot spots. Both locales boast long expanses of white-sand beaches, backed by lush forests, and are popular with surfers.

Farther north up the Nicoya Peninsula coast lies Punta Islita, one of the country's most exclusive, isolated boutique beach resorts.

Exploring southern Costa Rica

The hot, humid southern region of Costa Rica is remote and undeveloped. It's characterized by dense rain forests and rugged coastlines. Much of the area is protected in Corcovado National Park, the largest single expanse of lowland tropical rain forest in Central America, and its newly created sister the Piedras Blancas National Park.

On the inside of the Osa Peninsula lies the Golfo Dulce, or "Sweet Gulf." This large and beautiful body of water is a great place for fishing, kayaking, and dolphin spotting.

Several wonderful remote ecolodges are spread around the shores of the Golfo Dulce and on the Osa Peninsula, bordering Corcovado National Park. Some may find the area solitary, but if you like your ecotourism raw and challenging, you'll want to visit this region.

Chilling on the Caribbean coast

Most of the Caribbean coast is a wide, steamy lowland laced with rivers and blanketed with rain forests and banana plantations. The culture here is predominantly Afro-Caribbean, with many residents speaking English or a Caribbean dialect. The northern section of this coast is accessible only by boat or small plane and is the site of Tortuguero National Park, which is known for its nesting sea turtles and riverboat trips through its network of jungle canals and lagoons.

The towns of Cahuita and Puerto Viejo, on the southern half of the Caribbean coast, are popular beach destinations — and they are home to, or close to, some of the best and least crowded beaches in the country. Small coral reefs also dot the coastlines off each town, giving this region some of the best snorkeling in Costa Rica.

No large resorts are to be found here, and although the towns of Cahuita and Puerto Viejo can bustle at times, this area is remote and isolated and will really give you a sense of getting away from it all.

Scheduling Your Time

Although visiting several destinations during one trip is certainly possible, Costa Rica doesn't lend itself well to stringing together five or so destinations in a week. If you want to visit several destinations, you have to factor in travel time. It takes four to eight hours to drive between San

José and most popular destinations and approximately the same amount to drive between the different spots.

Commuter flights cut down the travel time considerably, but they add on cost and some logistical challenges because you often have to fly in and out of San José as a hub. So, if the flights don't line up, you may end up adding an extra overnight in San José.

Many folks are content to spend a week or more at one resort, and this is a good option in Costa Rica, especially up in Guanacaste, where you can enjoy the comforts of a beach resort combined with the ability to take day trips that range from horseback rides near the Rincón de la Vieja volcano, to rafting trips on the Corobicí River, to sailboat outings, hikes, and canopy tours. A similar amount of activities and tour options are available in Manuel Antonio and to a slightly lesser extent from the remote ecolodges of the Osa Peninsula.

Narrowing down your choices

If you're looking for some unadulterated beach time and plenty of sun and fun, Guanacaste is often your best choice. If you want to mix your beach time with a bit more adventure and a trip into the rain forest, Manuel Antonio is a great option.

For a more intense exploration of the tropical rain and cloud forests you should visit one or more of the following destinations: Monteverde, the Osa Peninsula and Golfo Dulce, or Tortuguero.

For a simple loop that hits three major and distinct destinations, I always recommend that folks head straight for La Fortuna and the Arenal volcano, then head over to Monteverde, and finish by dropping down to the coast at Manuel Antonio.

In Chapter 4, I outline several different possible itineraries to help you plan the perfect trip to Costa Rica, given your particular interests, budget, and time constraints.

Revealing the Secrets of the Seasons

Costa Rica's high season runs from mid-December to late April, which coincides almost perfectly with the chill of winter in the United States, Canada, and Europe. The high season also coincides almost perfectly with the country's dry season. If you want some unadulterated time on a tropical beach and less rain during your rain-forest experience, this is the time to come. During this period (and especially around the Christmas holidays), tourism is in full swing — prices are higher, attractions are more crowded, and reservations need to be made in advance.

In order to drum up business during the rainy season, locals sometimes refer to it as the *green season*. The adjective is appropriate. At this time of year, even brown and barren Guanacaste becomes lush and verdant. I personally love traveling around Costa Rica during the rainy season (but then again, I'm not trying to flee winter in Chicago). It's easy to find or at least negotiate reduced rates, there are far fewer fellow travelers, and the rain is often limited to a few hours each afternoon (although you can occasionally get socked in for a week at a time).

Understanding Costa Rica's climate

Costa Rica is a tropical country with distinct wet and dry seasons. However, some regions receive rain all year, and others are very dry and sunny for most of the year. Temperatures in Costa Rica are rarely as extreme. The average annual daytime temperature for much of the country ranges between 71°F (21.7°C) and 81°F (27°C). Moreover, temperatures vary primarily with elevation, not with seasons: On the coasts, it's hot all year with daytime temperatures hovering between 90°F (32.2°C) and 96°F (35.5°C). But up in the mountains, it can be cool at night any time of year, with temperatures dipping into the mid-60s (15–17 Celsius). At the highest elevations (3,000–3,600m/9,840–11,808 ft.), frost is common.

The dry season, considered summer by Costa Ricans, is from mid-November to April. In Guanacaste, the dry northwestern province, the dry season lasts several weeks longer than in other places. Even in the rainy season, days often start sunny, with rain falling in the afternoon and evening. The wet or rainy season (or green season) is from May to mid-November. Costa Ricans call this time of year their winter.

For most of the wet season, the rains are often limited to a brief but substantial downpour during the late afternoon. However, from mid-August through October, the rain can be hard, heavy, and seemingly relentless for long stretches.

In general, the best time of year to visit weather-wise is in December and early January, when everything is still green from the rains, but the sky is clear.

Costa Rica's Caribbean coast breaks all the rules mentioned in this section. It can rain pretty much any time of the year here. However, the one semidependable period when the Caribbean coast often enjoys clear skies and calm seas is between mid-September and late October, when the rest of the country is experiencing some of the worst effects of the rainy season.

Some of the country's rugged dirt roads become downright impassable without four-wheel-drive during the rainy season.

Avoiding the crowds

Keep in mind that tourism to Costa Rica peaks during the Christmas holidays, spring break, and Easter week. Stay at home during these seasons if you don't want to fight crowds and pay top dollar. However, you'll generally get good weather, uncrowded beaches and resorts, and decent price breaks, if you visit from late April through early June, or from late November through mid-December.

Perusing a Calendar of Events

Some of the events listed here may be considered more of a *happening* than a well-organized event — there's not, for instance, a Virgin of Los Angeles PR committee that readily dispenses information. If I haven't listed a contact number, your best bet is to call the **Costa Rican Tourist Board (ICT)** at ☎ **800-343-6332** in the United States, or 223-1733 in Costa Rica, or visit www.visitcostarica.com.

January

Some of the best young tennis players from around the region and around the world come to San José and the **Copa del Café (Coffee Cup).** Matches are held at the Costa Rica Country Club (☎ **228-9333**). First week in January.

March

Orchid growers throughout the world gather to show their wares, trade tales and secrets, and admire the hundreds of species on display at the **National Orchid Show.** The show takes place at a different venue each year in the Central Valley. Contact the Costa Rican Tourist Board for precise location and dates.

April

Costa Rica is a predominantly Roman Catholic country and **Holy Week** is celebrated with fervor. Religious processions are held in cities and towns throughout the country. The week before Easter.

July

Annexation of Guanacaste Day is celebrated each year in Liberia with Tico-style bullfights, folk dancing, horseback parades, rodeos, concerts, and other events. On and around July 25.

August

Over 100,000 people make the annual pilgrimage from San José to the basilica in Cartago every year in honor of the **Fiesta of the Virgin of Los Angeles.** Even those who don't make the 24km (15-mile) trek take the day off to honor the country's virgin saint. August 2.

September

School children across the country take to the streets in marching bands heavy on xylophones and snare drums to celebrate **Costa Rica's**

Independence Day. Many of the parades are nighttime affairs, replete with fireworks. September 15.

If you're visiting Costa Rica this time of year, **International Beach Clean-Up Day** is a good excuse to chip in and help clean up the Costa Rican shoreline. Third Saturday of September.

October

Limón's **Carnaval,** or **Día de la Raza,** is a miniature Mardi Gras, complete with floats and dancing in the streets, that commemorates Columbus's dropping anchor off this Caribbean port city in 1502. The weekend closest to October 12.

December

The streets of downtown San José belong to horses and their riders for **El Tope,** each December 26. The next day, those same streets are taken over by carnival floats, marching bands, and street dancers, for **Carnival.**

Costa Rican bullfights and a hodgepodge of carnival rides, games of chance, and fast-food stands are set up at the fairgrounds in Zapote, a San José neighborhood. The **Festejos Populares (Popular Fiestas)** are a rowdy and raucous affair. Last week in December.

Chapter 4

Following an Itinerary: Five Great Options

osta Rica boasts plenty of things to see and do. You can use the following itineraries as precise guides or as rough outlines to help you structure your time and plan your trip.

Seeing Costa Rica's Highlights in One Week

The timing is tight, but this itinerary packs a lot into a weeklong vacation.

Day 1

Arrive and get settled in San José. If you have time, visit the **Centro Nacional de Arte y Cultura** (National Arts and Culture Center), the **Museo de Oro Banco Central** (Gold Museum), and/or the **Teatro Nacional** (National Theater). Have dinner at **Bakea** in Barrio Amón. See Chapters 11 and 12.

Day 2

Rent a car and head to the **Arenal volcano.** Settle in to your hotel and spend the afternoon at the **Tabacón Hot Springs** working out the kinks from the road. In the evening, either sign up for a volcano-watching tour, or do so yourself, either from the comfort of your hotel room's balcony, or from one of the better volcano viewing spots I lay out for you in Chapter 18.

Day 3

Spend the morning doing something adventurous, like **white-water rafting, mountain biking, canyoning,** or **horseback riding** and then **hiking** to the **La Fortuna waterfall.** Make sure you give yourself at least four hours of daylight, though, to drive around **Lake Arenal** to **Monteverde.** Stop to shop for gifts, artwork, and souvenirs at **Toad Hall,** which is located on the road between Tabacón and Nuevo Arenal. After you get to Monteverde, settle into your hotel and head for a sunset drink at **El Sapo Dorado.** See Chapters 17 and 18.

Day 4

Wake early and take a guided tour of the **Monteverde Cloud Forest Reserve.** Be sure to stop in at the **Hummingbird Gallery** next-door to the entrance after your tour. Spend the afternoon visiting several of the area's attractions, which include the **Butterfly Garden, Orchid Garden, Monteverde Serpentarium, Frog Pond of Monteverde,** and **World of Insects.** See Chapter 17.

Day 5

Use the morning to take one of the zip-line **canopy tours** here, but be sure to schedule it early enough that you can hit the road by noon for your drive to **Manuel Antonio.** Settle into your hotel and head for a sunset drink at one of the several roadside restaurants with **spectacular views over the rain forest to the sea.** You can drop off your car at any point now and just rely on taxis and tours. Adobe, Alamo, Economy, and Payless Rent-a-Car all have offices in downtown Quepos, but check with your car-rental company in advance about any drop-off fees. See Chapter 15.

Day 6

In the morning take a boat tour of the **Damas Island Estuary,** and then reward yourself for all this hard touring with an afternoon lazing on one of the beautiful beaches inside **Manuel Antonio National Park.** If you just can't lie still, be sure to hike the loop trail through the rain forest here and around **Cathedral Point.** See Chapter 15.

Day 7

Fly back to **San José** in time to connect with your departing flight home.

Touring the Best of Costa Rica in Two Weeks

If you've got two weeks, you'll be able to hit all the highlights mentioned in the preceding section and more, all at a more relaxed pace, to boot.

It's a real judgment call, but you may want to substitute a two- to three-day trip to Tortuguero for either the Guanacaste or southern zone section listed here, or whittle down a day here or there along the way in order to squeeze in Tortuguero.

Days 1 and 2

Spend as in days 1 and 2 of "Seeing Costa Rica's Highlights in One Week," earlier in this chapter.

Day 3

Spend the morning doing something adventurous, like **white-water rafting, mountain biking, canyoning,** or **horseback riding** and then **hiking** to the **La Fortuna waterfall.** If you're really active you can schedule a second adventure for the afternoon or take time to visit the town of La Fortuna and the new **Butterfly and Orchid Garden** there. In the evening return to the Hot Springs, spend more time watching the volcano, or combine both. See Chapters 17 and 18.

Day 4

Drive around **Lake Arenal** to **Monteverde.** Stop to shop for gifts, artwork, and souvenirs at **Toad Hall,** which is located on the road between Tabacón and Nuevo Arenal. After you get to Monteverde, settle into your hotel and head to **El Sapo Dorado** for a sunset drink. See Chapters 17 and 18.

Day 5

Wake early and take a guided tour of the **Monteverde Cloud Forest Reserve.** Be sure to stop in at the **Hummingbird Gallery** next-door to the entrance after your tour. Spend the afternoon visiting several of the area's attractions, which include the **Butterfly Garden, Orchid Garden, Monteverde Serpentarium, Frog Pond of Monteverde,** and **World of Insects.** See Chapter 17.

Day 6

Use the morning to take one of the zip-line **canopy tours** here, but be sure to schedule it early enough that you can hit the road by noon for your drive to **Manuel Antonio.** Settle into your hotel and head for a drink or dinner at one of the several roadside restaurants with **spectacular sunset views over the rain forest to the sea.** You can drop off your car at any point now and just rely on taxis and tours. The major rental-car agencies all have offices in the area, but check with your specific car-rental company in advance about any drop-off fees. See Chapters 15 and 17.

Day 7

In the morning take a boat tour of the **Damas Island Estuary,** and then reward yourself for all this hard touring with an afternoon lazing on one of the beautiful beaches inside **Manuel Antonio National Park.** If you just can't lie still, be sure to hike the loop trail through the rain forest here and around **Cathedral Point.** See Chapters 15 and 16.

Days 8, 9, and 10

Fly from **Quepos** and **Manuel Antonio** to either **Golfito, Puerto Jiménez,** or **Drake Bay,** and settle into one of the remote **ecolodges** of the **southern zone.** You'll need these three days to really experience the many natural wonders of this region. Aside from **hiking in the rain forest,** you'll be able to take **scuba or snorkel outings, sport-fishing trips, kayak adventures,** and **surfing lessons.** See Chapter 20.

Days 11, 12, and 13

You've had enough nature and adventure — it's time to enjoy some pampering. From the southern zone fly straight up to **Guanacaste** and spend your final days enjoying the pleasures of one of Costa Rica's **Gold Coast** beaches. If just lying on the beach or poolside is too mellow, you can take advantage of the scores of tour and activity options. Otherwise, break out that novel you've been too busy to open and enjoy. See Chapters 13 and 14.

Day 14

Fly back to **San José** in time to connect with your departing flight home.

Discovering Costa Rica with Kids

Costa Rica is not a particularly kid-friendly destination, even if it's not especially *un*friendly. Still, a few attractions or activities are geared toward the very young, and the country does have a few resorts with well-developed children's programs. Youngsters and teens, especially those with strong adventurous and inquisitive traits, will do great here.

The biggest challenges for families traveling with children are travel distances and the time it takes to move around within the country, which is why I recommend flying in and out of Liberia, and basing yourself in Guanacaste. The Guanacaste area is ripe with activities, adventures, and attractions for the whole family. And everyone will enjoy the fact that this option drastically cuts down on travel time.

Day 1

Fly into Liberia. From here, it's a 30- to 45-minute drive to any of the many area beach resorts. I recommend either the **Four Seasons Resort** or the **Allegro Papagayo** resort. Both have excellent children's programs, as well as tons of activity and tour options. See Chapter 13.

Day 2

Get to know and enjoy the facilities and activities offered up at your hotel or resort. Check out the **children's program** and any scheduled activities or tours that particularly appeal to anyone in your family. Feel free to adapt the following days' suggestions accordingly. See Chapters 13 and 14.

Day 3

The whole family will enjoy a rafting tour on the gentle **Corobicí River.** This trip is appropriate for all ages except infants. There'll be plenty of opportunities to watch birds and other wildlife along the way. See Chapter 14.

Day 4

Drop off the kids with the **children's program** for at least one full day, and treat yourselves to a **sailboat cruise.** You'll spend some time cruising the coast, take a break or two to snorkel, and probably stop for lunch at a deserted beach. See Chapter 14.

Day 5

It's time to head for the hills, which are mostly volcanoes in this neck of the woods. Book a full-day outing to **Hacienda Guachipilín,** near the **Rincón de la Vieja volcano.** Older and more adventurous children can sign up for a **horseback ride** or **canopy tour.** Younger children should get a kick out of visiting this working farm and cattle ranch. See Chapter 14.

Day 6

Use this day to satisfy any lingering whims. Some will want to just laze on the beach or by the pool. Others may want to try a **surf or boogieboard lesson.** If the kids feel left out, taking the whole brood out on a boat may be a good idea. You won't want for options. See Chapter 14.

Day 7

Use any spare time you have before your flight to buy last-minute **souvenirs** at your resort or in town, or just laze on the beach or by the pool. Fly home out of Liberia.

Having a High-Octane Week of Adventures

Costa Rica is a major adventure-tourism destination. Adventure opportunities range from white-water rafting and kayaking, to zip-line canopy tours. The following itinerary packs a lot of punch into one week but doesn't even scratch the surface. You can also find excellent mountain biking, windsurfing, kiteboarding, and sport fishing. Feel free to modify the following itinerary to include any of these activities.

Day 1

Arrive and get settled in San José. If you have time, visit the **Centro Nacional de Arte y Cultura,** the **Museo de Oro Banco Central,** and/or the **Teatro Nacional.** See Chapter 12.

Day 2

Begin a two-day white-water rafting expedition on the **Pacuare River,** and then camp out at a rustic lodge on the river's edge. See Chapter 12.

Day 3

Finish running the **Pacuare River,** and arrange for a transfer to **La Fortuna** at the end of your rafting trip. Settle into your hotel and head to the **Tabacón Hot Springs** for a soothing soak and to watch the volcano. See Chapter 18.

Day 4

Go **canyoning** with **Pure Trek Canyoning** in the morning, and then hop on some horses or mountain bikes in the afternoon and be sure to stop at the **La Fortuna Waterfall.** Take the short hike down to the base of the falls, and take a dip in one of the pools there. See Chapter 18.

Day 5

Arrange a **taxi-to-boat-to-horse** transfer over to **Monteverde.** Settle in quickly at your hotel and take a zip-line **canopy tour** in the afternoon. See Chapter 17.

Day 6

Wake up early and take a guided tour of the **Monteverde Cloud Forest Reserve.** Be sure to bring a packed lunch. After the guided tour, spend the next few hours continuing to explore the trails through the cloud forest here. See if you can spot a **quetzal** on your own. Take a late-afternoon bus or transfer back to San José. See Chapter 17.

Day 7

Unfortunately, you'll most likely be on an early flight home from San José. If you have a few hours to kill, head for a hike or jog around the **La Parque Sabana** (La Sabana Park) downtown, or, better yet, try to get yourself in a pickup soccer game. See Chapter 12.

Getting the Most out of a Week on the Gold Coast

Face it, for many the idea of touring around from place to place and checking in and out of a different hotel every day or two is just too much work for a vacation.

If you want to be able to settle into one hotel or resort, yet still have an adventure-packed, fun, and relaxing vacation, the following itinerary should be right up your alley.

Day 1

Fly into Liberia. From here it's a 30- to 45-minute drive to any of the area's many beach resorts. Choose one according to your budget, making sure to plan on taking a variety of tours during your stay. Check into your hotel, and use the rest of the day to unwind and shake off the weariness of travel. See Chapter 13.

Day 2

Get to know and enjoy the facilities and activities offered up at your hotel or resort. Take advantage of any free classes or water-sports equipment. If your hotel is near a town, spend the afternoon exploring the local scene. See Chapter 13.

Day 3

It's time to head for the hills, which are mostly volcanoes in this neck of the woods. Book a full-day outing to the **Rincón de la Vieja volcano.** Be sure to hike the short loop trail around the bubbling mud pots here, and sign on for either a **horseback ride** or **canopy tour.** See Chapter 14.

Day 4

Shopping options are very limited in Costa Rica, but one of the most interesting outings is to the small Guanacaste village of **Guaitil,** where the locals have developed a unique ceramic style, using local mud, dyes, and wood-burning kilns. In the afternoon, rent a scooter and **explore some of the other beaches** near your resort. See Chapter 14.

Day 5

Take a **rafting trip** on the gentle **Corobicí River.** You'll have plenty of opportunities to watch birds and other wildlife on this outing. If it's **turtle nesting** season, take a night tour to **Playa Grande** to see the giant leatherback turtles nest. See Chapter 14.

Day 6

You're at the ocean, so take advantage of it. Book a **sailing tour, sport fishing outing,** or **surf lesson,** or just laze on the beach or by the pool. See Chapter 14.

Day 7

Use any spare time you have before your flight home from Liberia to buy last-minute **souvenirs,** or continue to laze on the beach or by the pool. See Chapter 13.

Part II

Planning Your Trip to Costa Rica

The 5th Wave   By Rich Tennant

"The closest hotel room to Costa Rica I could get you for that amount of money would be in Boca Raton."

In this part . . .

This is the place to come when you finally decide to take the plunge and book your trip. You'll find all the nuts-and-bolts information necessary to actually make arrangements. From planning a budget, to managing your money and changing cash into colones, to scoring a deal, this part has it all. You'll also find information on how to get to Costa Rica, and then how to get around after you're there.

Later on, you'll find suggestions and recommendations for a variety of travelers with particular needs, from families traveling with children, to travelers with disabilities, to gay and lesbian tourists looking for the inside scoop, to lovers looking to tie the knot in a tropical paradise.

Chapter 5

Managing Your Money

"So, how much is this trip to Costa Rica going to cost me, anyway?"

This is an important question, and one you'll want to address before packing your bags. As far as destinations go, Costa Rica is relatively inexpensive. Still, a perfect vacation can be tailored to meet just about any budget here. Although bargains do abound, there are also plenty of places to lap up the luxury. In this chapter, I tell you how much things cost and offer you tips that can help you save big on some of the major expenses.

Planning Your Budget

With a little planning, mapping out a trip to Costa Rica to fit any budget is easy. Airfare and hotels will probably end up being your largest cash outlays. Other things, like rental cars and dining, are relatively inexpensive in Costa Rica.

Your choice of activities will also determine how much you spend: Relaxing on the beach and taking self-guided hikes in one of Costa Rica's national parks are both easy on the wallet. But guided tours and organized activities — like white-water rafting trips, sport-fishing outings and zip-line canopy tours — can quickly add substantial costs to your vacation (see Table 5-1).

Table 5-1	What Things Cost in Costa Rica
Item/Activity	*Price*
Taxi from the airport to downtown San José	$12
Cup of coffee	75¢
Bottle of beer	$2.50
Compact rental car (per day)	$35
Four-wheel-drive rental car (per day)	$55
White-water-rafting trip on the Pacuare River	$90
Zip-line canopy tour	$35–$45
Admission to the Gold Museum	$4
A day at the beach	Free!
A sunset cruise	$35–$55
Luxury room for two at the Four Seasons Resort (Papagayo)	$435–$545
Rain-forest bungalow for two at Bosque del Cabo (Osa Peninsula), all meals and taxes included	$280–$310
Oceanview condo for four at Villas Nicolas (Manuel Antonio)	$160–$240
Moderate room for two at Hotel Grano de Oro (San José)	$90–$125
Budget room for two at La Colina Lodge (Monteverde), breakfast included	$45
Gourmet dinner for two at Bakea (San José)	$50
Oceanfront dinner for two at Camarón Dorado (Guanacaste)	$30
Costa Rican *casado* (blue-plate special)	$3

Transportation

The cost of your flight to Costa Rica will be one of your major expenses, especially during the high season. Airfares are almost impossible to predict and can change at the drop of a hat. Still, to give you an idea of what to expect, here's a sampling of potential fares from season to season: If you're going to Costa Rica in the off season — say, May or anytime between September and November — you may be able to snag a round-trip ticket for as little as $375 or $450 from any major U.S. hub. If you're traveling in the high season (late Dec–Apr, or July–Aug), you'll pay more — probably in the $500 to $800 range.

Expect to pay a little more if you're departing from a city that's not a major airline hub. If you're traveling to Costa Rica over the Christmas holidays or during other peak periods, expect to pay full fare. After you get to Costa Rica, your in-country transportation costs should be low.

 You can score any number of money-saving deals, especially if you consider an all-inclusive package. See Chapter 6 for more details on travel packages. I also tell you how to save on airfares in that chapter.

Internal Costa Rican flights

Many popular destinations inside Costa Rica are a four- to eight-hour drive from San José. Luckily, the country is served by a dependable network of internal commuter flights. One-way fares from San José to most other destinations run from $45 to $85. See Chapter 7 for details.

Car rentals

Rental cars are relatively inexpensive in Costa Rica. You can often get a compact for as little as $30 to $35 a day, or even less if you visit during the off season. If you need a larger car, or four-wheel-drive vehicle, expect to pay more like $45 to $65 per day. Weekly rates almost always save you a bundle.

Because driving distances to most destinations are substantial, don't forget to factor in the cost of gas. Currently, a liter of premium gas costs 360 colones, or roughly $2.96 per gallon.

 You'll seldom save by waiting to rent your car; generally, prices only go up as your pickup date approaches — especially in the busy travel seasons. Book as far in advance as possible for the best rate. Also see "Cutting Costs — but Not the Fun," later in this chapter, as well as Chapter 7, for additional money-saving tips.

Lodging

Although Costa Rica has a few luxury resorts and several excellent high-end boutique hotels, its strong suit is affordable small- to midsize hotels. Real budget hounds will have no problem finding clean and comfortable accommodations for under $75 per night. The best deals, though, can be found in the $80- to $120-per-night range, where Costa Rica really shines.

In this book, I recommend a range of lodging choices in each destination to suit just about any budget. I also include many helpful tips on how to save money, regardless of your budget. For one thing, booking a package deal can be a huge money saver when it comes to hotels. For more information on packages, see Chapter 6. For additional cost-cutting measures, see "Cutting Costs — but Not the Fun," later in this chapter.

 So that you don't encounter any unwanted surprises at check-out time, be sure to account for the 16.39 percent in taxes that will be added to your final hotel bill when planning your budget.

Dining

Dining options and quality have really improved in recent years in Costa Rica. What's more, prices remain relatively low to downright cheap, compared to those found in the United States and Europe.

Even at some of the best restaurants in Costa Rica, main dishes rarely cost over $20, and most average between $10 and $15. Things get much more affordable at the local Tico restaurants, where full meals can often be had for under $7.

At any of the beach destinations, fresh seafood is plentiful and cheap. A grilled whole snapper should only run you $8 to $10 at most seaside restaurants.

If you're staying in one spot for an extended stay, a good way to save on dining expenses is to book a room with a kitchenette. Kitchen facilities are a virtual must if you're traveling with kids.

Sightseeing

This is an area where you have to budget carefully. Most of the tours and activities in Costa Rica require an individual guide or guided tour. Options include guided hikes through the rain or cloud forests, white-water-rafting tours, sail and snorkel outings, and zip-line canopy tours. Rates on these range from $25 to $50 for a half-day outing, to $55 to $120 for full-day tours.

Other popular attractions found at various destinations include butterfly farms, serpentariums, and botanical gardens. Admission fees to these attractions run from $5 to $10 per person. Admission fees to national parks run from $6 to $8.

The only real museums in the country are found in San José, and admission to these is generally under $5.

This book lists exact prices for activities, entertainment, admission fees, and the like, so you can budget your money realistically. If there's a way to land a bargain, I include that information, too.

Shopping and nightlife

These two areas are the most flexible parts of your budget. Your shopping options will be very limited in Costa Rica. Most of what you'll be able to buy are simple souvenirs and inexpensive handcrafts.

Costa Rica also has very limited nightlife options. There are virtually no major shows or theaters to tempt you. And tickets to those shows are very inexpensive, in any case. Most clubs and discos charge a very modest admission fee, or none at all.

Cutting Costs — but Not the Fun

I don't care how much money you have — nobody wants to spend more than one has to. In this section, I give you some tips on how to avoid spending more of your hard-earned cash than is necessary.

Getting the best airfares

Getting the best airfare to Costa Rica is such a huge topic that I dedicate the better part of a chapter to it. Before you even start scanning for fares, see Chapter 6. That chapter also discusses how to find money-saving package deals.

Avoiding paying full price for your hotel room

A huge gap often exists between hotels' official *rack rates* (the published, full-price rates) and what you actually pay, so don't be scared off at first glance. What's more, savvy travelers can find ways to further widen the margin.

The best way to avoid paying the full rack rate when booking your hotel is stunningly simple: Book directly with the hotel and ask for a cheaper or discounted rate. You may be pleasantly surprised — I have been, many times. **Remember:** Hotels sell the majority of their rooms for far below their rack rates. Moreover, they're accustomed to paying travel agents and wholesalers hefty commissions. If you book directly, they're saving that commission (as much as 30 percent). But you have to take the initiative and ask because no one is going to *volunteer* to save you money.

Another good way to save money on lodging is to buy a package. Packages can include airfare, hotel, and car, and sometimes other extras, in one low price; for details on scoring a good-value package, see Chapter 6.

Here are a few more potentially money-saving tips on hotels:

✔ **Rates are generally lowest in spring and fall.** The time of year you decide to visit may affect your bargaining power more than anything else. During the peak seasons — basically mid-December through mid-April and throughout the summer — demand is high and hotels are less likely to offer discounted rates. In the slower seasons — generally mid-April through mid-June and September through mid-December — when demand is down, they're often very willing to negotiate. In fact, many places drop rates by 10 to 30 percent automatically in the less-busy times of year. If you haven't decided when you want to visit Costa Rica yet, see Chapter 3.

✔ **Inquire about the hotel's own package deals.** Even if you're not traveling on an all-inclusive package (see Chapter 6), you may be able to take advantage of packages offered by hotels, resorts, and condos directly. Properties often list these deals on their Web sites, but not always, so it never hurts to ask additional questions about available specials.

✔ **If you're booking a hotel that belongs to a chain, contact the hotel directly in addition to going through central reservations.** See which one gives you the better deal. Sometimes, the local reservationist knows about packages or special rates, but the hotel may neglect to tell the central booking line.

✔ **Reserve a hotel room with a kitchenette, or a condo with a full kitchen, and do your own cooking.** You may miss the pampering that room service provides, but you can save lots of money. Even if you prepare only breakfast and an occasional picnic lunch in the kitchen, you'll save significantly in the long run. Plus, if the beach is right outside your door, you won't ever have to leave it to go on restaurant runs.

✔ **Ask if your kids can stay in the room with you.** A room with two double beds usually doesn't cost any more than one with a queen-size bed. And many hotels won't charge you the additional-person rate if the additional person is pint-size and related to you. Even if you have to pay $10 or $15 extra for a rollaway bed, you'll save hundreds by not taking two rooms

✔ **Surf the Web to save.** A surprising number of hotels advertise great packages via their Web sites, and some even offer Internet-only special rates. In addition to surfing the hotel's own sites, you may want to try using a general travel-booking site like **Expedia.com, Travelocity.com, Hotels.com,** or **Orbitz.com** to book your hotel or a pay-one-price package that also includes airfare. Acting much like airline consolidators, these sites can sometimes offer big discounts on rooms as well. See Chapter 8 for a more complete discussion of how to use the Web to find a great hotel bargain.

Cutting other costs

Here are a few more useful money-saving tips:

✔ **Surf the Web to save on your rental car, too.** In addition to surfing car-rental agencies' own sites, you may want to try comparing rates through a general travel booking site like **Expedia.com, Travelocity.com, Orbitz.com,** or **Sidestep.com.** This one-stop-shopping method can save you more than money — it can save you time, too.

✔ **Don't rent a gas guzzler or four-wheel-drive vehicle.** Renting a smaller car is cheaper, and you save on gas to boot. Unless you're traveling with a large group, or you really need to go off-road, don't go beyond the economy size. See Chapter 7 for more tips on booking a car.

✔ **Travel midweek.** If you can travel on a Tuesday, Wednesday, or Thursday, you may find cheaper flights to your destination. When you ask about airfares, see if you can get a cheaper rate by flying on a different day. For more tips on getting a good fare, see Chapter 6.

✔ **Try a package tour.** For many destinations, you can book airfare, hotel, ground transportation, and even some sightseeing just by making one call to a travel agent or packager, for a price much lower than if you put the trip together yourself. (See Chapter 6 for more on package tours.)

✔ **Reserve a room with a refrigerator and coffeemaker.** You don't have to slave over a hot stove to cut a few costs; many hotels have minifridges and coffeemakers. Buying supplies for breakfast will save you money — and probably calories.

✔ **Always ask for discount rates.** Membership in AAA, frequent-flier plans, trade unions, AARP, or other groups may qualify you for savings on car rentals, plane tickets, hotel rooms, and even meals. Ask about everything; you may be pleasantly surprised.

✔ **Skip the souvenirs.** Your photographs and your memories could be the best mementos of your trip. If you're concerned about money, you can do without the T-shirts, key chains, salt-and-pepper shakers, shot glasses, and other trinkets.

Handling Money

You're the best judge of how much cash you feel comfortable carrying or what alternative form of currency is your favorite. That's not going to change much on your vacation. True, you'll probably be moving around more and incurring more expenses than you generally do, and you may let your mind slip into vacation gear and not be as vigilant about your safety as when you're in work mode. But, those factors aside, the only type of payment that won't be quite as available to you away from home is your personal checkbook.

Unlocking the mystery of the colón

The unit of currency in Costa Rica is the **colón.** In mid-2005, there were approximately 470 colones to the U.S. dollar, but because the colón is in a constant state of devaluation, you can expect this rate to change. Because of this devaluation and accompanying inflation, *this book lists prices in U.S. dollars only.* To check the very latest exchange rates before you leave home, point your browser to www.xe.com/ucc.

There are paper notes in denominations of 1,000, 2,000, 5,000, and 10,000 colones.

Currently, two types of coins are in circulation. The older and larger nickel-alloy coins come in denominations of 5, 10, and 20 colones. There are even smaller denominations, but because of their evaporating value, you'll probably never see or have to handle them. In 1997, the government introduced gold-hued 5-, 10-, 25-, 50-, 100-, and 500-colón coins. They're smaller and heavier than the older coins, and the government is supposed to eventually phase out the other currency, although that plan has seemingly stalled. See Table 5-2.

Table 5-2	The Colón, the U.S. Dollar, the Euro, and the British Pound		
Colones	*U.S. $*	*E.U.* €	*British £*
10	.02	.02	.01
25	.05	.04	.03
100	.21	.16	.10
500	1.06	.82	.56
5,000	10.64	8.17	5.55
10,000	21.28	16.34	11.11
25,000	53.20	40.86	27.78
50,000	106.38	81.70	55.56
100,000	212.76	163.40	111.11
500,000	1,063.83	817.02	555.60

You'll hear people refer to a *rojo* or *tucán,* which are slang terms for the 1,000- and 5,000-colón bills, respectively. One-hundred-colón denominations are called *tejas,* so *cinco tejas* is 500 colones.

Exchanging money

If you fly into the Juan Santamaria International Airport in San José, you'll find a **Global Exchange** money-exchange booth just as you clear customs and immigration. However, these folks offer a good 10 percent less money than the official bank rate.

Several ATM machines are available at the airport, including one inside the baggage-claim area. These will give you the current official bank-exchange rate. However, the local machines charge between $1 and $2 per transaction, and depending upon your card, bank, and type of account, you may face an additional charge from your home bank.

You can also change money at all state-owned banks. However, the service at these banks is often slow and tedious. This simple transaction can often take as long as an hour and cause unnecessary confusion and anxiety. I don't recommend it.

Fortunately, you don't have to rely on the state's banks. There are much more efficient private banks around San José and in some of the larger provincial towns and cities. These private banks are kicking the state banks' butts, providing fast service at reasonable commissions, with short or no lines.

Hotels will often exchange money and cash traveler's checks as well; there usually isn't much of a line, but they may shave a few colones off the exchange rate.

When you change money, ask for some small bills and some 100-colón coins. Petty cash will come in handy for tipping and public transportation. Consider keeping the change separate from your larger bills so it's readily accessible and so you're less of a target for theft.

Unless you can secure a decent exchange rate, you really don't need to change dollars into colones in advance of your trip because the airport taxis all accept U.S. dollars.

Be very careful about exchanging money on the streets; doing so is extremely risky. In addition to forged bills and short counts, street money-changers frequently work in teams that can leave you holding neither colones nor dollars. When receiving change in colones, checking the larger-denomination bills is a good idea; they should have protective bands or hidden images that appear when held up to the light.

Using ATMs and carrying cash

The easiest and best way to get cash away from home is from an ATM. ATMs are quite common throughout Costa Rica, particularly in San José, and at most major tourist destinations around the country. You'll find them at almost all banks and most shopping centers. Still, make sure you have some cash at the start of your trip, never let yourself run totally out of spending money, and definitely stock up on funds before heading to any of the more remote destinations in the country. Outside San José and any of the more developed beach destinations, it's still best to think of your ATM card as a backup measure because machines are not nearly as readily available or dependable as you may be accustomed to, and you may encounter compatibility problems.

The **Cirrus** (☎ 800-424-7787; www.mastercard.com) and **PLUS** (☎ 800-843-7587; www.visa.com) networks span the globe; look at the back of your bank card to see which network you're on, then call or check online for ATM locations at your destination. Be sure you know your personal identification number (PIN) before you leave home and be sure to find out your daily withdrawal limit before you depart. Also keep in mind that many banks impose a fee every time your card is used at a different bank's ATM, and that fee can be higher for international transactions (up to $5 or more) than for domestic ones (where they're rarely more than $1.50). On top of this, the bank from which you withdraw cash may charge its own fee. To compare banks' ATM fees within the U.S., go to www.bankrate.com. For international withdrawal fees, ask your bank.

See the Quick Concierge appendix for additional information on ATMs.

Charging ahead with credit cards

Credit cards are a safe way to carry money: They provide a convenient record of all your expenses, and they generally offer relatively good exchange rates. You can also withdraw cash advances from your credit cards at banks or ATMs, provided you know your PIN. If you've forgotten yours, or didn't even know you had one, call the number on the back of your credit card and ask the bank to send it to you. It usually takes five to seven business days, though some banks will provide the number over the phone if you tell them your mother's maiden name or some other personal information.

Keep in mind that when you use your credit card abroad, most banks assess a 2 percent fee above the 1 percent fee charged by Visa, MasterCard, or American Express for currency conversion on credit charges. But credit cards still may be the smart way to go when you factor in things like exorbitant ATM fees and higher traveler's check exchange rates (and service fees).

Some credit card companies recommend that you notify them of any impending trip abroad so that they don't become suspicious when the card is used numerous times in a foreign destination and block your charges. Even if you don't call your credit card company in advance, you can always call the card's toll-free emergency number if a charge is refused — a good reason to carry the phone number with you. But perhaps the most important lesson here is to carry more than one card with you on your trip; a card might not work for any number of reasons, so having a backup is the smart way to go.

Toting traveler's checks

These days, traveler's checks are less necessary because most cities have 24-hour ATMs that allow you to withdraw small amounts of cash as needed. However, keep in mind that you'll likely be charged an ATM withdrawal fee if the bank is not your own, so if you're withdrawing money every day, you may be better off with traveler's checks — provided that you don't mind showing identification every time you want to cash one.

You can get traveler's checks at almost any bank. **American Express** offers denominations of $20, $50, $100, $500, and (for cardholders only) $1,000. You'll pay a service charge ranging from 1 to 4 percent You can also get American Express traveler's checks over the phone by calling ☎ **800-221-7282;** AMEX gold and platinum cardholders who use this number are exempt from the 1 percent fee.

Visa offers traveler's checks at Citibank locations nationwide, as well as at several other banks. The service charge ranges between 1.5 percent and 2 percent; checks come in denominations of $20, $50, $100, $500, and $1,000. Call ☎ **800-732-1322** for information. AAA members can obtain Visa checks without a fee at most AAA offices or by calling ☎ **866-339-3378. MasterCard** also offers traveler's checks. Call ☎ **800-223-9920** for a location near you.

If you choose to carry traveler's checks, be sure to keep a record of their serial numbers separate from your checks in the event that they're stolen or lost. You'll get a refund faster if you know the numbers.

Taking Taxes into Account

There is a 13 percent tax on most goods and services in Costa Rica. Restaurants charge 13 percent tax and also add on a 10 percent service charge, for a total of 23 percent more on your bill. On restaurant menus, look for the letters *i.v.i.* next to the prices, which means the tax is included or factored into the listed price. Otherwise, tax may be added onto your bill later. All hotels charge 16.3 percent tax, which is the 13 percent tax, plus a 3.3 percent special hotel tax.

There is a $26 departure tax for all visitors leaving by air.

Dealing with a Lost or Stolen Wallet

Be sure to contact all your credit card companies the minute you discover your wallet has been lost or stolen and file a report at the nearest police precinct. Your credit card company or insurer may require a police-report number or record of the loss. Most credit card companies have an emergency toll-free number to call if your card is lost or stolen; they may be able to wire you a cash advance immediately or deliver an emergency credit card in a day or two. Call the following emergency numbers in Costa Rica:

- ✔ **American Express (for lost cards):** ☎ **0800-012-3211**
- ✔ **American Express (for lost traveler's checks):** ☎ **0800-242-8585**
- ✔ **MasterCard:** ☎ **0800-011-0184**
- ✔ **Visa:** ☎ **0800-011-0130**

Most credit cards carry a phone number you can call collect 24 hours a day from anywhere on the globe. It's a good idea to jot down this number in a safe place separate from your wallet and valuables before you travel.

If your ATM card doesn't work and you need cash in a hurry, **Western Union** (☎ 800-777-7777 in Costa Rica; www.westernunion.com) has numerous offices around San José and in several major towns and cities around the country.

Identity theft and fraud are potential complications of losing your wallet, especially if you've lost your driver's license along with your cash and credit cards. Notify the major credit-reporting bureaus immediately; placing a fraud alert on your records may protect you against liability for criminal activity. The three major U.S. credit-reporting agencies are **Equifax** (☎ 800-766-0008; www.equifax.com), **Experian** (☎ 888-397-3742; www.experian.com), and **TransUnion** (☎ 800-680-7289; www.transunion.com). Finally, if you've lost all forms of photo ID, call your airline and explain the situation; they might allow you to board the plane if you have a copy of your passport or birth certificate and a copy of the police report you've filed.

Chapter 6

Getting to Costa Rica

● ●

In This Chapter

▶ Finding the best airfares
▶ Considering a tour
▶ Taking advantage of package deals

● ●

*G*etting there may not *really* be half the fun, but it's a necessary step — and a big part of the planning process. How can you beat the high cost of international airfares? Should you reserve a package deal or book the elements of your vacation separately?

In this chapter, I give you all the information you need to make the trip decision that's right for you.

Flying to Costa Rica

The majority of international flights arrive at San José's Juan Santamaria International Airport, but an increasing number are beginning to land in Liberia at the Daniel Olduber International Airport in the northern province of Guanacaste.

The following major airlines fly between mainland North America and one of Costa Rica's two airports:

✔ **Air Canada** (☎ 888-247-2262; www.aircanada.ca) flies from Toronto to San José's Juan Santamaria International Airport.

✔ **American Airlines** (☎ 800-433-7300; www.americanair.com) flies from Los Angeles, Miami, JFK in New York, and Dallas–Fort Worth to San José's Juan Santamaria International Airport. It also has three weekly direct flights from Miami to the Daniel Olduber International Airport in Liberia.

✔ **America West** (☎ 800-363-2957; www.americawest.com) flies direct from Phoenix to San José's Juan Santamaria International Airport.

✔ **Continental Airlines** (☎ 800-525-0280; www.continental.com) has daily flights from Houston and Newark to San José's Juan

Santamaria International Airport, as well as three weekly flights
from Houston to the Daniel Olduber International Airport in Liberia.

✔ **Delta Air Lines** (☎ **800-221-1212**; www.delta.com) flies twice daily
direct from Atlanta to San José's Juan Santamaria International
Airport, as well as six times each week from Atlanta to the Daniel
Olduber International Airport in Liberia.

✔ **US Airways** (☎ **800-622-1015**; www.usairways.com) has direct
flights between Charlotte, North Carolina, and both major airports
in Costa Rica.

✔ **United Air Lines** (☎ **800-241-6522**; www.ual.com) flies direct from
Los Angeles and Washington, D.C., to San José's Juan Santamaria
International Airport.

Getting the best airfare

Competition among the major airlines is unlike that of any other industry. Every airline offers virtually the same product (basically, a coach
seat is a coach seat is a . . .), yet prices can vary by hundreds of dollars.

Business travelers who need the flexibility to buy their tickets at the last
minute and change their itineraries at a moment's notice — and who
want to get home before the weekend — pay (or at least their companies
pay) the premium rate, known as the *full fare*. But if you can book your
ticket far in advance, stay over Saturday night, and are willing to travel
midweek (Tues, Wed, or Thurs), you can qualify for the least expensive
price — usually a fraction of the full fare. On most flights, even the shortest hops within the United States, the full fare is close to $1,000 or more,
but a 7- or 14-day advance-purchase ticket may cost less than half of that
amount. Obviously, planning ahead pays.

The airlines also periodically hold sales, in which they lower the prices
on their most popular routes. These fares have advance-purchase
requirements and date-of-travel restrictions, but you can't beat the
prices. As you plan your vacation, keep your eyes open for these sales,
which tend to take place in seasons of low travel volume — mid-April
through mid-June and September through mid-December. You almost
never see a sale around the peak summer vacation months of July and
August, or around Thanksgiving or Christmas, when many people fly,
regardless of the fare they have to pay.

Consolidators, also known as *bucket shops,* are great sources for international tickets, although they usually can't beat the Internet on fares
within North America. Start by looking in Sunday newspaper travel sections; U.S. travelers should focus on the *New York Times, Los Angeles
Times,* and *Miami Herald.* For a less-developed destination like Costa
Rica, small travel agents who cater to immigrant communities in large
cities often have the best deals.

Bucket-shop tickets are usually nonrefundable or rigged with stiff cancellation penalties, often as high as 50 percent to 75 percent of the ticket price, and some put you on charter airlines with questionable safety records.

One consolidator specializing in travel to Latin America is **Latin Air Discount** (☎ 213-383-8906; www.latindiscountair.com). Several reliable consolidators are worldwide and available on the Net. **STA Travel** (☎ 800-781-4040; www.statravel.com), the world's leader in student travel, offers good fares for travelers of all ages. **FlyCheap** (☎ 800-359-2432; www.1800flycheap.com) is owned by package-holiday megalith MyTravel and so has especially good access to fares for sunny destinations like Costa Rica. **Air Tickets Direct** (☎ 800-778-3447; www.air ticketsdirect.com) is based in Montreal and leverages the currently weak Canadian dollar for low fares.

Booking your flight online

The "big three" online travel agencies, **Expedia** (www.expedia.com), **Travelocity** (www.travelocity.com), and **Orbitz** (www.orbitz.com) sell most of the air tickets bought on the Internet. (Canadian travelers should try www.expedia.ca and www.travelocity.ca; U.K. residents can go for expedia.co.uk and opodo.co.uk.) Each has different business deals with the airlines and may offer different fares on the same flights, so shopping around is wise. Expedia and Travelocity will also send you an **e-mail notification** when a cheap fare becomes available to your favorite destination. Of the smaller travel agency Web sites, **SideStep** (www.sidestep.com) receives good reviews from users. It's a browser add-on that purports to "search 140 sites at once" but in reality only beats competitors' fares as often as other sites do.

Great **last-minute deals** are available through free weekly e-mail services provided directly by the airlines. Most of these deals are announced on Tuesday or Wednesday and must be purchased online. Most are only valid for travel that weekend, but some (such as Southwest's) can be booked weeks or months in advance. Sign up for weekly e-mail alerts at airline Web sites or check mega-sites that compile comprehensive lists of last-minute specials, such as **Smarter Travel** (www.smartertravel.com). For last-minute trips, **www.site59.com** in the United States and **www.last minute.com** in Europe often have better deals than the major-label sites.

If you're willing to give up some control over your flight details, use an *opaque fare service* like **Priceline** (www.priceline.com) or **Hotwire** (www.hotwire.com). Both offer rock-bottom prices in exchange for travel on a "mystery airline" at a mysterious time of day, often with a mysterious change of planes en route. The mystery airlines are all major, well-known carriers — and the possibility of being sent from Philadelphia to Chicago via Tampa is remote. But your chances of getting a 6 a.m. or 11 p.m. flight are pretty high. Hotwire tells you flight prices before you buy; Priceline usually has better deals than Hotwire, but you have to play their "name our price" game. *Note:* In 2004, Priceline added nonopaque

---

Frommers.com: The complete travel resource

For an excellent travel-planning resource, we highly recommend **Frommers.com** (www.frommers.com), voted Best Travel Site by *PC Magazine*. We're a little biased, of course, but we guarantee that you'll find the travel tips, reviews, monthly vacation giveaways, bookstore, and online-booking capabilities thoroughly indispensable. Among the special features are our popular **Destinations** section, where you'll get expert travel tips, hotel and dining recommendations, and advice on the sights to see for more than 3,500 destinations around the globe; the **Frommers.com Newsletter,** with the latest deals, travel trends, and money-saving secrets; our **Community** area featuring **Message Boards,** where Frommer's readers post queries and share advice (sometimes even our authors show up to answer questions); and our **Photo Center,** where you can post and share vacation tips. When your research is done, the **Online Reservations System** (www.frommers.com/book_a_trip) takes you to Frommer's preferred online partners for booking your vacation at affordable prices.

---

service to its roster. You now have the option to pick exact flights, times, and airlines from a list of offers — or opt to bid on opaque fares as before.

 Great last-minute deals are also available directly from the airlines themselves through a free e-mail service called *E-savers*. Each week, the airline sends you a list of discounted flights, usually leaving the upcoming Friday or Saturday and returning the following Monday or Tuesday. You can sign up for all the major airlines at one time by logging on to **Smarter Travel** (www.smartertravel.com), or you can go to each individual airline's Web site. Airline sites also offer schedules, flight booking, and information on late-breaking bargains.

Joining an Escorted Tour

Pay-one-price discount package tours are one thing, but escorted tours are a different animal altogether. Costa Rica is a friendly and accessible country for independent travel, but in some instances an escorted tour can be helpful. Many escorted tours to Costa Rica are built around a specific theme or adventure — bird-watching or mountain biking, for example. They often carry knowledgeable and experienced guides with them.

Or, you may be one of the many people who love escorted tours. The tour company takes care of all the details and tells you what to expect at each leg of your journey. You know your costs up front and, in the case of the tame ones, you don't get many surprises. Escorted tours can take you to the maximum number of sights in the minimum amount of time with the least amount of hassle.

If you decide to go with an escorted tour, I strongly recommend purchasing travel insurance, especially if the tour operator asks you to pay up front. But don't buy insurance from the tour operator! If the tour operator doesn't fulfill its obligation to provide you with the vacation you paid for, you have no reason to believe that the operator willfulfill its insurance obligations either. Get travel insurance through an independent agency. (I tell you more about the ins and outs of travel insurance in Chapter 10.)

When choosing an escorted tour, along with finding out whether you have to put down a deposit and when final payment is due, ask a few simple questions before you buy:

- **What is the cancellation policy?** Can they cancel the trip if they don't get enough people? How late can you cancel if you're unable to go? Do you get a refund if you cancel? If they cancel?

- **How jam-packed is the schedule?** Does the tour schedule try to fit 25 hours into a 24-hour day, or does it give you ample time to relax by the pool or shop? If getting up at 7 a.m. every day and not returning to your hotel until 6 or 7 p.m. at night sounds like a grind, certain escorted tours may not be for you.

- **How large is the group?** The smaller the group, the less time you spend waiting for people to get on and off the bus. Tour operators may be evasive about this, because they may not know the exact size of the group until everybody has made reservations, but they should be able to give you a rough estimate.

- **Is there a minimum group size?** Some tours have a minimum group size and may cancel the tour if they don't book enough people. If a quota exists, find out what it is and how close they are to reaching it. Again, tour operators may be evasive in their answers, but the information may help you select a tour that's sure to happen.

- **What exactly is included?** Don't assume anything. You may have to pay to get yourself to and from the airport. A box lunch may be included in an excursion, but drinks may be extra. Beer may be included but not wine. How much flexibility do you have? Can you opt out of certain activities, or does the bus leave once a day, with no exceptions? Are all your meals planned in advance? Can you choose your entree at dinner, or does everybody get the same chicken cutlet?

Depending on your recreational passions, I recommend one of the following tour companies:

- **Abercrombie & Kent** (☎ **800-323-7308;** www.abercrombiekent. com) is a luxury-tour company that offers several tours to Costa Rica. It specializes in nine-day highlight tours hitting Monteverde, Arenal, and Tortuguero. Service is personalized and the guides are top-notch. The cost is around $2,500 to $3,000 per adult, not including international airfare.

✔ **Butterfield & Robinson** (☎ 800-678-1147; www.butterfield.com) is another company specializing in the very high-end market. One of its most interesting options is a trip designed for families with children over 8 years old. The trip provides a wealth of activities and adventures for parents and kids to enjoy both together and apart. An eight-day/seven-night trip costs around $5,700 per person.

✔ **Costa Rica Expeditions** (☎ 257-0766; www.costarica expeditions.com) is a Costa Rica–based company that offers everything from a ten-day escorted tour covering the whole country, to three-day/two-night and two-day/one-night tours of Monteverde Biological Cloud Forest Reserve, Tortuguero National Park, and Corcovado National Park, where it runs its own lodges. It also offers one- to two-day white-water-rafting trips and other excursions.

✔ **Overseas Adventure Travel** (☎ 800-493-6824; www.oattravel. com) offers good-value natural history and soft adventure itineraries, with optional add-on excursions. Tours are limited to 16 people and are guided by naturalists. All accommodations are in small hotels, lodges, or tent camps. The "Real Affordable Costa Rica" 13-day package lives up to its name at $1,495 per person, including round-trip airfare from Miami.

Choosing a Package Tour

For lots of destinations, package tours can be a smart way to go. In many cases, a package tour that includes airfare, hotel, and transportation to and from the airport costs less than the hotel alone on a tour you book yourself. That's because packages are sold in bulk to tour operators, who resell them to the public. It's kind of like buying your vacation at a buy-in-bulk store — except the tour operator is the one who buys the 1,000-count box of garbage bags and resells them 10 at a time at a cost that undercuts the local supermarket.

Package tours can vary quite a bit. Some offer a better class of hotels than others; others provide the same hotels for lower prices. Some book flights on scheduled airlines; others sell charters. In some packages, your choice of accommodations and travel days may be limited. Some let you choose between escorted vacations and independent vacations; others allow you to add on just a few excursions or escorted day trips (also at discounted prices) without booking an entirely escorted tour.

To find package tours, check out the travel section of your local Sunday newspaper or the ads in the back of national travel magazines such as *Travel + Leisure, National Geographic Traveler,* and *Condé Nast Traveler.*

Every destination, including Costa Rica, usually has a few packagers that are better than the rest because they buy in even bigger bulk. The time you spend shopping around is likely to be well rewarded.

Apple Vacations (www.applevacations.com) is a large package wholesaler with a host of all-inclusive options flying in and out of Liberia. You can either book directly online at their Web site, or they'll direct you to an approved travel agent near you. Weeklong, all-inclusive getaways can start as low as $1,100 including airfare, during the high season.

Costa Rica Experts (☎ **800-827-9046** or 773-935-1009; www.crexpert.com) offers a large menu of à la carte and scheduled departures, as well as day trips and adventure packages.

Liberty Travel (☎ **888-271-1584;** www.libertytravel.com) is one of the biggest packagers in the Northeast and usually boasts a full-page ad in Sunday papers. At press time, Liberty was offering several value packages, with or without air, to various upscale all-inclusive and boutique properties in Costa Rica. Calling the toll-free number immediately connects you to the Liberty Travel store nearest your home.

Vacation Express (☎ **800-309-4717;** www.vacationexpress.com) is a large packager with excellent deals on air-only, air and hotel, and all-inclusive options to Costa Rica.

Another good source of package deals is the airlines themselves. Most major airlines offer air/land packages, including **Air Canada Vacations** (☎ 800-662-3221; www.aircanadavacations.com), **American Airlines Vacations** (☎ 800-321-2121; www.aavacations.com), **Delta Vacations** (☎ 800-221-6666; www.deltavacations.com), **Continental Airlines Vacations** (☎ 800-301-3800; www.covacations.com), and **United Vacations** (☎ 888-854-3899; www.unitedvacations.com). Several big **online travel agencies** — Expedia, Travelocity, Orbitz, Site59, and Lastminute.com — also do a brisk business in packages. If you're unsure about the pedigree of a smaller packager, check with the Better Business Bureau in the city where the company is based, or go online to www.bbb.org. If a packager won't tell you where it's based, don't fly with them.

If you're booking a last-minute getaway, you may be able to score a stellar deal through **Site 59** (www.site59.com), which books all-inclusive travel packages as much as 60 percent off what the major packagers charge. The catch? You can only price and purchase your trip between 3 hours and 14 days before your departure, and all destinations are not available from all departure points. Still, if you're just dying to get away on the spur of the moment, it's worth checking out. You may also want to check out **TravelHub** (www.travelhub.com) for last-minute package deals.

Be aware that some travel packagers are likely to book you on their own charter flights rather than on commercial flights on major airlines. Which airline the packager uses doesn't really make a difference, unless you have a particular allegiance to a specific airline (or to collecting miles in a frequent-flier program). Be sure that you know which airline you're flying when you book. If you really do want to fly with a specific airline, that doesn't rule out a packager. In fact, just about any packager will be happy to book you a land-only vacation that lets you book your own airfare separately (even the airline packagers will do this; see the list of packagers mentioned earlier).

 Choosing between a travel agent and a packager isn't an either/or proposition; in fact, your travel agent can be your best source in sorting through the various deals that are available. If you're an AMEX customer, you may consider going through **American Express Travel Service,** which can book travel packages through various vendors, including Continental Vacations and Delta Vacations. To locate the office (or official travel-agent representative) nearest you, call ☎ **800-297-3429** or go online to www.americanexpress.com and click "Find a Travel Service Location." You can also use the site's online locator to find an agent who specializes in Costa Rican travel.

Ditto for members of the American Automobile Association, who have access to the **AAA Travel Agency,** which can also book excellent value package deals. Visit www.aaa.com to find the regional office nearest you.

Weighing your options

 With the multitude of packages on the market, you may need some help weighing the various merits of each one. Follow these tips as you sift your way through the options:

- ✔ **Read up on Costa Rica.** Read through the hotel listings in this book and select the places that sound interesting. Compare the rates that I list with the packagers' prices to best gauge which packagers are really offering a good deal and which have simply gussied up the rack rates to make their full-fare offer sound like a smart buy. Remember that the amount you save depends on both the property and the packager; some packagers can offer bigger savings on some properties than on others. Many packagers are selling the same pool of hotels, so be sure to comparison-shop.

- ✔ **Compare apples to apples.** When comparing packages, make sure that you know *exactly* what's included in the quoted price, and what's not. Don't assume anything: Some packagers include everything — including value-added extras like free continental breakfast, and tour and dining discounts — and others don't even include airfare. Additionally, when considering package prices, be sure to factor in add-on costs if you're flying from somewhere other than a major airline hub — some packagers price packages directly from your hometown, and some require additional premiums for airfares from your hometown to their Costa Rican gateway.

- ✔ **Before you commit to a package, make sure you know how much flexibility you have.** Some packagers require ironclad commitments, but others charge only minimal fees for changes or cancellations.

Consider the possibility that your travel plans may change and select a packager with the degree of flexibility that suits your needs. And if you pay up front for a complete vacation package that carries stiff cancellation penalties, consider buying travel insurance that will reimburse you in case an unforeseen emergency prevents you from traveling. (See Chapter 10 for more on this topic.)

✔ **Don't believe in fairy tales.** Unfortunately, shady dealers and fly-by-night operations are out there. If a package appears too good to be true, it probably is. Any knowledgeable travel agent should be able to help you determine whether a specific packager is on the level or not.

Chapter 7

Getting Around Costa Rica

● ●

In This Chapter
▶ Flying south
▶ Renting a car
▶ Busing it around Costa Rica

● ●

Getting around Costa Rica is relatively simple and you have various options for transportation. In this chapter, I give you the general lowdown on how to book and save money on car rentals, as well as the scoop on commuter airlines and local buses.

To visit many of the top spots in Costa Rica, taking a quick little commuter flight is the best, and sometimes only, option. Luckily, an excellent network of commuter flights is serviced by two reliable local airlines.

If you're going to crash on the beach for the week or visit just one area, you probably won't need to rent a car. But if you want to travel around the country and explore a few different destinations, renting a car is inexpensive and easy.

Finally, if you really want to keep your budget in line, local buses, and a couple of regularly scheduled minivan lines, are the way to go. That said, buses are by far the slowest and least comfortable means of transportation.

Flying Is Fastest

Many of Costa Rica's most popular destinations are a four- to eight-hour drive from San José. Luckily, excellent and affordable commuter airline service is offered to all these spots.

One-way fares from San José to most popular destinations run between $45 and $85. Flight times are generally between 20 minutes and a little over an hour.

Costa Rica's two principal local commuter airlines are:

✔ **Sansa** (☎ **221-9414**; www.flysansa.com)

✔ **Nature Air** (☎ **800-235-9272** in the United States or Canada; ☎ 299-6000 in Costa Rica; www.natureair.com)

Sansa operates from a separate terminal at San José's Juan Santamaría International Airport, while **Nature Air** operates from the small **Tobís Bolaños International Airport** in Pavas, 6.4km (4 miles) from San José. The ride from downtown to Pavas takes about ten minutes, and a metered taxi fare should cost $6 to $8. The ride from the airport to downtown is a different story: Most taxis refuse to use their meters, and the standard fee is set at double the metered rate, around $10 to $12.

In the last few years, some of Nature Air's return flights have started stopping first at the Juan Santamaría International Airport, enabling folks to make outgoing connections on international flights.

Sansa offers an in-country "air pass" at $199 for one week and $249 for two weeks. Theoretically, these allow for unlimited flights inside Costa Rica, although limited seating, overbooking, and preference given to full-price ticket buyers may make these air passes a slightly less appealing option.

Renting a Car

Renting a car in Costa Rica is no idle proposition. The roads are riddled with potholes, most rural intersections are unmarked, and, for some reason, sitting behind the wheel of a car seems to turn peaceful Ticos into homicidal maniacs.

This reality check isn't meant to scare you off from driving in Costa Rica. If you plan to visit more than one destination, and you're comfortable facing the aforementioned challenges, renting a car is a great way to go.

Despite what you may have heard, you probably don't absolutely need a four-wheel-drive vehicle in Costa Rica. Monteverde is the only major destination where four-wheel-drive is more or less mandatory, because roads generally aren't paved here. The rest of the country can be reached by paved roads.

Still, many visitors enjoy the extra clearance afforded by a four-wheel-drive vehicle. Moreover, a four-wheel-drive vehicle does allow you more freedom to venture off the beaten path.

The following companies rent cars in Costa Rica:

✔ **Alamo:** ☎ **800-462-5266**; www.alamo.com

✔ **Avis:** ☎ **800-230-4898**; www.avis.com

✔ **Budget:** ☎ **800-527-0700;** www.budget.com

✔ **Dollar:** ☎ **800-800-4000;** www.dollar.com

✔ **Hertz:** ☎ **800-654-3131;** www.hertz.com

✔ **National:** ☎ **800-227-7368;** www.nationalcar.com

✔ **Thrifty:** ☎ **800-847-4389;** www.thrifty.com

Getting the best deal

Rental cars are relatively inexpensive in Costa Rica. You can often get a compact car for as little as $30 to $40 a day, sometimes even less if you hit on a bargain or visit during the off season. If you need a larger car or a four-wheel-drive vehicle, expect to pay more on the order of $45 to $65 per day. Weekly rates almost always save you a bundle.

Car-rental rates vary even more than airline fares. The price depends on the size of the car, the length of time you keep it, where and when you pick it up and drop it off, where you take it, and a host of other factors. Keeping in mind a few key factors may save you hundreds of dollars.

✔ Weekend rates may be lower than weekday rates. If you're keeping the car five or more days, a weekly rate should be cheaper than the daily rate. Ask if the rate is the same for pickup Friday morning as it is Thursday night.

✔ Check whether the rate is cheaper if you pick up the car at a location in town rather than at the airport. In San José, I recommend picking up and dropping off your car at the airport because the city is a confusing and inhospitable place for visiting drivers.

✔ Find out whether age is an issue. Many car-rental companies add on a fee for drivers under 25, while some don't rent to them at all.

✔ If you see an advertised price in your local newspaper, be sure to ask for that specific rate; otherwise you may be charged the standard (higher) rate. Don't forget to mention membership in AAA, AARP, and trade unions. These memberships usually entitle you to discounts ranging from 5 percent to 30 percent.

✔ Check your frequent-flier accounts. Not only are your favorite (or at least most-used) airlines likely to have sent you discount coupons, but most car rentals add at least 500 miles to your account.

✔ As with other aspects of planning your trip, using the Internet can make comparison shopping for a car rental much easier. You can check rates at most of the major agencies' Web sites. Plus, all the major travel sites — **Travelocity** (www.travelocity.com), **Expedia** (www.expedia.com), **Orbitz** (www.orbitz.com), and **Smarter Living** (www.smarterliving.com), for example — have search engines that can dig up discounted car-rental rates. Just enter the car size you want, pickup and return dates, and location, and the server returns a price. You can even make the reservation through any of these sites.

✔ Consider booking your car as part of a complete travel package. Package deals not only save you dollars on airfare and accommodations but also on your rental cars, too. This one-stop shopping can help streamline the trip-planning process. For more on package deals, see Chapter 6.

✔ Join the rental company's preferred customer program. Most companies offer such promotions (such as National's Emerald Club). You may be able to snag a bargain rate or have a better shot at an upgrade if you're a member. Some companies make the process of picking up your car more hassle-free for members, too. And membership can work just like the airlines' frequent-flier plans: Renting from the same company several times can land you a free day or other perks.

In addition to the standard rental prices, other optional charges apply to most car rentals (and some not-so-optional charges, such as taxes). The Collision Damage Waiver (CDW), which requires you to pay for damage to the car in a collision, is covered by many credit card companies. Check with your credit card company before you go so you can avoid paying this hefty fee (as much as $20 a day). If you plan on renting a four-wheel-drive vehicle or a van, be sure to ask if those vehicles are covered. If you plan on driving to Monteverde or any other remote destination, also ask if you're covered for off-road travel; some of Costa Rica's more remote destinations are reached via some very rough dirt roads.

The car-rental companies also offer additional *liability insurance* (if you harm others in an accident), *personal accident insurance* (if you harm yourself or your passengers), and *personal effects insurance* (if your luggage is stolen from your car). Your insurance policy on your car at home probably covers most of these unlikely occurrences. However, if your own insurance doesn't cover you for rentals or if you don't have auto insurance, definitely consider the additional coverage (ask your car-rental agent for more information). Unless you're toting around the Hope diamond, and you don't want to leave that in your car trunk anyway, you can probably skip the personal effects insurance, but driving around without liability or personal accident coverage is never a good idea. Even if you're a good driver, other people may not be, and liability claims can be complicated.

Some companies also offer *refueling packages,* in which you pay for your initial full tank of gas up front, and can return the car with an empty gas tank. The prices can be competitive with local gas prices, but you don't get credit for any gas remaining in the tank. If you reject this option, you pay only for the gas you use, but you have to return the car with a full tank or face charges of $5 to $6 a gallon for any shortfall. If you usually run late and a fueling stop may make you miss your plane, you're a perfect candidate for the fuel-purchase option.

Before driving off with a rental car, be sure that you inspect the exterior and point out every tiny scratch, dent, tear, or any other damage. It's a common practice with many Costa Rican car-rental companies to claim that you owe payment for minor dings and dents that the company finds when you return the car.

 Although rental cars no longer bear special license plates, they're still readily identifiable to thieves and are frequently targeted. (Nothing is ever safe in a car in Costa Rica, although parking in guarded parking lots helps.) Transit police also sometimes target tourists. Never pay money directly to a police officer who stops you for any traffic violation.

Busing It around Costa Rica

Buses are by far the most economical way to get around the country, but they can be slow, uncomfortable, and a hassle if you have a lot of luggage. Costa Rican buses are inexpensive and they go nearly everywhere. There are two types: **Local buses** are the cheapest and slowest; they stop frequently and are generally a bit dilapidated. **Express buses** run between San José and most beach towns and major cities; these tend to be newer units and more comfortable, although very few are so new or modern as to have bathroom facilities.

Grayline (☎ 220-2126; www.graylinecostarica.com) and **Interbus** (☎ 283-5573; www.costaricapass.com) run regularly scheduled departures in passenger vans and small buses to and from most of the major tourist destinations in the country. Both charge between $17 and $38 for a one-way trip, depending on the distance to your destination.

For more detailed information on how to get to various destinations, see the various destination chapters that follow.

 Both Grayline and Interbus offer pickup and drop-off at a wide range of hotels. This means that if you're the first person picked up or the last person dropped off, you may have to sit through a long period of subsequent stops before finally hitting the road or reaching your destination. I've heard some horror stories about both lines concerning missed or severely delayed connections and rude drivers.

 Be very careful with your bags and belongings on public buses and around public bus stations. Tourists are prime targets for thieves and pickpockets, and these are places where they're easy picking. Try to always keep an eye on your belongings. If you must store your luggage out of sight, check on it during intermediary stops when others are loading and off-loading more baggage, just to be safe.

Chapter 8

Booking Your Accommodations

. . . .

In This Chapter

▶ Figuring out what kind of accommodations are right for you
▶ Checking out prices
▶ Getting the best room at the best rate

. . . .

Costa Rica is a rich and varied destination. You can spend a week of utter luxury at a full-service beach resort, or some time trekking through the rain forest while staying at an isolated ecolodge. This chapter helps you zero in on the type of accommodation best suited to your needs and tastes.

Costa Rica offers excellent options for every budget if you just know where to look — and I include the best of them in the chapters that follow. At the end of this chapter I give specific tips on how to find the best rate and best room, no matter what your budget is. For more-general tips on how to save, check out Chapter 5.

Getting to Know Your Options

Before you book your accommodations, you need to figure out what kind of place you want and how much you want to spend. Your options range from large-scale luxury resorts to basic budget *cabinas* (simple, rustic Costa Rican hotels). In between these extremes you'll find numerous small- to midsize hotels, ranging from moderate to downright decadent, as well as a whole host of ecolodges in remote, wild destinations.

Table 8-1 gives you an idea of what you can expect to pay in each price category.

Table 8-1	Key to Hotel Dollar Signs*	
Dollar Sign(s)	*Price Range*	*What to Expect*
$	Less than $75 per night	Budget — in this range you'll find everything from very basic to quite comfortable options, but often lacking amenities like air-conditioning, televisions, and in-room telephones.
$$	$75–$124	Moderate — midpriced room, often in a charming small- to midsize hotel. You'll start to get more amenities in this price range, but air-conditioning, televisions, and in-room phones are still sometimes missing.
$$$	$125–$199	Expensive — a high-quality hotel room with plenty of amenities.
$$$$	$200–$349	Very expensive — a high-quality room in a full-service resort, or intimate boutique hotel.
$$$$$	$350 or more per night	Ultraluxurious — only a few properties in Costa Rica charge this much. For this price, you'll get a huge room, suite, or private bungalow; an impressive view; and excellent service.

Each range of dollar signs, from one ($) to five ($$$$$), represents the median rack-rate price range for a double room per night during the high season, not factoring in the 16.39 percent hotel tax.

Relaxing at a large resort

Relatively few large-scale resorts exist in Costa Rica. Only the new Four Seasons Resort caters to the ultra-high-end traveler. Aside from a few exceptions in San José, most of the large resorts are beach resorts (there are none in the remote rain- and cloud-forest destinations). Most are located in the northwestern province of Guanacaste.

A resort (or resort hotel) offers everything that your average hotel offers — plus much more. Every resort hotel is different, of course, but you can expect such amenities as pools (often more than one) with poolside bar service; an activities desk; a fitness center and often a full-service spa; a variety of restaurants, bars, and lounges; a 24-hour front desk; concierge, valet, and bell services; twice-daily maid service; room service; tennis and sometimes golf; a business center; extensive children's programs; and more comforts. Beach resorts all offer direct beach access, with beach chairs and umbrellas, and often beach-toy rentals and a host of ocean activities.

Many luxury resorts also boast an increasing slate of in-room extras, such as CD players and big TVs with Nintendo systems, on-screen Web access, and VCRs or DVD players, and even Internet access.

Although large resorts often carry the heftiest rack rates, you can often score good deals if you book these as part of a package (see Chapter 6) because the large resorts often presell a chunk of their rooms in bulk to packagers and wholesalers. Many large resorts also feature special offers and package deals on their own Web sites.

Hanging at a hotel

Most hotels in Costa Rica tend to be smaller and have fewer facilities than your typical resort. In many cases, midpriced hotels don't offer air-conditioning. Still, many are very comfortable and feature a whole host of facilities, amenities, and activity options. Although many have a small swimming pool, in general, you shouldn't expect more than one restaurant or bar, or the myriad amenities that come with a full-fledged resort.

Unless otherwise noted, hotel pools and tennis courts are outdoors.

You'll find proportionally few chain hotels in Costa Rica, although Barceló, Best Western, Clarion, Comfort, Marriott, Meliá, Occidental, and Radisson are all represented.

Enjoying intimacy at a boutique hotel or B&B

Boutique hotels are smaller — with maybe 10 to 40 rooms — and more intimate than your average hotel. Bed-and-breakfasts are even smaller still. In both cases, the rooms are often more stylish and less cookie-cutter and usually have more amenities than those found at similarly priced hotels. The service also tends to be more attentive and personalized.

Throughout the book, I've listed the best boutique hotels Costa Rica has to offer. Several of these have banded together under the banner of **Small Distinctive Hotels of Costa Rica** (☎ 258-0150; www.distinctive hotels.com).

Getting close to nature at an ecolodge

Costa Rica is one of the world's great natural destinations. Bird-watchers, neophyte naturalists, and professional biologists flock here to spot wildlife and learn about the natural wonders of Costa Rica's many national parks and bioreserves. Ecosystems range from the high-altitude cloud forests of Monteverde, to the lowland rain forests of Manuel Antonio and the Osa Peninsula, to the jungle canals of Tortuguero. In all these remote destinations, you'll find small, isolated nature lodges or ecolodges. Some rival any accommodation in the country for a sense of style and personal attention, with a fair amount of luxury thrown in besides. (However, very few have air-conditioning or televisions in the rooms. In general, you shouldn't need the former and should be able to do without the latter here.) All have on-staff naturalist guides and a host of tour and hiking options.

Choosing a cabina

Cabinas are Costa Rica's cut-rate accommodations. Many are simple cinder-block rooms, with concrete floors, and no air-conditioning. The better ones, however, can be quite cozy, and may have wood or tile floors, firm beds, plenty of space, an overhead fan, and perhaps even air-conditioning and/or a television. Many cabinas feature either communal or private cooking areas, or laundry facilities. Cabinas are also great places to mingle with Costa Ricans. Throughout the book, I've only included the cream of the crop of the cabina field.

Finding the Best Room Rate

The *rack rate* is the maximum rate a hotel charges for a room. It's the rate you get if you walk in off the street and ask for a room for the night. You sometimes see these rates printed on the fire/emergency exit diagrams posted on the back of your door.

Hotels are happy to charge you the rack rate, but you can almost always do better. Perhaps the best way to avoid paying the rack rate is surprisingly simple: Just ask for a cheaper or discounted rate. You may be pleasantly surprised.

Room rates (even rack rates) change with the season, as occupancy rates rise and fall. But even within a given season, room prices are subject to change without notice, so the rates quoted in this book may be different from the actual rate you receive when you make your reservation. Be sure to mention membership in AAA, AARP, frequent-flier programs, and any other corporate-rewards programs you can think of when you call to book. You never know when the affiliation may be worth a few dollars off your room rate.

In all but the smallest accommodations the rate you pay for a room depends on many factors — chief among them being how you make your reservation. A travel agent may be able to negotiate a better price with certain hotels than you can get by yourself. (That's because the hotel often gives the agent a discount in exchange for steering his business toward that hotel.)

 A great way to get a great deal on a hotel room, especially at the large resorts, is to book it as part of an all-inclusive travel package that includes airfare and hotel, and sometimes other extras, in one low price. For details on how to find the best package deals, see Chapter 6.

Surfing the Web for Hotel Deals

Shopping online for hotels is generally done one of two ways: through the hotel's own Web site, or through an independent booking agency (or a fare-service agency like Priceline). These Internet hotel agencies have multiplied in mind-boggling numbers as of late, competing for the business of millions of consumers surfing for accommodations around the world. This competitiveness can be a boon to consumers who have the patience and time to shop and compare the online sites for good deals — but shop they must, for prices can vary considerably from site to site. And keep in mind that hotels at the top of a site's listing may be there for no other reason than that they paid money to get the placement.

Of the "big three" sites, **Expedia** offers a long list of special deals and "virtual tours" or photos of available rooms so you can see what you're paying for (a feature that helps counter the claims that the best rooms are often held back from bargain booking Web sites). **Travelocity** posts unvarnished customer reviews and ranks its properties according to the AAA rating system. Also reliable are **Hotels.com** and **Quikbook.com.** An excellent free program, **TravelAxe** (www.travelaxe.net), can help you search multiple hotel sites at once, even ones you may never have heard of — and conveniently lists the total price of the room, including the taxes and service charges. Another booking site, **Travelweb** (www.travelweb.com), is partly owned by the hotels it represents (including the Hilton, Hyatt, and Starwood chains) and is, therefore, plugged directly into the hotels' reservations systems — unlike independent online agencies, which have to fax or e-mail reservation requests to the hotel, a good portion of which get misplaced in the shuffle.

More than once, travelers who have booked through online agencies have arrived at their hotel, only to be told that they have no reservation. To be fair, many of the major sites are undergoing improvements in service and ease of use, and Expedia will soon be able to plug directly into the reservations systems of many hotel chains — none of which can be bad news for consumers. In the meantime, **get a confirmation number** and **make a printout** of any online booking transaction.

In the opaque Web site category, **Priceline** and **Hotwire** are even better for hotels than for airfares; with both, you're allowed to pick the neighborhood and quality level of your hotel before offering up your money. Priceline's hotel product even covers Europe and Asia, though it's much better at getting 5-star lodging for 3-star prices than at finding anything at the bottom of the scale. On the downside, many hotels stick Priceline guests in their least desirable rooms. Be sure to go to BiddingForTravel.com before bidding on a hotel room on Priceline; the site features a fairly up-to-date list of hotels that Priceline uses in major cities. For both Priceline and Hotwire, you pay up front, and the fee is nonrefundable. *Note:* Some hotels do not provide loyalty program credits or points or other frequent-stay amenities when you book a room through opaque online services.

For more tips on getting what you want using Priceline, check out *Priceline.com For Dummies* by Sascha Segan (Wiley Publishing, Inc.).

Reserving the Best Room

After you make your reservation, asking one or two more pointed questions can go a long way toward making sure you get the best room in the house:

> ✔ **Always ask for a corner room.** They're usually larger, quieter, and have more windows and light than standard rooms, and they don't always cost more.

> ✔ **Ask if the hotel is renovating.** If it is, request a room away from the renovation work.

> ✔ **Inquire about the location of the restaurants, bars, and discos in the hotel — all sources of annoying noise.**

If you aren't happy with your room when you arrive, talk to the front desk. If they have another room, they should be happy to accommodate you, within reason.

Chapter 9

Catering to Special Travel Needs or Interests

· ·

In This Chapter

▶ Bringing the kids along

▶ Finding travel tips for seniors, folks with disabilities, and gays and lesbians

▶ Tying the knot in Costa Rica

· ·

> **C**osta Rica is an exotic and foreign destination that is well-suited to all sorts of travelers. Still, travelers come in a variety of ages, sizes, and types. Some may wonder how Costa Rica is for families traveling with kids? What will it be like for same-sex couples? Is it hospitable to older travelers, or those with disabilities? Can I get married there? If you have any of these questions, you've turned to the right chapter. In the following, I give you the details of what to expect and how to best prepare for any or all of these circumstances.

Traveling with the Brood: Advice for Families

If you have enough trouble getting your kids out of the house in the morning, dragging them thousands of miles away may seem like an insurmountable challenge. But family travel can be immensely rewarding, giving you new ways of seeing the world through smaller pairs of eyes.

Costa Rica is an excellent destination for children, especially those who are inquisitive and adventurous. Most children will be fascinated by the wildlife. Imagine, this is a place where grown adults come to study and collect insects, frogs, and snakes. So kids will feel right at home. Older children can learn to surf and fly through the air on a zip-line canopy tour.

Hotels in Costa Rica often give discounts for children under 12, and children under 3 or 4 are usually allowed to stay for free. Discounts for children and the cutoff ages vary according to the hotel. In general, don't assume that your kids can stay in your room for free, but be sure to ask.

Many hotels, villas, and cabinas come equipped with kitchenettes or full kitchen facilities. These can be a real money saver for those traveling with children, and I list many of these accommodations in the destination chapters that follow.

Cabinas are Costa Rica's version of cheap lodging. They're very inexpensive and very basic — often just cinder-block buildings divided into small rooms. They cater primarily to Tico families on vacation. See Chapter 8 for more information.

Hotels offering regular, dependable babysitting service are few and far between. If you'll need babysitting, make sure that your hotel offers it, and be sure to ask whether the babysitters are bilingual. In many cases, they aren't; this language difference usually isn't a problem with infants and toddlers, but it can cause problems with older children.

Familyhostel (☎ 800-733-9753; www.learn.unh.edu/familyhostel) takes the whole family, including kids ages 8 to 15, on moderately priced domestic and international learning vacations. Lectures, field trips, and sightseeing are guided by a team of academics.

You can find good family-oriented vacation advice on the Internet from sites like the **Family Travel Forum** (www.familytravelforum.com), a comprehensive site that offers customized trip planning; **Family Travel Network** (www.familytravelnetwork.com), an award-winning site that offers travel features, deals, and tips; **Traveling Internationally with Your Kids** (www.travelwithyourkids.com), a comprehensive site that offers customized trip planning; and **Family Travel Files** (www.thefamilytravelfiles.com), which offers an online magazine and a directory of off-the-beaten-path tours and tour operators for families.

Look for the Kid Friendly icon as you flip through this book. I use it to highlight hotels, restaurants, and attractions that are particularly welcoming or suited to families traveling with kids. Zeroing in on these listings can help you plan your trip more efficiently.

All visitors to Costa Rica, including children, need to carry a current passport.

Making Age Work for You: Tips for Seniors

Although senior citizens are respected and honored in Costa Rican society, they're seldom offered official discounts or perks. Still, mention the fact that you're a senior citizen when you make your travel reservations. Although all the major U.S. airlines except America West have cancelled their senior-discount and coupon-book programs, many hotel chains still offer discounts for seniors.

Always carry an ID card with you, especially if you've kept your youthful glow.

Learning Spanish or just brushing up

A trip to Costa Rica is a perfect opportunity to learn Spanish or brush off the rusty high school Spanish you've let slide. Costa Rica boasts scores of language institutes. Most offer intensive courses combined with cultural activities and adventure outings. Many can set you up with a home-stay, where you stay and eat meals with a local Costa Rican family.

Whereas in the past, most language schools were based in San José, you can now find them in most of the popular tourist destinations. Courses tend to be weekly and can have anywhere from four to six hours of language instruction per day.

Here's a list of some well respected language schools you might contact:

✔ **Centro Panamericano de Idiomas** (☎ 866-528-3424 in the United States, or 265-6306 in Costa Rica; www.cpi-edu.com) has three campuses: one in the quiet suburban town of Heredia, another in Monteverde, and a new facility in Playa Flamingo. A one-week program with four hours of class per day and a home-stay with a Costa Rican family costs $380.

✔ **Costa Rican Language Academy** (☎ 866-230-6361 in the United States, or 280-1685 in Costa Rica; www.spanishandmore.com), which is located in San José, has classes only Monday through Thursday, to give students a chance to make longer weekend excursions. The academy also integrates Latin dance and Costa Rican cooking classes into the program. A one-week class with four hours of class per day, plus a home-stay, costs $300.

✔ **Costa Rica Spanish Institute** (☎ 800-771-5184 in the United States, or 253-2117 in Costa Rica; www.cosi.co.cr) offers small classes in the San Pedro neighborhood of San José, as well as a program at the Pacific beach of Manuel Antonio. The cost is $380 per week with a home-stay in San José; at the beach, it's $425, with room and board extra.

✔ **La Escuela Idiomas D'Amore** (☎/fax 262-367-8598 in the United States, or ☎/fax 777-1143 in Costa Rica; www.escueladamore.com) is situated in the lush surroundings of Manuel Antonio National Park. A two-week conversational Spanish course, including a home-stay and two meals daily, costs $980. Fifteen percent of your tuition is donated to the World Wildlife Fund.

✔ **Wayra Instituto de Español** (☎/fax 653-0359; www.spanish-wayra.co.cr) is located in the beach town of Tamarindo. A week of classes, four hours per day, will run you $230. With a home-stay, the cost is $350.

Members of **AARP** (formerly known as the American Association of Retired Persons), 601 E St. NW, Washington, DC 20049 (☎ 888-687-2277 or 202-434-2277; www.aarp.org), get discounts on hotels (including chains represented in Costa Rica), airfares, and car rentals. AARP offers members a wide range of benefits, including *AARP: The Magazine* and a monthly newsletter. Anyone over 50 can join.

Many reliable agencies and organizations target the 50-plus market. **Elderhostel** (☎ 877-426-8056; www.elderhostel.org) runs regular educational trips to Costa Rica for travelers age 55 and over (and a spouse or companion of any age). Most tours last about three weeks, and many include airfare, accommodations in student dormitories or modest inns, meals, and tuition. **INTRAV** (☎ 800-456-8100; www.intrav.com) is a high-end tour operator that caters to the mature, discerning traveler, not specifically seniors, with trips around the world, including Costa Rica.

Recommended publications offering travel resources and discounts for seniors include the quarterly magazine *Travel 50 & Beyond* (www.travel50andbeyond.com); *Travel Unlimited: Uncommon Adventures for the Mature Traveler,* by Alison Gardner; *101 Tips for Mature Travelers,* available from Grand Circle Travel (☎ 800-221-2610 or 617-350-7500; www.gct.com); *The 50+ Traveler's Guidebook,* by Anita Williams and Merrimac Dillon; and *Unbelievably Good Deals and Great Adventures That You Absolutely Can't Get Unless You're Over 50,* by Joan Rattner Heilman.

Accessing Costa Rica: Advice for Travelers with Disabilities

A disability shouldn't stop anyone from traveling. More options and resources are available than ever before. Still, Costa Rica does present specific challenges to travelers with disabilities. Although Costa Rica has an Equality of Opportunities for People with Disabilities law, and some facilities are beginning to be adapted, in general, there are relatively few handicapped-accessible buildings. In San José or elsewhere, sidewalks are crowded and uneven. Few hotels offer wheelchair-accessible accommodations, and there are no public buses thus equipped. In short, people with disabilities often have difficulty getting around in Costa Rica.

Many travel agencies offer customized tours and itineraries for travelers with disabilities. **Flying Wheels Travel** (☎ 507-451-5005; www.flyingwheelstravel.com) offers escorted tours and cruises that emphasize sports and private tours in minivans with lifts. Another good operator offering tours in Costa Rica is **Accessible Journeys** (☎ 800-846-4537 or 610-521-0339; www.disabilitytravel.com). **Access-Able Travel Source** (☎ 303-232-2979; www.access-able.com) offers extensive access information and advice for traveling around the world with disabilities.

One local agency specializes in tours for travelers with disabilities and restricted ability. **Vaya Con Silla de Ruedas** (☎ 454-2810 or 391-5045; www.gowithwheelchairs.com) has a ramp- and elevator-equipped van and knowledgeable bilingual guides. It charges very reasonable prices and can provide anything from simple airport transfers to complete multiday tours.

Organizations that offer assistance to disabled travelers include the **MossRehab** (www.mossresourcenet.org), which provides a library of accessible-travel resources online; **Society for Accessible Travel and Hospitality** (SATH; ☎ 212-447-7284; www.sath.org; annual membership fees: $45 adults, $30 seniors and students), which offers a wealth of travel resources for all types of disabilities and informed recommendations on destinations, access guides, travel agents, tour operators, vehicle rentals, and companion services; and the **American Foundation for the Blind** (AFB; ☎ 800-232-5463; www.afb.org), a referral resource for the blind or visually impaired that includes information on traveling with Seeing Eye dogs.

For more information specifically targeted to travelers with disabilities, the community Web site **iCan** (www.icanonline.net/channels/travel/index.cfm) has destination guides and several regular columns on accessible travel. Also check out the quarterly magazine *Emerging Horizons* ($14.95 per year, $19.95 outside the United States; www.emerginghorizons.com); **Twin Peaks Press** (☎ 360-694-2462; http://disabilitybookshop.virtualave.net/blist84.htm), offering travel-related books for travelers with special needs; and *Open World Magazine,* published by SATH (subscription: $13 per year, $21 outside the United States).

Following the Rainbow: Resources for Gay and Lesbian Travelers

Costa Rica is a conservative Catholic country where public displays of same-sex affection are rare and considered somewhat shocking. Aside from the large resort hotels, some smaller hotels, a handful of bars and clubs, and one section of beach in Manuel Antonio, there are few places where same-sex shows of affection and contact are widely accepted. Still, gay and lesbian tourism to Costa Rica is robust, and gay and lesbian travelers are generally treated with respect. If you take into effect the local mores, you should not experience any harassment.

The best local source for current information on the gay and lesbian scene is **Uno@Diez**, on Calle 3 between avenidas 5 and 7 in downtown San José (☎ 258-4561; www.1en10.com), a coffeehouse, information outlet, gallery, and Internet cafe.

If you're doing your research online, check www.gaycostarica.com. A local tour agency specializing in gay and lesbian travel is **Tiquicia Travel** (www.tiquiciatravel.com). Two other agencies are **Gay Adventure Tours, Inc.** (☎ 888-206-6523; www.gayadventuretours.com) and **Above and Beyond Tours** (☎ 800-397-2681; www.abovebeyondtours.com), which offers gay and lesbian tours worldwide and is the exclusive gay and lesbian tour operator for United Airlines.

A note for female travelers

For lack of better phrasing, Costa Rica is a typically "macho" Latin American nation. Single women can expect a nearly constant stream of catcalls, hisses, whistles, and car horns, especially in San José. The best advice is to ignore the unwanted attention rather than try to come up with a witty rejoinder. Women should also be careful walking alone at night, both in San José and in more remote destinations. I definitely don't recommend hitchhiking. You may want to check out the award-winning Web site **Journeywoman** (www.journeywoman.com), a women's travel information network where you can sign up for a free e-mail newsletter and get advice on everything from etiquette and dress to safety.

The **International Gay and Lesbian Travel Association (IGLTA; ☎ 800-448-8550** or 954-776-2626; www.iglta.org) is the trade association for the gay and lesbian travel industry, and offers an online directory of gay- and lesbian-friendly travel businesses; go to its Web site and click on "Members."

The following travel guides are available at most travel bookstores and gay and lesbian bookstores, or you can order them from **Giovanni's Room** bookstore, 1145 Pine St., Philadelphia, PA 19107 (☎ **215-923-2960;** www.giovannisroom.com): *Frommer's Gay & Lesbian Europe,* an excellent travel resource (www.frommers.com); *Out and About* (☎ **800-929-2268** or 415-644-8044; www.outandabout.com), which offers guidebooks and a newsletter ($20/year; ten issues) packed with solid information on the global gay and lesbian scene; and the *Damron* guides (www.damron.com), with separate, annual books for gay men and lesbians.

Planning a Costa Rican Wedding

Whether you want to tie the knot on a beautiful beach at sunset, or surrounded by life's bounty under the canopy of giant rain-forest trees, Costa Rica offers some truly spectacular places to get married. What's more, your friends and family will love the excuse to take a tropical vacation, and you won't have to hop on a plane or experience any downtime before starting your honeymoon.

Getting married in Costa Rica is simple and straightforward. In most cases, all you need are current passports. You'll have to provide some basic information, including a copy of each passport, your dates of birth, your occupations, your current address, and the names and addresses of your parents. Two witnesses are required to be present at the ceremony. If you're traveling alone, your hotel, wedding consultant, or lawyer will provide the required witnesses.

Things are slightly more complicated if one or more of the partners was previously married. In such a case, the previously married partner must provide an official copy of the divorce decree. However, a couple of more draconian requirements exist specifically for recently divorced women. A bride-to-be cannot be remarried in Costa Rica within 300 days of her divorce, and if she was divorced less than 1 year before the current wedding date, she must present a negative pregnancy test.

Most travelers who get married in Costa Rica do so in a civil ceremony officiated by a local lawyer. After the ceremony, the lawyer records the marriage with Costa Rica's National Registry, which issues an official marriage certificate. This process generally takes between four and six weeks. Most lawyers or wedding coordinators then have the document translated and certified by the Costa Rican Foreign Ministry and at the embassy or consulate of your home country within Costa Rica before mailing it to you. From here, it's a matter of bringing this document to your local civil or religious authorities, if necessary.

Because Costa Rica is more than 90 percent Roman Catholic, arranging for a church wedding is usually easy in all but the most isolated and remote locations. To a lesser extent, a variety of denominational Christian churches and priests are often available to perform or host the ceremony. If you're Jewish, Muslim, Buddhist, or a follower of some other religion, bringing your own officiant is a good idea.

Officially, the lawyer must read all or parts of the Costa Rican civil code on marriage during your ceremony. This is a rather uninspired and somewhat dated legal code that, at some weddings, can take as much as 20 minutes to slog through. Most lawyers and wedding coordinators are quite flexible and can work with you to design a ceremony and text that fits your needs and desires. Insist on this.

Most of the higher-end and romantic hotels in Costa Rica have ample experience in hosting weddings. Many have an in-house wedding planner. Narrowing the list is tough, but I'd say the top choices include **Hotel Punta Islita** (Chapter 19), **Villa Caletas** (Chapter 16), **Makanda-by-the-Sea** (Chapter 15), **Flor Blanca Resort** (Chapter 19), and the **Four Seasons Resort** (Chapter 13). If you want a remote, yet luxurious, rain-forest lodge to serve as host and backdrop, try **La Paloma Lodge** (Chapter 20), **Bosque del Cabo Rainforest Lodge** (Chapter 20), or **Lapa Ríos** (Chapter 20). Another interesting option is **Punta Coral,** a private reserve owned by Calypso Tours (☎ **256-8787;** www.calypsotours.com).

If you're looking for service beyond what your hotel can offer, or if you want to do it yourself, check out www.weddingsincostarica.com, www.tropicaloccasions.com, or www.marcelogalli.com.

Chapter 10

Taking Care of the Remaining Details

*T*his chapter helps you shore up the final details — from getting a passport to purchasing travel insurance to mapping out strategies to stay connected while you're in Costa Rica.

Getting a Passport

A valid passport is the only legal form of identification accepted around the world. You can't cross an international border without it. Getting a passport is easy, but the process takes some time. For an up-to-date country-by-country listing of passport requirements around the world, go to the "Foreign Entry Requirement" Web page of the U.S. State Department at http://travel.state.gov.

Applying for a U.S. passport

If you're applying for a first-time passport, follow these steps:

1. **Complete a passport application in person at a U.S. passport office; a federal, state, or probate court; or a major post office.**

   To find your regional passport office, either check the **U.S. State Department** Web site (http://travel.state.gov) or call the **National Passport Information Center** (☎ 877-487-2778) for automated information.

2. **Present a certified birth certificate as proof of citizenship.**

   Bringing along your driver's license, state or military ID, or social security card is also a good idea.

3. **Submit two identical passport-size photos, measuring 2 x 2 inches in size.**

   You often find businesses that take these photos near a passport office. *Note:* You can't use a strip from a photo-vending machine because the pictures aren't identical.

4. **Pay a fee.**

   For people 16 and over, a passport is valid for ten years and costs $85. For those 15 and under, a passport is valid for five years and costs $70.

 Allow plenty of time before your trip to apply for a passport; processing normally takes three weeks but can take longer during busy periods (especially spring).

If you have a passport in your current name that was issued within the past 15 years (and you were over age 16 when it was issued), you can renew the passport by mail for $55. Whether you're applying in person or by mail, you can download passport applications from the U.S. State Department Web site at http://travel.state.gov. For general information, call the **National Passport Agency** (☎ 202-647-0518).

Applying for other passports

The following list offers more information for citizens of Australia, Canada, New Zealand, and the United Kingdom:

- ✔ **Australians** can visit a local post office or passport office, call the **Australia Passport Information Service** (☎ 131-232 toll-free from Australia), or log on to www.passports.gov.au for details on how and where to apply.

- ✔ **Canadians** can pick up applications at passport offices, at post offices, or from the central **Passport Office, Department of Foreign Affairs and International Trade,** Ottawa, ON K1A 0G3 (☎ 800-567-6868; www.ppt.gc.ca). Applications must be accompanied by two identical passport-size photographs and proof of Canadian citizenship. Processing takes five to ten days if you apply in person, or about three weeks by mail.

- ✔ **New Zealanders** can pick up a passport application at any New Zealand Passports Office or download it from the Web site. Contact the **Passports Office** at ☎ 0800-225-050 in New Zealand or 04-474-8100, or log on to www.passports.govt.nz.

- ✔ **United Kingdom** residents can pick up applications for a standard ten-year passport (five-year passport for children under 16) at passport offices, major post offices, or travel agencies. For information, contact the **United Kingdom Passport Service** (☎ 0870-521-0410; www.ukpa.gov.uk).

Playing It Safe with Travel and Medical Insurance

Three kinds of travel insurance are available: trip-cancellation insurance, medical insurance, and lost-luggage insurance. The cost of travel insurance varies widely, depending on the cost and length of your trip, your age and health, and the type of trip you're taking, but expect to pay between 5 percent and 8 percent of the vacation itself. Here is my advice on all three:

✔ **Trip-cancellation insurance** helps you get your money back if you have to back out of a trip, if you have to go home early, or if your travel supplier goes bankrupt. Allowed reasons for cancellation can range from sickness to natural disasters to the State Department declaring your destination unsafe for travel. (Insurers usually won't cover vague fears, though, as many travelers discovered who tried to cancel their trips in October 2001 because they were wary of flying.)

A good resource is **"Travel Guard Alerts,"** a list of companies considered high-risk by Travel Guard International (www.travel insured.com). Protect yourself further by paying for the insurance with a credit card — by law, consumers can get their money back on goods and services not received if they report the loss within 60 days after the charge is listed on their credit card statement.

Note: Many tour operators, particularly those offering trips to remote or high-risk areas, include insurance in the cost of the trip or can arrange insurance policies through a partnering provider, a convenient and often cost-effective way for the traveler to obtain insurance. Make sure the tour company is a reputable one, however: Some experts suggest you avoid buying insurance from the tour or cruise company you're traveling with, saying it's better to buy from a third-party insurer than to put all your money in one place.

✔ For travel overseas, most health plans (including Medicare and Medicaid) do *not* provide coverage, and the ones that do often require you to pay for services up front and reimburse you only after you return home. As a safety net, you may want to buy travel **medical insurance,** particularly if you're traveling to a remote or high-risk area where emergency evacuation is a possible scenario. If you require additional medical insurance, try **MEDEX Assistance** (☎ 410-453-6300; www.medexassist.com) or **Travel Assistance International** (☎ 800-821-2828; www.travelassistance.com; for general information on services, call the company's Worldwide Assistance Services, Inc., at ☎ 800-777-8710).

✔ **Lost-luggage insurance** is not necessary for most travelers. On domestic flights, checked baggage is covered up to $2,500 per ticketed passenger. On international flights (including U.S. portions of international trips), baggage coverage is limited to approximately $9.07 per pound, up to approximately $635 per checked bag. If you plan to check items more valuable than the standard liability, see whether your valuables are covered by your homeowner's policy, get baggage insurance as part of your comprehensive travel-insurance package, or buy Travel Guard's "BagTrak" product. Don't buy insurance at the airport — it's usually overpriced. Be sure to take any valuables or irreplaceable items with you in your carry-on luggage because many valuables (including books, money, and electronics) aren't covered by airline policies.

If your luggage is lost, immediately file a lost-luggage claim at the airport, detailing the luggage contents. For most airlines, you must report delayed, damaged, or lost baggage within four hours of arrival. The airlines are required to deliver luggage, as soon as it's found, directly to your house or destination free of charge.

For more information, contact one of the following recommended insurers: **Access America** (☎ 866-807-3982; www.accessamerica.com); **Travel Guard International** (☎ 800-826-4919; www.travelguard.com); **Travel Insured International** (☎ 800-243-3174; www.travelinsured.com); and **Travelex Insurance Services** (☎ 888-457-4602; www.travelex-insurance.com).

Staying Healthy When You Travel

Getting sick will ruin your vacation, so I *strongly* advise against it. (Of course, last time I checked, the bugs weren't listening to me any more than they probably listen to you.)

Staying healthy on a trip to Costa Rica is predominantly a matter of being a little cautious about what you eat and drink, and using common sense. Know your physical limits, and don't overexert yourself in the ocean, on hikes, or in athletic activities. Respect the tropical sun and protect yourself from it. Limit your exposure to the sun, especially during the first few days of your trip and, thereafter, from 11 a.m. to 2 p.m. Use a sunscreen with a high protection factor, and apply it liberally. Remember that children need more protection than adults do.

Because many folks experience minor gastrointestinal weirdness when visiting a foreign country, I recommend buying and drinking bottled water or soft drinks, but the water in San José and in most of the heavily visited spots is safe to drink. If your stomach is very sensitive, drink straight from the bottle or can (wiping it off first), avoid drinks with ice, and don't eat fruits or vegetables that you don't peel first, except at the better hotels and restaurants.

Talk to your doctor before leaving on a trip if you have a serious and/ or chronic illness. For conditions such as epilepsy, diabetes, or heart problems, wear a **MedicAlert identification tag** (☎ 888-633-4298;

www.medicalert.org), which immediately alerts doctors to your condition and gives them access to your records through MedicAlert's 24-hour hotline. Contact the **International Association for Medical Assistance to Travelers (IAMAT; ☎ 716-754-4883** or, in Canada, 416-652-0137; www.iamat.org) for tips on travel and health concerns in Costa Rica, and lists of local, English-speaking doctors. The United States **Centers for Disease Control and Prevention** (☎ **800-311-3435;** www.cdc.gov) provides up-to-date information on health hazards by region or country and offers tips on food safety.

Your chance of contracting any serious tropical disease in Costa Rica is slim, especially if you stick to the beaches or traditional spots for visitors. However, malaria, dengue fever, and leptospirosis all exist in Costa Rica, so it's a good idea to know what they are.

Malaria is found in the lowlands on both coasts and in the northern zone. Although it's rarely found in urban areas, it's still a problem in remote wooded regions and along the Caribbean coast. Malaria prophylaxes are available, but several have side effects, and others are of questionable effectiveness. Consult your doctor regarding what is currently considered the best preventive treatment for malaria. Be sure to ask whether a recommended drug will cause you to be hypersensitive to the sun; it would be a shame to come down here for the beaches and then have to hide under an umbrella the whole time. Because malaria-carrying mosquitoes usually come out at night, you should do as much as possible to avoid being bitten after dark. If you are in a malarial area, wear long pants and long sleeves, use insect repellent, and either sleep under a mosquito net or burn mosquito coils (similar to incense, but with a pesticide).

Of greater concern is dengue fever, which has had periodic outbreaks in Latin America since the mid-1990s. Dengue fever is similar to malaria and is spread by an aggressive daytime mosquito. This mosquito seems to be most common in lowland urban areas, and Puntarenas, Liberia, and Limón have been the worst-hit cities in Costa Rica. Dengue is also known as "bone-break fever" because it is usually accompanied by severe body aches. The first infection with dengue fever will make you very sick but should cause no serious damage. However, a second infection with a different strain of the dengue virus can lead to internal hemorrhaging and could be life threatening.

Many people are convinced that taking B-complex vitamins daily will help prevent mosquitoes from biting you. I don't think the American Medical Association has endorsed this idea yet, but I've run across it in enough places to think that there might be something to it.

One final tropical fever that I think you should know about (because I got it myself) is **leptospirosis.** There are more than 200 strains of leptospires, which are animal-borne bacteria transmitted to humans via contact with drinking, swimming, or bathing water. This bacterial infection is easily treated with antibiotics; however, it can quickly cause very high fever and chills, and should be treated promptly.

If you develop a high fever accompanied by severe body aches, nausea, diarrhea, or vomiting during or shortly after a visit to Costa Rica, consult a physician as soon as possible.

Costa Rica has been relatively free of the cholera epidemic that has spread through much of Latin America in recent years. This is largely due to an extensive public-awareness campaign that has promoted good hygiene and increased sanitation. Your chances of contracting cholera while you're here are very slight.

Staying Connected by Cellphone or E-Mail

The three letters that define much of the world's **wireless capabilities** are GSM (Global System for Mobiles), a big, seamless network that makes for easy cross-border cellphone use throughout Europe and dozens of other countries worldwide. In the United States, T-Mobile, AT&T Wireless, and Cingular use this quasi-universal system; in Canada, Microcell and some Rogers customers are GSM; and all Europeans and most Australians use GSM.

Costa Rica uses both GSM and TDMA (a separate system and protocol). The TDMA system in use in Costa Rica is not internationally compatible with any other TDMA phones or systems (so if you're on a system like Verizon in the United States, which uses TDMA, your phone won't work in Costa Rica). If your cellphone is on a GSM system, and you have a world-capable multiband phone such as many Sony Ericsson, Motorola, or Samsung models, you can make and receive calls across civilized areas on much of the globe, from Andorra to Uganda. Just call your wireless operator and ask for international roaming to be activated on your account. Unfortunately, per-minute charges can be high — usually ($1–$5).

So far, GSM world-phone owners cannot use an "unlocked" phone and local chip — no local provider can sell the GSM chip.

For many, **renting** a phone is a good idea. Although you can rent a phone from any number of overseas sites, including kiosks at airports and at car-rental agencies, I suggest renting the phone before you leave home. That way you can give loved ones and business associates your new number, make sure the phone works, and take the phone wherever you go.

Phone rental isn't cheap. You'll usually pay $40 to $50 per week, plus air-time fees of at least $1 a minute. The bottom line: Shop around.

Two good wireless rental companies are **InTouch USA** (☎ **800-872-7626;** www.intouchglobal.com) and **RoadPost** (☎ **888-290-1606** or 905-272-5665; www.roadpost.com). Give them your itinerary, and they'll tell you what wireless products you need. InTouch will also, for free, advise you on whether your existing phone will work overseas; simply call ☎ **703-222-7161** between 9 a.m. and 4 p.m. EST, or go to http://intouch global.com/travel.htm.

Renting a phone in Costa Rica is definitely an option, although due to a state monopoly on telecommunications, the entire cellphone rental industry exists in an area of legal limbo. Several firms rent cellphones to visiting tourists and businessmen, but it's probably illegal, and the Costa Rican telecommunications institute could theoretically crack down on them at any time. To date, they've been able to go about their business, albeit discreetly. None of the rental companies has a booth or office at the airport, so you'll have to contact them either beforehand or from your hotel. **Cell Service** (☎ **296-5553**; www.cellservicecr.com) and **GSM Rent A Cell** (☎ **231-5410**; www.gsmrentacell.com) both rent cellphones. Rates run around $6 per day or $35 per week for the rental, with charges of 70¢ per minute for local calls and $2 to $3 per minute for international calls.

Accessing the Internet Away from Home

You have any number of ways to check your e-mail and access the Internet on the road. Of course, using your own laptop — or even a personal digital assistant (PDA) or electronic organizer with a modem — gives you the most flexibility. But even if you don't have a computer, you can still access your e-mail and even your office computer from cybercafes.

It's hard nowadays to find a city that *doesn't* have a few cybercafes. Although there's no definitive directory for cybercafes — these are independent businesses, after all —places to start looking are at www.cybercaptive.com and www.cybercafe.com.

Most major tourist destinations in Costa Rica have several Internet cafes, and in those destinations that don't, most hotels will let you check your e-mail and surf the Web either for free or for a nominal charge.

Aside from formal cybercafes, most **youth hostels** nowadays have at least one computer on which you can get to the Internet. Avoid **hotel business centers** unless you're willing to pay exorbitant rates.

Most major airports now have **Internet kiosks** scattered throughout their gates. These kiosks, which you'll also see in shopping malls, hotel lobbies, and tourist information offices around the world, give you basic Web access for a per-minute fee that's usually higher than cybercafe prices. The kiosks' clunkiness and high price mean they should be avoided whenever possible.

To retrieve your e-mail, ask your **Internet service provider (ISP)** if it has a Web-based interface tied to your existing e-mail account. If your ISP doesn't have such an interface, you can use the free **mail2web** service (www.mail2web.com) to view and reply to your home e-mail. For more flexibility, you may want to open a free, Web-based e-mail account with **Yahoo! Mail** (http://mail.yahoo.com). (Microsoft's Hotmail is another popular option, but Hotmail has severe spam problems.) Your home ISP may be able to forward your e-mail to the Web-based account automatically.

If you need to access files on your office computer, look into a service called **GoToMyPC** (www.gotomypc.com). The service provides a Web-based interface for you to access and manipulate a distant PC from anywhere — even a cybercafe — provided your "target" PC is on and has an always-on connection to the Internet (such as with Road Runner cable). The service offers top-quality security, but if you're worried about hackers, use your own laptop rather than a cybercafe computer to access the GoToMyPC system.

If you're bringing your own computer, the buzzword in computer access is **Wi-Fi** (wireless fidelity), and more and more hotels, cafes, and retailers are signing on as wireless "hotspots" from where you can get high-speed connection without cable wires, networking hardware, or a phone line. You can get Wi-Fi connection one of several ways. Many laptops sold in the last year have built-in Wi-Fi capability (an 802.11b wireless Ethernet connection). Mac owners have their own networking technology, Apple AirPort. For those with older computers, an 802.11b/**Wi-Fi card** (around $50) can be plugged into your laptop.

You sign up for wireless access service much as you do cellphone service, through a plan offered by one of several companies that have made wireless service available in airports, hotel lobbies, and coffee shops, primarily in the United States (followed by the U.K. and Japan). **Boingo** (www.boingo.com) and **Wayport** (www.wayport.com) have set up networks in airports and high-class hotel lobbies. IPass providers also give you access to a few hundred wireless hotel lobby setups. Best of all, you don't need to be staying at the Four Seasons to use the hotel's network; just set yourself up on a nice couch in the lobby. The companies' pricing policies can be byzantine, with a variety of monthly, per-connection, and per-minute plans, but in general you pay around $30 a month for limited access — and as more and more companies jump on the wireless bandwagon, prices are likely to get even more competitive.

To locate **free wireless network** hotspots in cities around the world, go to www.personaltelco.net/index.cgi/WirelessCommunities.

Although Wi-Fi is in its infancy in Costa Rica, most business class hotels do offer dataports for laptop modems. You can bring your own cables, but most hotels rent them for around $10. **Call your hotel in advance** to see what your options are.

In addition, major ISPs have **local access numbers** around the world, allowing you to go online by simply placing a local call. Check your ISP's

Web site or call its toll-free number and ask how you can use your current account away from home, and how much it will cost. If you're traveling outside the reach of your ISP, the **iPass** network has dial-up numbers in most of the world's countries. You'll have to sign up with an iPass provider, who will then tell you how to set up your computer for your destination(s). For a list of iPass providers, go to www.ipass.com and click on "Individual Purchase." One solid provider is **i2roam** (☎ **866-811-6209** or **920-235-0475**; www.i2roam.com).

Wherever you go, bring a **connection kit** of the right power and phone adapters, a spare phone cord, and a spare Ethernet network cable — or find out whether your hotel supplies them to guests. Costa Rica uses 110-volt electricity, with U.S.-standard two- and three-prong outlets. Phone jacks are also U.S.-standard jacks.

Keeping Up with Airline Security Measures

With the federalization of airport security, security procedures at U.S. airports are more stable and consistent than ever. Generally, you'll be fine if you arrive at the airport **one hour** before a domestic flight and **two hours** before an international flight; if you show up late, tell an airline employee and she'll probably whisk you to the front of the line.

Bring a **current, government-issued photo ID** such as a driver's license or passport. Keep your ID at the ready to show at check-in, the security checkpoint, and sometimes even the gate. (Children under 18 do not need government-issued photo IDs for domestic flights, but they do for international flights to destinations such as Costa Rica.)

In 2003, the Transportation Security Administration (TSA) phased out **gate check-in** at all U.S. airports. And **E-tickets** have made paper tickets nearly obsolete. If you have an E-ticket, you can beat the ticket-counter lines by using airport **electronic kiosks** or even **online check-in** from your home computer.

Online check-in involves logging on to your airline's Web site, accessing your reservation, and printing out your boarding pass — and the airline may even offer you bonus miles to do so!

If you're using a kiosk at the airport, bring the credit card you used to book the ticket or your frequent-flier card. Print out your boarding pass from the kiosk and simply proceed to the security checkpoint with your pass and a photo ID. If you're checking bags or looking to snag an exit-row seat, you'll be able to do so using most airline kiosks. Even the smaller airlines are employing the kiosk system, but always call your airline to make sure these alternatives are available. **Curbside check-in** is also a good way to avoid lines, although a few airlines still ban curbside check-in; call before you go.

Security checkpoint lines are getting shorter than they were during 2001 and 2002, but some doozies remain. If you have trouble standing for long periods of time, tell an airline employee; the airline will provide a wheelchair. Speed up security by **not wearing metal objects** such as big belt buckles. If you have metallic body parts, a note from your doctor can prevent a long chat with the security screeners. Keep in mind that only **ticketed passengers** are allowed past security, except for folks escorting disabled passengers or children.

Federalization has stabilized **what you can carry on** and **what you can't**. The general rule is that sharp things are out, nail clippers are okay, and food and beverages must be passed through the x-ray machine — but security screeners can't make you drink from your coffee cup. Bring food in your carryon rather than checking it because explosive-detection machines used on checked luggage have been known to mistake food (especially chocolate, for some reason) for bombs. Travelers in the United States are allowed one carry-on bag, plus a "personal item" such as a purse, briefcase, or laptop bag. Carry-on hoarders can stuff all sorts of things into a laptop bag; as long as it has a laptop in it, it's still considered a personal item. The TSA has issued a list of restricted items; check its Web site (www.tsa.gov/public/index.jsp) for details.

Airport screeners may decide that your checked luggage needs to be searched by hand. You can now purchase luggage locks that allow screeners to open and relock a checked bag if hand-searching is necessary. Look for Travel Sentry–certified locks at luggage or travel shops and Brookstone stores (you can buy them online at www.brookstone.com). These locks, approved by the TSA, can be opened by luggage inspectors with a special code or key. For more information on the locks, visit www.travelsentry.org. If you use something other than TSA-approved locks, your lock will be cut off your suitcase if a TSA agent needs to hand-search your luggage.

Part III

San José and the Central Valley

"Nowhere have I seen such biodiversity of frogs, snakes, butterflies, and insects. And that's just in my coffee cup!"

In this part . . .

Located more or less in the geographic center of the country, San José is the political, social, cultural, and transportation hub of Costa Rica. This part tells you what to see and what to avoid in the city. It lists the best hotels and restaurants in San José in a range of price categories and a variety of locations.

After you're settled in, orientated, and well-fed, this part goes on to list a wide range of attractions and day trips in the city and surrounding Central Valley to keep you busy.

Chapter 11

Settling into San José

The prevailing rap is that San José is an unattractive, uninspiring, and somewhat dangerous city. And this reputation is, in part, true: Streets are burdened by traffic in a near-constant state of gridlock, sidewalks are poorly maintained and claustrophobic, and street crime is a problem.

Still, San José is the most cosmopolitan city in Central America. You can find a broad selection of small, elegant hotels in renovated historic buildings, as well as innovative new restaurants serving a wide range of international cuisines.

And things have been improving in recent years. Mayor Johnny Araya has led ambitious and controversial campaigns to rid the narrow sidewalks of illegal vendors, to reduce the clutter of billboards and overhead signs, and to bury a good share of the city's electrical and phone cables. A move to regulate bus and commuter traffic more efficiently has even begun.

San José also makes a great base for a variety of day trips and excursions. Within an hour or two, you can climb a volcano, go white-water rafting, hike through a cloud forest, and stroll through a butterfly garden — among many, many other activities.

For most visitors to Costa Rica, San José will invariably serve as a default hub or transfer point, unless you're flying in and out of Liberia. This chapter helps you plan your time in the capital and helps ease your way through the aforementioned pitfalls.

Getting There

San José is the transportation hub of Costa Rica. Most visitors arrive by air because for most airlines, San José is the gateway to Costa Rica. Flying is also the fastest and most comfortable way to get to San José. This section also covers arriving by bus and automobile. However, these are far less common options, given the long travel times involved and the often shabby conditions of the buses and roads.

Arriving by air

A great majority of international flights to Costa Rica land at the **Juan Santamaría International Airport** (☎ **437-2626** for 24-hour airport information), which is located near the city of Alajuela, about 20 minutes from downtown San José.

At press time, the airport was still in the midst of a major renovation and expansion. So far, the first phase of the new terminal has been completed, and all the major airlines have moved their desks into the terminal. The baggage claim and Customs and Immigration areas, which are modern and spacious, are not necessarily fast and efficient. Moreover, despite the major remodeling, chaos and confusion continue to greet arriving passengers the second they step out of the terminal. As in the past, you must abandon your luggage carts just before exiting the building and then face a gauntlet of aggressive taxi drivers and people offering to carry your bags. Fortunately, the official airport taxi service (see later in this section) has a booth inside the terminal after you clear customs. Most porters or skycaps wear a uniform identifying them as such, but sometimes "improvised" porters will try to earn a few dollars by carrying your bags. (Because the line of waiting taxis and shuttles is just steps away, your bags probably won't have to be carried.)

Tip porters about 75¢ per bag.

Keep a watchful eye on your bags. Thieves have historically preyed on newly arrived passengers and their luggage.

Getting from the airport to your hotel

You can get to and from the airport in several different ways, but I've listed them here starting with what's easiest:

- ✔ **By taxi:** If you have a lot of luggage, a cab is your best option. Try to stick with **Taxis Unidos Aeropuerto** (☎ **221-6865**), which operates a fleet of orange vans and sedans, charging fixed prices according to your destination. Head to its kiosk in the no-man's land just outside the exit door for arriving passengers. Here you can buy a prepaid voucher to the hotel or destination of your choice. It costs between $12 and $15 to most hotels downtown.

Despite Taxis Unidos's official monopoly at the airport, you'll usually find a handful of regular cabs (marked red sedans) and "pirate" or *pirata* cabs, freelance drivers using their own vehicles. A handful of these drivers and their touts await all arriving flights, and will be screaming "Taxi, my friend," or something similar, as you exit the terminal. You could use either of these latter options, and they tend to charge a dollar or two less, but I recommend using the official service for safety and standardized prices.

Don't worry if you haven't been able to exchange money for colones. The official taxi company, and most of the *piratas,* accept U.S. dollars.

✔ **By shuttle:** A couple of the large chain hotels, including the **Marriott** and **Hampton Inn,** have regular free shuttles to and from the airport. You can also take the **Grayline** (☎ 220-2126; www. graylinecostarica.com) or **Interbus** (☎ 283-5573; www.costa ricapass.com) shuttle-bus services. Grayline runs approximately every ten minutes and charges $10 per person to most downtown hotels. You can either book in advance or catch the bus at the curb just beyond the exit for international arriving passengers. Interbus charges $5 per person between 6 a.m. and 10 p.m. and $10 per person after hours. With Interbus, reserving in advance is best.

✔ **By bus:** Alajuela–San José buses stop right at the airport, run frequently, and will drop you off anywhere along Paseo Colón, or at a station near the Parque de la Merced (downtown, between calles 12 and 14 and avs. 2 and 4). You can take one of two separate lines: **Tuasa** buses are red; **Station Wagon** buses are beige/yellow. At the airport, you'll find the bus stop directly in front of the main terminal. Be sure to ask whether the bus is going to San José, or you may end up in Alajuela.

✔ **By rental car:** Quite a few car-rental agencies with desks and offices can be found at the airport, although if you're planning to spend a few days in San José itself, a car is a liability. (If you're heading immediately to the beach, though, picking up your car here is much easier than having to get it at a downtown office.)

Several car-rental agencies already have desks inside the new terminal, right where you exit Customs and Immigration; other agencies are still in limbo awaiting completion of airport remodeling, so be sure to contact them first to confirm that they'll have an agent or an office at the airport when you arrive.

The airport sits right off the main Interamerican Highway, and the only exit will put you right on the highway. Follow signs to San José if you're going downtown. Follow signs to Alajuela and San Ramón if you're heading straight to the beach or to a hotel either in Alajuela or north of the Interamerican Highway.

Arriving by bus

San José is connected to all other major Central American hub cities by a couple of bus lines. **Transnica** (☎ 223-4242; Calle 22, between avenidas 3 and 5) and **Tica Bus Company** (☎ 221-8954; www.ticabus.com; Avenida 4 between Calle 9 and Calle 11) both service San José directly from Panama City and Managua, with onward connections to most other major Central American cities. Neither will reserve a seat by telephone or the Internet, and schedules change frequently according to season and demand. Buy your ticket in advance — several days in advance if you plan to travel on weekends or holidays.

Buses arriving from Panama pass first through Cartago and San Pedro before letting passengers off in downtown San José; buses arriving from Nicaragua generally enter the city on the west end of town, on Paseo Colón. If you're staying here, you can ask to be let off before the final stop.

Arriving by car

If you're intrepid enough to be arriving by car, you'll be entering San José via the Interamerican Highway. If you arrive **from Nicaragua and the north,** you'll find that the highway brings you first past the airport and the city of Alajuela, to the western edge of downtown, right at the end of Paseo Colón, where it hits the Parque La Sabana. This area is well marked with large road signs, which direct you either to the downtown (CENTRO) or to the western suburbs of Rhormerser, Pavas, and Escazú. If you're heading downtown, just follow the flow of traffic and turn left on Paseo Colón.

If you're entering **from Panama and the south,** things get a little more complicated. The Interamerican Highway first passes through the city of Cartago and then through the San José suburbs of Curridabat and San Pedro before reaching downtown. This route is relatively well marked, and if you stick with the major flow of traffic, you should find San José without any problem. If you get lost, feel free to stop and ask directions. If you don't speak any Spanish, repeating the phrase "San José centro" should get you pointed toward downtown.

Orienting Yourself in San José

Downtown San José is laid out on a grid. *Avenidas* (avenues) run east and west, while *calles* (streets) run north and south. The center of the city is at **Avenida Central** and **Calle Central.** To the north of Avenida Central the avenidas have odd numbers beginning with Avenida 1; to the south, they have even numbers beginning with Avenida 2. Likewise, calles to the east of Calle Central have odd numbers, and those to the west have even numbers.

The main downtown artery is **Avenida 2,** which merges with Avenida Central on either side of the downtown area. West of downtown, Avenida Central becomes **Paseo Colón,** which ends at Parque La Sabana (La Sabana Park) and feeds into the highway to Alajuela, the airport, and the Pacific coast. East of downtown, Avenida Central leads to San Pedro and then to Cartago and the Interamerican Highway heading south. **Calle 3** takes you out of town to the north and puts you on the Guápiles Highway out to the Caribbean coast.

Introducing the neighborhoods

San José is sprawling. It's divided into dozens of neighborhoods known as *barrios.* Only a handful of these are of any interest or concern for visitors. This section gives you a quick rundown of the major barrios or neighborhoods in San José. Only the best-known barrios — meaning the ones that you're most likely to stay in or visit — are mentioned. Most are close to the central downtown area, but some are located in a few outlying neighborhoods.

Downtown

In San José's busy downtown, you'll find most of the city's museums, as well as a handful of small urban parks and open-air plazas. Many tour companies, restaurants, and hotels are also located here. Unfortunately, traffic noise and exhaust fumes make this one of the least pleasant parts of the city. Streets and avenues are usually bustling and crowded with pedestrians and vehicular traffic, and street crime is most rampant here. The section of Avenida Central between Calle Central and Calle 7 has been converted into a pedestrian mall, slightly improving things on this stretch.

Barrio Amón and Barrio Otoya

These two picturesque neighborhoods, just north and east of downtown, are the site of the greatest concentration of historic buildings in San José. Some of these have been renovated and turned into hotels and restaurants. If you're looking for character and don't mind the noise and exhaust fumes from passing cars and buses, this neighborhood makes a good base for exploring the city.

La Sabana/Paseo Colón

Paseo Colón, a wide boulevard west of downtown, is an extension of Avenida Central and ends at Parque La Sabana. Paseo Colón has several good, small hotels and numerous excellent restaurants. This is also where many of the city's car-rental agencies have their in-town offices. Parque La Sabana is a large urban park, with jogging paths, sports facilities and fields, an open-air sculpture garden, and a couple of small ponds.

San José

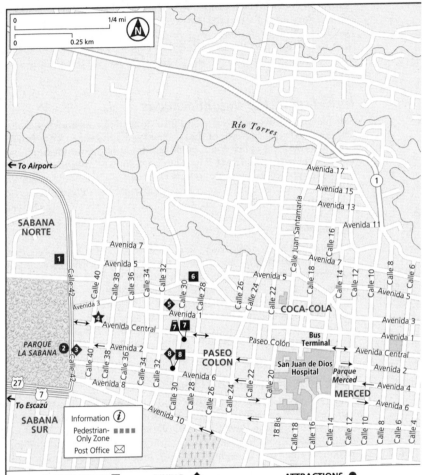

ACCOMMODATIONS ■
Britannia Hotel **15**
Clarion Amón Plaza **14**
Hotel Aranjuez **40**
Hotel Cacts **6**
Hotel Don Carlos **20**
Hotel Grano de Oro **8**
Hotel Le Bergerac **45**
Hotel Presidente **34**
Hotel Rosa del Paseo **7**
Hotel Santo Tomás **16**
Radisson Europa Hotel **10**
Tryp Corobicí **1**

DINING ◆
Bakea **18**
Café del Teatro Nacional **30**
Café Mundo **39**
Cafeteria 1830 **31**
Grano de Oro Restaurant **8**
La Cocina de Leña **12**
Machu Picchu **5**
Olio **47**
Soda Tapia **3**
Tin Jo **35**
Whappin' **48**

ATTRACTIONS ●
Centro Nacional de Arte
   y Cultura **38**
Museo de Arte Costarricense **2**
Museo de Jade Marco Fidel
   Tristán **21**
Museo de los Niños **9**
Museo de Oro Banco Central **29**
Museo Nacional de Costa Rica **36**
Spirogyra Butterfly Garden **13**
Teatro Nacional **30**

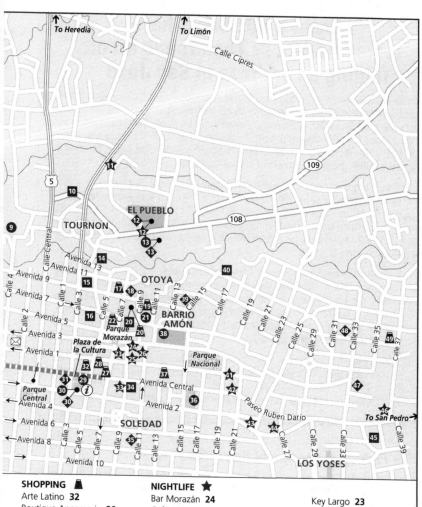

SHOPPING 🛍
Arte Latino **32**
Boutique Annemarie **20**
Galería 11-12 **49**
Galería Andrómeda **19**
Galería Jacobo "Karpio" **37**
TEORetica **17**
Galería Namu **22**
Malety **28**
Seventh Street Books **27**

NIGHTLIFE ⭐
Bar Morazán **24**
Café 83 Sur **44**
Casino Club Colonial **26**
Casino Del Rey **25**
Chelles **33**
El Cuartel de la Boca del Monte **41**
El Observatorio **42**
El Pueblo **12**
El Tobogán **11**
El Yos **46**

Key Largo **23**
Meridiano al Este **43**
Vertigo **4**

"I know a number is here somewhere . . .": The arcane art of finding an address in San José

Finding an address is one of the most confusing aspects of visiting Costa Rica in general, and San José in particular. Although street addresses and occasional building numbers are often listed for locations in downtown San José, they're almost never used. Addresses are given as a set of coordinates such as "Calle 3 between avenidas Central and 1." It's then up to you to locate the building within that block, keeping in mind that the building could be on either side of the street.

Many addresses or directions also include additional information, such as the number of meters or blocks from a specified intersection or some other well-known landmark. (Don't get hung up on exact measurements, in Costa Rica 100 meters = 1 block, 200 meters = 2 blocks, and so on.) These landmarks are what become truly confusing for visitors to Costa Rica because they're often simply restaurants, bars, and shops that would be familiar only to locals.

Things get even more confusing when the landmark in question no longer exists. The classic example of this is "the Coca-Cola," one of the most common landmarks used in addresses in the blocks surrounding San José's main market. The trouble is, the Coca-Cola bottling plant that it refers to is no longer there; the edifice is long gone, and one of the principal downtown bus depots stands in its place. Old habits die hard, though, and the address description remains.

You may also try to find someplace near the *antiguo higuerón* ("old fig tree") in San Pedro. This tree was felled years ago. In outlying neighborhoods, addresses can become long directions such as "50m south of the old church, then 100m east, then 20m south." Luckily for the visitor, most downtown addresses are more straightforward.

San Pedro, Los Yoses, and Barrio Escalante

Located just east of downtown San José, Los Yoses and Barrio Escalante are upper-middle-class neighborhoods that are home to many diplomatic missions and embassies. San Pedro is a little farther east and is the site of the University of Costa Rica. There are numerous college-type bars and restaurants all around the edge of the campus, as well as several good restaurants and small hotels in both neighborhoods.

Escazú and Santa Ana

Located in the hills west of San José, Escazú and Santa Ana are two fast-growing suburbs. Although the area is only 15 minutes from San José by taxi, it feels much farther away because of its relaxed atmosphere. This area has a large expatriate community, with many bed-and-breakfast establishments.

Heredia, Alajuela, and the Airport Area

Heredia and Alajuela are two colonial-era cities that lie closer to the airport than San José. Alajuela is the closest city to the airport, with Heredia lying about midway between Alajuela and the capital. Several quite beautiful high-end boutique hotels are found here. There are also several large, modern hotels located on, or just off, the Interamerican Highway close to the airport.

Street smarts: Where to get information after you arrive

The **Costa Rican Tourism Institute,** or **Instituto Costarricense de Turismo** (ICT; ☎ 443-2883) has a desk at the Juan Santamaría International Airport, located in the baggage claims area, just before Customs. You can pick up maps and browse brochures, and they may even lend you a phone to make or confirm a reservation. It's open Monday through Friday from 9 a.m. to 5 p.m., which is a little bit pathetic because such a large number of flights arrive either on the weekends or after 5 p.m.

If you're looking for the **main ICT visitor information center** in San José, it's located below the Plaza de la Cultura, at the entrance to the Oro Museum (Gold Museum), on Calle 5 between avenidas Central and 2 (☎ 222-1090). The people here are helpful, although the information they have to offer is rather limited. This office is also open Monday through Friday from 9 a.m. to 5 p.m. Another ICT information desk is located at the **main post office** (☎ 258-8762; Calle 2 between avenidas 1 and 3). This branch is open Monday through Friday from 8 a.m. to 4 p.m.

Getting Around San José

You've got plenty of options for getting around San José. In most instances, a taxi will be your best bet. But in this section, I also tell you how to navigate the city by bus, rental car, and foot.

By taxi

Taxis are an easy and inexpensive way to get around San José. Although taxis in San José have meters *(marías),* the drivers sometimes refuse to use them, particularly with foreigners, so you'll occasionally have to negotiate the price. Always try to get them to use the meter first (say "ponga la maría, por favor"). The official rate at press time is around 65¢ for the first kilometer (½ mile) and around 35¢ for each additional kilometer. If you have a rough idea of how far it is to your destination, you can estimate how much it should cost from these figures. After 10 p.m., taxis are legally allowed to add a 20 percent surcharge. Some of the meters are programmed to include the extra charge automatically, but be careful: Some drivers will use the evening setting during the daytime or to try to charge an extra 20 percent on top of the higher meter setting.

Tipping taxi drivers is not expected. Also, it's not uncommon for passengers to sit in the front seat with the driver.

Depending on your location, the time of day, and the weather (rain places taxis at a premium), it's relatively easy to hail a cab downtown. You'll always find taxis in front of the Teatro Nacional (National Theater) and around the Parque Central (Central Park) at Avenida Central and Calle Central. Taxis in front of hotels and the El Pueblo tourist complex usually try to charge more than others, although this is technically illegal. Most hotels will gladly call you a cab, either for a downtown excursion or for a trip back out to the airport. You can also get a cab by calling **Coopetaxi** (☎ 235-9966), **Coopeirazu** (☎ 254-3211), or **Coopeguaria** (☎ 227-9300). **Cinco Estrellas Taxi** (☎ 228-3159) is another company that is based in Escazú, but it services the entire metropolitan area and airport and claims to always have an English-speaking operator on call.

By bus

Bus transportation around San José is cheap — the fare is usually somewhere around 15¢ (although the Alajuela/San José buses that run in from the airport cost 60¢). However, be forewarned: Costa Rica's urban buses tend to be overcrowded, slow, and in poor condition. Moreover, they're often frequented by pickpockets and petty thieves. So if you do opt to take the local public transportation, be alert and careful.

The most important buses are those running east along Avenida 2 and west along Avenida 3. The **Sabana/Cementerio** bus runs from Parque La Sabana to downtown and is one of the most convenient buses to use. You'll find a bus stop for the outbound Sabana/Cementerio bus near the main post office on Avenida 3 near the corner of Calle 2 and another one on Calle 11 between avenidas Central and 1. This bus also has stops all along Avenida 2. **San Pedro** buses leave from Avenida Central between calles 9 and 11, in front of the Cine Capri, and take you out of downtown heading east. **Escazú**-bound buses leave from the Coca-Cola bus station, as well as from Avenida 6 and Calle 2, while buses for **Santa Ana** leave only from the Coca-Cola bus station. Alternatively, you can pick up both the Escazú and Santa Ana buses, as well as those bound for Alajuela and the airport, from the busy bus stop in front of the Centro Colón shopping center toward the western end of Paseo Colón.

Board buses from the front. The bus drivers can make change, although they don't like to receive large bills. *Remember:* Be especially mindful of your wallet, purse, or other valuables because pickpockets often work the crowded buses.

By car

In general, I consider it a liability for visitors to rent a car while in San José. The city streets are poorly marked and congested, Costa Rican drivers tend to be aggressive, and traffic laws as well as basic norms of road courtesy are generally ignored. Relying on taxis is much easier and more economical.

Renting a car in San José will cost you between $35 and $90 per day (the higher prices are for four-wheel-drive vehicles). Many car-rental agencies have offices at the airport, as well as downtown. Regardless, almost all will either meet you at the airport or deliver the car to any San José hotel. See Chapter 7 for more information on renting a car in Costa Rica.

On foot

Downtown San José is quite compact. Even so, aside from touring a few heavily trafficked tourist areas in broad daylight, I don't recommend exploring San José by foot. Street crime is a real problem, and most visitors stand out prominently and, thus, are targets. The best places to stroll around downtown are the two main plazas — Plaza de la Democracia and Plaza de la Cultura — and the pedestrian-only section of Avenida Central between Calle Central and Calle 7.

Where to Stay in San José

You'll find a wide range of hotel options in San José, ranging from comfortable and homey budget lodgings, to unique boutique hotels housed in restored colonial-era mansions, to large modern resort hotels. Most hotels in San José are moderately priced, including some of the best of the bunch.

If you're heading out to Guanacaste, the central Pacific, or the northern zone, you might consider a hotel either near or beyond the airport. Sure, you give up proximity to downtown, but you can cut as much as an hour off your travel time to any of these destinations.

Apart from the large, modern hotels and chains, few hotels in San José come with air-conditioning. Even many of the more expensive boutique hotels lack air-conditioning. The good news, given the mild, temperate climate, is that this is really not a problem for most. If you absolutely must have air-conditioning, be sure to inquire in advance if your room will have it or not.

The top hotels

The following list features a wide range of choices to suit any budget. I also list a selection of hotels from various neighborhoods, including hotels close to the airport and others just slightly out of downtown.

Prices for recommended hotels are designated with dollar signs — the more you see, the more expensive the hotel. Check the introduction to this book for how the dollar-sign system works. Also see Chapter 8 for tips on booking your accommodations.

Britannia Hotel
$$ Barrio Amón

This is the most luxurious of the many boutique hotels that have been created from restored old houses in Barrio Amón. Built in 1910, the large, low building, with its wraparound veranda, is also one of the area's most attractive hotels. Along with the restored old home, a four-story addition is separated from the original building by a narrow atrium. Rooms in the old section have hardwood floors and furniture; high ceilings and fans help keep them cool. In the deluxe rooms and junior suites, you get air-conditioning, one king- or two queen-size beds, and a hair dryer in the bathroom. The standards come with either one king or two twin beds. Although the street-side rooms have double glass, light sleepers will still want to avoid them. The quietest rooms are those toward the back of the newer addition. In what was once a wine cellar, you'll find a casual restaurant.

See map p. 102. Calle 3 and Av. 11, San José. ☎ *800-263-2618 in the United States, or 223-6667 in Costa Rica. Fax: 223-6411.* www.hotelbritanniacostarica.com. *Limited street parking. Rack rates: $89–$105 double; $117 junior suite. AE, MC, V.*

Clarion Amón Plaza
$$$–$$$$ Barrio Amón

This business-class hotel is larger and more modern than the nearby boutique options. Nothing particularly stands out about the property or rooms here; however, in terms of service, location, and price, this hotel gets my nod over the nearby Holiday Inn. The rooms are all spacious and well kept, and they come with plenty of amenities, including wireless Internet connections. The hotel features a small exercise room and a lovely open-air sidewalk restaurant. You're also close to all the downtown action here.

See map p. 102. Av. 11 and Calle 3 bis, San José. ☎ *800-575-1253 in the United States, or 257-0191 in Costa Rica. Fax: 257-0284.* www.hotelamonplaza.com. *Free parking. Rack rates: $120–$145 double; $160–$265 suite. AE, DC, MC, V.*

Costa Rica Hotel Marriott
$$$$–$$$$$ Near the airport

Hands down, the Marriott is the top large luxury resort hotel in the San José area. The hotel is designed in a mixed colonial style, with hand-painted Mexican tiles; antique red-clay roof tiles; weathered columns; and heavy wooden doors, lintels, and trim. The centerpiece is a large open-air interior patio, which somewhat replicates Old Havana's Plaza de Armas. The rooms are all comfortable and well appointed, with either a king-size or two double beds, two telephones, a working desk, an elegant wooden armoire holding a large television, plenty of closet space, a comfortable sitting chair and ottoman, and a small "Juliet" balcony. The bathrooms are up to par but seem slightly small for this price. Amenities are plentiful, and service here reaches a level of attention to detail uncommon in Costa Rica. Kids love the two large pools, and this is one of the few San José options with dependable babysitting services.

San Antonio de Belén. ☎ *888-236-2427 in the United States and Canada, or 298-0844 in Costa Rica. Fax: 298-0033.* www.marriott.com. *Free parking. Rack rates: $236 double; $266 executive level; $550 master suite; $1,000 presidential suite. AE, DC, MC, V.*

Finca Rosa Blanca Country Inn
$$$–$$$$ Santa Bárbara de Heredia

Finca Rosa Blanca is an eclectic architectural confection set amid the lush, green hillsides of a coffee plantation. Square corners seem to have been prohibited in the design of this beautiful hotel. Instead, you'll find turrets and curving walls of glass, arched windows, and a semicircular built-in couch. Everywhere the glow of polished hardwood blends with blindingly white stucco walls and brightly painted murals. Inside, plenty of original artwork lines the walls, and each room is decidedly unique. Las Mascaras (The Masks) has a variety of masks adorning the walls, while La Ventana (The Window) features a hand-painted mural of a window over the room's queen-size bed. If breathtaking bathrooms are your idea of the ultimate luxury, consider splurging on the master suite, which has a stone waterfall that cascades into a tub in front of a huge picture window. This suite also has a spiral staircase that leads to the top of a turret, where the master bedroom is located. The two separate villas have the same sense of eclectic luxury, with small kitchenettes and quite a bit of space and privacy. All rooms are nonsmoking. The small outdoor pool sits on a gentle hillside, and a Jacuzzi rests on the roof of the main building.

Santa Bárbara de Heredia. ☎ *269-9392. Fax: 269-9555.* www.fincarosablanca. com. *Free parking. Rack rates: $185–$280 double. Extra person $30. Rates include breakfast. AE, MC, V.*

Hotel Aranjuez
$ Barrio Amón

This is the best and most popular budget option close to downtown. Located on a quiet and safe street on the outskirts of the Barrio Amón neighborhood, this humble hotel is made up of five contiguous houses. The rooms are all simple and clean, although some are a little dark. Both the rooms and bathrooms vary greatly in size, so be very specific when reserving, or ask to see a few rooms when you arrive. The cheapest rooms here share a couple of communal bathrooms. The best features, aside from the convivial hostel-like atmosphere, are the lush and shady gardens; the hanging orchids, bromeliads, and ferns decorating the hallways and nooks; and the numerous open lounge areas furnished with chairs, tables, and couches — great for lazing around and sharing travel tales with your fellow guests. The hotel has a couple of computers, as well as a wireless network, and offers guests free Internet and e-mail services.

See map p. 102. Calle 19, between avs. 11 and 13, San José. ☎ *877-898-8663 in the United States, or 256-1825 in Costa Rica. Fax: 223-3528.* www.hotelaranjuez.com. *Free parking. Rack rates: $25–$42. Rates include breakfast buffet. V.*

Hotel Don Carlos
$–$$ Barrio Amón

If you're looking for an affordable, small hotel that is unmistakably Costa Rican and hints at the days of the planters and coffee barons, this is the place for you. Located in an old residential neighborhood, only blocks from the business district, the Don Carlos is popular with both vacationers and businesspeople. A large reproduction of a pre-Columbian carved-stone human figure stands outside the front door of this gray inn, which was a former president's mansion. Inside you'll find many more such reproductions, as well as orchids, ferns, paintings, and parrots. The rooms are distinct and vary greatly in size, so be specific when you reserve, or ask if it's possible to see a few when you check in. You'll also find a soothing ten-person Jacuzzi and an outdoor orchid garden and atrium where breakfast is served. The gift shop here is one of the largest in the country, and guests have free use of the hotel's Internet access.

See map p. 102. 779 Calle 9, between avs. 7 and 9, San José. ☎ *221-6707. Fax: 255-0828.* www.doncarloshotel.com. *Free parking. Rack rates: $70–$80 double. Rates include continental breakfast. AE, MC, V.*

Hotel Grano de Oro
$$–$$$$ Paseo Colón

San José boasts dozens of old homes that have been converted into boutique hotels, but this one is my favorite. Located on a quiet side street off Paseo Colón, this small hotel offers a variety of room types to fit most budgets and tastes. I prefer the patio rooms, which have French doors opening onto private patios. However, if you want a room with more space, ask for one of the deluxe rooms, which also have large, modern, tiled baths with big tubs. All rooms are nonsmoking. Throughout all the guest rooms, you find attractive hardwood furniture, including old-fashioned wardrobes in some rooms. For additional luxuries, you can stay in one of the suites, which have whirlpool tubs. If you don't grab a suite, you still have access to the hotel's two rooftop Jacuzzis. The hotel's gorgeous patio-garden restaurant serves excellent international cuisine and some of the best desserts in the city.

See map p. 102. Calle 30, no. 251, between avs. 2 and 4, 150m (1½ blocks) south of Paseo Colón, San José. ☎ *255-3322. Fax: 221-2782.* www.hotelgranodeoro.com. *Free parking. Rack rates: $90–$125 double; $150–$255 suite. AE, MC, V.*

Hotel Le Bergerac
$–$$ Los Yoses

With all the sophistication and charm of a small French inn, the Hotel Le Bergerac has ingratiated itself with business travelers and members of various diplomatic missions. These guests have found a tranquil environment in a quiet suburban neighborhood, spacious and comfortable accommodations, personal service, and gourmet meals. Still, you don't have to be a diplomat or business traveler to enjoy this hotel's charms. Le Bergerac is composed of three houses with courtyard gardens in between. Almost all the rooms are quite large, and each is a little different. My favorite rooms are those with private patio gardens or balconies.

See map p. 102. Calle 35, no. 50, San José. ☎ *234-7850. Fax: 225-9103.* www. bergerachotel.com. *Free parking. Rack rates: $68–$110 double. Rates include full breakfast. AE, DC, MC, V.*

Hotel Presidente
$$–$$$$ Downtown

This modern business-class hotel is a good midrange option in the heart of downtown. Although the hotel's eight stories practically qualify it for skyscraper status, very few of the rooms have any view to speak of; those with north-facing windows are your best bet. Rooms are all clean and modern and feature the basic amenities you'd expect. Most rooms come with one double and one single bed. If you want more space, opt for one of the junior suites. The master suite is a massive two-bedroom, featuring a wide-screen TV in the living room and a private eight-person Jacuzzi. A very popular casual cafe-style restaurant is located just off the street.

See map p. 102. Av. Central and Calle 7, San José. ☎ *222-3022. Fax: 221-1205.* www. hotel-presidente.com. *Free parking. Rack rates: $75 double; $105 junior suite; $250 suite. Rates include full breakfast buffet. AE, MC, V.*

Hotel Santo Tomás
$–$$ Downtown

Even though it's on a busy downtown street, this converted mansion is a quiet oasis inside. Built over 100 years ago by a coffee baron, the house has been lovingly restored and maintained by its owner, Thomas Douglas. Throughout the hotel you'll enjoy the deep, dark tones of well-aged and well-worked wood. The rooms vary in size, but most are fairly spacious and have a small table and chairs. All rooms are nonsmoking, although smoking is permitted in some of the common areas. Skylights in some bathrooms will brighten your morning, and firm beds provide a good night's sleep. The hotel has a couple of patio areas, as well as a lounge and combination breakfast room and outdoor bar. A small kidney-shaped pool rests outside with a Jacuzzi above it; the two are solar heated and connected by a tiny waterslide. The staff and management are extremely helpful with tour arrangements and any other needs or requests, and the restaurant here is excellent.

See map p. 102. Av. 7, between calles 3 and 5, San José. ☎ *255-0448. Fax: 222-3950.* www.hotelsantotomas.com. *No parking. Rack rates: $70–$105 double. Rates include breakfast buffet. MC, V.*

Peace Lodge
$$$$–$$$$$ Varablanca

The rooms here just might be some of the most impressive in the country — the bathrooms in the deluxe units easily earn that distinction alone. The lodge is an outgrowth of the popular La Paz Waterfall Gardens, which features a host of attractions and activities to please the whole family (see Chapter 12 for more information). The rooms are large and feature sparkling wood floors and trim, handcrafted four-poster beds, beautiful stone fireplaces, intricately sculpted steel light fixtures, and a host of other creative touches and details. Every room has a private balcony fitted with a mosaic-tiled Jacuzzi. The aforementioned deluxe bathrooms come with a second oversize Jacuzzi set under a skylight in the middle of an immense room that features a full interior wall planted with ferns, orchids, and bromeliads and fed by a functioning waterfall system. The lodge is located about 45 minutes from the airport and makes a good first stop if your itinerary takes you next to La Fortuna and Arenal volcano, or to the Puerto Viejo de Sarapiqui region.

6km (3¾ miles) north of Varablanca on the road to San Miguel. ☎ *482-2720 or 225-0643.* www.waterfallgardens.com. *Free parking. Rack rates: $225–$285 double; $375 villa. Rates include breakfast and entrance to La Paz Waterfall Gardens. Rates lower in the off season; higher during peak weeks. AE, MC, V.*

Vista del Valle Plantation Inn
$$$ Alajuela

If you have little need for San José and are looking for a comfortable base for exploring the rest of Costa Rica, consider this fine little country inn. The architecture has a strong Japanese influence. The rooms are all either independent or duplex villas. All are open and airy, with lots of windows letting in lots of light. You also find plenty of varnished woodwork, small kitchenettes (in some), and comfortable wraparound decks here. My favorites are the Mona Lisa and Ylang-Ylang suites, which are octagonal in shape and set on the edge of the bluff with impressive views over the Río Grande and its steep-walled canyon. The grounds are wonderfully landscaped, with several inviting seating areas set among a wealth of flowering tropical plants. You can lounge around the lovely outdoor pool, take a hike or horseback ride, and even play tennis here. The hotel is located 20 minutes north of the Juan Santamaría International Airport, and staying here can cut as much as an hour off your travel time to the Pacific coast beaches, Arenal volcano, and the Monteverde cloud forest.

40km (27 miles) north of San José, just off the Interamerican Highway. ☎ *450-0800 or* ☎*/fax 451-1165.* www.vistadelvalle.com. *Free parking. Rack rates: $145–$165 villa. Rates include full breakfast. Rates lower in the off season. AE, MC, V.*

Xandari Resort & Spa
$$$–$$$$ Alajuela

Xandari is yet another architecturally stunning small hotel not far from the airport. Set on a high hilltop above the city of Alajuela, Xandari commands wonderful views of the surrounding coffee farms and the Central Valley below. The villas are huge private spaces with high-curved ceilings, stained-glass windows, and handmade fine furniture. All come with both an outdoor patio with a view and a private covered *palapa* (straw umbrella), as well as a smaller interior terrace with chaise lounges. Most have king-size beds; the rest have two queens. All rooms boast spacious living rooms with rattan sofas and chairs, as well as small kitchenettes. The owners are artists, and their original works and innovative design touches abound. The hotel grounds contain several miles of trails that pass by at least five jungle waterfalls, as well as lush gardens and fruit orchards. The adjacent "spa village" features a series of private thatch-roofed treatment rooms, many with their own Jacuzzi, and most with stunning views. A wide range of spa and beauty treatments is offered, in addition to yoga and other fitness classes.

5km (3 miles) outside (east) of downtown Alajuela, off the road to Poás volcano. ☎ *800-686-7879 in the United States, or 443-2020 in Costa Rica. Fax: 442-4847.* www. xandari.com. *Free parking. Rack rates: $180–$260 double. Rates include continental breakfast and airport shuttle. $20 for extra person over 12; $10 for children 3–11; children under 3 stay free in parent's room. Rates lower in the off season. AE, MC, V.*

Runner-up hotels

If all the hotels in the preceding section are full, try one of these very good hotels.

Courtyard by Marriott San José

$$$ **Escazú**   A tidy and comfortable business-class hotel in the western suburb of Escazú, the Courtyard has the added bonus of having numerous dining and nightlife options in an adjacent strip- mall. *Next to the Plaza Itzkatsu, off the Prospero Fernandez Highway, Escazú.* ☎ *888-236-2427 in the United States and Canada, or 208-3000 in Costa Rica. Fax: 288-0808.* www. marriott.com.

Hampton Inn & Suites

$$–$$$ **Airport area**   This international chain is one of the closest hotels to the airport. It's very convenient if you're arriving late or leaving early. *Autopista General Cañas, by the airport.* ☎ *800-426-7866 in the United States, or 443-0043 in Costa Rica. Fax: 442-9532.* www.hamptoninn.com.

Hotel Alta

$$$–$$$$ **Santa Ana**   This small boutique hotel is infused with old-world charm. Most of the rooms here have wonderful views of the Central Valley from private balconies; the others have nice garden patios. *Alto de las Palomas, old road to Santa Ana.* ☎ *888-388-2582 in the United States and Canada, or 282-4160 in Costa Rica. Fax: 282-4162.* www.thealtahotel.com.

Hotel Cacts

$ **Paseo Colón**   This interesting budget hotel is housed in an attractive tropical contemporary home. Rooms vary considerably in size, so it's always best to check out a few first, if possible. *Av. 3 bis, no. 2845, between calles 28 and 30.* ☎ *221-2928 or 221-6546. Fax: 221-8616.*

Hotel Rosa del Paseo

$$ Paseo Colón   This hotel is housed in a beautiful old stucco home built more than 110 years ago. Try to grab one of the rooms on the second floor, which feature wooden floors and front doors that open onto the open-air central courtyard. *2862 Paseo Colón, between calles 28 and 30.* ☎ *257-3225. Fax: 223-2776.* www.rosadelpaseo.com.

Orquídeas Inn

$–$$ Alajuela   This little boutique inn is just ten minutes from the airport on the road heading out of Alajuela to Grecia and the Poás volcano. The rooms are all spacious and comfortable, with tile floors, private bathrooms, and colorful Guatemalan bedspreads. *Alajuela.* ☎ *433-9346. Fax: 433-9740.* www.orquideasinn.com.

Radisson Europa Hotel

$$$–$$$$ Downtown   This business-class hotel is a good choice for anyone looking for a big, dependable luxury hotel near downtown San José. The hotel features a very well-equipped gym that is part of the local Multispa chain. *Calle Blancos, behind La República building.* ☎ *800-333-3333 in the United States, or 257-3257 in Costa Rica. Fax: 257-8221.* www.radisson.com.

Real InterContinental San José

$$$–$$$$$ Escazú   This is a modern and luxurious large-scale business-class hotel. The hotel is located just across from a large, modern shopping-mall complex, which is nice if you want access to the shopping, restaurants, and a six-plex movie theater. *Autopista Próspero Fernández, across from the Multiplaza mall, Escazú.* ☎ *289-7000. Fax: 289-8930.* www.grupo real.com.

Tryp Corobicí

$$$–$$$$ La Sabana   Located just past the end of Paseo Colón, the Corobicí offers all the amenities you would expect at a large airport hotel, with one added bonus: It's much closer to downtown. Joggers will enjoy the nearby Parque La Sabana, and the Corobicí claims to have the largest health spa in Central America. *Autopista General Cañas, Sabana Norte.* ☎ *888-485-2676 in the United States, or 232-8122 in Costa Rica. Fax: 231-5834.* www. solmelia.com.

Where to Dine in San José

Although the Costa Rican cuisine and the local dining scene are easily disparaged and dismissed, recently some creative chefs have been trying to educate and enlighten the Costa Rican palate, particularly in San José. Many have begun using fresh local ingredients in new and exciting ways. The early results are quite promising. In addition, many excellent restaurants now serve international cuisines ranging from Italian and Asian, to Peruvian and even Indian. I list the best of the local restaurant scene in this section, with options ranging from typical Tico fare to eclectic fusion cuisine.

Reservations are only necessary in a handful of upscale or very popular restaurants, and in these cases I note the fact in the restaurant's information section.

You'll find several good restaurants in the downtown, Barrio Amón, and San Pedro neighborhoods. Escazú and Santa Ana, two popular upscale suburbs, boast the greatest number of interesting, recent restaurant openings.

See Chapter 2 for information on Costa Rican cuisine, and Chapter 5 for information on budgeting for meals.

Bakea
$$$–$$$$ Barrio Amón   INTERNATIONAL

Bakea is eclectic across the board, from its architecture to its cuisine. Housed in an old historic downtown home, it has one room with a Plexiglas floor, and underfoot lighting revealing the original foundations. A separate intimate dining room, a courtyard patio done in a postmodern, industrial-chic style, and a main dining room that is at once casual and elegant round out the décor. The owner-chef, Camila Peréz-Ratton, is trained in classical French cooking, which she has updated with a host of modern and local flourishes. I particularly like the filete multicolor, a tenderloin cut bathed in a guava glaze served over polenta and accompanied by caramelized tomatoes. Try the signature cahuita y caramelo dessert, a standout chocolate-banana tart with a molten chocolate center and macadamia pieces thrown in for good measure.

See map p. 102. Av. 7 and Calle 11, Casa 956. ☎ ***221-1051.*** *Reservations recommended. Main courses: $8–$18. AE, MC, V. Open: Tues–Sat noon to midnight.*

Café del Teatro Nacional
$$ Downtown   COFFEEHOUSE

Housed in a spacious room off the main lobby of the Teatro Nacional (National Theater), this is an elegant little coffeehouse. Even if there's no show on during your visit, you can enjoy a light meal, sandwich, dessert, or cup of coffee here, while soaking up the neoclassical atmosphere. The theater was built in the 1890s from the designs of European architects, and the Art Nouveau chandeliers, ceiling murals, and marble floors and tables are pure Parisian. The ambience is French-cafe chic, but the marimba music drifting in from outside the open window and the changing art exhibits by local artists will remind you that you're still in Costa Rica. On sunny days, outdoor seating opens up at wrought-iron tables on the side of the theater.

See map p. 102. Av. 2 between calles 3 and 5, in the Teatro Nacional. ☎ ***221-3262.*** *Sandwiches $3– $5; main courses $5–$11. AE, MC, V. Open: Mon–Fri 9 a.m.–5 p.m.; Sat 9 a.m.–4 p.m.*

Café Mundo
$$–$$$ **Barrio Amón** **INTERNATIONAL**

Wood tables and Art Deco wrought-iron chairs are spread spaciously around several rooms in this former colonial mansion. Additional seating is available on the open-air veranda and in the small gardens both in front of and behind the cafe. This was one of the first places in San José to mix creative cuisine with an ambience of casual elegance, and although the food quality has suffered a bit following the departure of the original chef, it's still a beautiful and lively spot to grab a meal. The appetizers include vegetable tempura, crab cakes, and chicken satay, alongside more traditional Tico standards such as *patacones* (fried plantain chips) and fried yuca. A long list of pastas and pizzas, as well as more substantial main courses, round out the menu. One room here boasts colorful wall murals by Costa Rican artist Miguel Cassafont. This place is almost always filled with a broad mix of San José's gay, bohemian, theater, arts, and university crowds.

See map p. 102. Calle 15 and Av. 9, 200m (2 blocks) east and 100m (1 block) north of the INS building. ☎ *222-6190. Reservations recommended. Main courses $5–$18. AE, MC, V. Open: Mon–Thurs 11 a.m.–11 p.m.; Fri 11 a.m. to midnight; Sat 5 p.m. to midnight.*

Cafeteria 1830
$–$$ **Downtown** **INTERNATIONAL**

Fronting the Plaza de la Cultura, the open-air section of this simple hotel restaurant is perhaps the best people-watching spot in the city. A wrought-iron railing, white columns, and arches create an old-world atmosphere. And a marimba band often plays right in front. It's open 24 hours a day. Stop by for breakfast and watch the plaza vendors set up their booths, or peruse the *Tico Times* over coffee while you have your shoes polished. The menu is basic and the food is unspectacular, but you won't find a better place downtown to bask in the tropical sunshine while you sip a beer or have a light lunch. This is also a great place to come just before or after a show at the Teatro Nacional.

See map p. 102. In the Gran Hotel Costa Rica, Av. 2 between calles 1 and 3. ☎ *221-4011. Sandwiches $3–$6; main courses $4–$19. AE, DC, MC, V. Open: Daily 24 hours.*

Grano de Oro Restaurant
$$$ **Paseo Colón** **CONTINENTAL**

This is one of the most elegant and romantic restaurants in the city. Both indoor and courtyard seating is offered, but when the weather's nice, you'll definitely want the latter. The menu features a wide range of meat and fish dishes. The *lomito piemontes* is two medallions of filet mignon stuffed with Gorgonzola cheese in a sherry sauce, while the *lomito Diana* comes with fresh pears and a thick brandy reduction. If you opt for fish, I recommend the macadamia-encrusted corvina, which is served with a light and tangy orange sauce. Be sure to save room for the *Grano de Oro* pie, a decadent dessert with various layers of chocolate and coffee mousses and creams.

See map p. 102. Calle 30, no. 251, between avs. 2 and 4, 150m (1½ blocks) south of Paseo Colón. ☎ **255-3322**. Reservations recommended. Main courses $8–$20. AE, MC, V. Open: Daily 6 a.m.–10 p.m.

La Cava Grill
$$–$$$ Escazú   COSTA RICAN/STEAKHOUSE

This is a cozy and casual joint housed underneath the popular, yet over-priced and overrated, Le Monastère restaurant. Although the décor is much less ornate, the service much less formal, and the menu much less French, the view is still just as spectacular. Grab one of the window seats here on a clear night and enjoy the sparkle of the lights below. The menu features a range of simply prepared meat, poultry, and fish. More-adventurous diners can try the *tepesquintl,* or *paca,* a large rodent that is actually quite tasty. You'll find live music and a festive party most weekend nights in the attached bar.

Escazú, 1.5km (1 mile) south of Centro Comercial Paco; follow the signs to Le Monastère. ☎ **289-4404**. Reservations recommended. Main courses $6–$14. AE, MC, V. Open: Mon–Sat 5 p.m. to midnight.

La Cocina de Leña
$$$ Downtown   COSTA RICAN

La Cocina de Leña ("The Wood Stove") is designed as a faux-rustic recre-ation of a rural Costa Rican farmhouse. Stacks of firewood line the shelves, long stalks of bananas hang from pillars, tables are suspended from the ceiling by heavy ropes, and the menus are printed on paper bags. If you're adventurous, you could try some of the more unusual dishes — perhaps oxtail stew served with yuca and *plátano* might appeal to you. If not, plenty of steaks and seafood dishes are featured on the menu. The *chilasuilas* are delicious tortillas filled with fried meat. Black-bean soup with egg is a Costa Rican standard and is mighty fine here; the corn soup with pork is equally satisfying. For dessert, try the *tres leches* cake or the more unusual sweetened *chiverre,* which is a type of squash that looks remarkably like a watermelon.

See map p. 102. Centro Comercial El Pueblo. ☎ **255-1360** or 223-3704. Reservations recommended. Main courses $6–$24. AE, MC, V. Open: Daily 11 a.m.–11 p.m.

La Luz
$$$–$$$$ Santa Ana   FUSION

La Luz serves up some of the more adventurous food in Costa Rica, mixing fresh local ingredients with the best of a whole host of international ethnic cuisines. The fiery garlic prawns are sautéed in ancho-chile oil and sage and served over a roasted-garlic potato mash. Then the whole thing is served with a garnish of fried leeks and a tequila-lime butter and cilantro-oil sauce. I also enjoy the beef tenderloin in a strawberry-balsamic reduc-tion, served over a champagne-infused risotto. The glass-walled dining room is one of the most elegant in town, with a view of the city lights. The wait staff is attentive and knowledgeable. On top of all this, you get nightly specials and a wide selection of inventive appetizers and desserts.

In the Hotel Alta, on the old road to Santa Ana. ☎ 282-4160. Reservations recommended. Main courses $7–$24. AE, DC, MC, V. Open: Daily 7 a.m.–3 p.m. and 6–10 p.m.

Machu Picchu
$$ Paseo Colón   PERUVIAN

Machu Picchu is an unpretentious little hole-in-the-wall that has become one of the most popular restaurants in San José. One of my favorite entrees is the *causa limeña,* lemon-flavored mashed potatoes stuffed with shrimp. The ceviche is excellent, as is the *ají de gallina,* a dish of shredded chicken in a fragrant cream sauce, and octopus with garlic butter. For main dishes, I recommend *corvina a lo macho,* sea bass in a slightly spicy tomato-based seafood sauce. Be sure to ask for a pisco sour, a classic Peruvian drink made from *pisco,* a grape liquor. These folks have a sister restaurant by the same name, but with much less ambience, over in San Pedro (☎ 283-3679).

See map p. 102. Calle 32, between avs. 1 and 3, 150m (1½ blocks) north of the KFC on Paseo Colón. ☎ 222-7384. Reservations recommended. Main courses $4–$15. AE, DC, MC, V. Open: Mon–Sat 11 a.m.–3 p.m. and 6–10 p.m.

Olio
$–$$ Los Yoses   TAPAS

Exposed brick walls, dark-wood wainscoting, and stained-glass lamps imbue this place with character and romance. Couples will want to grab a table in a quiet nook, while groups tend to gravitate toward the large main room or the bar. The extensive tapas menu features traditional Spanish fare, as well as bruschetta, antipasti, and a Greek *mezza* plate. For a main dish, I recommend the chicken Vesubio, which is marinated first in a balsamic vinegar reduction and finished with a creamy herb sauce, or the *arrollado siciliano,* which is a thin filet of steak rolled around spinach, sundried tomatoes, and mozzarella cheese and topped with a pomodoro sauce. The midsize wine list features modestly priced wines from Italy, France, Spain, Germany, Chile, Greece, and even Bulgaria.

See map p. 102. Barrio California, 200m (2 blocks) north of Bagelman's. ☎ 281-0541. Main courses $5–$12. AE, DC, MC, V. Open: Mon–Fri 11:30 a.m.–1 a.m.; Sat 4 p.m. to midnight.

Soda Tapia
$ Paseo Colón   COSTA RICAN

The food is unspectacular, dependable, and quite inexpensive at this landmark local restaurant. Seating is offered inside the brightly lit dining room, as well as on the sidewalk-style patio fronting the parking area. Dour but efficient waitstaff take the order you mark down on your combination

Taking in the view

Although myriad unique experiences can be had in Costa Rica, one of my favorites is dining on the side of a volcano, with the lights of San José shimmering below. These hanging restaurants, called *miradores,* are a resourceful response to the city's topography. Because San José is set in a broad valley surrounded on all sides by volcanic mountains, people who live in these mountainous areas have no place to go but up — so they do, building roadside restaurants vertically up the sides of the volcanoes.

The food at most of these establishments usually isn't spectacular, but the views often are, particularly at night, when the whole wide valley sparkles in a wash of lights. The town of **Aserri,** 10km (6¼ miles) south of downtown San José, is the king of miradores, and **Mirador Ram Luna** (☎ 230-3060) is the king of Aserri. Grab a window seat and, if you have the fortitude, order a plate of *chicharrones* (fried pork rinds). Live music — usually folk, pop, or jazz — is frequently played here. You can hire a cab for around $9, or take the Aserri bus at Avenida 6 between calles Central and 2. Just ask the driver where to get off.

You can also find miradores in the hills above Escazú and in San Ramón de Tres Ríos and Heredia. The most popular is **Le Monastère** (☎ 289-4404; closed Sun), an elegant converted church serving somewhat overrated French and Belgian cuisine in a spectacular setting above the hills of Escazú. I recommend coming here just for the less formal **La Cava Grill** (see the listing earlier in this chapter), which often features live music, ranging from folk pop to jazz. I also like **Mirador Tiquicia** (☎ 289-5839), which occupies several rooms in a sprawling old Costa Rican home and has live folkloric dance shows on Thursdays.

menu/bill. This place is great for late-night eats or for before or after a visit to Parque La Sabana or Museo de Arte Costarricense (Costa Rican Art Museum).

See map p. 102. Calle 42 and Av. 2, across from the Museo de Arte Costarricense.
☎ *222-6734. Sandwiches $2–$3.50; main dishes $4–$8. MC, V. Open: Mon–Thurs 6 a.m.–2 a.m.; Fri 6 a.m. to midnight; Sat open 24 hours; Sun midnight to 2 a.m.*

Tin Jo
$$–$$$ Downtown   CHINESE/PAN-ASIAN

This is the best, if not only true, Pan-Asian restaurant in San José. Tin Jo has a wide and varied menu, with an assortment of Cantonese and Szechuan staples, as well as a range of Thai, Japanese, and Malaysian dishes, and even some Indian food. The delicious pineapple shrimp in coconut-milk curry is served in the hollowed-out half of a fresh pineapple. Other dishes not to miss include the salt-and-pepper shrimp, beef teriyaki, and Thai curries. Tin Jo is also a great option for vegetarians. For dessert, try the sticky rice with mango, or banana tempura. The waiters here are some of the most attentive in Costa Rica. The décor features artwork and textiles from across Asia, and you'll have real tablecloths and cloth napkins. The lively atmosphere, extensive menu, and excellent service also make this a great choice for families traveling with kids.

See map p. 102. Calle 11, between avs. 6 and 8. ☎ 221-7605 or 257-3622. Reservations recommended. Main courses $5–$14. AE, MC, V. Open: Mon–Sat 11:30 a.m.–3 p.m. and 5:30–10 p.m. (Fri–Sat kitchen open till 11 p.m.); Sun 11:30 a.m.–10 p.m.

Whappin'
$$ Barrio Escalante   COSTA RICAN/CARIBBEAN

You don't have to go to Limón or Cahuita to get good home-cooked Costa Rican Caribbean food. The menu features a range of regional chicken, beef, or fish dishes, and almost all come with a side of the classic Caribbean-style rice and beans cooked in coconut milk. I usually go with the whole red snapper covered in a spicy sauce of sautéed onions. A small bar rests at the entrance and some simple tables spread around the restaurant, with an alcove here and there. Everything is very simple, and the prices are quite reasonable. After a dinner of fresh fish, with rice, beans, and *patacones* (fried plantain chips), the only letdown is that the beach is some four hours away.

See map p. 102. Barrio Escalante, 200m (2 blocks) east of El Farolito. ☎ 283-1480. Main courses: $4–$12. AE, MC, V. Open: Mon–Sat noon to 3 p.m. and 6–11 p.m.

Fast Facts: San José

American Express

American Express Travel Services is represented in Costa Rica by ASV Olympia (Oficentro La Sabana, Sabana Sur; ☎ 242-8585), which can issue traveler's checks and replacement cards and provide other standard services. To report lost or stolen American Express traveler's checks within Costa Rica call ☎ 242-8585 or 257-0155.

ATM Locators

ATMs are widely available around San José. Before you leave home, ask your bank to print out a list of ATMs that accept your bankcard or MasterCard or Visa cards. Or check out the following sites: www.visaeu.com/personal/atm_locator/main.html or www.mastercard.com/cardholder services/atm.

Business Hours

Banks are usually open Monday through Friday from 9 a.m. to 4 p.m., although many have begun to offer extended hours. Offices are open Monday through Friday from 8 a.m. to 5 p.m. (many close for one hour at lunch). Stores are generally open Monday through Saturday from 9 a.m. to 6 p.m. (many close for one hour at lunch). Stores in modern malls generally stay open until 8 or 9 p.m. and don't close for lunch. Most bars are open until 1 or 2 a.m.

Currency Exchange

Although a new Global Exchange money exchange office rests in the area just beyond Customs and Immigration at the Juan Santamaría International Airport, in general, few true money-exchange operations exist in San José. You can change money at all state-owned banks and private banks, although the service at some banks is slow and tedious. Hotels will often exchange money and cash traveler's checks as well, without much waiting involved. However, they might shave a few colones off the exchange rate.

Be very careful about exchanging money on the streets; it's extremely risky. In addition to forged bills and short counts, street money-changers frequently work in teams that can leave you holding neither colones nor dollars.

The best way to get cash in Costa Rica, is with an ATM machine connected to your debit-card account at home.

Dentists

You can call your consulate and ask the duty officer to recommend a dentist. Many bilingual dentists also advertise in the *Tico Times*. Because treatments are so inexpensive in Costa Rica, dental tourism has become a popular option for people needing extensive work.

Doctors

Call your consulate and ask the duty officer to recommend a doctor in San José, or see "Hospitals."

Embassies/Consulates

If you have a passport, immigration, legal, or other problem, contact your consulate. The following embassies and consulates are located in San José: United States Embassy, in front of Centro Commercial, on the road to Pavas (☎ 519-2000, or 220-3127 after hours in case of emergency); Canadian Consulate, Oficentro Ejecutivo La Sabana, Edificio 5 (☎ 242-4400); and British Embassy, Paseo Colón between calles 38 and 40 (☎ 258-2025). Australia and New Zealand do not have embassies in San José.

Emergencies

In case of any emergency, dial ☎ 911 (which should have an English-speaking operator). If 911 doesn't work, you can contact the police at ☎ 222-1365 or 221-5337, and they may be able to find someone who speaks English. For an ambulance, you can also call ☎ 128; and to report a fire, call ☎ 118.

Hospitals

Clínica Bíblica, Avenida 14 between calles Central and 1 (☎ 522-1000; www.clinica biblica.com), is conveniently located close to downtown and has several English-speaking doctors. The Hospital CIMA (☎ 208-1000; www.hospitalsan jose.net), located in Escazú on the Próspero Fernández Highway, which connects San José and the western suburb of Santa Ana, has the most modern facilities in the country.

Information

The Costa Rican Tourism Institute, or Instituto Costarricense de Turismo (ICT; ☎ 443-2883), has a desk at the Juan Santamaría International Airport, located in the baggage-claims area, just before Customs. You can pick up maps and browse brochures, and they may even lend you a phone to make or confirm a reservation. It's open Monday through Friday from 9 a.m. to 5 p.m., which is a little bit pathetic because such a large number of flights arrive either on the weekends or after 5 p.m.

If you're looking for the main ICT visitor information center in San José, it's located below the Plaza de la Cultura, at the entrance to the Museo de Oro (Gold Museum), on Calle 5 between avenidas Central and 2 (☎ 222-1090). The people here are friendly, although the information they have to offer is rather limited. This office is also open Monday through Friday from 9 a.m. to 5 p.m. Another ICT information desk is at the main post office, Calle 2 between avenidas 1 and 3 (☎ 258-8762). The main post office is open Monday through Friday from 8 a.m. to 4 p.m.

Internet Access

Internet cafes can be found all over San José. Rates run between $1 and $3 per hour. Many hotels either have their own Internet cafe or allow guests to send and receive e-mail. If your hotel doesn't provide the service and no Internet cafe is close by, you can try Racsa, Avenida 5 and Calle 1 (☎ 287-0087; www.racsa.co.cr), the state Internet monopoly, which also sells prepaid cards in 5-, 10-, and 15-hour denominations for connecting your laptop to the Web via a local phone call. Some knowledge of configuring your computer's dial-up connection is necessary. Be sure to factor in the phone-call charge if calling from a hotel.

Laundry and Dry Cleaning

Self-service laundry facilities are uncommon in San José, and hotel services can be expensive. Sixaola (☎ 240-7667) and Tyson (☎ 225-7549) are two dependable laundry and dry-cleaning chains with outlets all over town. The latter will even pick up and deliver your clothes free of charge.

Mail

The main post office *(correo)* is on Calle 2 between avenidas 1 and 3 (☎ 800-900-2000 toll-free in Costa Rica, or 202-2900; www.correos.go.cr) and is open Monday through Friday from 8 a.m. to 5:30 p.m. and Saturday from 7:30 a.m. to noon. At press time, mailing a postcard or letter to the United States cost 120 colones (26¢), and mailing a letter or postcard to Europe cost 140 colones (28¢). Given the Costa Rican postal service's track record, I recommend paying an extra 430 colones (94¢) to have anything of any value certified. Better yet,

use an international courier service or wait until you get home to post it.

Maps

The Costa Rican Tourist Board (Instituto Costarricense de Turismo, ICT, see "Information" earlier in this section for locations) can usually provide you with decent maps of both San José and Costa Rica. Other sources in San José are Seventh Street Books, Calle 7 between avenidas Central and 1 (☎ 256-8251); Librería Lehmann, Avenida Central between calles 1 and 3 (☎ 223-1212); and Librería Universal, Avenida Central and calles Central and 1 (☎ 222-2222).

Police

Dial ☎ 911 or ☎ 222-1365 for the police. They should have someone who speaks English.

Restrooms

These are known as *sanitarios* or *servicios sanitarios.* You might also hear them called *baños.* They are marked *damas* (women) and *hombres* or *caballeros* (men). Public restrooms are rare to nonexistent, but most big hotels and public restaurants will let you use their restrooms. If you're downtown, public restrooms are located at the entrance to the Museo de Oro (Gold Museum).

Safety

Pickpockets and purse slashers are rife in San José, especially on public buses, in the markets, on crowded sidewalks, and near hospitals. Leave your passport, money, and other valuables in your hotel safe, and carry only as much as you really need when you go out. Making a photocopy of your passport's opening pages and carrying that with you is a good idea. If you do carry anything valuable with you, keep it in a money belt or special passport bag around your neck. Day packs are a prime target of brazen pick-pockets throughout the city. One common scam involves someone dousing you or your pack with mustard or ice cream. Another scamster (or two) will then quickly come to your aid — they're usually much more interested in cleaning you out than cleaning you up.

Stay away from the red-light district north-west of the Central Market. Also, be advised that the Parque Nacional (National Park) is not a safe place for a late-night stroll. Other precautions include walking around corner vendors, not between the vendor and the building. The tight space between the vendor and the building is a favorite spot for pickpockets. Never park a car on the street, and never leave anything of value in a car, even if it's in a guarded parking lot. Don't even leave your car unat-tended by the curb in front of a hotel while you dash in to check on your reservation. With these precautions in mind, you should have a safe visit to San José.

Taxes

All hotels charge 16.3 percent tax. Restaurants charge 13 percent tax and also add on a 10 percent service charge, for a total of 23 percent more on your bill. A $26 departure tax is charged to all visitors leav-ing by air.

Taxis

Taxis are plentiful in San José. Depending on your location, the time of day, and the weather (rain places taxis at a premium), it's relatively easy to hail a cab downtown. You'll always find taxis in front of the Teatro Nacional and around the Parque Central at Avenida Central and Calle Central. You can also get a cab by calling Coopetaxi (☎ 235-9966), Coopeirazu (☎ 254-3211), or Coopeguaria (☎ 227-9300). Cinco Estrellas Taxi (☎ 228-3159) is another company that is based in Escazú, but it services the entire

metropolitan area and airport and claims to always have an English-speaking operator on call.

Although they have meters *(marías)*, the drivers sometimes refuse to use them, particularly with foreigners, so you'll occa-sionally have to negotiate the price. Always try to get them to use the meter first (say "ponga la maría, por favor"). The official rate at press time is around 65¢ for the first kilometer (½ mile) and around 35¢ for each additional kilometer. If you have a rough idea of how far it is to your destination, you can estimate how much it should cost from these figures. After 10 p.m., taxis are legally allowed to add a 20 percent surcharge. For more information, see "Getting Around San José" earlier in this chapter.

Telephone/Fax

Costa Rica has an excellent phone system, with a dial tone similar to that heard in the United States. A phone call within Costa Rica costs around 10 colones (3¢) per minute. Pay phones take either a calling card or 5-, 10-, or 20-colón coins. Calling cards are becoming more prominent, and coin-operated phones are getting harder to find. You can purchase calling cards in a host of gift shops and pharmacies. However, several competing calling-card companies exist, and certain cards work only with certain phones. CHIP calling cards work with a computer chip and just slide into specific phones, although these phones aren't widely available. Better bets are the 197 and 199 calling cards, which are sold in varying denominations. These have a scratch-off PIN and can be used from any phone in the country. In general terms, the 197 cards are sold in smaller denominations and are used for local calling, while the 199 cards are deemed international and are easier to find in larger denominations. That said, you can use either card to make any call, as long as the card can cover the costs. Another perk of the 199 cards is the fact that you can get the instructions in English. For local calls, calling from your hotel is often easiest, although you'll likely be charged around 150 to 300 colones (32¢–63¢) per call.

Numbers beginning with 0800 and 800 within Costa Rica are toll-free, but calling an 800 number in the States from Costa Rica is not toll-free. In fact, it costs the same as an overseas call.

You can make international phone calls, as well as send faxes, from the ICE office, Avenida 2 between calles 1 and 3, in San José (☎ 255-0444). The office is open daily from 7 a.m. to 10 p.m. Faxes cost around $1.50 per page to the United States. (Many hotels also offer the same service for a fee.) Radiográfica, Calle 1 and Avenida 5 in San José (☎ 287-0087), also has fax service.

Water

Tap water in San José is perfectly safe, but if you're prone to stomach problems, you may prefer to drink bottled water. If you aim to err on the side of caution, avoid ordering drinks with ice and eating uncooked fruits or vegetables, unless you peel them yourself.

Chapter 12

Exploring San José

- -

In This Chapter

▶ Taking a guided tour of San José
▶ Checking out the top attractions in San José
▶ Finding the best places to shop
▶ Experiencing San José's nightlife
▶ Heading out of town for a day trip

- -

*M*ost visitors try to get out of San José as fast as possible so they can spend more time on the beach or off in the rain forests and cloud forests. But if you'll be in San José for longer than an overnight stay, there are plenty of sights and activities to keep you busy. Some of the best and most modern museums in Central America are here, with a wealth of fascinating pre-Columbian artifacts. Several great things to see and do also lie just outside San José in the Central Valley.

Seeing San José by Guided Tour

You shouldn't have any reasons to take a guided tour of San José. It's so compact that you can easily visit all the major sights on your own. The best attractions are all described earlier in this chapter, and I give you a few suggested itineraries later in this chapter. However, if you want to take a city tour, which will run you between $15 and $35, try one of these companies: **Horizontes Travel** (☎ 222-2022; www.horizontes.com); **Grayline Tours** (☎ 220-2126; www.graylinecostarica.com); or **Swiss Travel Service** (☎ 282-4898; www.swisstravelcr.com). These same companies also offer a whole range of day trips out of San José (see "Taking a Day Trip out of San José," later in this chapter). Almost all the major hotels have tour desks, and most of the smaller hotels will also help arrange tours and day trips.

Be sure to check out the map in Chapter 11 for help locating the following listings.

The Top Attractions: Gold Underground and Jade in the Skies

Centro Nacional de Arte y Cultura
(National Arts and Culture Center)
Downtown

Occupying a full city block, this was once the National Liquor Factory. Now it houses the offices of the Cultural Ministry, several performing-arts centers, and the Museum of Contemporary Art and Design. The latter has done an excellent job of promoting cutting-edge Costa Rican and Central American artists while also featuring impressive traveling international exhibits, including large retrospectives by Mexican painter José Cuevas and Ecuadorian painter Oswaldo Guayasamín. If you're looking for modern dance, experimental theater, or a lecture on Costa Rican video, this a good place to check. Allow around two hours to take in all the exhibits here.

See map p. 102. Calle 13 between avs. 3 and 5. ☎ 257-7202 or 257-9370. www.madc. ac.cr. Bus: Any downtown bus. Admission: $1; free for children under 12. Museum open: Tues–Sat 10 a.m.–5 p.m.

Museo de Arte Costarricense (Museum of Costa Rican Art)
La Sabana

Formerly the country's first major airport terminal, this museum houses a collection of works in all media by Costa Rica's most celebrated artists. On display are some exceptionally beautiful pieces in a wide range of styles, demonstrating how Costa Rican artists have interpreted and imitated the major European movements over the years. In addition to the permanent collection of sculptures, paintings, and prints, regular temporary exhibits are staged here. If the second floor is open during your visit, be sure to go up and have a look at the conference room's bas-relief walls, which chronicle the history of Costa Rica from pre-Columbian times to the present. The newest addition here is an outdoor sculpture garden. So far, the collection is small, but it does include at least one representative work by José Sancho, Jorge Jiménez Deredia, Max Jiménez, and Francisco Zuñiga. Moreover, the outdoor setting is lovely. You can easily spend an hour or two at this museum — more if you take a stroll through the neighboring park.

See map p. 102. Calle 42 and Paseo Colón, Parque La Sabana Este. ☎ 222-7155. Bus: Sabana-Cementerio. Admission: $5 for adults, free for children and students; free for everyone on Sundays. Open: Tues–Fri 10 a.m.–6 p.m., Sat 11 a.m.–6 p.m., Sun 11 a.m.–4 p.m.

Museo de Jade Marco Fidel Tristán (Jade Museum)
Downtown

Jade was the most valuable commodity among the pre-Columbian cultures of Mexico and Central America, worth more than gold. This modern museum displays a huge collection of jade artifacts dating from 500 B.C. to A.D. 800. Many are large pendants that were parts of necklaces and are primarily human and animal figures. An extensive collection of pre-Columbian polychromed terra-cotta vases, bowls, and figurines is also on display. Some of these pieces are amazingly modern in design and exhibit a surprisingly advanced technique. Particularly fascinating is a vase that incorporates real human teeth and a display that shows how jade was embedded in human teeth merely for decorative reasons.

Most of the identifying labels and explanations are in Spanish, but a few are in English. This museum is housed on the 11th floor of one of the few downtown skyscrapers. Before you leave, be sure to check out the splendid view of San José from the lounge area. Allow an hour or two to visit this museum.

See map p. 102. Av. 7 between calles 9 and 9B, 11th floor, INS Building. ☎ *287-6034. Bus: Any downtown bus. Admission: $2 for adults, free for children under 12. Open: Mon–Fri 8:30 a.m.–3:30 p.m.*

Museo de los Niños (Children's Museum)
Downtown

A former barracks and then prison, this museum houses an extensive collection of exhibits designed to edify and entertain children of all ages. Experience a simulated earthquake, or make music by dancing across the floor. Many of the exhibits encourage hands-on play. If you're traveling with children, you'll definitely want to come here, and you might want to visit even if you don't have kids with you. This museum sometimes features limited shows of "serious" art and is also the home of the National Auditorium. You can spend anywhere from one to four hours here, depending on how much time your children spend at each exhibit. Be careful, though: The museum is large and spread out, and losing track of a family member or friend is easy.

This museum is located a few blocks north of downtown, on Calle 4. It's within easy walking distance of downtown sites, but you may want to take a cab because you'll have to walk right through the worst part of the red-light district to get here.

See map p. 102. Calle 4 and Av. 9. ☎ *258-4929.* www.museocr.com. *Bus: Any downtown bus. Admission: $2 for adults, $1.50 for students and children under 18. Open: Tues–Fri 8 a.m.–4 p.m., Sat–Sun 10 a.m.–5 p.m.*

Museo de Oro Banco Central (Gold Museum)
Downtown

Located directly beneath the Plaza de la Cultura, this unusual underground museum houses one of the largest collections of pre-Columbian gold in the Americas. On display are more than 20,000 troy ounces of gold, in more than 2,000 objects. The sheer number of small pieces can be overwhelming and seem redundant, but the unusual display cases and complex lighting systems show off every piece to its utmost. This museum complex also includes a gallery for temporary art exhibits, separate coin and stamps museums, a modest gift shop, and a branch of the Costa Rican Tourist Institute's information center. Plan to spend between one and two hours here.

See map p. 102. Calle 5, between avs. Central and 2, underneath the Plaza de la Cultura. ☎ *243-4202.* www.museosdelbancocentral.org. *Bus: Any downtown bus. Admission: $4 for adults, $1.50 for students, 75¢ for children under 12. Open: Tues–Sun 10 a.m.–4:30 p.m.*

Museo Nacional de Costa Rica (National Museum)
Downtown

Costa Rica's most important historical museum is housed in a former army barracks that was the scene of fighting during the civil war of 1948. You can still see hundreds of bullet holes on the turrets at the corners of the building. Inside this traditional Spanish-style courtyard building, you will find displays on Costa Rican history and culture from pre-Columbian times to the present. In the pre-Columbian rooms, you'll see a 2,500-year-old jade carving that is shaped like a seashell and etched with an image of a hand holding a small animal.

Among the most fascinating objects unearthed at Costa Rica's numerous archaeological sites are many *metates,* or grinding stones. This type of grinding stone is still in use today throughout Central America; however, the ones on display here are more ornately decorated than those you'll see anywhere else. Some of the *metates* are the size of a small bed and are believed to have been part of funeral rites. A separate vault houses the museum's collection of pre-Columbian gold jewelry and figurines. In the courtyard, you'll be treated to a wonderful view of the city and see some of Costa Rica's mysterious stone spheres. Taking in the lion's share of the collection here takes about two hours.

See map p. 102. Calle 17, between avs. Central and 2, on the Plaza de la Democracia. ☎ *257-1433. Bus: Any downtown bus. Admission: $5 for adults, $2 for students and children under 12. Open: Tues–Sat 8:30 a.m.–4 p.m., Sun 9 a.m.–4 p.m. Closed Dec 25 and Dec 31.*

Spirogyra Butterfly Garden
Downtown

This butterfly garden is smaller and less elaborate than Butterfly Farm (see the listing later in this chapter), but it provides a good introduction to the life cycle of butterflies. Moreover, it's a calm and quiet oasis in a noisy and crowded city, quite close to downtown. You'll spend anywhere from a half-hour to several hours here, depending on whether you have lunch or refreshments at the small coffee shop and gallery. You'll be given a self-guided tour booklet when you arrive, and an 18-minute video is shown continuously throughout the day. You'll find Spyrogyra near El Pueblo, a short taxi ride from the center of San José.

See map p. 102. 100m (1 block) east and 150m (1½ blocks) south of El Pueblo Shopping Center. ☎/fax 222-2937. www.infocostarica.com/butterfly. *Bus: Calle Blancos bus from Calle 3 and Av. 5. Admission: $6. Open: Daily 8 a.m.–4 p.m. (cafe open till 7:30 p.m.).*

More Cool Things to See and Do

San José has several very pleasant and inviting downtown parks and plazas. Most are very close to one or more major attractions, and they make excellent spots to take a break and soak in the sunshine and local color.

The largest of these is the **Parque La Sabana** (La Sabana Park) on the western edge of downtown. This sprawling park has a network of trails and paths used by bikers, joggers, and pedestrians, as well as basketball and tennis courts, football (soccer) fields, and baseball diamonds. You'll also find a small outdoor sculpture garden, but this is not to be confused with the sculpture garden found at the neighboring **Museo de Arte Costarricense** (Museum of Costa Rican Art). The park boasts excellent spots to have a picnic, particularly on the banks of the small ponds.

In the heart of downtown, the **Plaza de la Cultura** occupies the space between the **Teatro Nacional** (National Theater) and busy Avenida Central. Stepped down on several levels, you'll find ample park benches, which are great places from which to people watch. If you have some spare change, buy a handful of popcorn to feed the pigeons. Underneath this plaza, you'll find the **Museo de Oro Banco Central** (Gold Museum). On the western edge of this plaza sits the Gran Hotel Costa Rica, with it's inviting outdoor **Cafeteria 1830** (see Chapter 11).

A few blocks east of the Plaza de la Cultura, the **Plaza de la Democracia** occupies a full city block. This concrete affair is a bit stark and dour, with just a few undersized trees and a massive bronze sculpture of Don Pepe Figueres. Moreover, it's often very run-down and unkempt. However, the plaza does offer a few well-placed benches. The plaza is bordered on one side by the **Museo Nacional de Costa Rica** (National Museum), and an extensive **outdoor market** of handicrafts and other assorted souvenirs.

The **Parque Central** (Central Park) is a full city block located off Avenida 2, in front of the **Teatro Melico Salazar** (Melico Salazar Theater). In the center of this park is a large gazebo, which on rare occasions hosts live music concerts. This park is a very popular lunchtime spot for local workers.

Set between the Legislative Assembly and the National Library, the **Parque Nacional** (National Park) is perhaps the shadiest and most lush of the downtown city parks, forgetting the Parque La Sabana, which is in another class. At the northeast corner of this park sits the main entrance to the **Museo Nacional de Arte y Cultura** (National Arts and Culture

Center). This park is delightful on a sunny day, with numerous benches and a series of bronze busts of famous historical figures. Be careful at night, however — this park is taken over by prostitutes and transvestites after dark.

Finally, **Parque Morazán** (Morazán Park) is another popular downtown park, featuring a central gazebo and a series of benches and small patches of grass. With several major governmental offices and businesses nearby, this is also a popular lunchtime meeting spot for local workers. I actually prefer the neighboring diminutive **Parque España** (Spain Park), which is shadier, with large stands of bamboo and other mature trees. Parque España fronts the INS Building, which houses the **Museo de Jade Marco Fidel Tristán** (Jade Museum), as well as an alternative entrance to the **Museo Nacional de Arte y Cultura** (see earlier in this section).

Be especially on guard for pickpockets and street crime while in downtown San José.

Visiting attractions just outside the city

Several wonderful attractions lie within easy reach of downtown San José. Most are able to provide transportation at a reasonable rate. Others can be reached by public transportation. Or most can be reached by taxi for between $15 and $30 each way.

In addition to the places listed here, other exciting adventures and day trips are available out of San José. For a rundown of these, see "Taking a Day Trip out of San José," later in this chapter.

Butterfly Farm
Alajuela

This is the best butterfly farm and exhibit in the metropolitan area. At any given time, you may see around 30 of the 80 different species of butterflies raised here. The butterflies live in a large enclosed garden similar to an aviary and flutter about the heads of visitors during tours of the gardens. You should be certain to spot glittering blue morphos (a large fleet-winged butterfly with iridescent blue pigment on its wings) and a large butterfly that mimics the eyes of an owl.

The admission includes a two-hour guided tour. In the demonstration room, you see butterfly eggs, caterpillars, and pupae. There are cocoons trimmed in a shimmering gold color and cocoons that mimic a snake's head to frighten away predators. The last guided tour of the day begins at 3 p.m.

If you reserve in advance, the Butterfly Farm has three daily bus tours that run from many major San José hotels, the cost, including round-trip transportation and admission to the garden, is $25 for adults, $20 for students, and $13 for children under 12. Buses pick up passengers at more than 20 different hotels in the San José area.

In front of Los Reyes Country Club, La Guácima de Alajuela. ☎ **438-0400.** www. butterflyfarm.co.cr. *Admission: $15 for adults, $10 for students, $7 for children 5–12, and free for children under 5. Open: Daily 8:30 a.m.–5 p.m.*

Café Britt Farm
Heredia

Café Britt is one of the leading coffee exporters in Costa Rica, and the company has put together an interesting tour and stage production at its farm. Here, you can see how coffee is grown. You also visit the roasting and processing plant to learn how a coffee "cherry" is turned into a delicious roasted bean. Tasting sessions are offered for visitors to experience the different qualities of coffee. A restaurant and a store are on-site, so you can buy coffee and coffee-related gift items. The entire tour, including transportation, takes about three to four hours. Allow some extra time and an extra $10 for a visit to their nearby working plantation and mill. You can even strap on a basket and go out coffee picking during harvest time. The folks here offer several full-day options that combine a visit to the Britt Farm with a stop at Poás volcano, the Butterfly Farm (see the preceding listing), or the Rain Forest Aerial Tram Caribbean (see "Canopy tours and the rain-forest aerial tram," later in this chapter). They've also begun offering mountain-bike tours in this hills of Heredia above their farm, ending with lunch or refreshments at their restaurant.

North of Heredia on the road to Barva. ☎ **277-1600.** www.coffeetour.com. *Admission: $29 per person, including transportation from downtown San José, and a coffee drink and snack; add $10 for full buffet lunch; subtract $10 if you have your own transportation. Tours: Daily 9 and 11 a.m., and 3 p.m. during the high season; reduced schedule in the off season. Store and restaurant open: Daily 8:30 a.m.–5 p.m. year-round.*

INBio Park
Heredia

Run by the National Biodiversity Institute (Instituto Nacional de Biodiversidad, or INBio), this place is part museum, part educational center, and part nature park. In addition to watching a 15-minute informational video, visitors can tour two large pavilions explaining Costa Rica's biodiversity and natural wonders and hike on trails that re-create the ecosystems of a tropical rain forest, dry forest, and premontane forest. A two-hour guided hike is included in the entrance fee, and self-guided tour booklets are also available. Other features are a good-size butterfly garden, as well as a Plexiglas viewing window into the small lagoon. One of my favorite attractions here is the series of wonderful animal sculptures donated by one of Costa Rica's premiere artists, José Sancho. If you get hungry, try the simple cafeteria-style restaurant for lunch or the on-site coffee shop. You can easily spend two to three hours here.

400m (4 blocks) north and 250m (2½ blocks) west of the Shell station in Santo Domingo de Heredia. ☎ **507-8107.** www.inbio.ac.cr. *Admission: $12 for adults, $6 for children under 13; rates slightly lower in the off season. Open: Daily 7:30 a.m.–4 p.m. INBio Park can arrange round-trip transportation from downtown for $10 per person.*

Lankester Gardens
Cartago

Costa Rica has more than 1,400 varieties of orchids, and no fewer than 800 species are on display at this botanical garden in Cartago province. Created in the 1940s by English naturalist Charles Lankester, the gardens are now administered by the University of Costa Rica. The primary goal is to preserve the local flora, with an emphasis on orchids and bromeliads. Paved trails meander from open, sunny gardens into shady forests. In each environment, different species of orchids are in bloom. An information center and gift shop round out the offerings, and the trails are well tended and well marked. Plan to spend between one and three hours here if you're interested in flowers and gardening; you can run through it more quickly if you're not.

Paraíso de Cartago. ☎ **552-3247.** *Take the Cartago bus from San José, and then the Paraíso bus from a stop 100m (1 block) south and 75m (¾ block) west of the Catholic church ruins in Cartago (ride takes 30 to 40 minutes). Admission: $5 adults, $1 children. Open: Daily 8:30 a.m.–4:30 p.m. Closed all national holidays.*

La Paz Waterfall Gardens
Varablanca, Heredia

The namesake attraction here consists of a series of trails through primary and secondary forest alongside the La Paz River, with lookouts over a series of powerful falls, including the namesake La Paz Fall. The trails include lookouts and suspended walkways that give you an intimate, and sometimes wet, view of the falls. An orchid garden, a hummingbird garden, and a huge butterfly garden — they claim it's the largest in the world — round out the attractions. A small serpentarium featuring a mix of venomous and nonvenomous native snakes, and several terrariums containing various frogs and lizards have recently been added. A trout pond was under construction at press time, and future plans include the opening of a wider network of trails and the option of taking horseback riding tours. I find the admission fee a little steep, but everything is wonderfully done and the trails and waterfalls are beautiful. A buffet lunch will run you an extra $11 at the large cafeteria-style restaurant. This is a good stop after a morning visit to the Poás volcano. Plan to spend between two and four hours here.

6km (3¾ miles) north of Varablanca on the road to San Miguel, Heredia. ☎ **482-2720** *or 225-0643.* www.waterfallgardens.com. *Take a Puerto Viejo de Sarapiquí bus from Calle 12 and Av. 9 (make sure it passes through Varablanca and La Virgen), and ask to be let off at the entrance. These buses are infrequent, and coordinating your* *return can be difficult, so coming in a rental car or arranging transport is best. Admission: $22 for adults, $12 for children and students with valid ID. Open: Daily 8:30 a.m.–5:30 p.m.*

Zoo Ave
Alajuela

This zoo is, by far, the best-run one in the country. The zoo began as a bird sanctuary and rescue center. Dozens of scarlet macaws, reclusive owls, majestic raptors, several different species of toucans, and a host of brilliantly colored birds from Costa Rica and around the world make this one exciting place to visit. Bird-watching enthusiasts will be able to get a closer look at birds they may have seen in the wild. But there is much more to see here. There are also large iguana, deer, tapir, puma, and monkey exhibits — and look out for the 3.6m (12-ft.) crocodile. Zoo Ave houses only injured, donated, or confiscated animals. Walking the paths and visiting all the exhibits here takes about two hours.

La Garita, Alajuela. ☎ **433-8989.** www.zooave.org. *Catch one of the frequent Alajuela buses on Av. 2 between calles 12 and 14. In Alajuela, transfer to a bus for Atenas and get off at Zoo Ave before you get to La Garita. Fare is 55¢. Admission: $9 for adults, $2 for children under 12. Open: Daily 9 a.m.–5 p.m.*

Suggested one-, two-, and three-day sightseeing itineraries

San José is a compact city, with a limited number of major attractions. You can easily knock off almost all of them in a few days. Here are some sample itineraries covering one-, two-, and three-day stays in San José. See Chapter 11 and earlier in this chapter for specific listing information.

If you have one day

On **Day One,** start your day by having coffee and breakfast at the **Cafeteria 1830,** on the outdoor patio of the Gran Hotel Costa Rica, on the edge of the **Plaza de la Cultura.** After breakfast, visit the **Museo de Oro Banco Central** (Gold Museum, and see if you can get tickets for a performance that night at the **Teatro Nacional** (National Theater). From the Plaza de la Cultura, stroll up Avenida Central to the **Museo Nacional** (National Museum). Have lunch at Café Mundo. If it's a nice day, be sure to grab one of the outdoor tables near a flowing fountain.

After lunch, head over to the nearby **Centro Nacional de Arte y Cultura** (National Arts Center), but only if you have the energy for another museum. After all this culture, some shopping at the open-air stalls at the **Plaza de la Democracia** is in order. Try dinner at **Bakea** before going to the **Teatro Nacional.** After the performance, let your day come full circle with a cup of coffee or a nightcap at the **Cafeteria 1830** before calling it a night.

If you have two days

On **Day Two,** you're probably best off taking one of the day trips outside of San José described in the "Taking a Day Trip out of San José" section, later in this chapter. Alternatively, you could spend the day further exploring the capital. Start by heading out on Paseo Colón to the **Museo de Arte Costarricense** (Museum of Costa Rican Art) and **Parque La Sabana** (La Sabana Park). Intrepid travelers can do some shopping at the **Mercado Central.** You can pick up the fixings for a **picnic lunch** at the Mercado Central, or at any supermarket in town.

After lunch, if you've brought kids along, you'll want to visit the **Museo de Los Niños** (Children's Museum) or the **Spyrogyra Butterfly Garden.** Otherwise, this is a good time to tour the **Museo de Jade Marco Fidel Tristán** (Jade Museum). If you want to get more shopping in, be sure to save some time for the nearby **Galeria Namu.** For dinner, grab a taxi and head for one of the *miradores* (see "Taking In the View" in Chapter 11) for dinner, and enjoy the spectacular view of the lights of San José twinkling below you.

If you have three days

On **Day Three,** head out to the **Poás volcano** and then visit the **La Paz Waterfall Gardens,** returning through the hills of Heredia, with a stop at **INBio Park** if you have the time and energy. Alternatively, you could head to the **Irazú volcano, Lankester Gardens,** and the colonial city of **Cartago.** Start your day at the volcano and work your way back toward San José. If you want to try an organized tour, try a cruise to **Isla Tortuga** in the Gulf of Nicoya, a **white-water-rafting** trip on the Pacuare River, or a visit to the **Rain Forest Aerial Tram Caribbean.**

Shopping: Gold Beans and Painted Oxcarts

Serious shoppers will probably be disappointed in Costa Rica. Aside from coffee and miniature reproductions of working oxcarts, you'll find few distinctly Costa Rican wares. To compensate for its own relative lack of goods, Costa Rica does a brisk business in selling crafts and clothing imported from Guatemala, Panama, and Ecuador.

Best shopping areas

San José's principal shopping district is bounded by avenidas 1 and 2, from about Calle 14 in the west to Calle 13 in the east. For several blocks west of the Plaza de la Cultura, **Avenida Central** is a pedestrian-only street mall where you can find store after store of inexpensive clothes for men, women, and children. Depending on the mood of the police that day, you may find a lot of street vendors as well.

Most shops in the downtown district are open Monday through Saturday from about 8 a.m. to 6 p.m. Some shops close for lunch, while others remain open (it's just the luck of the draw for shoppers, although fewer and fewer stores are closing for lunch these days). When you do purchase something, you'll be happy to find that the sales and import taxes have already been figured into the display price.

Do not buy any kind of sea-turtle products (including jewelry); wild birds; lizard, snake, or cat skins; corals; or orchids (except those grown commercially). International laws prohibit trade in endangered wildlife, and such goods will be confiscated at the airport. No matter how unique, beautiful, insignificant, or inexpensive it may seem, your purchase will directly contribute to the further hunting of endangered species.

Visiting a Costa Rican market

There are several large markets near downtown, but by far the largest is the **Mercado Central,** located between avenidas Central and 1 and calles 6 and 8. Although this dark maze of stalls is primarily a food market, inside you'll find all manner of vendors, including a few selling Costa Rican souvenirs, leather goods, and musical instruments. Be especially careful about your wallet or purse and any prominent jewelry — very skilled pickpockets frequent this area. All the streets surrounding the Mercado Central are jammed with produce vendors selling from small carts or loading and unloading trucks. It's always a hive of activity, with crowds of people jostling for space on the streets. Your best bet is to visit on Sundays or on weekdays; Saturdays are particularly busy. In the hot days of the dry season, the aromas can get quite heady.

You'll also find a daily street market on the west side of the **Plaza de la Democracia.** The market boasts two long rows of outdoor stalls selling T-shirts, Guatemalan and Ecuadorian handicrafts and clothing, small ceramic *ocarinas* (small musical wind instruments), and handmade jewelry. The atmosphere here is much more open than at the Mercado Central, which I find just a bit too claustrophobic.

Finally, two other similar options downtown include **La Casona,** Calle Central between avenidas Central and 1 (☎ 222-7999), a three-story warren of crafts and souvenir shops, and **El Pueblo,** a tourism complex built in the style of a mock colonial-era village, with a wide range of restaurants, gift shops, art galleries, bars, and discos.

Heading to a mall

With globalization and modernization taking hold in Costa Rica, much of the local shopping scene has shifted to large mega-malls. Modern multi-level affairs with cineplexes, food courts, and international brand-name stores are becoming more ubiquitous. The biggest and most modern of these malls include the **Mall San Pedro, Multiplaza, Terra Mall,** and **Mall Real Cariari.** Although they lack the charm of the small shops found around San José, they're a reasonable option for one-stop shopping; most contain at least one or two local galleries and crafts shops, along with a large supermarket, which is always the best place to stock up on local coffee, hot sauces, liquors, and other nonperishable foodstuffs.

What to look for and where to find it

If the large markets and malls don't have what you're looking for, perhaps one of the specialty shops or galleries listed in the following sections will fill the bill.

You may be able to negotiate prices down a little bit, but bargaining is not a traditional part of the vendor culture here, so you'll have to work hard to save a few dollars.

Art galleries

Arte Latino (Calle 5 and Av. 1; ☎ 258-3306) carries original artwork in a variety of media, featuring predominantly Central American themes. Some of it is pretty gaudy, but this is a good place to find Nicaraguan and Costa Rican "primitive" paintings. The gallery also has storefronts in the Multiplaza Mall in Escazú and at the Mall Cariari, which is located on the Interamerican Highway, about halfway between the airport and downtown, across the street from the Hotel Herradura.

For an outstanding gallery dealing mainly in high-end Costa Rican art, head to **Galería 11–12** (Av. 15 and Calle 35, Casa 3506, in Barrio Escalante; ☎ 280-8441; www.galeria11-12.com). The collection here ranges from neoclassical painters such as Teodorico Quirós to modern masters such as Francisco Amighetti and Paco Zuñiga, to current stars such as Rafa Fernández, Fernando Carballo, and Fabio Herrera. These folks recently opened a second gallery in Escazú, at the Plaza Itskatzu, just off the main highway, next to the Courtyard San José hotel.

Galería Jacobo Karpio (Av. 1, Casa 1352, between calles 11 and 13; ☎ 257-7963) handles some of the more adventurous modern art to be found in Costa Rica. Karpio has a steady stable of prominent Mexican, Cuban, and Argentine artists, as well as some local talent.

TEORetica (Av. 7 and Calle 11; ☎ 233-4881) is a small downtown gallery, run by Virginia Pérez-Ratton, one of the more adventurous and internationally respected collectors and curators in Costa Rica. You'll often find very interesting and cutting-edge exhibitions here.

Galería Andrómeda (Calle 9 at Av. 9; ☎ 223-3529) is a small, personal gallery featuring contemporary local artists of good quality. There are usually prints and paintings by several artists on display, and prices are very reasonable.

Books

The best bookstore for English-language books is **Seventh Street Books** (Calle 7, between avs. Central and 1; ☎ 256-8251). They have an especially good selection of natural history books and field guides.

Handicrafts

The quality of Costa Rican handicrafts is generally very low, and the offerings are limited. The most typical items you'll find are hand-painted wooden **oxcarts.** These come in a variety of sizes, and the big ones can be shipped to your home for a very reasonable price.

Notable exceptions to the generally meager crafts offerings include the fine wooden creations of **Barry Biesanz** (☎ 289-4337; www.biesanz.com). His work is sold in many of the finer gift shops around, but beware: Biesanz's work is often imitated, so make sure that what you buy is the real deal (he generally burns his signature into the bottom of the piece). **Lil Mena** is a local artist who specializes in working with and painting on handmade papers and rough fibers. You'll find her work in a number of shops around San José.

You may also run across **carved masks** made by the indigenous Boruca people of southern Costa Rica. These full-size balsa-wood masks come in a variety of styles, both painted and unpainted, and run anywhere from $10 to $70, depending on the quality of workmanship. **Cecilia "Pefi" Figueres** makes practical ceramic wares that are lively and fun. Look for her brightly colored abstract and figurative bowls, pitchers, and coffee mugs at some of the better gift shops around the city.

Scores of shops around San José sell a wide variety of crafts, from the truly tacky to the divinely inspired. Here are some that sell more of the latter and fewer of the former.

Biesanz Woodworks (Escazú; ☎ 289-4337; www.biesanz.com; call for directions and off-hour appointments) produces a wide range of high-quality items, including bowls, jewelry boxes, humidors, and some wonderful sets of wooden chopsticks. Biesanz Woodworks is actively involved in reforestation, so you can even pick up a hardwood seedling here.

Occupying two floors at the Hotel Don Carlos, **Boutique Annemarie** (Calle 9, between avs. 7 and 9; ☎ 221-6063) has an amazing array of wood products, leather goods, papier-mâché figurines, paintings, books, cards, posters, and jewelry. You'll see most of this stuff at the other shops, but not in such quantities or in such a relaxed and pressure-free environment. Don't miss this shopping experience.

Galería Namu (Av. 7 between calles 5 and 7; ☎ 256-3412; www.galerianamu.com) has some very high-quality arts and crafts, including excellent Boruca and Huetar carved masks and "primitive" paintings, many painted by rural women. It also carries a good selection of the ceramic work of Cecilia "Pefi" Figueres. This place organizes tours to visit various indigenous tribes and artisans as well.

Jewelry

Part working jewelry factory, part shopping center, part tourist trap, **Plaza Esmeralda** (Sabana Norte, 800m [8 blocks] north of Jack's in Pavas; ☎ 296-0312; www.plaza-esmeralda.com) is a good place to come to buy replicas of pre-Columbian jewelry. The several shops here carry a wide range of typical tourist souvenirs and locally produced arts and craftworks at fair prices. Visitors are treated to a 15-minute guided tour where you can see some of the jewelry being manufactured.

Leather goods

In general, Costa Rican leather products are not of the highest grade or quality, and prices are not particularly low — but take a look and see for yourself.

Del Río (☎ 262-1415) is a local leather-goods manufacturer, with stores in most of the city's modern malls. It also offers free hotel pickups and transfers to its factory outlet in Heredia.

Malety (Av. 1 between calles 1 and 3; ☎ 221-1670) is another good place to shop for locally produced leather bags, briefcases, purses, wallets, and other such items. A second store is located on Calle 1 between avenidas Central and 2.

Liquor

The national drink is **guaro,** a rough, clear liquor made from sugar cane. The most popular brand is **Cacique,** which you'll find at every liquor store and most supermarkets. Costa Ricans drink their *guaro* straight or mixed with club soda or Fresca. When drinking it straight, it's customary to follow a shot with a bite into a fresh lime covered in salt.

Costa Ricans also drink a lot of rum. The premier Costa Rican rum is **Centenario,** but I recommend that you opt for the Nicaraguan **Flor de Caña** or Cuban **Havana Club,** which are both far superior rums.

Because of the trade embargo, bringing Havana Club into the United States is illegal.

Several brands and styles of coffee-based liqueurs are also produced in Costa Rica. **Café Rica** is similar to Kahlúa, and you can also find several types of coffee cream liqueurs. The folks at **Café Britt** produce their own line of coffee liqueurs, which are quite good. You can buy them in most supermarkets, liquor stores, and tourist shops.

Music

A CD of Costa Rican music makes a great souvenir. **Editus** is an inventive trio (guitar, violin, and percussion) that has several albums out. They've won two Grammy awards for their collaborations with Rubén Blades on the albums *Tiempos* and *Mundo.*

Taking a trip to Sarchí for some local crafts

Sarchí is Costa Rica's main artisan town. The colorfully painted miniature oxcarts that you see all over the country are made here. Oxcarts such as these were once used to haul coffee beans to market. Today, although you may occasionally see oxcarts in use, most are purely decorative. However, they remain a well-known symbol of Costa Rica. In addition to miniature oxcarts, many carved wooden souvenirs are made here with rare hardwoods from the nation's forests. Dozens of shops are located within a few blocks of each other in town, and all have similar prices.

If you're driving, take the Interamerican Highway north. After passing the airport and the turnoff for Jacó and Manuel Antonio, look for the marked exit for Grecia and Sarchí. It's about a 30-minute drive from the airport to Sarchí. A taxi should charge around $30 each way from downtown.

About five buses leave San José for Sarchí from Avenida 3 between calles 16 and 18. Alternatively, you can take any Grecia bus from this same station. In Grecia, they connect with the Alajuela-Sarchí buses, which leave every 30 minutes from Calle 8 between avenidas Central and 1 in Alajuela. The fare is 75¢.

You should also see discs by **Cantoamérica,** which plays upbeat dance music ranging from salsa to son to calypso to meringue. Jazz pianist **Manuel Obregón** has several excellent albums out, including *Simbiosis,* on which he improvises along with the sounds of Costa Rica's wildlife, waterfalls, and weather, as well as his work with the *Papaya Orchestra,* a collaboration and gathering of musicians from around Central America.

 Son is a style of dance music, predominantly Cuban in origin. It mixes some African and Cuban rhythms with Spanish dance music.

Papaya Music (www.papayamusic.com), produces and distributes an excellent range of local music, including everyone from Obregon to **Malpais,** a local pop-rock band, to a broad selection of traditional folk music, including one of my favorite local discs, *Dr. Bombodee,* by the Costa Rican–born calypsonian Walter "Gavitt" Ferguson.

Many gift shops around the country carry a small selection of Costa Rican music. You can also find music stores in all the modern malls mentioned in the "Heading to a mall" section, earlier in this chapter.

Living It Up After Dark: From the Theaters to a Bitter Street

Catering to a mix of tourists, college students, and just generally party-loving Ticos, San José has a host of options to meet the nocturnal needs of visitors and residents alike. You'll find plenty of interesting clubs and bars, a wide range of theaters, and some very lively discos and dance salons.

To find out what's going on in San José while you're in town, pick up either the *Tico Times* (English) or *La Nación* (Spanish), two local newspapers. The former is a good place to find out where local expatriates are hanging out; the latter's "Viva" and "Tiempo Libre" sections have extensive listings of discos, movie theaters, and live music.

The performing arts

Theater is very popular in Costa Rica, and downtown San José is studded with small theaters. However, tastes tend toward the burlesque, and the crowd pleasers are almost always simplistic sexual comedies. The **National Theater Company** (☎ 257-8304) is an exception, tackling works from Lope de Vega to Lorca to Mamet. Similarly, the small independent group **Abya Yala** (☎ 240-6071) also puts on several cutting-edge avant-garde shows each year. Almost all the theater offerings are in Spanish, although the **Little Theater Group** (☎ 355-1623) is a long-standing amateur group that periodically stages orks in English. Check the *Tico Times* to see if anything is running during your stay.

Costa Rica has a strong modern-dance scene. Both the **University of Costa Rica** (☎ 207-4595) and the **National University** (☎ 256-4838) have modern-dance companies that perform regularly in various venues in San José. In addition to the university-sponsored companies, you should check out some of the various smaller independent companies. **Los Denmedium** and **Diquis Tiquis** are particularly good.

The **National Symphony Orchestra** (☎ 236-6669) is a respectable orchestra by regional standards, although its repertoire tends to be rather conservative. The symphony season runs March through November, with concerts roughly every other weekend at the **Teatro Nacional** (National Theater; Avenida 2 between calles 3 and 5 (☎ 221-3756) and the **Auditorio Nacional** (National Auditorium; ☎ 222-7647), located at the Museo de Los Niños (see the listing earlier in this chapter). Tickets cost between $3 and $15 and can be purchased at the box office.

Visiting artists also stop in Costa Rica from time to time. Recent concerts have featured old rocker Deborah Harry, opera legend Luciano Pavarotti, reggae star Sean Paul, Puerto Rican heartthrob Luis Miguel, pop-opera phenom Andrea Bocelli, Chilean rockers La Ley, and salsa star Marc Anthony, whose wife, Jennifer Lopez, even joined him onstage for a moment. Many of these concerts and guest performances take place in San José's two historic theaters, the **Teatro Nacional** (see earlier in this section) and the **Teatro Melico Salazar** (Avenida 2 between calles Central and 2; ☎ 221-4952), as well as at the **Auditorio Nacional** (see earlier in this section). Really large shows are sometimes held at football (soccer) stadiums or at the amphitheater at the Hotel Herradura.

Dance clubs and discos

Ticos love to dance, and you'll find plenty of places to hit the dance floor in San José. Salsa and merengue are the main beats that move people here, but you'll also find clubs specializing in more-modern dance music such as house. Many of the dance clubs, discos, and salons feature live music on the weekends.

In general, bars open anywhere from mid- to late-afternoon and stay open to anywhere from midnight to 2 a.m. Most discos and dance halls follow similar hours, although a very few will open as late as 8 p.m. Some bars and discos do stay open as late as 4 a.m.

A good place to sample a range of San José's nightlife is in **El Pueblo,** a shopping, dining, and entertainment complex done up like an old Spanish village. It's just across the river to the north of town. The best way to get there is by taxi; all the drivers know El Pueblo well. Within the alleyways that wind through El Pueblo are a dozen or more bars, clubs, and discos — plus an indoor football (soccer) playing field. **Cocoloco** (☎ 222-8782) features nightly "fiestas," **Discoteque Infinito** (☎ 223-2195) has three different environments under one roof, and **Twister** (☎ 222-5746) and **Friends** (☎ 223-5283) are happening party spots. Across the street, you'll find **La Plaza** (☎ 257-1077), one of my favorite dance spots.

Most of the places listed in this section demand a nominal cover charge; sometimes it includes a drink or two.

Café 83 Sur (1 block south of the Nicaraguan Embassy, on Avenida 2; ☎ 221-2369) is a restaurant, lounge, and dance joint with various rooms and environments to suit your mood. A live DJ, playing a current mix of dance music, is almost always on hand.

The dance floor at **El Tobogán** (2 blocks north and 1 block east of the La República main office, off the Guápiles Highway; ☎ 223-8920) is about the size of a football field, yet it still fills up. This is a place where Ticos come with their loved ones and dance partners. The music is a mix of classic Latin dance rhythms — salsa, cumbia, and merengue. It's open only on the weekends (till about 2 a.m.), but a live band is always playing, and sometimes the music's very good.

Tucked inside a nondescript office building and commercial center on Paseo Colón, **Vertigo** (Edificio Colón, Paseo Colón; ☎ 257-8424) has quickly become one of the more popular places for rave-style, late-night dancing and partying. The dance floor is huge, the ceilings are high, and electronic music rules the roost. It's open daily till 4 a.m.

The bar scene

There seems to be something for every taste in San José. Lounge lizards will be happy in most hotel bars in the downtown area, while students and the young at heart will have no problem mixing in at the livelier spots around town, especially out in San Pedro.

The best part of the San José bar scene is something called a *boca*, the equivalent of a tapa in Spain: a little dish of snacks that arrives at your table when you order a drink. Although this is a somewhat dying tradition, especially in the younger, hipper bars, you'll still find *bocas* alive and well in the older, more traditional Costa Rican drinking establishments. In most, the *bocas* are free, but in some, where the dishes are more sophisticated, you'll have to pay for the treats.

A recent remodel and ownership change have made **Bar Morazán** (Avenida 3 and Calle 9; ☎ 221-9527) one of the classiest downtown watering holes. Exposed brick walls and risqué traffic signs provide most of the décor. The crowd is a broad mix of downtown workers, tourists, young hipsters, and gay partiers.

Chelles (Av. Central and Calle 9; ☎ 221-1369) makes up for its lack of ambience with plenty of tradition and its diverse and colorful clientele. The lights are bright, the chairs surround simple Formica-topped card tables, and mirrors adorn most of the walls. Simple sandwiches and meals are served, and pretty good *bocas* come with the drinks. Plus, this place is open 24 hours every day.

El Cuartel de la Boca del Monte (Av. 1 between calles 21 and 23; ☎ 221-0327) began life as an artist-and-bohemian hangout, and over the years it has evolved into the leading meat market for the young and well heeled. However, artists still come, as do local and foreign-exchange students, young working stiffs, and tourists. Live music is usually offered here on Monday, Wednesday, and Friday nights, and when it's playing, the place is packed shoulder to shoulder.

You can easily miss the narrow entrance to **El Observatorio** (Calle 23 between avs. Central and 1; ☎ 223-0725). Owned by a local filmmaker, the décor includes a heavy dose of cinema motifs. The space is large, with high ceilings, and one of the best (perhaps only) smoke extraction systems of any popular bar, making the air pleasant to breathe, despite the fact that 80 percent of the clientele are chain smokers. Occasional live music or movie screenings are featured, and a pretty good menu of appetizers and main dishes, drawn from various world cuisines, is on hand.

Housed in a beautiful old mansion just off Parque Morazán in the heart of downtown, **Key Largo** (Calle 7 between avs. 1 and 3; ☎ 221-0277) is worth a visit if just to take in the scene and admire the dark-stained carved wood ceilings. However, be forewarned, this has historically been, and still is, one of the city's prime hangouts for prostitutes and their potential customers.

Meridiano al Este (Av. Central, across from La Bomba La Primavera, Barrio California; ☎ 256-2705) may just be the best spot in San José to catch live music. Owned by some of the members of the Grammy

Award–winning group Editus, this place actually took acoustic and sight-line considerations into account during the design phase, unlike most other bars that host live music in town.

Hanging out in San Pedro

The 2-block stretch of **San Pedro** just south of the University of Costa Rica has been dubbed La Calle de Amargura, or the "Street of Bitterness," and it's the heart and soul of this eastern suburb and college town. Bars and cafes are mixed in with bookstores and copy shops. After dark, the streets here are packed with teens, punks, students, and professors barhopping and just hanging around. You can walk the strip until some-place strikes your fancy, or you can try one of the places listed in this section.

The **Jazz Café** (next to the Banco Popular on Av. Central; ☎ 253-8933) is consistently one of the more happening spots in San Pedro and one of my favorites, although low ceilings and poor air circulation make it almost unbearably smoky most nights. Wrought-iron chairs, sculpted busts of famous jazz artists, and creative lighting give the place ambi-ence. Live music is featured here most nights.

Set on a busy corner in the heart of the University district, **Terra U** (2 blocks east and 1½ blocks north of the Church in San Pedro; ☎ 225-4261) is quickly becoming one of the most popular bars in the area. Part of this is due to the inviting, open-air, street-front patio area, which pro-vides a nice alternative to the all-too-common smoke-filled rooms found at most other trendy spots.

Hard rockers, metal freaks, ravers, and rowdy young crowds tend to con-gregate at the **Sand Bar** (☎ 225-9229), in the Centro Comercial Cocorí, and **El Yos** (☎ 283-0095), located 75m (¾ block) west of the Automercado in Los Yoses. The latter club often has live music or DJs.

You can get here by heading out (east) on Avenida 2, following the flow of traffic. You'll first pass through the neighborhood of **Los Yoses** before you reach a big traffic circle with a big fountain in the center (La Fuente de la Hispanidad). The **Mall San Pedro** is located on this traffic circle. Heading straight through the circle (well, going around it and continuing on what would have been a straight path), you'll come to the **Church of San Pedro,** about 4 blocks east of the circle. The church is San Pedro's major landmark.

Casinos

Gambling is legal in Costa Rica; however, there are some idiosyncrasies involved in gambling *à la Tica*.

If blackjack is your game, you'll want to play rummy. The rules are almost identical, except that the house doesn't pay one and a half times on blackjack — instead, it pays double on any three of a kind or three-card straight flush — even if it pushes you over 21.

If you're looking for roulette, what you'll find here is a bingo-like spinning cage of numbered balls. The betting is the same, but some of the glamour is lost.

You'll also find a version of five-card-draw poker, but the rule differences are so complex that I advise you to sit down and watch for a while and then ask some questions before joining in. That's about all you'll find — no craps tables or baccarat are on hand.

In the past few years, some controversy has arisen over slot machines — mechanical slot machines are currently outlawed — but you will be able to play electronic slots and poker games. Most of the casinos here are quite casual and small by international standards. You may have to dress up slightly at some of the fancier hotels, but most are accustomed to tropical-vacation attire.

Casinos are located at several of the mid- to large-scale hotels, as well as some stand-alone casinos downtown. **Casino Club Colonial** (Av. 1 between calles 9 and 11; ☎ **258-2807**) and **Casino Del Rey** (Av. 1 and Calle 9, inside the Hotel Del Rey; ☎ **257-7800**) are two good options, virtually next door to each other.

Taking a Day Trip out of San José

San José makes an excellent base for exploring the beautiful Central Valley and the surrounding mountains. A wide range of organized day trips are offered, ranging from visits to some pre-Colombian ruins to a host of adventure activities.

Guided tours and adventures

For most visitors, the best way to take advantage of a day trip or adventure outside of San José is as part of a guided tour or outing.

A number of companies offer a wide variety of primarily nature-related day tours out of San José. The best of these include **Costa Rica Expeditions** (☎ **257-0766**; www.costaricaexpeditions.com), **Costa Rica Sun Tours** (☎ **296-7757**; www.crsuntours.com), and **Horizontes Tours** (☎ **222-2022**; www.horizontes.com).

Before signing on for a tour of any sort, find out how many fellow travelers will be accompanying you, how much time will be spent in transit and eating lunch, and how much time will actually be spent doing the primary activity. I've had complaints about tours that were rushed, that spent too much time in a bus or on secondary activities, or that had a cattle-car, assembly-line feel to them.

The tours below are arranged by type of activity. In addition to these, many other tours exist, some of which combine two or three different activities or destinations.

Bungee jumping

Nothing is unique about bungee jumping in Costa Rica, but the sites here are quite beautiful. If you've always had the bug, **Tropical Bungee** (☎ 248-2212; www.bungee.co.cr) helps folks jump off an 80m (262-ft.) bridge for $60 per person, and $30 for a second jump. Transportation is provided free from San José twice daily. These folks also offer paragliding tours.

Canopy tours and the rain-forest aerial tram

Getting off the ground and up into the treetops is the latest fad in Costa Rican tourism, and scores of such tours abound around the country. You have several options relatively close to San José. The folks at the **Original Canopy Tours** (☎ 257-5149; www.canopytour.com) have their **Mahogany Park** operation, located about one hour outside of San José. The tour here features ten platforms, and at the end, you have the choice of taking a cable to a ground station or doing an 18m (60-ft.) rappel down to finish off. The tour takes about two hours and costs $45.

A less adventurous option is the **Rain Forest Aerial Tram Caribbean** (☎ 257-5961; www.rainforesttram.com), built on a private reserve bordering Braulio Carillo National Park. The tramway takes visitors on a 90-minute ride through the treetops, where they have the chance to glimpse the complex web of life that makes these forests unique. Well-groomed trails are located throughout the rain forest and you may want to stop at the restaurant on-site, so a trip here can easily take up a full day. The cost for tours, including transportation from San José and either breakfast or lunch, is $79. Alternatively, you can drive or take one of the frequent Guápiles buses — they leave every half-hour throughout the day and cost $2 — from the new Caribbean bus terminal (Gran Terminal del Caribe) on Calle Central, 1 block north of Avenida 11. Ask the driver to let you off in front of the *teleférico.* If you're driving, head out on the Guápiles Highway as if driving to the Caribbean coast. Watch for the tram's roadside welcome center — it's hard to miss. For walk-ins, the entrance fee is $50; students and anyone under 18 pay $25.

Because the Rain Forest Aerial Tram Caribbean is a popular tour for groups, I highly recommend that you have an advance reservation in the high season and, if possible, a ticket. Otherwise, you may end up waiting a long time for your tram ride or may even be shut out. The tram can handle only about 80 passengers per hour, so scheduling is tight; the folks here try to schedule as much as possible in advance.

Day cruises

If you want to really enjoy the beach and the tropics, take a cruise to lovely Tortuga Island in the Gulf of Nicoya. These full-day tours entail an early departure for the two-and-a-half-hour chartered bus ride to Puntarenas, where you board your vessel for a one-and-a-half-hour cruise to Tortuga Island. Then you get several hours on the picturesque island, where you can swim, lie on the beach, play volleyball, or try a canopy tour, followed by the return journey.

The original and most dependable company running these trips is **Calypso Tours** (☎ 256-2727; www.calypsotours.com). The tour costs $99 per person and includes round-trip transportation from San José, a basic continental breakfast during the bus ride to the boat, all drinks on the cruise, and an excellent buffet lunch on the beach at the island. The Calypso Tours main vessel is a massive motor-powered catamaran. A second vessel runs a separate tour to a private nature reserve at **Punta Coral.** The beach is much nicer at Tortuga Island, but the tour to Punta Coral is much more intimate, and the restaurant, hiking, and kayaking are all superior here.

Exploring pre-Columbian ruins

Although Costa Rica lacks the kind of massive pre-Columbian archaeological sites found in Mexico, Guatemala, or Honduras, it does have **Guayabo National Monument,** a small excavated town that today is just a small collection of building foundations, cobbled streets, aqueducts, and a small plaza. **Costa Rica Sun Tours** (☎ 296-7757; www.crsuntours.com) offers a day trip here for around $125 per person.

Choosing the volcano trip that's right for you

Poás, Irazú, and Arenal volcanoes are three of Costa Rica's most popular destinations, and the first two are easy day trips from San José. Although numerous companies offer day trips to Arenal, I don't recommend them because you'll spend at least three and a half hours on travel in each direction. You usually arrive when the volcano is hidden by clouds and leave before the night's darkness shows off its glowing eruptions. For more information on Arenal volcano, see Chapter 18.

Tour companies offering trips to Poás and Irazú include **Costa Rica Expeditions** (☎ 257-0766; www.costaricaexpeditions.com), **Costa Rica Sun Tours** (☎ 296-7757; www.crsuntours.com), and **Horizontes Tours** (☎ 222-2022; www.horizontes.com). Prices range from $25 to $35 for a half-day trip, and from $50 to $90 for a full-day trip.

The 3,378m (11,080-ft.) **Irazú volcano** is historically one of Costa Rica's more active volcanoes, although it's relatively quiet these days. It last erupted on March 19, 1963, on the day that President John F. Kennedy arrived in Costa Rica. A good paved road passes right to the rim of the crater, where a desolate expanse of gray sand nurtures few plants and the air smells of sulfur. The landscape here is often compared to that of the moon. You'll get fabulous views of the fertile Meseta Central and Orosi Valley as you drive up from Cartago, and if you're very lucky, you may be able to see both the Pacific Ocean and the Caribbean Sea. Clouds usually descend by noon, so get here as early in the day as possible.

A visitor center with information on the volcano and natural history can be found at the entrance to the park, just off the parking lots. A short trail leads to the rim of the volcano's two craters, their walls a maze of eroded gullies feeding onto the flat floor far below. This is a national park, with an admission fee of $7 charged at the gate. Dress in layers; this may be the tropics, but it can be cold up at the top if the sun's not out. The park restaurant, at an elevation of 3,022m (9,912 ft.), with walls of windows looking out over the valley far below, claims to be the highest restaurant in Central America.

If you don't want to take an organized tour, buses leave for Irazú volcano Saturday, Sunday, and holidays at 8 a.m. from Avenida 2 between calles 1 and 3 (across the street from the entrance to the Gran Hotel Costa Rica). The fare is $5 round-trip, with the bus leaving the volcano at 2 p.m. To make sure that the buses are running, call ☎ 534-4125. If you're driving, head northeast out of Cartago toward San Rafael, and then continue driving uphill toward the volcano, passing the turnoffs for Cot and Tierra Blanca en route.

Poás volcano is 37km (23 miles) from San José on narrow roads that wind through a landscape of fertile farms and dark forests. As at Irazú, a paved road runs right to the top, although you'll have to hike in about 1km (½ mile) to reach the crater. The volcano stands 2,640m (8,659 ft.) tall and is located within a national park, which preserves not only the volcano but also dense stands of virgin forest. Poás's crater, said to be the second largest in the world, is more than a mile across. Geysers in the crater sometimes spew steam and muddy water 180m (590 ft.) into the air, making this the largest geyser in the world. An information center is located at the entrance to the park, just off the parking lots. Here you can see a slide show about the volcano, and you'll find well-groomed and well-marked hiking trails through the cloud forest that rings the crater. About 15 minutes from the parking area, along a forest trail, is an overlook onto beautiful Botos Lake, which has formed in one of the volcano's extinct craters.

Be prepared when you come to Poás: This volcano is often enveloped in dense clouds. If you want to see the crater, you'll want to come early and during the dry season. Moreover, it can get cool up here, especially when the sun isn't shining, so dress appropriately. Admission to the national park is $7 at the gate.

In case you don't want to go on a tour, a daily bus (☎ 442-6900) leaves from Avenida 2 between calles 12 and 14 at 8:30 a.m. and returns at 2 p.m. The fare is $4 round-trip. The bus is often crowded, so arrive early. If you're driving, head for Alajuela and continue on the main road through town and follow signs for Fraijanes. Just beyond Fraijanes, you'll connect with the road between San Pedro de Poás and Poasito; turn right toward Poasito, and continue to the rim of the volcano.

Mountain biking

The best bicycle riding is well outside of San José — on dirt roads where you're not likely to be run off the highway by a semi, or run head-on into someone coming around a blind curve in the wrong lane. Several companies run a variety of one-day and multiday tours out of San José. The one-day tours usually involve a round-trip bus or van ride out of downtown to the primary destination. These destinations include the small towns of Sarchí and Turrialba, as well as the Irazú and Poás volcanoes. Several of these tours are designed to be either entirely or primarily descents. **Costa Rica Biking Adventure** (☎ 225-6591; www.bikingincostarica.com) offers a variety of mountain-biking tours using high-end bikes and gear. A one-day trip should cost between $70 and $150 per person.

Rafting, kayaking, and river trips

Dozens of tumultuous rivers cascade down from the Costa Rican mountains. Several have become very popular for white-water rafting and kayaking. If I had to choose just one day trip to do out of San José, it would be a white-water-rafting trip. For between $75 and $95, you can spend a day rafting through lush tropical forests; multiday trips are also available. Some of the most reliable rafting companies are **Aventuras Naturales** (☎ 800-514-0411 in the United States, or 225-3939 in Costa Rica; www.toenjoynature.com), **Costa Rica White Water** (☎ 257-0766; www.costaricaexpeditions.com), **Exploradores Outdoors** (☎ 222-6262; www.exploradoresoutdoors.com) and **Ríos Tropicales** (☎ 233-6455; www.riostropicales.com). These companies all ply a number of rivers of varying difficulties, including the popular **Pacuare** and **Reventazón rivers.**

Of all of Costa Rica's white-water rivers, the **Pacuare River** is the most popular and arguably the most spectacular. Class III and IV rapids weave through predominantly uninhabited forest, and toucans fly overhead. Near the end of the run, the river passes through a narrow steep-walled canyon.

The Sarapiquí River is also a popular waterway for day trips out of San José. **Ecoscapes Highlights Tour** (☎ 297-0664; www.ecoscapetours.com) runs a jam-packed trip here that combines a stop at the La Paz waterfall, a visit to a banana plantation, a rain-forest hike, and a boat ride on the river for $79 per person, including round-trip transportation, breakfast, and lunch.

Part IV

Guanacaste and Environs

The 5th Wave   By Rich Tennant

JERRY FAILS TO HEED THE DIVE GUIDE'S REQUEST THAT NO ONE EAT A HEAVY LUNCH BEFORE THE DIVE

Hey— who's gonna know?

In this part . . .

The northwestern province of Guanacaste is home to Costa Rica's greatest array of beach towns and resort destinations. This part gives you insights into choosing the right beach and resort to fit your travel needs and wants. From the quiet isolated beaches of Playa Hermosa and Pan de Azucar, to the bustling surfer town of Tamarindo, to the mega-resorts of the Papagayo Peninsula, this part helps you choose the perfect destination on Costa Rica's Gold Coast.

After you've chosen where to go, this part goes on to list a wide range of activities to keep you busy while in Guanacaste.

Chapter 13

Going for Gold in Guanacaste

In This Chapter

▶ Arriving in Guanacaste

▶ Finding your way around Guanacaste

▶ Choosing where to stay and dine in Guanacaste

Guanacaste has earned its reputation as Costa Rica's "Gold Coast." Occupying the northwest corner of the country, Guanacaste is the driest and most consistently sunny region in Costa Rica. Not surprisingly, it is home to many of the country's most popular beaches and resorts.

Guanacaste province is named after the shady trees that still shelter the herds of cattle that roam the dusty inland savanna here. In addition to the beaches, resorts, and cattle ranches, Guanacaste has several active volcanoes and one of the last remnants of tropical dry forest left in Central America.

Hotel options range from large, luxurious resorts and all-inclusives, to isolated beachfront bed-and-breakfasts and small inns. Guanacaste currently boasts three championship golf courses, and more are allegedly in the works.

During the dry season, the hillsides in Guanacaste turn brown and barren. Dust from dirt roads blankets the trees in many areas, and the scenery seems far from tropical. Driving these dirt roads without air-conditioning and closed windows can be extremely unpleasant.

On the other hand, if you happen to visit this area in the rainy season, the hillsides are a beautiful, rich green, and the sun usually shines all morning, giving way to an afternoon shower — just in time for a nice siesta.

Getting There

Whether you fly directly to Liberia, or take a commuter flight from San José, the fastest and easiest way to get to Guanacaste is by air. I highly recommend it. If you want the freedom and flexibility of a car, you can always rent one in Guanacaste. However, if you're touring the country by car, or want to save money, you can also drive or take a bus. You'll find detailed information on all these options in the following sections.

By air

The **Daniel Oduber Airport** (☎ 668-1117; airport code: LIR) in Liberia is a small, modern international airport that receives a steady stream of scheduled commercial and charter flights throughout the year.

Major commercial airlines with regularly scheduled service include

- ✔ **American Airlines** (☎ 800-433-7300; www.aa.com) has three weekly direct flights between Miami and Liberia.

- ✔ **Continental** (☎ 800-525-0280; www.continental.com) has three weekly direct flights between Houston and Liberia.

- ✔ **Delta** (☎ 800-241-4141; www.delta.com) has six weekly direct flights between its Atlanta hub and Liberia.

- ✔ **US Airways** (☎ 800-622-1015; www.usairways.com) has one weekly direct flight between Charlotte and Liberia.

In addition, numerous commercial charter flights arrive from various North American and European cities throughout the high season. Check with your travel agent.

 A small, commuter airstrip also lies in Tamarindo. Most of the beaches in Guanacaste are between a 25- and 55-minute drive from the Liberia airport. If you're going to Playa Hermosa, Playa Ocotal, or the Papagayo Peninsula, you're best off flying into Liberia. Playa Flamingo, Playa Brasilito, Playa Conchal, and Sugar Beach, are slightly closer to Tamarindo, but the differences are almost negligible. Of course, if you're going to Tamarindo (or Playa Grande), and coming from San José, flying into and out of Tamarindo is your best option.

Sansa (☎ 221-9414; www.flysansa.com) and **Nature Air** (☎ 800-235-9272 in the United States and Canada, 299-6000 in Costa Rica; www.natureair.com) are two local commuter airlines with daily service to both Liberia and Tamarindo. The flight takes about 50 minutes and costs between $70 and $80 each way.

By bus

Grayline (☎ 220-2126; www.graylinecostarica.com) and **Interbus** (☎ 283-5573; www.costaricapass.com) are two private bus companies running fleets of modern minivans to all the major destinations in Costa Rica. Both service all the different beaches mentioned in this chapter. The fare is $25 each way on either line.

Both companies will pick you up at most San José–area hotels and drop you off at any of the hotels in this region. However, if you're the first pickup, or last drop-off on the route, you may be in for a long and tedious wait.

You can also take inexpensive Costa Rican bus lines to many Guanacaste beaches. Tickets cost between $5 and $6, and the trips take between five and six hours. You can buy tickets on the bus or just prior to departing at the station. In most cases, getting a confirmed ticket in advance is very hard and usually unnecessary.

The following is a listing of the schedules, terminal locations, and contact information of the major bus companies servicing the major beach destinations of Guanacaste:

- ✔ **Playa del Coco:** Pulmitan buses (☎ 222-1650) leave San José for Playa del Coco at 8 a.m. and 2 and 4 p.m. daily from Calle 24 between avenidas 5 and 7.

- ✔ **Playa Hermosa and Playa Panamá:** Tralapa buses (☎ 221-7202) leave San José daily at 3:25 p.m. from Calle 20 between avenidas 3 and 5, stopping first at Playa Hermosa and next at Playa Panamá.

- ✔ **Playa Brasilito, Playa Flamingo, and Playa Potrero:** Tralapa buses (☎ 221-7202) leave San José daily at 8 and 10:30 a.m. and 3 p.m. from Calle 20 between avenidas 3 and 5, stopping at playas Brasilito, Flamingo, and Potrero, in that order.

- ✔ **Tamarindo:** Tracopa buses (☎ 222-2666) leave San José for Tamarindo at 11:30 a.m. and 3:30 p.m., departing from Calle 14 between avenidas 3 and 5.

Alternatively, Pulmitan express buses (☎ 222-1650, or 666-0458 in Liberia) leave San José for Liberia roughly every hour between 6 a.m. and 8 p.m. from Calle 24 between avenidas 5 and 7. The ride to Liberia is four hours. After you're in Liberia, you can transfer to a local bus to your destination of choice at the main Liberia bus station. In general, three to four daily buses run between Liberia and the various Guanacaste beach destinations.

No direct bus service exists to either Playa Ocotal or Playa Grande. Playa del Coco is very close to Playa Ocotal, and a cab ride from the bus station there should be just about $5. Playa Grande is about a 20-minute ride from Tamarindo, and a taxi should charge you around $15 for this trip.

By car

Driving to Guanacaste from San José is a relatively easy and straight shot, with only two major routes.

If you're going to any of the more northern beaches, take the Interamerican Highway west from San José, and follow the signs for Nicaragua and the Guanacaste beaches. Turn left at the major cross-roads at the entrance to Liberia. This intersection is very well marked, and will point you toward Santa Cruz and the various Guanacaste beaches. Driving to Liberia from San José takes approximately three and a half to four hours. From Liberia, it's another 25 to 55 minutes to most of the beaches in this area.

After the turnoff, the road to the Papagayo Peninsula is prominently marked 8km (5 miles) south of the Liberia airport. At the corner here, you'll see a massive Do It Center hardware store and lumberyard.

If you're going on to Playa Hermosa and Playa Panamá, continue on a little farther and, just past the village of Comunidad, turn right. In about 11km (6¾ miles), you'll come to a fork in the road; take the right fork. These roads are relatively well-marked, and a host of prominent hotel billboards should make it easy enough to find the beach.

If you continue farther on the road to Santa Cruz, just beyond the town of Belén you'll see the turnoff for Playa Conchal, Playa Flamingo, Playa Brasilito, Sugar Beach, and Tamarindo.

If you're going to Tamarindo, Playa Conchal, Playa Brasilito, or Sugar Beach, the most direct route is by way of the Tempisque River bridge. Take the Interamerican Highway west from San José. Forty-seven kilometers (29 miles) past the turnoff for Puntarenas, you'll see signs for the turnoff to the bridge. After crossing the river, follow the signs for Nicoya and Santa Cruz. Continue north out of Santa Cruz until just before the village of Belén, where you'll find the turnoff for the various beaches. In another 20km (12 miles), you'll hit the village of Huacas. Take the left fork for Playa Tamarindo, and head straight for the road to Playa Flamingo, Playa Brasilito, Playa Conchal, and Sugar Beach.

Orienting Yourself in Guanacaste

The province of Guanacaste occupies the bulk of Costa Rica's northwestern land mass, from the northern section of the Nicoya Peninsula up to the Nicaraguan border. For tourists, most of Guanacaste's appeal lies with its miles and miles of beautiful beaches. The capital of Guanacaste is the city of Liberia, where you'll find the Daniel Oduber International Airport. The city itself holds little appeal for most tourists. In fact, although much of Guanacaste province is inland, the only major attraction here for visitors is the Rincón de la Vieja volcano and the surrounding Rincón de la Vieja National Park.

Introducing the neighborhoods

The beaches of Guanacaste come in various shapes and sizes. Some are protected and calm, while others feature strong surf. Some are quite developed, while others are home to just a few hotels and small resorts.

Here's a quick rundown of Guanacaste's principal beach destinations, running (more or less) from north to south.

Papagayo Peninsula

The turnoff for this long narrow peninsula is the first you'll hit heading west from the Liberia airport. So far, only two major hotels have opened up here, the Allegro Papagayo Resort and the Four Seasons Resort Costa Rica. The peninsula features several stunning and often deserted beaches, including **Playa Nacascolo,** which is inside the property of the Four Seasons Resort — but all beaches in Costa Rica are public, so you cannot be denied entry. Almost all the beaches here are very well protected, with little or no wave action.

Playa Hermosa and Playa Panama

Surrounded by steep forested hills, this curving gray-sand beach is long and wide and rarely crowded. It's also relatively protected and is consistently one of the region's calmest beaches for swimming. Fringing the beach is a swath of trees that stays surprisingly green right through the dry season. The shade provided by these trees, along with the calm protected waters, is a big part of the beach's appeal. **Playa Hermosa** has no large hotels or developments.

Beyond Playa Hermosa, you'll find the still underdeveloped **Playa Panamá** and, farther on, the calm waters of **Bahía Culebra,** a large protected bay dotted with small, semiprivate patches of beach and ringed with mostly intact dry forest. After years of neglect and abuse, Playa Panamá has finally been cleaned up and cars and camping have been severely restricted, making this a beautiful beach once again.

Playa del Coco and Playa Ocotal

Playa del Coco was one of the first beaches in Guanacaste to be developed, and it has long been a popular destination with middle-class Ticos and weekend revelers from San José. It's also a prime scuba-diving spot. The beach, which has grayish-brown sand, is quite wide at low tide and almost nonexistent at high tide. In between high and low tides, it's just right.

Playa Ocotal is a tiny pocket cove featuring a small salt-and-pepper beach bordered by high bluffs. It's quite beautiful. When the water is calm, you'll find good snorkeling around some rocky islands close to shore here. You'll see a fair amount of residential development here, as well as a couple of small hotels and resorts.

Playas Conchal, Brasilito, Flamingo, and Pan de Azúcar

Playa Conchal is the first in a string of beaches stretching north along this coast. For decades this was the semiprivate haunt of a few beach cognoscenti. The unique beach here is made up primarily of soft crushed shells. Nearly every place you could walk, turn, or lay down your towel was shell-collectors' heaven. Unfortunately, as Conchal developed and its popularity spread, unscrupulous builders have brought in dump trucks to haul away the namesake seashells for landscaping and construction, and the impact is noticeable.

Just beyond Playa Conchal to the north, you'll come to **Playa Brasilito,** a tiny beach town and one of the few real villages in the area. The soccer field is in the center of the village, and around its edges you'll find a couple of little *pulperías* (general stores). Playa Brasilito is popular both with Ticos and budget travelers from abroad. You'll find a few hotels and a couple of campsites here.

Playa Flamingo is located on a long spit of land that forms part of Potrero Bay. The beach here is a beautiful stretch of white sand. Despite a fair amount of development, Playa Flamingo feels sleepy and forgotten. You'll get a sense that the boom has passed it by.

If you continue along the road from Brasilito without taking the turn for Playa Flamingo, you'll soon come to **Playa Potrero.** The sand here is a brownish gray, but the beach is long, deserted, and quite calm for swimming. You can see the hotels of Playa Flamingo across the bay. Drive a little farther north, and you'll find the still undeveloped **Playa La Penca** and, finally, **Playa Pan de Azúcar,** a beautiful little salt-and-pepper beach with one lone small resort hotel backing it, Hotel Sugar Beach (see the listing later in this chapter).

Playa Grande and Tamarindo

Playa Grande is a long, isolated, and sparsely developed stretch of beach with strong surf. It's very popular with surfers, which can make the beach unsuitable for swimming at times. Playa Grande is one of the principal nesting sites for the giant leatherback turtle, the largest turtle in the world. I almost hate to mention places to stay in Playa Grande because the steady influx of tourists and development could doom this beach as a turtle-nesting site.

Tamarindo is a boomtown and one of the most popular beaches on the Gold Coast. Tamarindo boasts a mixture of hotels in a variety of sizes and price ranges and an eclectic array of restaurants, as well as several seemingly out-of-place modern strip malls.

Ongoing development continues to spread up the hills inland from the beach and south beyond to **Playa Langosta.** The beach itself is a long, wide swath of white sand that curves gently from one rocky headland to another. Behind the beach are low, dry hills that can be a dreary brown

in the dry season but that instantly turn green with the first brief showers of the rainy season. Fishing boats bob at their moorings at the south
end of the beach, and brown pelicans fish just outside the breakers.

The southernmost beaches

The beaches south of Tamarindo are some of the least developed on this
coast. All are fairly exposed to the open ocean and, thus, popular with
surfers. In order, heading south, you'll find the beaches of Avellanas,
Playa Negra, and Junquillal. All feature just a few small hotels and simple
restaurants. These are great places to get away from it all.

Rincón de la Vieja National Park

This national park begins on the flanks of the Rincón de la Vieja volcano
and includes this volcano's active crater. Down lower, you'll find an area
of geothermal activity with fumaroles, geysers, and hot mud pools that
create a bizarre, otherworldly landscape. In addition to hot springs and
mud pots, you can explore waterfalls, a lake, and volcanic craters. The
bird-watching here is excellent, and the views across the pasturelands to
the Pacific Ocean are stunning.

Finding information after you arrive

A small information kiosk will greet you at the Liberia airport, but invariably your best bet for information will be your hotel front desk, concierge,
or tour desk. Tour desks are available at almost every hotel in the region,
as well as tour offices in most major beach towns.

Getting Around Guanacaste

The best way to get around Guanacaste is by taxi or rental car, or as part
of an organized tour. For information on the many available tour options,
see Chapter 14.

By taxi

Taxis are available at the airport and in all the major beach towns. Any
hotel in the area can call you a taxi. Rates range from $3 to $5 for short
rides, to $25 to $40 for longer jaunts between more-distant towns and
destinations.

By car

Many of the major car-rental agencies have offices at the Liberia airport
and around Guanacaste. Reserving in advance with a company's U.S. or
international reservations office is probably best, but you can also rent a
car for a day or more by calling after you're in Costa Rica. Any of the following car-rental companies will deliver your car to any Guanacaste area
hotel:

- ✔ **Alamo** (☎ **800-462-5266** in the United States and Canada, or 668-1111 in Liberia, or 653-0727 in Tamarindo; www.alamo.com)

- ✔ **Avis** (☎ **800-230-4898** in the United States and Canada, or 666-7585 in Liberia; www.avis.com)

- ✔ **Budget** (☎ **800-527-0700** in the United States and Canada, or 668-1118 in Liberia, or 653-4381 in Tamarindo; www.budget.com)

- ✔ **Dollar** (☎ **800-800-4000** in the United States and Canada, or 668-1061 in Liberia; www.dollar.com)

- ✔ **Payless** (☎ **800-582-7432** in the United States and Canada, or 667-0511 in Liberia; www.paylesscr.com)

By foot

Most of the beach destinations here are small and easily navigable — in and of themselves — by foot. You can even sometimes walk between two beach towns or destinations — say, from Playa Conchal to Playa Brasilito, or from Tamarindo to Playa Langosta. However in most cases, you'll need to find some sort of motorized transportation to get between the different beach destinations.

By bus

Public buses are not a practical means for most tourists to get around Guanacaste. Although regular local buses connect most of the major beach towns and destinations with Liberia, you'll find virtually no connections among the different beach towns and destinations.

Where to Stay in Guanacaste

Guanacaste is Costa Rica's fastest-developing tourist destination, and the region boasts hotel options to suit any budget and any vacation style. Here are the best choices in a broad range of categories.

Allegro Papagayo Resort
$$–$$$ Papagayo Peninsula

This midpriced resort is an excellent choice if you're looking for an affordable all-inclusive vacation at a large modern resort, with a wide range of facilities and activities. The rooms are all identical in size — comfortable enough, but by no means extravagant — and housed in 14 different three-story buildings spread over a steep hillside overlooking the sea. The rooms on the upper floors in the buildings higher up the hill have the best views. All come with two queen-size beds or one king-size bed, a small private balcony, and the full complement of modern amenities. The beach is an isolated patch of hard-packed salt-and-pepper sand that almost disappears at high tide. The waters here are very protected, and the drop-off is very gradual. You can walk out for a hundred yards or more, and still have

Guanacaste

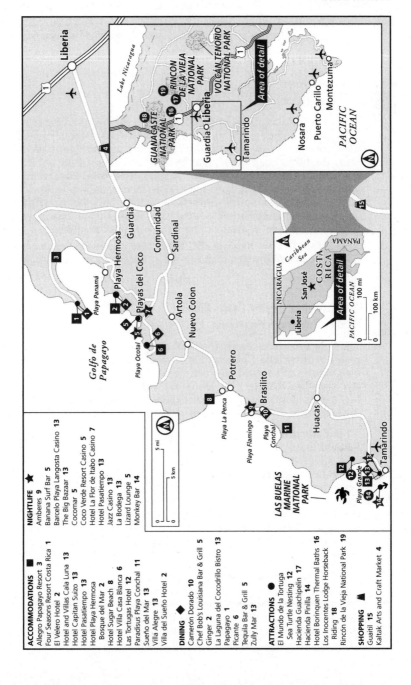

ACCOMMODATIONS ■
Allegro Papagayo Resort **3**
Four Seasons Resort Costa Rica **1**
El Velero Hotel **2**
Hotel and Villas Cala Luna **13**
Hotel Capitan Suizo **13**
Hotel Pasatiempo **13**
Hotel Playa Hermosa
Bosque del Mar **2**
Hotel Sugar Beach **8**
Hotel Villa Casa Blanca **6**
Las Tortugas Hotel **12**
Paradisus Playa Conchal **11**
Sueño del Mar **13**
Villa Alegre **13**
Villa del Sueño Hotel **2**

DINING ◆
Camarón Dorado **10**
Chef Bob's Louisiana Bar & Grill **5**
Ginger **2**
La Laguna del Cocodrillo Bistro **13**
Papagayo **1**
Picante **6**
Tequila Bar & Grill **5**
Zully Mar **13**

ATTRACTIONS ●
El Mundo de la Tortuga
Sea Turtle Nesting **12**
Hacienda Guachipelin **17**
Hacienda Pinilla **14**
Hotel Borinquen Thermal Baths **16**
Los Inocentes Lodge Horseback
Riding **18**
Rincón de la Vieja National Park **19**

SHOPPING ▣
Guaitíl **15**
Kaltak Arts and Craft Market **4**

NIGHTLIFE ★
Amberes **9**
Banana Surf Bar **5**
Barcelo Playa Langosta Casino **13**
The Big Bazaar **13**
Cocomar **5**
Coco Verde Resort Casino **5**
Hotel La Flor de Itabo Casino **7**
Hotel Pasatiempo **13**
Jazz Casino **13**
La Bodega **13**
Lizard Lounge **5**
Monkey Bar **14**

water around waist level. Still, most folks will want to spend their beach time at the hotel's "Fun Club" on a beautiful nearby white-sand beach.

See map p. 159. Playa Manzanillo. ☎ **248-2323.** *Fax: 221-9095.* www.occidental hotels.com. *Rack rates: $200–$330 double. Rates include all food and drinks, a range of activities, and taxes. AE, DC, MC, V.*

El Velero Hotel
$ Playa Hermosa

This little hotel is the best choice right on the beach in Playa Hermosa. White walls and polished tile floors give El Velero a Mediterranean flavor. The guest rooms are large, and those on the second floor have high ceilings. The furnishings are simple, though, and some of the bathrooms are a bit small. The hotel has its own popular little restaurant, which offers a good selection of meat, fish, and shrimp dishes, as well as weekly barbecue fests. Various tours, horseback riding, and fishing trips can be arranged through the hotel; however, the most popular excursions are the full-day and sunset cruises on the hotel's namesake sailboat.

See map p. 159. Playa Hermosa. ☎/fax **672-0016.** www.costaricahotel.net. *Rack rates: $72 double. Rates lower in the off season, higher during peak periods. AE, MC, V.*

Four Seasons Resort Costa Rica
$$$$$ Papagayo Peninsula

The Four Seasons is easily the most luxurious and impressive large-scale resort in Costa Rica. The resort is set near the very end of a long peninsula on a narrow spit of land between two white-sand beaches. The majority of the rooms are in three long, four-story, oceanfront buildings. The architecture here is stunning, with most buildings featuring flowing roof designs and other touches imitating the forms of turtles, armadillos, and butterflies.

All the rooms are very spacious, with wood floors, rich wood furnishings, tasteful fixtures and decorations from around the world, marble bathrooms with a deep tub and separate shower, luscious cotton sheets and bathrobes, and a large private balcony. The rooms on the third and fourth floors have the best views and cost a little more. The others have either garden views or partial ocean views, even though every room faces the sea. On the rocky hill at the end of the peninsula are the resort's suites and villas. These are all similarly appointed, but with even more space and often a private pool, a Jacuzzi, or an open-air gazebo for soaking in the views.

The resort also features the renowned service of the Four Seasons (including family-friendly amenities such as kid-size bathrobes and childproof rooms), one of the best-equipped full-service spas in the country, a truly spectacular golf course that offers ocean views from 15 of its 18 holes, and several excellent dining options. Of the hotel's restaurants, **Papagayo** (see the listing later in this chapter), serving Nuevo Latino cuisine, is my favorite.

Tamarindo

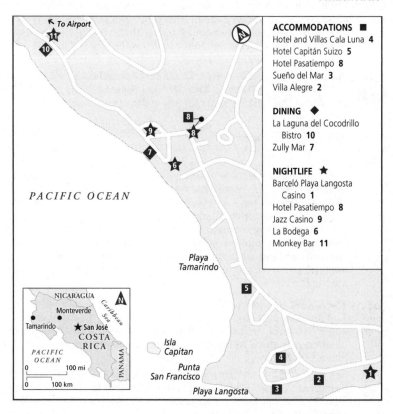

ACCOMMODATIONS ■
Hotel and Villas Cala Luna **4**
Hotel Capitán Suizo **5**
Hotel Pasatiempo **8**
Sueño del Mar **3**
Villa Alegre **2**

DINING ◆
La Laguna del Cocodrillo
　Bistro **10**
Zully Mar **7**

NIGHTLIFE ★
Barceló Playa Langosta
　Casino **1**
Hotel Pasatiempo **8**
Jazz Casino **9**
La Bodega **6**
Monkey Bar **11**

See map p. 159. Papagayo Peninsula. ☎ *800-819-5053 or 212-688-2440 in the United States, or 696-0098 in Costa Rica. Fax: 696-0010.* www.fourseasons.com/costarica. *Rack rates: $435–$545 double; $985 executive suite; $1,150–$4,950 suites and villas. Rates lower in the off season, higher during peak weeks. Children stay free in parent's room. AE, DC, MC, V.*

Hotel and Villas Cala Luna
$$$–$$$$$ Tamarindo

If you're looking for serious luxury in Tamarindo, stay in one of the two- or three-bedroom villas here, which are the size of a small home and just as well equipped. The living rooms are huge, with high-peaked ceilings, couches, tables and chairs, satellite televisions, and complete sound systems. The full kitchens come with microwave ovens and cappuccino machines — even washing machines. If this isn't enough, each villa has its own private swimming pool. The bedrooms are spacious and elegant, with either a king-size bed or two double beds. Everything is done in soft pastels with hand-painted accents, and the red-tile roofs and Mexican tile floors add elegance while keeping things cool. Rooms in the hotel are spacious and similarly well done, with their own terraces, but you'll have to share the hotel's main swimming pool with the rest of the guests. The hotel isn't right on the beach; you have to cross the street and walk a short path to reach the ocean.

See map p. 161. Playa Tamarindo. ☎ **653-0214.** *Fax: 653-0213.* www.calaluna.com. *Rack rates: $155–$175 double; $345–$440 villa. Rates for rooms, but not villas, include continental breakfast. Rates slightly higher during peak weeks. AE, MC, V.*

Hotel Capitán Suizo
$$$ Tamarindo

This well-appointed beachfront hotel is located on the quiet southern end of Tamarindo. The rooms are housed in a series of two-story buildings. The lower rooms have air-conditioning and private patios; the upper units have plenty of cross-ventilation and inviting balconies. All have large bathrooms and sitting rooms with fold-down futon couches. In effect, all the rooms are really junior suites, with separate sitting/living-room areas. The spacious individual bungalows are spread around the shady grounds; these all come with a tub in the bathroom and an inviting outdoor shower among the trees.

The hotel's free-form pool is the best I've found outside of a large resort. The shallow end slopes in gradually, imitating a beach, and a separate children's pool rests nearby. Perhaps this hotel's greatest attribute is its location just steps from one of the calmer and more isolated sections of Playa Tamarindo.

See map p. 161. Playa Tamarindo. ☎ **653-0353** *or 653-0075. Fax: 653-0292.* www.hotelcapitansuizo.com. *Rack rates: $140–$160 double; $195 bungalow. Rates include continental breakfast. Rates lower in the off season, higher during peak periods. AE, MC, V.*

Hotel Pasatiempo
$–$$ Tamarindo

A popular, and at times rowdy, midrange option, this hotel is set back from the beach a couple of hundred meters in a grove of shady trees. Most of the rooms are housed in duplex buildings, but each room has its own private patio with a hammock or chairs. The rooms boast plenty of space, and some even sleep five people. The two suites are very comfortable and well-equipped. Each room bears the name of a different beach, and the bedroom walls feature hand-painted murals. A small yet very inviting pool sits in the center of the complex.

The restaurant here serves excellent fresh fish, as well as pizza and Tex-Mex specialties. This rancho-style affair also has a pool table, a nightly happy hour, cable television with live sporting events, good snacks, and occasional live music.

Playa del Coco

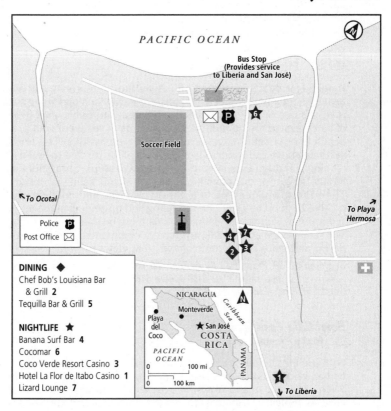

PACIFIC OCEAN

Bus Stop
(Provides service
to Liberia and San José)

Soccer Field

↖To Ocotal

To Playa
Hermosa

Police

Post Office

DINING ◆
Chef Bob's Louisiana Bar
  & Grill **2**
Tequilla Bar & Grill **5**

NIGHTLIFE ★
Banana Surf Bar **4**
Cocomar **6**
Coco Verde Resort Casino **3**
Hotel La Flor de Itabo Casino **1**
Lizard Lounge **7**

NICARAGUA

Monteverde

Playa
del
Coco

★San José

COSTA
RICA

PACIFIC
OCEAN

Caribbean Sea

PANAMA

0   100 mi
0   100 km

↓ To Liberia

See map p. 161. Playa Tamarindo. ☎ *653-0096. Fax: 653-0275.* www.hotel
pasatiempo.com. *Rack rates: $64–$89 double; $84–$99. Rates slightly higher
during peak periods. AE, MC, V.*

Hotel Playa Hermosa Bosque del Mar
$ Playa Hermosa

Tucked away under shady trees, this sprawling beachfront spread is under
new ownership and has gotten a major remodel and upgrade. Most of the
rooms have been entirely redone, with new tile floors and contemporary
furniture and fixtures. These rooms have air-conditioning, and I was told
they would soon have televisions as well. However, some of the more-basic
older rooms are still available for bargain hunters. The open-air restaurant
has a rustic tropical feel, with unfinished tree trunks holding up the roof.
This hotel has a prime location, with plenty of beachfront on the quiet southern end of Playa Hermosa. A swimming pool is due to open in late 2005, and
eight to ten new deluxe rooms, with kitchenettes, are soon to be added.

See map p. 165. Playa Hermosa. ☎ *672-0046. Fax: 672-0019.* www.hotelplaya hermosa.com. *Rack rates: $55–$75 double. Rates lower in the off season, higher during peak periods. MC, V.*

Hotel Sugar Beach
$$–$$$ **Playa Pan de Azúcar**

Hotel Sugar Beach is located on a beautiful, semiprivate salt-and-pepper beach about a ten-minute drive north of Playa Flamingo along a rough dirt road. It's one of the only hotels in the area, and that's what gives it most of its charm, in my opinion — it boasts lots of seclusion and privacy. The beach is on a small cove surrounded by rocky hills. The hotel itself is perched above the water. Nature lovers will be thrilled to find wild howler monkeys and iguanas almost on their doorsteps. Snorkelers should be happy here, too; this cove has some good snorkeling in the dry season. The rooms, which come in a variety of sizes and configurations, have received a good amount of remodeling and upgrading in recent years, and several new suites and deluxe rooms have been added in the past year. The main lodge and restaurant have a commanding view from a hillside perch, and many of the rooms have great views as well.

See map p. 159. Playa Pan de Azúcar. ☎ *654-4242. Fax: 654-4239.* www.sugar-beach.com. *Rack rates: $110–$155 double; $165–$190 suite. Rates include continental breakfast. Rates lower in the off season. AE, MC, V.*

Hotel Villa Casa Blanca
$$ **Playa Ocotal**

With friendly, helpful owners, beautiful gardens, and attractive rooms, this bed-and-breakfast is one of my favorite options in the area. Located about 500m (1,640 ft.) inland from the beach, it's built in the style of a Spanish villa. All the guest rooms feature fine furnishings and are well kept. Some are a tad small, but others are quite spacious and even have kitchenettes. The suites are higher up and have ocean views. My favorite has a secluded patio with lush flowering plants all around.

A little rancho serves as an open-air bar and breakfast area, and beside this is a pretty little lap pool with a bridge over it. Another separate rancho serves as a sort of lounge/recreation area and has a satellite television. An inviting hot tub and sitting area awaits you near the pool. These folks manage several rental houses and condos in the area, so if you plan to stay for a week or more, or if you need lots of room, ask about these.

See map p. 159. Playa Ocotal. ☎ *670-0518. Fax: 670-0448.* www.costa-rica-hotels-travel.com. *Rack rates: $80 double; $105–$125 suite. Rates include breakfast buffet. Rates lower in the off season, higher during peak periods. AE, MC, V.*

Las Tortugas Hotel
$$–$$$ **Playa Grande**

Playa Grande is best known for the leatherback turtles that nest here, and much of the beach is now part of Las Baulas National Park, which was

Playa Hermosa

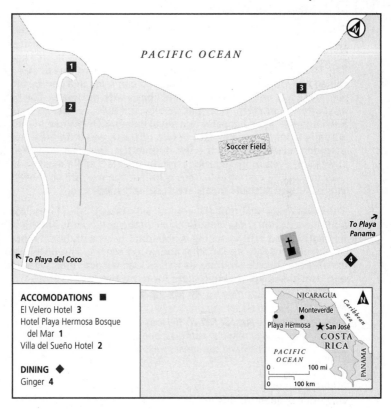

PACIFIC OCEAN

1

2

3

Soccer Field

To Playa
Panama

To Playa del Coco

4

ACCOMODATIONS ■
El Velero Hotel **3**
Hotel Playa Hermosa Bosque
del Mar **1**
Villa del Sueño Hotel **2**

DINING ◆
Ginger **4**

NICARAGUA
Monteverde
Playa Hermosa ★ San José
COSTA
RICA
PACIFIC
OCEAN
0   100 mi
0   100 km

created to protect the turtles. However, this beach and this hotel are also very popular with surfers. Several of the rooms are quite large, and most have interesting stone floors and shower stalls. The upper suite has a curving staircase that leads to its second room. A few canoes on the nearby estuary are available for gentle paddling among the mangroves.

The owners here led the fight to have the area declared a national park and continue to do everything possible to protect the turtles. As part of the hotel's turtle-friendly design, a natural wall of shrubs and trees shields the beach from the restaurant's light and noise, and the swimming pool is shaped like a turtle.

See map p. 159. Playa Grande. ☎ ***653-0423*** *or* ☎ */fax 653-0458.* www.cool.co.cr/ usr/turtles. *Rack rates: $50–$80 double; $100–$125 suite. Rates lower in the off season, slightly higher during peak weeks. V (5 percent surcharge for credit-card purchase).*

Paradisus Playa Conchal
$$$$–$$$$$ Playa Conchal

This sprawling all-suite, all-inclusive resort is large and luxurious. From the massive open-air reception building down to the free-form swimming pool (the largest in Central America), everything here is on a grand scale. The rooms feature either one king-size bed or two queen-size beds in a raised bedroom nook. Down below, you can relax in a comfortable sitting area, with a couch, coffee table, and chairs with ottomans. The bathrooms are large and modern, with marble tiles, full tubs, bidets, and a telephone. Each unit has a garden patio or a small balcony. Only three of the buildings actually front the ocean, and in two of these you'll find the resort's two presidential suites, which have double the living area of the standard suites and even more luxurious appointments. Unlike most all-inclusives, only one of the restaurants here is buffet; the rest are sit-down à la carte affairs, although these meals are decidedly mediocre.

The hotel has a beautiful golf course, with broad, open holes; rolling hills; and the occasional sea view. Because of the golf course and its ponds and wetlands, good bird-watching is abundant here, with healthy populations of parrots, roseate spoonbills, and wood storks. The hotel also has an excellent children's program, as well as loads of activities, with both water- and land-based sports equipment for guest use.

See map p. 159. Playa Conchal. ☎ **888-336-3542** *in the United States, or 654-4123 in Costa Rica. Fax: 654-4181.* www.solmelia.com. *Rack rates: $498–$800 double; $598–$1,100 royal suites; $1,500–$1,800 presidential suites. Rates include all meals, drinks, taxes, a wide range of activities, and use of nonmotorized land- and water-sports equipment. Golf and spa services extra. AE, MC, V.*

Sueño del Mar
$$$–$$$$ Playa Langosta

This small bed-and-breakfast has charming little touches and innovative décor: four-poster beds made from driftwood; African dolls on the windowsills; Kokopeli candleholders; and open-air showers with sculpted angelfish, hand-painted tiles, and lush tropical plants. Fabrics are from Bali and Guatemala. Somehow all of this works well together, and the requisite chairs and lounges nestled under shade trees right on the beach add the crowning touch.

The two casitas have their own kitchen, veranda, and sleeping loft. The honeymoon suite is a spacious second-floor room, with wraparound screened-in windows, a delightful open-air bathtub and shower, and an ocean view. The beach right out front is rocky and a bit rough, but it does reveal some nice, quiet tidal pools at low tide; it's one of the better sunset-viewing spots in Costa Rica. Breakfasts are huge and elaborate. No children under 12 are allowed unless your party rents out the whole hotel.

See map p. 161. Playa Langosta. ☎ **653-0284.** *Fax: 653-0558.* www.sueno-del-mar.com. *Rack rates: $185 double; $210–$295 suite or casita. Rates include full breakfast. Rates lower in the off season, higher during peak periods. MC, V.*

Villa Alegre
$$$ Playa Langosta

This small bed-and-breakfast on Playa Langosta is a well-run and homey option. The rooms are each decorated in the theme of a different country. In the main house, Guatemala, Mexico, and the United States are all represented. Of these, Mexico is the biggest and best, with a recently expanded open-air bathroom and shower. Every room has its own private patio, courtyard, or balcony. The villas are quite spacious and luxurious, with full kitchenettes. My favorite is the Japanese villa, with its subtle design touches and great woodwork. The Russian and the United States villas are truly wheelchair-accessible and -equipped, with ramps and modified bathrooms. The beach is just 90m (295 ft.) or so away through the trees, and a very pleasant little pool can be found here as well. Breakfasts are delicious and abundant.

See map p. 161. Playa Tamarindo. ☎ **653-0270.** *Fax: 653-0287.* www.villaalegre costarica.com. *Rack rates: $145 double; $195 villa. Rates include full breakfast. Rates lower in the off season. AE, MC, V.*

Villa del Sueño Hotel
$–$$ Playa Hermosa

This small hotel provides excellent value and attentive service in a beautiful setting. Although Villa del Sueño is not right on the beach (it's about 90m/295 ft. from the sand), its well-groomed lawns and gardens feel like an oasis in the dust and heat of a Guanacaste dry season. All the rooms have cool tile floors, high hardwood ceilings, ceiling fans, and well-placed windows for cross-ventilation. The second-floor superior rooms have more space, larger windows, and air-conditioning. A small pool and open-air bar rest in the center courtyard. Meals are served in the main building's open-air restaurant, which even has a stage for live music, generally folk rock, during much of the high season. The folks here manage a neighboring condominium development, which has additional apartment and efficiency units available for nightly and weekly rental.

See map p. 165. Playa Hermosa. ☎ */fax:* **672-0026.** www.villadelsueno.com. *Rack rates: $59–$89 double. Rates lower in the off season, higher during peak periods. AE, MC, V.*

Where to Dine in Guanacaste

Camarón Dorado
$$ Playa Brasilito   SEAFOOD

With tables and kerosene torches set right in the sand just steps from the crashing surf, this is one of my favorite restaurants in the area. More tables are available in the simple, open-air dining room, for those who don't want sand in their shoes. The service is semiformal, with the attentive waitstaff bringing you a bowl of flower-infused water so that you can wash your hands even before you order. The seafood is fresh, wonderfully prepared, and reasonably priced. When I asked to see the wine list, two waiters came over carrying about 12 different bottles between them.

See map p. 159. Playa Brasilito ☎ *654-4028. Reservations recommended in high season. Main courses: $5–$21. MC, V. Open: Daily 11 a.m.–10 p.m.*

Chef Bob's Louisiana Bar & Grill
$$–$$$ Playa del Coco   SEAFOOD

This place serves some of the freshest and best prepared seafood around. In addition to the daily catch cooked to order and a host of Cajun specialties, you can get seared yellowfin tuna with a ginger-sesame sauce, blackened mahimahi, or broiled grouper with Veracruz sauce. Several types of jambalaya, some pasta dishes, and a full complement of meat and poultry selections round out the menu. The choicest tables are on the second-floor open-air deck overlooking the main street of Playa del Coco, although tables can also be found in an enclosed little dining room nearby.

See map p. 163. Playa del Coco, 200m (2 blocks) before the beach on the main road. ☎ *670-0882. Main courses: $7–$24. AE, MC, V. Open: Daily 11 a.m.–10 p.m.*

Ginger
$$ Playa Hermosa   TAPAS

Ginger is at once the hippest and one of the more creative restaurants in the region. The architecture and décor are stylish and modern, with sharp angles and loads of chrome and glass. The food is an eclectic mix of modern takes on wide-ranging international fare, all served as tapas, meant to be shared while sampling some of the many cocktails and wines served here. Still, you can easily make a full meal of a night here. Order the house special ginger-glazed chicken wings, along with some spring rolls, and a plate of fresh mahimahi marinated in vodka and Asian spices. You can also order more-traditional Mediterranean and Spanish-style tapas, as well as delicious desserts.

See map p. 165. Playa Hermosa, on the main road. ☎ *672-0041. Tapas: $3–$8. AE, MC, V. Open: Tues–Sun 5–10 p.m.*

La Laguna del Cocodrillo Bistro
$$$$ Tamarindo   FUSION

Yet another new entry in the field of fine dining and fusion cuisine, this small restaurant has impressed me every time I've eaten here. Beautiful presentations, hearty portions, and a creative use of ingredients are the norm. Start things off with their almond-, basil-, and garlic-crusted goat cheese, served with an almond-pesto and balsamic vinegar reduction. For a main dish, try the fresh mahimahi, which is first blackened and then served with a honey-curry relish. Be sure to save room for dessert, which are always excellent. The open-air restaurant space is very small, but when the weather permits, more tables are set up under the trees in their beachfront garden area.

See map p. 161. Tamarindo, on the main road, toward the north end of town. ☎ *653-0255. Reservations recommended. Main courses: $13–$22. MC, V. Open: Mon–Sat 6–10 p.m.*

Papagayo
$$$$$ Four Seasons Resort   NUEVO LATINO

The luxurious Four Seasons Resort (see the listing earlier in this chapter) boasts one of the best Nuevo Latino ("New Latin") restaurants in Costa Rica. The menu is always long and creative, but it changes regularly and features daily specials. I thoroughly enjoyed my *ancho chile*–crusted rack of lamb served with a *mole poblano* sauce. The tamarind-crusted ahi tuna is also excellent and comes with jalapeño corn pudding and a mango salsa. The large dining room has high ceilings and low lighting, and it features some equally large artworks by renowned Costa Rican painters. However, the best seats, weather permitting, are those at the few outdoor garden tables.

See map p. 159. At the Four Seasons Resort, Papagayo Peninsula. ☎ *696-0006. Reservations necessary. Main courses: $22–$35. AE, MC, V. Open: Daily 6–10 p.m.*

Picante
$$ Playa Ocotal   INTERNATIONAL

You'll enjoy excellent fresh fish and daily specials in the large, open-air, poolside restaurant at this modest little resort and condominium project. Beyond the pool and down a steep little hill, you can see the Pacific Ocean. The menu is pretty simple and straightforward, with a selection of fresh seafood dishes, big burgers, excellent fish sandwiches, and large creative salads. The daily chalkboard specials are usually more creative and eclectic, ranging from sesame-seared tuna to mahimahi topped with a homemade curry sauce.

See map p. 169. At Bahia Pez Vela resort, Playa Ocotal. ☎ *670-0901. Main courses: $5–$14. MC, V. Open: Daily 10 a.m.–10 p.m.*

Tequila Bar & Grill
$$ Playa del Coco   MEXICAN

This is a simple and rustic restaurant serving good Mexican food and magnificent margaritas — in fact, 20 different types of margaritas can be sampled here. Because this is a fishing town, I recommend the seafood tacos and fajitas, although they both come in chicken and beef varieties. Main-course meals include pork chops in a chipotle barbecue sauce and grilled chicken with tomatillo and lime, as well as some fish dishes. Definitely grab one of the open-air street-side tables, if you get here early enough to snag one.

See map p. 163. Playa del Coco, 150m (492 ft.) before the beach on the main road. ☎ *670-0741. Main courses: $5–$14. No credit cards. Open: Thurs–Tues noon to 10 p.m.*

Zully Mar
$$ Tamarindo COSTA RICAN/SEAFOOD

This place has an enviable location, right on the beach in the center of Tamarindo. Recent improvements in the food and service have once again made this a top spot in town. The food and menu are not fancy, nor extensive, but the fresh fish and seafood specials are all well prepared and reasonably priced. You can also get a range of Costa Rican standards, as well as decent pizzas. The restaurant is a simple, open-air affair, but it runs lengthwise along the beach, so quite a few tables with good views of the sea can be found.

See map p. 161. Tamarindo, on the beach, across from the Hotel Zullymar. ☎ *653-0023. Reservations not necessary. Main courses: $5–$17. MC, V. Open: Daily 11 a.m.–10 p.m.*

Fast Facts: Guanacaste

Ambulance

Call ☎ 128.

ATMs

You'll find ATMs in Liberia, Playa Flamingo, Playa del Coco, and Tamarindo, as well as at the Daniel Oduber Airport in Liberia.

Country Code and City Code

The country code for Costa Rica is **506.** Costa Rica does not use city or area codes. To call from the United States, dial 011-506 plus the seven-digit number. From within Costa Rica, you simply dial the seven-digit number.

Currency Exchange

Most hotels will exchange money for you at decent rates. To get official rates, head to one of the banks in Tamarindo, Flamingo, Playa del Coco, or Liberia.

Fire

Call ☎ 118.

Hospitals

The Liberia Hospital (☎ 666-0011) is the best hospital in the area. A smaller hospital lies in the city of Santa Cruz. Most of the beach towns have some sort of health clinic.

Information

See "Orienting Yourself in Guanacaste," earlier in this chapter.

Internet Access

Internet cafes can be found in all the major beach towns of Guanacaste. Rates run between $1 and $3 per hour.

Pharmacies

Each of the beach towns and destinations has a pharmacy or two. Ask at your hotel for the nearest and best-stocked option.

Police

Call ☎ 911.

Post Office

Small post offices are open in most of the major beach towns. Alternatively, most hotels can mail your letters and postcards for you.

Taxis

Taxis meet all incoming flights at the Daniel Oduber Airport in Liberia, and at the small airstrip in Tamarindo. Though taxi services can be found in all the beach towns, it's almost always better to have your hotel call a cab for you, instead of hoping to find one in the street.

Chapter 14

Exploring Guanacaste

● ●

In This Chapter

▶ Scoping out the many tour and activity options in Guanacaste

▶ Buying something beyond tourist trinkets

▶ Enjoying Guanacaste's nightlife

● ●

*G*uanacaste is vast. Though you may be content to pass your days soaking in the sun and taking the occasional dip in the ocean or pool, you'll have plenty to choose from if you're feeling more active.

Although the tours and adventures listed in this chapter are best done as part of a guided excursion, if you have your own rental car, or you want to hire a taxi or private guide, you can certainly set them up independently.

Seeing Guanacaste by Guided Tour

Nearly all the hotels and resorts in Guanacaste have a tour desk or can help you arrange a variety of popular day tours and activities. Prices range from $35 to $120 per person, depending on the length of the tour and the activity or activities involved.

Be careful before signing up for a trip to a more distant destination. Find out how much time will be spent on travel and how much time will be spent enjoying the attraction and activities. I personally don't recommend the day trips to Arenal volcano or Monteverde, for example, because the trip is three to four hours each way in a bus or minivan. Still, some folks are willing to put up with that much travel time for the chance to visit these very worthwhile places. See Chapters 17 and 18 for more information on Arenal and Monteverde.

Finding out how many other folks will be on the tour with you is also a good idea. If you're going on a rafting trip, or any other tour where the group will be broken down into smaller units, group size is not critical. But on any nature tour, hike, or other guided activity, I recommend ten persons per guide as a maximum, with six or fewer persons per guide as optimal. If you're the last person in line on an overcrowded nature hike, you're unlikely to see the wildlife pointed out to those at the front of the line.

Visits to other lo   es and destinations, as well as rafting trips, are best done on guided   urs. Other activities, including sport fishing and surfing, are best d   on your own.

See the maps   Chapter 13 for help locating the following listings.

The Top A ractions

Rincón   la Vieja National Park

This n   onal park begins on the flanks of the **Rincón de la Vieja volcano** and i   ades the volcano's active crater. Fumaroles, geysers, and hot pools can   be observed here. In addition to hot springs and mud pots, you can   plore waterfalls, a lake, and volcanic craters. The bird-watching is ex   lent, and the views across the pasturelands to the Pacific Ocean are s   ning.

   eral excellent trails run inside the Rincón de la Vieja National Park.   ore-energetic hikers can tackle the 8km (5 miles) up to **the summit** and   xplore the several craters and beautiful lakes up here. On a clear day, you'll be rewarded with a fabulous view of the plains of Guanacaste and the Pacific Ocean below. The easiest hiking is the gentle **Las Pailas loop.** This 3km (1¾-mile) trail is just off the Las Espuelas Park entrance and passes by several bubbling mud pots and steaming fumaroles. This trail crosses a river, so you'll have to either take off your shoes or get them wet. The whole loop takes around two hours.

My favorite hike here is to the **Blue Lake** and **La Cangrejo waterfall.** This 5km (3-mile) trail passes through several different life zones, including dry forest, transitional moist forest, and open savanna. A variety of birds and mammals are commonly sighted. Pack a lunch; at the end of your two-hour hike in, you can picnic at the aptly named Blue Lake, where a 30m (98-ft.) waterfall empties into the small pond with crystal-blue hues that are amazing.

You can visit Rincón de la Vieja National Park as part of a guided tour, or with a four-wheel-drive rental vehicle.

See map p. 159. The Las Espuelas park entrance is 25km (16 miles) northeast of Liberia, down a badly rutted dirt road. To reach the park entrance, drive about 5km (3 miles) north of Liberia and turn right on the dirt road to the park. The turnoff is well marked. In about 12km (7½ miles), you'll pass through the small village of Curubandé. Continue on this road for another 6km (3¾ miles) until you reach the Hacienda Lodge Guachipelin. The lodge is private property, and the owners charge a $2 toll to pass through their gate and continue on to the park. Pay the toll, pass through the lodge's gate, and continue for another 4km (2½ miles) until you reach the park entrance. ☎ *661-8139. Admission: $7. Open: Daily 7 a.m.–3 p.m.*

Rio Corobicí Rafting

This class II river makes for very gentle rafting, although you'll also find a few mild rapids. The *put in,* the spot where the rafting starts, is located just off the Interamerican Highway beside the Restaurant Rincón Corobicí, about 40km (25 miles) south of Liberia. Along the way, you might see many of the area's more exotic animal residents: howler monkeys, iguanas, caimans, coatimundis, otters, toucans, parrots, motmots, trogons, and many other species of birds. Aside from your binoculars and camera, a bathing suit and sunscreen are the only things you'll need.

All the tour agencies and tour desks in the area can book this for you, or you can call **Safaris Corobicí** (☎/fax **669-6191;** www.nicoya.com), and set it up for yourself. These folks offer a variety of options, including separate trips on the Bebedero River. For a much wetter and wilder ride, the folks at **Hacienda Guachipelin** (see later in this chapter) offer white-water inner-tube trips on the narrow Río Negro, near their lodge.

Safaris Corobicí. Main office is on the Interamerican Highway, at kilometer marker 193, 40km (25 miles) south of Liberia, and about 1km (⅔ mile) south of the Restaurant Rincón Corobicí. ☎/fax **669-6191.** www.nicoya.com. *Admission: $37 for a two-hour float; $60 for a half-day trip, including lunch. Open: Daily 8 a.m.–4 p.m.*

Hacienda Guachipelin

This working cattle and horse ranch is located 23km (14 miles) northeast of Liberia on the edge of Rincón de la Vieja National Park.

This is one of the closest lodges to the thermal springs (10km/6¼ miles) and bubbling mud pots (5km/3 miles) of Rincón de la Vieja National Park, and horseback rides are offered to the geothermal areas, as well as to various lakes, the top of a nearby dormant volcano, and some beautiful waterfalls. You can augment your day's adventure by strapping on a climbing harness and sliding over cables back and forth over a deep canyon — it's one of my favorite canopy tours in the country, although they call it a "Canyon Tour."

If you decide to visit this place on your own, be sure to call and make a reservation in advance.

See map p. 159. Hacienda Guachipelin. 23km (14 miles) northeast of Liberia on the edge of Rincón de la Vieja National Park. To reach the lodge, drive about 5km (3 miles) north of Liberia and turn right on the dirt road to Rincón de la Vieja National Park. The turnoff is well marked. In about 12km (7½ miles), you'll pass through the small village of Curubandé. Continue on this road for another 6km (3¾ miles) until you reach the Hacienda Guachipelin. If you're staying at the lodge or doing a tour here, you shouldn't have to pay the $2 toll collected at the lodge gate. ☎ **666-8075.** www.guachipelin.com. *Admission: Tours, $15–$70 per person; Rio Negro Tubing, $45; horseback tours, $20–$30; Canyon Tour, $45; one-day adventure pass, $70. Open: Daily 7:30 a.m.–5 p.m. (for tours).*

Hotel Borinquen Thermal Baths

Another popular day trip from Guanacaste is to visit the mud pots and thermal waters at the Hotel Borinquen. Set at the foot of a deep valley on the flanks of the Rincón de la Vieja volcano, this place has several natural hot-spring pools of differing temperatures, a natural sauna, and an area for full-body mud baths given with hot volcanic mud, recently collected from steaming volcanic mud pots. After a mud bath and some hot soaking, you can lounge by the large free-form swimming pool. Hotel Borinquen is set on the edge of the rain forest beside gentle creeks, with trails to the mud pots and into the forest. Excellent hiking and horseback riding can be found here, and some nice waterfalls are nearby.

See map p. 159. Drive 26km (16 miles) north of Liberia along the Interamerican Highway. Take the turnoff toward Cañas Dulces, and follow the signs. The hotel is approximately 22km (14 miles) from the highway along a rough dirt road. ☎ **253-5080** *for reservations, or 690-1900 at the lodge.* www.borinquenresort.com. *Admission: $25 per person for use of the hot pools, sauna, and mud baths; $70 per person for full-day adventure, including canopy tour, horseback ride, and use of the spa.*

Los Inocentes Lodge Horseback Riding

Set up near the Nicaraguan border and bordering Guanacaste National Park, Los Inocentes Lodge is popular with bird-watchers and naturalists interested in exploring the local dry and transitional forests. Horseback riding through the ranch is the most popular activity here, and they have an excellent stable of well-kept and well-trained horses. You'll get a great view of Orosi volcano from the lodge. Tours here are similar to those at Hacienda Guachipelin, although you won't have the hot springs or canopy tour options. For those not interested in mounting a horse, Los Inocentes also offers guided nature tours in a tractor-pulled wagon, as well as hikes.

See map p. 159. Drive 20km (12 miles) north of Liberia towards La Cruz. Just before entering the town of La Cruz, you'll see a well-marked turnoff on your right. Los Inocentes is 14km (8¾ miles) from this turnoff. ☎ **679-9190.** www.losinocentes lodge.com. *Admission: $72 for a two-hour horseback (or tractor) ride and lunch; $84 for a full-day horseback ride and lunch.*

El Mundo de la Tortuga Sea Turtle Nesting

Giant leatherback sea turtles nest on Playa Grande between late September and late February. The turtles come ashore to lay their eggs only at night. During the nesting season, you'll be inundated with opportunities to sign up for the nightly tours, which usually cost around $35 to $45 per person.

The best tours these days are run through and include a stop at **El Mundo de la Tortuga,** a small turtle museum/exhibit at Playa Grande. At the museum, you can take the half-hour self-guided tour by picking up a cassette player and choosing a tour cassette in English, Spanish, German, or

Italian. Afterward, you can watch television while waiting for your group to head out to the beach. The museum opens each afternoon at 4:30 p.m. and stays open until the turtle tours are done for the night.

Do-it-yourselfers can drive over to Playa Grande and book a tour directly with either **El Mundo de la Tortuga** (☎/fax **653-0471**; $25) or the **National Parks Service** (☎ **653-0470**; $13). The Parks Service operates out of a small shack next to the turtle museum and opens each evening at around 6 p.m. to begin taking reservations. Whomever you decide to go with, try to make a reservation in advance because only a limited number of people are allowed on the beach at one time. Spots fill up fast, and if you don't have a reservation, you may have to wait until really late, or you may not be able to go out onto the beach.

Between July and November, the smaller Olive Ridley sea turtles nest on several other beaches in Guanacaste, including the northern beaches inside Santa Rosa National Park, and the more southern beach of Ostional. When the Olive Ridleys are nesting, tours are available to these beaches as well. The Olive Ridley nestings, or *arribadas,* are unique because they come ashore in massive numbers, even during the daytime. *Note:* No flash photography is allowed because any sort of light can confuse the turtles and prevent them from laying their eggs; guides must use red-tinted flashlights.

Turtle nesting is a natural, unpredictable, and rare event. You may have to wait your turn for hours, hike quite a ways, and even accept the possibility that no nesting mothers will be spotted that evening. Moreover, with the vast development in this area, the number of nesting turtles has dropped and the number of tourists has skyrocketed. Do not expect an intimate experience.

See map p. 159. Located on the main beach access road to Playa Grande 200m (2 blocks) before it hits the ocean; 100m (1 block) before the hotel Las Tortugas. ☎/fax 653-0471. Admission: $25, including turtle tour. Open: 4:30 p.m.–2 a.m. (roughly) during turtle season (late Sept–late Feb).

More Cool Things to See and Do

All the options listed in this section are probably best done on your own, either in a rental car or by taxi. However, most of the hotel tour desks and independent tour operators can book you almost any of the tours or adventures listed here as well.

Visiting some of the lesser-known beaches

Although none of the beaches in Guanacaste ever gets truly crowded, it is still possible and profoundly rewarding to find your own patch of sand on one of the more isolated or less developed beaches in this area, such as one of the following:

✔ At the northern end of the province, the Papagayo Peninsula has a number of very remote and undeveloped beaches to choose from. **Playa Nacascolo,** which sits within the property of the Four Seasons Resort, is one of the top beaches in this area. All beaches in Costa Rica are public property and open to anyone, and the Four Seasons provides parking and access for people visiting Playa Nacascolo.

✔ Farther south, **Playa Panamá** is a long and lovely beach with just one or two simple restaurants and a couple of hotels.

✔ You'll find a real treasure trove of remote beaches around the Playa Flamingo and Playa Conchal area. From these popular spots, several largely unexplored beaches lie in either direction, including **Playa La Penca, Playa Prieta, Playa Pan de Azúcar, Playa Real,** and a few that are, for all intents and purposes, unnamed.

✔ Although Tamarindo is easily the most developed and crowded beach in the area, just to the north of it, **Playa Grande** is seldom crowded, and to the south, beaches like **Playa Avellanas, Playa Negra,** and **Playa Junquillal** are known to only a few cognoscenti.

✔ If you head to Playa Avellanas, be sure to have a drink or lunch at **Lola's on the Beach** (☎ **658-8097**) and check out the restaurant's namesake 700-pound pig. Despite being immense, Lola will actually wade out into the surf at times.

If you're feeling really adventurous, rent an ATV. These rugged and easy-to-drive vehicles are available to rent at all the major beach destinations and cost $65 to $100 for the day.

Going under: Scuba diving

Some of Costa Rica's best diving can be had around the offshore islands and underwater rock formations of Guanacaste. Most hotel and tour desks can arrange a dive trip for you. Many also offer certification courses or shorter resort courses, the latter of which will get you some basic instruction and a controlled dive in the shortest amount of time.

A two-tank dive should run between $65 and $125 per person, depending primarily on the distance traveled to the dive sites.

An interesting stop on your way to Liberia

If you're driving to or from Guanacaste, be sure to take a brief break to check out the **Catholic Church** in Cañas. Well-known painter, installation artist, and local prodigal son Otto Apuy has designed and directed the envelopment of the entire church in colorful mosaic. The work uses whole and broken tiles in glossy, vibrant colors to depict both religious and abstract themes. The church is located in the center of town, just a few blocks off the Interamerican Highway.

If you don't set up your dive trip through your hotel, several very reputable dive operations are in the area. The best of these are

- **Diving Safaris de Costa Rica** (☎ 877-853-0538 in the United States, or 672-0012; www.costaricadiving.net), in Playa Hermosa. These folks have a large shop and offer a wide range of trips to numerous dive spots. They also offer night dives, multiday packages, certification classes, and Nitrox dives, done with specialized oxygen-enriched tanks.

- **Resort Divers** (☎ 672-0106; www.resortdivers-cr.com) has set up shop at several of the hotels in this area.

- **Rich Coast Diving** (☎ 800-434-8464 in the United States and Canada, or 670-0176 in Costa Rica; www.richcoastdiving.com) is an excellent operator based in Playa del Coco.

Hoisting sail

The winds off Costa Rica's Pacific coast are somewhat fickle and can often be slight to nonexistent. However, from December through March, they can be quite strong, with impressive gusts. Still, plenty of sailing options abound if you want to head to sea here.

A host of different boats take out day charters ranging from a few hours to a full day. Many include some food and drinks, as well as a break or two for some swimming or snorkeling. Some will take you to a deserted beach, and others let you throw a line overboard for fishing.

Rates run around $40 to $60 per person for a few hours or a sunset cruise, $65 to $120 per person for longer outings.

If your hotel can't line up a sail for you, here are a few good boats to check out:

- *Blue Dolphin* (☎ 653-0867; www.sailbluedolphin.com), a 12m (40-ft.) catamaran based out of Tamarindo

- *Cool Runnings* (☎ 672-0103; www.sailcoolrunnings.com), a 13.8m (46-ft.) trimaran anchored off Playa Hermosa

- *Samonique III* (☎ 388-7870; www.costarica-sailing.com), a 15.6m (52-ft.) ketch sailing out of Tamarindo

- *Shannon* (☎ 654-5201; www.flamingobeachcr.com), a 15.6m (52-ft.) cutter working out of Playa Flamingo

Hanging ten: Surfing and surf lessons

The Guanacaste coast is home to some of Costa Rica's best and most consistent surf breaks. Whether you're already a pro or you're looking to get your feet wet, you'll find beaches and breaks that are just right for you.

✔ Tamarindo is by far the best place for those looking to learn how to surf. There are several good surf schools in town, as well as a variety of surf shops where you can rent a board. Check out **Tamarindo Surf School** (☎ 653-0923; www.tamarindosurfschool.com); **Witch's Rock Surf Camp** (☎ 653-1262; www.witchsrocksurf camp.com); or **Chicasurf** (☎ 827-7884), a surf school for women.

✔ Experienced surfers will probably want to rent a car and head to the less crowded beaches south of Tamarindo, including **Playa Avellanas** and **Playa Negra,** or just north of Tamarindo to **Playa Grande.**

✔ Another option is to take a boat trip to the isolated point breaks of **Witch's Rock** and **Ollie's Point,** which are deep inside the remote Santa Rosa National Park. **Diving Safaris de Costa Rica** (☎ 672-0012) and **Aqua Sport** (☎ 672-0050) offer trips for up to six surfers for around $250, including lunch, leaving from Playa Hermosa.

Landing a big one

The waters off Guanacaste's coast are teaming with fish and world-class sport-fishing opportunities. Anglers can land marlin and sailfish, as well as tuna, dorado, roosterfish, and more.

A half-day of fishing, with boat, captain, food, and tackle, should cost between $200 and $600 for two to four passengers; a full day should run between $500 and $1,600. The wide range in prices reflects a wide range in the size of the boats, equipment, and distance traveled.

Although fishing is good all year, the peak season for billfish is between mid-April and August.

A host of boats and captains dot the Guanacaste coast. The Flamingo Marina, the area's largest marina, is currently closed, but, at press time, was due to open soon. Another marina will be built in the coming years on the Papagayo Peninsula. Some of the better operators include

✔ **Agua Rica Yacht Charters** (☎ 877-589-0539 in the United States and Canada, or 670-0473 in Costa Rica; www.aguaricacharters.com) in Playa del Coco

✔ **Capullo Sportfishing** (☎ 653-0048; www.capullo.com) in Tamarindo

✔ **Oso Viejo** (☎ 654-5201; www.flamingobeachcr.com) in Playa Flamingo

✔ **Warren Sellers Sportfishing** (☎ 877-776-7834 in the United States and Canada, or 653-0186 in Costa Rica; www.wssportfishing.com) in Tamarindo

Teeing off: Golf in Guanacaste

Golf is just beginning to take off in Costa Rica, but you'll find three of the country's best courses in Guanacaste.

The **Paradisus Playa Conchal** (☎ 888-336-3542 in the United States, or 654-4123 in Costa Rica; www.solmelia.com) is home to an excellent golf course featuring a few wonderful views of the ocean. This Robert Trent Jones–designed resort course is currently still open to the walk-in public, but as the all-inclusive resort itself gets more popular, it may restrict public access.

Currently, it costs $140 in greens fees for as many rounds as you can squeeze into one day, including a cart. If you tee off after 1 p.m., it's just $90.

South of Tamarindo, **Hacienda Pinilla** (☎ 680-7000; www.hacienda pinilla.com) is a beautiful 18-hole links-style course. The course is currently accepting golfers staying at hotels around the area, with advance reservations. Greens fees run around $150 for 18 holes, including a cart.

Finally, the most impressive course in the country is the new Arnold Palmer–designed course at the **Four Seasons Resort** (☎ 800-819-5053 or 212-688-2440 in the United States, or 696-0098 in Costa Rica; www.fourseasons.com/costarica). This stunning and challenging course features ocean views from 15 of its 18 holes. However, the course is only open to hotel guests.

Canopy tours

If you want to try one of the zip-line canopy tours, your best bet in this area is the **Canyon Tour** operation at **Hacienda Guachipelin** (☎ 666-8075; www.guachipelin.com). This tour has a little bit of everything, with treetop platforms, as well as cables crisscrossing a deep mountain canyon, some suspended bridges, a couple of pendulum swings, and two rappels.

However, if you don't want to head that far afield, there are several other options spread around Guanacaste:

- ✔ **Congo Trail Canopy Tour** (☎ 666-4422) is located near Playa del Coco and Playa Hermosa, and has 11 platforms connected by a series of cables.

- ✔ **Tamarindo Long Lines Canopy Tour** (☎ 653-0597) has just four cables connecting seven platforms. However, one of the cables is one of the longest in the country, at 500m (1,600 ft).

- ✔ **Witch's Rock Canopy Tour** (☎ 666-7546) is located just before the Allegro Papagayo Resort (Chapter 13). The two-and-a-half-hour tour covers 3km (1¾ miles) of cables and suspended bridges touching down on 24 platforms.

Horseback riding

If you don't want to take one of the full-day tours to one of the remote lodges listed in the "The Top Attractions" section earlier in this chapter, you can still ride a horse for an hour or more at most beach destinations in Guanacaste. Rates run from $10 to $20 per hour.

Be careful, many of the folks offering horseback riding, especially those plying the beaches themselves, are using poorly trained and poorly kept animals. Be sure you feel comfortable with the condition and training of your mount.

If your hotel tour desk can't arrange this for you, the following companies are all reputable, with good horses:

- ✔ **Casagua Horses** (☎ 653-8041)
- ✔ **Brasilito Excursions** (☎ 654-4237)
- ✔ **Flamingo Equestrian Center** (☎ 654-4089)

Shopping for Local Treasures

Simply put, the shopping scene in Guanacaste is disappointing. Mostly, you'll find hotel gift shops and simple souvenir stands. A couple of large souvenir shops, catering to large-scale tourist traffic, pop up along the highway between the Guanacaste beaches. The best of these is **Kaltak Arts and Craft Market** (☎ 667-0696), located on the main road between Liberia and the beach towns 19km (11.8 miles) from Liberia, 5km (3 miles) from the airport.

The ceramic wares produced in the small village of **Guaitil** are a notable exception to Guanacaste's standard trinkets. These low-fired works feature locally produced dyes and traditional indigenous design motifs. You'll find plates and bowls and a variety of functional pieces here.

Guaitil is located 12km (7½ miles) inland from the city of Santa Cruz. The road is paved the entire way. Many of the hotels and tour desks around Guanacaste offer tours to Guaitil.

However, if you don't take the trip out to the village itself, be sure to stop at one or more of the many roadside stands selling Guaitil pottery all along the road between Liberia and the Guanacaste beaches.

Living It Up After Dark

All the various beach towns and large resorts have their own bar and disco scenes throughout most of the high season. If you want to venture away from your hotel or resort, Tamarindo is by far the most raucous town on this coast.

Popular spots include **La Bodega** (☎ 653-0742), located on the little traffic circle; the **Monkey Bar** (☎ 653-0114), at the Best Western Vista Villas; and the bar at the **Hotel Pasatiempo** (Chapter 13), which has a giant television for sporting events and sometimes features live music.

Popular with Ticos, Playa del Coco is another of Costa Rica's livelier beach towns after dark. On the road into town, you'll find **Banana Surf Bar** (☎ 670-0708), a comfortable second-floor affair with good *bocas*) and some outdoor tables on the veranda overlooking Coco's main street. Lately they've been getting folks dancing to a modern mix of hip-hop, trance, and other dance rhythms. Closer to the beach is the **Lizard Lounge** (☎ 370-2186), which has a popular pool table and a laid-back tropical vibe. **Cocomar** (☎ 670-0167) is the main disco and dance hall in town. It's located just off the little park right on the beach. (If these directions don't get you there, just follow the loud music.)

If you're into gaming, there are several casinos around Guanacaste. In Playa del Coco, you can head to the small casinos at either the **Coco Verde Resort** (☎ 670-0494) or the **Hotel La Flor de Itabo** (☎ 670-0292). In Playa Flamingo, **Amberes** (☎ 654-4001) has a small casino as well.

The best casinos in the area are in Tamarindo, where you'll find the popular **Jazz Casino** (☎ 653-0406) in downtown Tamarindo and another out in Playa Langosta at the **Barceló Playa Langosta** resort (☎ 653-0363).

Part V
Manuel Antonio and Environs

The 5th Wave
By Rich Tennant

In this part . . .

In addition to being home to Costa Rica's most popular national park, Manuel Antonio National Park, Manuel Antonio is the heart of Costa Rica's central Pacific coast. This part gives you the lowdown on the highlights to be found in the Manuel Antonio area. Then it tells you about other interesting options to be found up and down this coast, from the breathtaking luxury of the hillside villas at Villa Caletas, to the remote beaches and small resorts south of Dominical.

Chapter 15

Enjoying Magnificent Manuel Antonio

Manuel Antonio is Costa Rica's single most popular destination. It's a virtual one-stop shop of the best that Costa Rica has to offer: beautiful beaches, lush rain forests, abundant wildlife, oodles of adventure opportunities, excellent restaurants, and romantic boutique hotels.

The relatively compact Manuel Antonio National Park is the crowning jewel of this area. Its several nearly perfect small beaches are connected by gentle trails that meander through a rain forest that is home to endangered squirrel monkeys, three-toed sloths, purple-and-orange crabs, and hundreds of other species of birds, mammals, and plants.

However, Manuel Antonio's popularity means it tends to be more crowded than most of Costa Rica's other beach destinations. Development here is leaving a noticeable footprint. What was once a smattering of small hotels tucked into the forested hillside has become a seemingly unbroken string of lodgings, souvenir shops, restaurants, bars, and adventure outfitters lining the winding road between Quepos and the national-park entrance.

Still, this remains one of the most beautiful locations in the entire country. Gazing down on the blue Pacific from high on the hillsides of Manuel Antonio, it's almost impossible not to appreciate the surrounding beauty — from the offshore, rocky islands dotting the vast expanse of blue ocean to the rich, deep green of the rain forest sweeping down to the water.

Getting There

You can fly, drive, or be driven to Manuel Antonio. The small airstrip in Quepos is served by a host of daily commuter flights from San José, and this is by far the easiest means of getting there. If you want the independence of your own car, you can drive to Quepos and Manuel Antonio in about four hours along paved roads. Finally, you can take a bus or private minivan service. I list more details about all these options in the following sections.

By air

Nature Air (☎ **800-235-9272** in the United States and Canada, ☎ **299-6000** in Costa Rica; www.natureair.com) and **Sansa** (☎ **221-9414**; www.flysansa.com) both have several daily flights from San José to the small Quepos airport. The flight takes just 30 minutes and costs between $45 and $50 each way.

Nature Air flies from the Tobías Bolaños International Airport in Pavas, while Sansa leaves from San José's Juan Santamaría International Airport. The flight's duration is 30 minutes; the fare is $44 each way.

Both Sansa and Nature Air provide airport-transfer service coordinated with their arriving flights. The service costs around $4 per person each way, depending on exactly where your hotel is located. Speak to your airline's agent when you arrive to confirm your return flight and to coordinate a pickup at your hotel for that day, if necessary.

Private cars and official taxis, which are painted red, will also be waiting outside the airport to be hailed. Expect to be charged between $8 and $12 per car for up to four people, depending on the distance to your hotel and your bargaining abilities.

By car

Several routes can take you to Manuel Antonio from San José.

The most popular route is a narrow and winding two-lane road, the "old highway," over and through mountains. This road is equal parts scenic and harrowing — it's not uncommon to encounter buses and trucks passing on blind curves, or to find yourself at the back of a long line of cars stuck behind a slow-moving truck, crawling up one of the steep hills.

Begin this route by taking the Interamerican Highway west out of San José and exiting just west of Alajuela near the town of Atenas. Follow any of the numerous signs to any hotel in Jacó or Manuel Antonio. The old highway meets the Costanera (Coastal) highway a few kilometers west of Orotina. From here it's a straight and flat shot down the coast. You'll hit Playa Herradura first, and then Jacó, before getting to Manuel Antonio.

If you're coming from anywhere in northern Costa Rica, your best option is to take the Interamerican Highway, get off at the Puntarenas exit, and follow signs to Caldera. From there, head south on the Costanera Highway. The section between Puntarenas and the exit for Orotina has been in terrible shape in recent years and is pocked with nearly constant, and often very deep, potholes.

However, the option of continuing on the Interamerican Highway until the exit near Atenas is much too long to make it a worthwhile alternative.

One last driving option is the route beginning in Ciudad Colón, a western suburb of San José. From here, you can head out to Puriscal and join the Costanera Highway either near Parrita or Orotina. This route is really only an option if you're departing from or returning to Escazu and Santa Ana, and it takes about 15 to 30 minutes longer than the more popular route mentioned earlier.

The route that heads to Parrita is the shortest, but some sections here are not paved and others are in rough shape. Nevertheless, locals often use it, especially during the dry season. Four-wheel-drive vehicles are recommended, but normal two-wheel-drive sedans can usually make it.

The route to Orotina is paved the entire way. But it is slightly longer than the Parrita route, and not as well marked. I like this route because it often has far less traffic, and virtually no truck traffic, as there is a narrow suspension bridge near Orotina that cannot support large trucks or buses.

Whether you decide to take the Parrita or the Orotina route, you'll hit the small port city of **Quepos** when you finally get close to Manuel Antonio. To continue on to Manuel Antonio, cross the bridge into town and take the lower road (to the left of the high road). In 4 blocks, turn left; you'll be on the road to Manuel Antonio. This road winds through Quepos a bit for about 10 to 15 minutes before starting over the hill to all the hotels and the national park.

See Chapter 16 for advice on a good crocodile-sightseeing stop during your drive.

By bus

Express and **local buses** (☎ **223-5567** in San José, **777-0101** in Quepos) to Manuel Antonio leave San José throughout the day from the Coca-Cola bus terminal at Calle 16 between avenidas 1 and 3.

The ride takes around three and a half hours and costs $4.50 on the express bus. The local buses cost a little less but take a bit longer. They're also usually older buses and much less comfortable. I highly recommend taking an express bus.

The express buses go all the way to the national-park entrance and will drop you off at any of the hotels along the way. The local buses will drop you off at the main bus terminal in Quepos.

Grayline (☎ 220-2126; www.graylinecostarica.com) and **Interbus** (☎ 283-5573; www.costaricapass.com) both have regular service to Quepos and Manuel Antonio. The fare with either of these operators is $25.

In the busy winter months, tickets sell out well in advance, especially on weekends. If you can, purchase your ticket several days in advance. However, you must buy your Quepos-bound tickets in San José and your San José return tickets in Quepos.

If you're staying in Manuel Antonio, you can buy your return ticket for a direct bus in advance in Quepos. The main bus station is in downtown Quepos, next to the main market. If you've bought your ticket in advance, you can wait along the road to be picked up. No particular bus stop exists; just make sure you're out to flag down the bus and give it time to stop — you don't want to be standing in a blind spot when the bus comes flying around some tight corner.

Orienting Yourself in Manuel Antonio

Manuel Antonio is a general term that often refers to one or more of the following: the small city of Quepos, Manuel Antonio National Park, and the winding road that connects these two.

Quepos is a small port city at the mouth of the Boca Vieja Estuary. A 7km (4⅓-mile) road connects Quepos to Manuel Antonio National Park. All along the road, you'll find the many hotels, restaurants, and shops that are considered part of Manuel Antonio — as opposed to Quepos. For all intents and purposes, the road ends at the national-park entrance, although a small side street branches off it here, where you'll find some more hotels and restaurants.

The Costanera Highway South that connects Jacó to Quepos passes through the town and continues on toward Dominical. Just outside the city center, you'll find the small Quepos airstrip, as well as the local hospital.

Manuel Antonio and Quepos don't have official tourist information offices, but a few tour-booking agencies masquerade as such. Most hotels have a knowledgeable front-desk staff, concierge, or in-house tour desk that can answer any questions. Also, keep an eye out for *Quepolandia,* a free, bi-monthly local tourist magazine that is loaded with information, articles, and advertisements; it's available at a host of local souvenir shops, restaurants, and hotel lobbies.

Getting Around

Getting around and between Quepos and Manuel Antonio is easy. Taxis are plentiful, and regular local bus service runs throughout the day.

The bus between Quepos and Manuel Antonio takes 15 minutes each way and runs roughly every half-hour from 6 a.m. to 7 p.m. daily, with one late bus leaving Quepos at 10 p.m. and returning from Manuel Antonio at 10:25 p.m.

The buses, which leave from the main bus terminal in Quepos, near the market, go all the way to the national-park entrance before turning around and returning. You can flag down these buses from any point on the side of the road. The fare is 35¢.

A taxi from Quepos to Manuel Antonio (or any hotel along the road toward the park) costs between $2 and $4. The return trip from the park to your hotel should cost only 75¢ per person. I know that this system doesn't make much sense, but this is a fixed price, so watch out for drivers who try to charge more. At night, or if the taxi must leave the main road (for hotels such as La Mariposa and Makanda-by-the-Sea), the charge is a little higher. If you need to call a taxi, dial ☎ **777-1695** or 777-0425.

You can also rent a car from **Adobe** (☎ **777-4242**), **Alamo** (☎ **777-3344**), **Economy** (☎ **777-5353**), or **Payless Rent-a-Car** (☎ **777-0115**) for around $50 a day. All have offices in downtown Quepos, but with advance notice, they'll have someone meet you at the airport with your car for no extra charge.

There's little reason to rent a car in Quepos and Manuel Antonio because taxis are cheap and plentiful. Moreover, most tours and many attractions include transportation in their outings and admissions. The only good reason to rent a car in town is if you want to explore the coastline north and south of Quepos. In that case, a rental car is your best option.

Car break-ins are common here. If you rent a car, never leave anything of value in it unless you intend to stay within sight of the car at all times. Instead, park in one of the parking lots just outside the park entrance that cost around $3 for the whole day. And although these lots are your safest bet, you still shouldn't leave anything of value exposed in the car's interior. Instead, use the trunk, or bring your valuables with you.

Spending the Night

Manuel Antonio's growing popularity has brought increased development and ever-expanding crowds of beachgoers. This means that you'll find scores of hotels, in all sizes and price ranges. The best (and most expensive hotels) usually boast rooms with private balconies, featuring the classic Manuel Antonio forest-to-ocean views.

Getting a bewitching view of the Manuel Antonio forest has its own set of drawbacks. If you want this great view, you probably can't stay on the beach — in fact, you probably won't be able to walk to the beach. This means that you'll be driving back and forth, taking taxis, or riding the public bus a lot.

Also keep in mind that it's hot and humid here, and it rains a lot. Of course, the rain is what keeps Manuel Antonio lush and green, and this wouldn't be the tropics if things were otherwise.

If you're traveling on a rock-bottom budget or you're mainly interested in sportfishing, you should stay in Quepos instead of Manuel Antonio.

Hotel Costa Verde
$$–$$$ Manuel Antonio

This longstanding and constantly evolving hotel offers good values, ocean views, and a relatively close proximity to the area's beaches and national park. Rooms come in a wide range of sizes and prices. Some of the buildings are located quite a hike from the hotel's reception and restaurants, so be sure you ask exactly what type of room you'll be staying in and where it's located. The best rooms here have ocean views, kitchenettes, private balconies, and loads of space. Though some of these don't have air-conditioning, that's no problem because they feature huge screened walls to encourage cross-ventilation. If you want to splurge, try the enormous penthouse suite with a commanding view of the spectacular surroundings.

Three small pools are set into the hillside, with views out to the ocean, and the hotel has a couple of miles of private trails through the rain forest. Costa Verde is located more than halfway down the hill to Manuel Antonio, about a ten-minute walk from the beach.

See map p. 191. Manuel Antonio. ☎ *866-854-7958 in the United States and Canada, or 777-0584 in Costa Rica. Fax: 777-0560.* www.costaverde.com. *Rack rates: $89–$165 double. Rates lower in the off season, higher during peak weeks. AE, MC, V.*

Hotel Malinche
$ Quepos

This downtown Quepos hotel is the best budget option in town. Look for the Hotel Malinche's arched brick entrance on the first street to your left as you come into Quepos. Inside, you'll find bright rooms with louvered windows. The rooms are small but have hardwood or tile floors and clean bathrooms. Although it's almost always very warm, if not downright hot in Quepos, be forewarned that most of the rooms have cold-water showers. The more expensive rooms are newer and larger, and have air-conditioning, TVs, and on-demand heated showerheads.

Quepos. ☎ *777-0093. Fax: 777-1833. Rack rates: $25–$50 double. V.*

Hotel Plinio
$ Manuel Antonio

This hotel is built into a steep hillside, so it's a bit of a climb from the parking lot up to the guest rooms and restaurant. When you're up top, though, you'll think you're in a treehouse. The spacious rooms feature floors and walls of polished hardwood, and you'll even find rooms with tree-trunk

Manuel Antonio

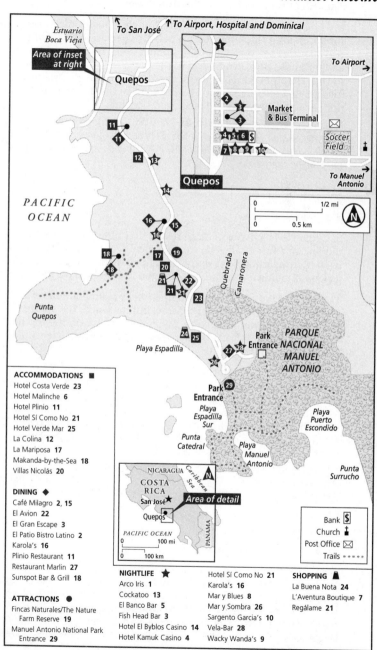

ACCOMMODATIONS ■
Hotel Costa Verde **23**
Hotel Malinche **6**
Hotel Plinio **11**
Hotel Sí Como No **21**
Hotel Verde Mar **25**
La Colina **12**
La Mariposa **17**
Makanda-by-the-Sea **18**
Villas Nicolás **20**

DINING ◆
Café Milagro **2, 15**
El Avion **22**
El Gran Escape **3**
El Patio Bistro Latino **2**
Karola's **16**
Plinio Restaurant **11**
Restaurant Marlin **27**
Sunspot Bar & Grill **18**

ATTRACTIONS ●
Fincas Naturales/The Nature
    Farm Reserve **19**
Manuel Antonio National Park
    Entrance **29**

NIGHTLIFE ★
Arco Iris **1**
Cockatoo **13**
El Banco Bar **5**
Fish Head Bar **3**
Hotel El Byblos Casino **14**
Hotel Kamuk Casino **4**

Hotel Sí Como No **21**
Karola's **16**
Mar y Blues **8**
Mar y Sombra **26**
Sargento Garcia's **10**
Vela-Bar **28**
Wacky Wanda's **9**

SHOPPING ▲
La Buena Nota **24**
L'Aventura Boutique **7**
Regálame **21**

pillars. The suites, built on either two or three levels, are the best value. The three-story suites have rooftop decks.

My favorite room is known as the "jungle house" and is set back in the forest. Behind the hotel rests a private reserve with 15km (9⅓ miles) of trails and, at the top of the hill, a 15m (49-ft.) tall observation tower with an incredible view. In addition to the popular **Plinio Restaurant** (see later in this chapter), lunches are served at the poolside grill. *Note:* Plinio is located just outside Quepos on the road to the national park, so it's a fair distance from the park entrance and beaches.

See map p. 191. Manuel Antonio. ☎ *777-0055. Fax: 777-0558.* www.hotelplinio.com. *Rack rates: $60–$70 double; $85–$110 suite or house. Rates include breakfast buffet in high season. Rates lower May–Nov but do not come with breakfast. V (7 percent surcharge).*

Hotel Sí Como No
$$$–$$$$ Quepos

Sí Como No is a lively midsize resort that offers an array of facilities and modern amenities, all with an ecologically conscious attitude. The wood used here is farm-grown, and although all the rooms have energy-efficient air-conditioning units, guests are urged to use them only when necessary.

The standard rooms (housed in the hotel's main building or in the ground floor of a villa) are quite acceptable, but it's worth the splurge for a superior or deluxe room or a suite. Most of these are on the top floors of the two- to three-story villas, with spectacular treetop views out over the forest and onto the Pacific.

This place is unique in that it is equally suited to families traveling with children and to couples looking for a romantic getaway. Two pools, including one with a long and winding waterslide for kids and another reserved for adults, rest outside. If they tire of swimming, kids will enjoy the wonderful little butterfly garden and frog farm just across the street. The hotel also has a full-service spa, a large modern theater featuring movies each night and several dining options.

See map p. 191. Manuel Antonio. ☎ *777-0777. Fax: 777-1093.* www.sicomono.com. *Rack rates: $170–$270 double. Rates include breakfast. Rates lower in the off season. Extra person $30. Children under 6 stay free in parent's room. AE, MC, V.*

Hotel Verde Mar
$–$$ Manuel Antonio

This hotel is a great choice for close proximity to the national park and the beach. From your room, it's just a short walk to Playa Espadilla via a raised wooden walkway. All the rooms here have plenty of space, nice wrought-iron queen-size beds, tile floors, a desk and chair, and a small porch. All but two of the rooms come with a basic kitchenette. Some of the larger rooms even have two queen-size beds. The hotel has no restaurant, but plenty are within walking distance. You'll even find a small pool here, for when the surf is too rough.

See map p. 191. Manuel Antonio. ☎ *777-1805. Fax: 777-1311.* www.verdemar.com. *Rack rates: $70–$90 double; $110 suite. Rates lower in the off season. AE, MC, V.*

La Colina
$–$$ Manuel Antonio

This casual little place started out as a quaint little B&B offering just four simple budget rooms. The hotel has grown considerably and now offers a variety of rooms in a variety of price ranges. Although the original rooms here are fairly small, each is decorated with style. They have cool tile floors, louvered French doors, and a good writing desk. Outside each room rests a small patio area with a few chairs. The newer suites are built on the highest spot on this property and have front and back balconies with views of both the ocean and the mountains, in addition to more space and natural light. All rooms are nonsmoking.

The hotel boasts a two-tiered swimming pool with a swim-up bar, and the restaurant here is pretty good. The hotel is on your right as you head out of Quepos toward Manuel Antonio, right at a sharp switchback on a steep hill (hence the name, which means "The Hill").

See map p. 191. Manuel Antonio. ☎ *777-0231. Fax: 777-1553.* www.lacolina.com. *Rack rates: $55–$120 double. Rates include full breakfast. Rates lower in the off season. AE, MC, V.*

La Mariposa
$$$$ Manuel Antonio

Perched on a ridge at the top of the hill between Quepos and Manuel Antonio, La Mariposa (The Butterfly) commands a mountains-to-the-sea vista of more than 270 degrees. This place has arguably the best view in town. However, La Mariposa has been transformed from an intimate and elegant boutique hotel, with just ten large, independent villas, into a hodgepodge of rooms, suites, and villas crowned by an awkward behemoth of a building towering over everything in sight. Although this is still one of Manuel Antonio's premier accommodations, I think the expansion and growth have cost this place some of its charm.

The best accommodations here are the premier suites, housed in two three-story buildings constructed over the foundation of a couple of the original villas. These rooms are large, well equipped, and tastefully decorated, with excellent views. Most of the surviving older villas have been split into separate junior suites and deluxe rooms, and they have received some long-overdue updating in recent years. I'd avoid the rooms in the four-story addition to the hotel's main building. Although these rooms are quite spacious and have great views, they don't have much charm or personality. One of the newest developments here is that televisions and high-speed Internet access have been added to some of the rooms, with more to follow.

See map p. 191. Manuel Antonio. ☎ *800-416-2747* in the United States, or 777-0355 in Costa Rica. Fax: 777-0050. www.lamariposa.com. Rack rates: $195 double; $215–$360 suite or villa; $430 penthouse suite. Rates lower in the off season. Extra person $20; children under 12 stay free. AE, MC, V.

Makanda-by-the-Sea
$$$$ Manuel Antonio

Makanda-by-the-Sea is a wonderfully luxurious collection of studio apartments and private villas. The villas are spread out over several thickly forested hillsides. Each is individually decorated with flair and a sense of style. If you combine villa number one with the three studios, you get one very large four-bedroom villa, great for a family or a small group — although children under 16 are not allowed, unless you rent out the whole hotel.

Every studio and villa comes with a full kitchenette, cable television, CD player, and either a terrace or a balcony. The grounds are well tended, intermixed with tropical flowers and Japanese gardens. A full breakfast is delivered to your room each morning. The hotel's pool and Jacuzzi combine intricate and colorful tile work with a view of the jungle-covered hillsides and the Pacific Ocean.

See map p. 191. Manuel Antonio. ☎ *888-625-2632* in the United States, or 777-0442 in Costa Rica. Fax: 777-1032. www.makanda.com. Rack rates: $230 studio; $300–$350 villa. Rates include full breakfast. Rates lower in the off season; higher during peak periods. V.

Villas Nicolás
$$–$$$ Manuel Antonio

These large villas offer plenty of bang for your buck. Built as terraced units up a steep hill in deep forest, they really give you the feeling that you're in the jungle. Most are quite spacious and well appointed, with wood or terracotta tile floors, throw rugs, and large bathrooms. Some units have separate living rooms and full kitchenettes, which make longer stays comfortable. Still, my favorite feature here is the balconies, which come with sitting chairs and a hammock. Some of these balconies are massive and have incredible views. In fact, the rooms highest up the hill have views that are worth even more money. Only some of the units have air-conditioning, but those without air-conditioning do come with fans. During the high season, the hotel opens an informal restaurant/bar near the pool that serves breakfast and sometimes lunch and dinner, depending on demand.

See map p. 191. Manuel Antonio. ☎ *777-0481*. Fax: 777-0451. www.villasnicolas. com. Rack rates: $85–$140 double. Weekly, monthly, and off-season (May–Nov) rates available. AE, MC, V.

Dining Locally

Manuel Antonio has the best restaurant scene outside of San José. Many of the hotel restaurants are quite good, with excellent views. Several restaurants stand out, and you'll find them listed in this section.

 I've got two words for you: "Eat fish." Quepos is a port town with a local fishing fleet, as well as numerous sportfishing boats. The local restaurants are awash in fresh-caught tuna, dorado, and snapper.

El Avion
$$ Manuel Antonio   SEAFOOD/INTERNATIONAL

Set on the edge of Manuel Antonio's hillside, with a great view of the ocean and surrounding forests, this restaurant is actually housed under some permanent tents and the right wing of a retired army transport plane, hence the name El Avion, which means "The Plane." This plane was actually shot down by the Sandinistas during the Contra War in neighboring Nicaragua. Today you can enjoy well-prepared seafood and steaks as you take in the unique surroundings and glow of history. Fresh tuna steaks are flash grilled and served with a teriyaki or fresh fruit sauce. Inside the fuselage, or the old body of the plane, you'll find a small bar.

See map p. 191. Manuel Antonio. ☎ *777-3378. Reservations recommended. Main courses: $8–$21. MC, V. Open: Daily 3–10 p.m.*

El Gran Escape
$$ Quepos   SEAFOOD

The fish here is fresh and expertly prepared, and the prices are reasonable. If that's not enough of a recommendation, the atmosphere is lively, the locals seem to keep coming back, and the service is darn good for a beach town in Costa Rica. Sturdy wooden tables and chairs fill up the large indoor dining room, and sportfishing photos and an exotic collection of masks fill up the walls. If you venture away from the fish, you can sample hearty steaks, giant burgers, and a wide assortment of delicious appetizers, including fresh tuna sashimi. El Gran Escape's Fish Head Bar is usually crowded and spirited, and if there's a game going on, it will be on the television here.

See map p. 191. On the main road into Quepos, on your left just after the bridge. ☎ *777-0395. Reservations recommended in the high season. Main courses: $5–$20. V. Open: Daily 6 a.m.–11 p.m.*

El Patio Bistro Latino
$$$ Quepos   NUEVO LATINO/FUSION

This little restaurant is an outgrowth of the popular coffeehouse and roasting company Café Milagro. By day you can get a wide range of coffee drinks and specialties, as well as simple breakfasts, fresh baked sweets, and a variety of salads, sandwiches, and light lunch dishes. By night, you'll find a small and regularly changing menu of inventive main dishes that take advantage of local ingredients and culinary traditions. So your fresh mahimahi may come steamed in a banana leaf with a spicy *mojo* (parsley and onion garnish), and your tenderloin could feature a tamarind glaze and be served over some roasted local sweet potatoes, called *camote*.

See map p. 191. Quepos. ☎ 777-4982. Reservations recommended. Main courses:$8–$18. V. Open: Daily 6 a.m.–10 p.m.

Karola's
$$–$$$ Manuel Antonio   SEAFOOD/INTERNATIONAL

The open-air dining room of this popular place is set in the crook of a jungle-covered hillside. The restaurant is located down a steep driveway and across a footbridge. Far below, you can see the ocean if you're here during the day. Grilled seafood is the specialty, but a wide range of international treats is also available, from sashimi, to fish burritos, to Caribbean chicken. I recommend starting things off with the Honduran tuna ceviche. Desserts are decadent, and you can order a variety of margaritas by the pitcher.

See map p. 191. Manuel Antonio. ☎ 777-1557. Reservations recommended. Main courses: $10–$22. V. Open: Daily 11 a.m.–10 p.m.

Plinio Restaurant
$$ Manuel Antonio   INTERNATIONAL

This open-air restaurant is about three stories up from its parking lot, so be prepared to climb some steps. It's worth it, though. The broad menu features an enticing mix of international dishes, with an emphasis on Asian fare. The chef uses locally and organically grown herbs and veggies. Thai, Indian, and Indonesian dishes are all excellently prepared, and vegetarian options are also offered, as well as nightly specials.

See map p. 191. In the Hotel Plinio, 1km (½ mile) out of Quepos toward Manuel Antonio. ☎ 777-0055. Reservations recommended in the high season. Main courses $5–$18. V (7 percent surcharge). Open: Daily 5–10 p.m.

Restaurant Marlin
$–$$ Manuel Antonio   SEAFOOD/COSTA RICAN

This is the best local restaurant down near the National Park entrance. Marlin has been serving fresh fish, hearty *casados,* as well as other Costa Rican and international fare for years. Everything is well-prepared and very reasonably priced. The restaurant has recently received a good amount of remodeling and upkeep, but it's still a casual open-air affair. In the evenings, they open the second-floor balcony, which is a great spot with a good view of the ocean.

See map p. 191. Facing Playa Espadilla, near the National Park entrance. ☎ 777-1134. Reservations not necessary. Main courses: $4.50–$15. MC, V. Open: Daily 7 a.m.–10 p.m.

Taking a coffee break

Although the area around Quepos and Manuel Antonio is not well-known as a coffee-growing region, you can still get excellent fresh-roasted coffee here from the folks at **Café Milagro** (☎ 777-0794). These folks have two storefront locations, one in downtown Quepos, just over the bridge, and another about midway along the Manuel Antonio road. Excellent fresh-roasted coffee drinks, baked goods, fruit drinks, and ice cream treats are the main draws here, but you can also get full breakfasts, as well as hearty sandwiches and good fresh salads. My favorite option is the selection of iced coffee drinks. Both shops sell fresh-roasted beans to take home with you and also feature well-stocked gift shops.

Sunspot Bar & Grill
$$$$ Manuel Antonio   INTERNATIONAL

If you want one of the most romantic dining experiences to be had in Manuel Antonio, dine here — you'll eat by candlelight, under a purple canvas tent, at one of a few poolside tables. The food's some of the best in town as well. The menu changes regularly but always features a selection of prime meats, poultry, and fresh fish, excellently prepared. The rack of lamb might get a light jalapeno-mint or tamarind glaze, and the chicken breast might be stuffed with feta cheese, Kalamata olives, and roasted red peppers, and topped with a blackberry sauce. Nightly specials and a good selection of salads, appetizers, and desserts round out the menu.

See map p. 191. At Makanda-by-the-Sea (see listing earlier in this chapter).
☎ *777-0442. Reservations necessary. Main courses $10–$25. AE, MC, V. Open: Daily 11 a.m.–10 p.m.*

Exploring Manuel Antonio

Manuel Antonio offers up a wealth of potential activities and attractions. You can spend time here doing everything from lazing on the beach or beside a pool, to hiking a rain-forest trail, to rappelling down the face of a jungle waterfall. If you want to head out or into the sea, you can learn to surf, try your hand sportfishing, or take a sunset cruise.

If you visit the park early in the morning, you can leave when the crowds begin to show up at midday. In the afternoon, you can lounge by your pool or on your patio. If you stay at a hotel partway up the hill from the park entrance, you'll have relatively easy access to the beach, you may get a view, and, best of all, you'll be out of earshot of the nearby disco.

If you steer clear of the peak months in Manuel Antonio (Dec–Mar), you'll miss most of the crowds. If you must come during the peak months, try to avoid the weekends, when the beaches inside and outside the park are packed with families from San José.

The top attractions

Fincas Naturales (The Nature Farm Reserve)

This new attraction is just across from (and run by) Hotel Sí Como No (see listing earlier in this chapter). A lovely bi-level **butterfly garden** is the centerpiece attraction here, but other attractions include a private reserve and a small network of well-groomed trails through the forest. A one-hour guided tour of the butterfly garden costs $15 per person, or $35 when combined with a one-hour guided hike through the forest.

See map p. 191. Located across from the Hotel Sí Como No, on the road between Quepos and Manuel Antonio. ☎ *777-0850.* www.butterflygardens.co.cr. *Admission: $15 for a 1-hour guided tour of the butterfly garden; $35 when combined with a 1-hour guided hike through the forest; $30 for 2-hour night tour. Open: Daily 8 a.m.–4 p.m., with the night tour leaving every evening at 5:30 p.m.*

Manuel Antonio National Park

Manuel Antonio is a small park with only three major trails. Most visitors come primarily to lie on one of the beaches and check out the white-faced monkeys, which sometimes seem as common as tourists.

Playa Espadilla Sur (as opposed to Playa Espadilla, which is just outside the park) is the first beach within the actual park boundaries. It's usually the least-crowded beach in the park and one of the best places to find a quiet shade tree to plant yourself under. However, if there's any surf, this is also the roughest beach in the park.

If you want to explore further, you can walk along Playa Espadilla Sur or follow a trail through the forest parallel to **Playa Manuel Antonio,** which is the most popular beach inside the park. This beach is a short, deep crescent of white sand backed by lush rain forest. The water here is sometimes clear enough to offer good snorkeling along the rocks at either end, and it's usually fairly calm. At low tide, Playa Manuel Antonio shows a very interesting relic: a circular stone turtle trap left by its pre-Columbian residents.

From Playa Manuel Antonio, another slightly longer trail leads to **Puerto Escondido,** where you'll spot a blowhole that sends up plumes of spray at high tide. Be careful when hiking beyond Puerto Escondido: What seems like easy beach hiking at low tide becomes treacherous to impassable at high tide.

From either Playa Espadilla Sur or Playa Manuel Antonio, you can take a circular hike around a high promontory bluff. The farthest point on this hike, which takes about 25 minutes round-trip, is **Punta Catedral,** where the view is spectacular. The trail is a little steep in places, but anybody in average shape can do it. I have done it in sturdy sandals, but you might want to wear good hiking shoes. This is a good place to spot monkeys, although you're more likely to see a white-faced monkey than a rare squirrel monkey.

Another good place to see monkeys is the trail inland from Playa Manuel Antonio. This is a linear trail and mostly uphill, but not too taxing. It's great to spend hours exploring the steamy jungle and then take a refreshing dip in the ocean.

A guide is not essential here, but unless you're experienced in rain-forest hiking, you'll see and learn a lot more with one. A two- or three-hour guided hike should cost between $25 and $35 per person. Almost any of the hotels in town can help you set up a tour of the park. If you decide to explore the park on your own, a basic map is usually available at the park entrance for $1.

You'll find the principal park entrance at **Playa Espadilla,** the beach at the end of the road from Quepos. To reach the park station, you must cross a small, sometimes polluted stream that's little more than ankle-deep at low tide but that can be knee- or even waist-deep at high tide. It's even reputed to house a crocodile or two. For years, locals have talked about building a bridge over this stream; in the meantime, you'll have to either wade it or pay a boatman a small voluntary tip for the very quick crossing.

Just over the stream, you'll find the small ranger station. The Park Service allows only 600 visitors to enter each day, which could mean that you won't get in if you arrive in midafternoon during the high season.

See map p. 191. 5km (3 miles) south of Quepos, 181km (112 miles) southwest of San José. Admission: $7. Open: Tues–Sun 7 a.m.–4 p.m.

More cool things to see and do

✔ **Enjoying the beaches outside the park: Playa Espadilla,** the gray-sand beach just outside the Manuel Antonio National Park boundary, is a wonderful place to enjoy sun, sand, sea, and local scenery. Because no entrance fee is charged, this is the area's most popular beach with locals and visiting Ticos.

This beach is often perfect for board surfing and bodysurfing, but at times it can be a bit rough for casual swimming. It's actually a better spot to learn how to surf. Several open-air shops rent surfboards and boogie boards along the road fronting this beach. Rates run between $5 and $10 per hour and around $30 to $40 per day. If you want a lesson, check in with Burro at **Burro's Surf Shop** (☎ 777-1413) in Quepos, or the **Manuel Antonio Surf School** (☎ 777-4842), which has a roadside kiosk on the road to Manuel Antonio.

Some shops by the water also rent beach chairs and beach umbrellas, both of which aren't available inside the park. A full-day rental of a beach umbrella and two chaise lounges costs around $10.

As you walk north along the beach, away from the national-park entrance, and beyond a rock outcropping, you'll come to a section of the beach that is "clothing optional" and very popular with the local and visiting gay and lesbian population.

✔ **Getting muddy on an ATV:** If you want to try riding a four-wheel-drive all-terrain vehicle (ATV), check in with the folks at **Fourtrax Adventures** (☎ 777-1825; www.fourtraxadventure.com). Their principal tour is a three-hour adventure through African palm plantations, rural towns, and secondary forest to a jungle waterfall, where you stop for a dip. You cross several rivers and a long suspension bridge. Either breakfast or lunch is served, depending on the timing. Cost is $95 per ATV. A second rider on the same ATV costs just $15.

You could also try the folks at **Adrenaline Tours** (☎ 777-0117; www.adrenalinetours.com), which runs a very similar tour.

✔ **Getting up close and personal with a mangrove:** One of my favorite tours in the area is a mangrove tour of the **Damas Island estuary** with Jorge Cruz. These trips generally include lunch, a stop on Damas Island, and roughly three to four hours of cruising the waterways. You're certain to see loads of wildlife on the tour. Contact **Iguana Tours** (☎ 777-1262; www.iguanatours.com) to set up this tour. The cost is $60.

✔ **Landing a big one: Quepos** is one of Costa Rica's billfish centers, and sailfish, marlin, and tuna are all common in this town's waters. In the past year or so, fresh- and brackish-water fishing in the area's mangroves and estuaries has also become popular.

If you're into sportfishing, try hooking up with **Blue Fin Sportfishing** (☎ 777-1676; www.bluefinsportfishing.com), **Blue Water** (☎ 800-807-1585 in the United States and Canada, or 777-4841 in Costa Rica; www.sportfishingincostarica.com), or **High Tec Sportfishing** (☎ 777-3465; www.hightecsportfishing.com).

A full day of fishing should cost between $450 and $1,600, depending on the size of the boat, distance traveled, tackle provided, and amenities. You'll find a lot of competition here, so it pays to shop around and investigate.

If you catch some fresh tuna or dorado, many restaurants in the area, including El Gran Escape (see the listing earlier in this chapter), will cook your fresh catch for you.

✔ **Playing Tarzan:** Tarzan never had it so good. Canopy tours involve putting on a climbing harness and a pulley system that lets you ride along a series of zip-lines connecting treetop platforms. Sometimes the trip involves a rappel down from the forest heights, while other times the trip ends with the final platform at ground level. Either way, thrills are guaranteed.

The most adventurous canopy tours in the area are offered by **Canopy Safari** (☎ 777-0100; www.canopysafari.com) and **Dream Forest Canopy Tour** (☎ 777-4567). The **Titi Canopy Tour** (☎ 777-1020) is a mellower setup, better suited to first-timer or timid adventurers. A canopy tour should run you between $45 and $65 per person.

If you're looking for even more adventure, the folks at **Pacific Ecotours** (☎ 777-4567) run a canyoning tour, which is a hike and scramble down through a mountain river. The trip includes four rappels down the face of waterfalls and several stops to dive into and swim in natural jungle pools. This half-day tour, including lunch, costs $75.

✔ **Playing tropical cowboy:** If your tropical fantasy is to ride a horse down a beach between jungle and ocean, contact **Stable Equus** (☎ 777-0001), which charges $35 for a two-hour ride in Manuel Antonio. This stable treats its animals more humanely than other stables in the area and is also concerned with keeping horse droppings off the beaches.

Brisas del Nara (☎ 779-1235; www.horsebacktour.com) offers full- and half-day horseback excursions that pass through both primary and secondary forest and feature a swimming stop at a jungle waterfall. A full-day tour with these folks, including breakfast and lunch, costs $55 per person ($45 half-day).

✔ **Riding the back roads on a mountain bike:** If you want to do some mountain biking while you're here, check in with **Estrella Tour** (☎/fax 777-1286; estrellatour@hotmail.com), in downtown Quepos. Well-maintained bikes rent for around $20 per day. You can also do a number of different guided tours according to skill level for between $45 and $95 per day, as well as multiday expeditions.

✔ **Riding the wild white water of a jungle river:** The Savegre and Naranjo rivers start in the rain-forested mountains above Quepos. They provide class II to IV white-water river rafting adventures, depending upon which section you run, and how much it's been raining of late.

Several rafting companies ply both these rivers. Among them **Iguana Tours** (☎ 777-1262; www.iguanatours.com), **H2O Adventures** (☎ 777-4092; www.aventurash2o.com), and **Amigos del Río** (☎ 777-0082) are the best. All offer full-day rafting trips for around $85 to $100. Large multiperson rafts are used during the rainy season, and single-person *duckies* (inflatable kayaks) are broken out when the water levels drop. All of these companies also offer half-day rafting adventures and sea-kayaking trips for around $65.

✔ **Setting out to sea:** Among the many boating options available around Quepos and Manuel Antonio are excursions in search of dolphins and sunset cruises. The choice of vessels range from large charter sailboats, to comfortable motorized cruisers, to jet skis.

Learning Spanish: A school with a view

La Escuela de Idiomas D'Amore (☎/fax 777-1143; www.escueladamore.com) runs language-immersion programs out of a former hotel with a fabulous view, on the road to Manuel Antonio. A two-week conversational Spanish course, including a home stay and two meals daily, costs $980.

In addition to **Iguana Tours** (see the preceding bullet), **Sunset Sails** (☎ 777-1304) and **Planet Dolphin** (☎/fax 777-1467; www.planet dolphin.com) offer a range of boat outings on a range of vessels for between $40 and $65 per person. Most of the tours include a snorkel break and, if you're lucky, dolphin sightings.

If you want to add some exhilaration to your sea venture, **Jungle Coast Jets** (☎ 777-1706) offers two-hour jet-ski tours for $99 per person. This tour plies the same waters and includes some snorkeling and the possibility of a dolphin encounter.

✔ **Taking a break to rejuvenate body and soul:** Quite a few massage therapists and a couple of excellent day spas can be found around Manuel Antonio. The best of these are **Sea Glass Spa** (☎ 777-2607; www.seaglassspa.com), located down a winding road on the ocean side just before Villas Nicolás, and **Serenity Spa** (☎ 777-0777), located in the Hotel Sí Como No. A wide range of treatments, wraps, and facials are available at both of these places.

Shopping for Local Treasures

If you're looking for souvenirs, you'll find plenty of beach towels, beachwear, and handmade jewelry in a variety of small shops in Quepos and at impromptu stalls down near the national park. For a good selection in one spot, try **La Buena Nota** (☎ 777-1002; www.labuenanota.com), which is on the road to Manuel Antonio, fairly close to the national park entrance. This shop is jam-packed with all sorts of beachwear, souvenirs, used books, and U.S. magazines and newspapers.

For higher-end gifts, check out **L'Aventura Boutique** (☎ 777-1019), on Avenida Central in Quepos. This small shop has a nice collection of woodwork by Barry Biesanz, banana-fabric works by Lil Mena, and pottery by Cecilia "Pefi" Figueres. The Hotel Sí Como No's **Regálame** gift shop is also pretty well stocked.

Living It Up After Dark

Discos are becoming almost as common in Manuel Antonio as capuchin monkeys. Night owls and dancing fools have a lot to choose from.

Down near the beach, folks get going at the **Mar y Sombra** (☎ 777-0003). This is my favorite spot — you can walk off the dance floor and right out onto the beach, and they usually don't charge a cover. For real late-night action, the local favorite appears to be the **Arco Iris** (no phone), which is located just before the bridge heading into town. Admission is usually around $2.50.

The bars at **Karola's** restaurant (see listing earlier in this chapter) and the **Hotel Sí Como No** (see listing earlier in this chapter) are good places to hang out and meet people in the evenings. You can also check out the **Vela-Bar** (☎ 777-0413) and **Cockatoo** (no phone), which often have a strong gay and lesbian crowd.

Back in Quepos, **El Banco Bar** (☎ 777-0478), **Mar y Blues** (☎ 777-4130), **Sargento Garcia's** (☎ 777-2960), **Wacky Wanda's** (☎ 777-2245), and the **Fish Head Bar** at El Gran Escape (see listing earlier in this chapter) are the most popular hangouts.

If you enjoy the gaming tables, the **Hotel Kamuk** (☎ 777-0811) in Quepos and the **Hotel El Byblos** (☎ 777-0411) on the road to Manuel Antonio both have small casinos and will even foot your cab bill if you try your luck and lay down your money.

If you want to see a flick, check out what's playing at **Hotel Sí Como No's** little theater, although you have to eat at the restaurant or spend a minimum at the bar to earn admission.

Fast Facts: Manuel Antonio

Ambulance
Call ☎ 128.

ATMs
You'll find several ATMs in Quepos, as well as one at Banca Promerica, which is located about midway along the road to the national park.

Country Code and City Code
The country code for Costa Rica is **506**. Costa Rica doesn't use city or area codes. To call from the United States, dial 011-506 plus the seven-digit number. From within Costa Rica, you simply dial the seven-digit number.

Currency Exchange
Most hotels will exchange money for you at decent rates. To get official rates, head to one of the banks in Quepos or to Banca Promerica, which is located about midway along the road to the national park.

Fire
Call ☎ 118.

Hospitals
The Quepos Hospital (☎ 777-0922) is located just outside of town, on the road to the airport and Dominical.

Information

Manuel Antonio and Quepos don't have official information offices. Most hotels have a tour desk, concierge, or helpful front desk where you can ask questions.

Internet Access

Several Internet cafes are located in Quepos, and a few are strung along the road to the national park. Many hotels also have their own in-house Internet cafes or wireless service. Rates run from $1 to $3 per hour.

Newspapers

Several gift shops around town and various hotels can get you current or day-late editions of the *Miami Herald, New York Times,* or *USA Today,* as well as all the local papers, such as the *Tico Times.* Also, keep an eye out for *Quepolandia,* a bimonthly tourist magazine that has a wealth of information and local advertising.

Pharmacies

Several well-stocked pharmacies can be found in downtown Quepos. A pharmacy even rests amongst the cluster of shops and restaurants near the national-park entrance.

Police

Call ☎ **911** or 777-2117.

Post Office

You'll find a post office in downtown Quepos (☎ 777-1471). Alternatively, most hotels can mail your letters and postcards for you.

Taxis

Taxis are plentiful in Quepos and Manuel Antonio. If you don't feel like flagging one down on the street, have your hotel call one for you or dial ☎ 777-1695 or 777-0425.

Chapter 16

Living the Lush Life on the Central Pacific Coast

. . . .

In This Chapter

▶ Getting to and deciding where to settle on the central Pacific coast

▶ Seeing scarlet macaws in Carara National Park

▶ Dining in style on the central Pacific coast

▶ Heading south to Dominical and the beaches south of Dominical

▶ Exploring isolated beaches south of Dominical

. . . .

*T*he central Pacific coast is home to some of the closest beaches to San José. In addition to Manuel Antonio (see Chapter 15), this coast boasts the popular fun-in-the-sun **Jacó** and the surfer stalwart **Playa Hermosa.** Although these two beach destinations are often busy and bustling with Tico weekenders and itinerant surfers, the rest of the destinations covered in this chapter are rather underdeveloped and uncrowded.

For some luxury, you could head to the exclusive resort beach of **Playa Herradura,** which features a large golf and beach resort and full-service marina. In the hills above Playa Herradura sits Villa Caletas, one of the finest and most luxurious boutique hotels in the country.

If you're looking to get away from it all without spending too much, **Dominical** and the **beaches south of Dominical** should be your top choice on this coast. The rain-forested hills and mountains that back these beaches are stunningly beautiful.

This coast is also home to **Carara National Park,** one of the last places in Costa Rica where you can see the disappearing dry forest join the damp, humid forests that extend south down the coast. This park is a prime nesting spot for the endangered scarlet macaw.

The climate here is considerably more humid than that farther north, but it's not nearly as steamy as it is along the southern Pacific or Caribbean coasts. This area stays lush and green year-round, even during the dry season.

Jacó and Playa Herradura

For all intents and purposes, these are the two closest beaches to San José. Playa de Jacó is also the closest thing in Costa Rica to Fort Lauderdale during spring break. This long stretch of beach is strung with a dense hodgepodge of hotels in all price categories, cheap souvenir shops, seafood restaurants, and pizza joints.

The number-one attraction in Jacó is the surf, and this is definitely a surfer-dominated beach town. In fact, the beach here is not particularly appealing. It's made of dark-gray sand with lots of rocks, and it's often very rough. Still, young surfers, Tico weekenders, and a regular stream of snowbirds keep this town pretty full during the northern winter months.

Just north of Jacó lies the crescent-shaped beach of Playa Herradura. Like Jacó, the dark-brown-sand beach here is fairly unattractive, although it is calm and protected.

Jacó and Playa Herradura can be visited from San José as a day trip. It's only about two and a half hours from San José to Jacó and slightly less even to Playa Herradura. However, you're probably best off dedicating about one or two nights to take full advantage of this area.

Getting there

The best way to get to Jacó and Playa Herradura is to drive. If you don't want to rent a car, frequent bus and minivan services are available. The specifics of each are listed in the following sections.

By car

Several routes run to Jacó and Playa Herradura from San José. The most popular one is a narrow and winding two-lane road, the "old highway," over and through mountains. This road is equal parts scenic and harrowing — it's not uncommon to encounter buses and trucks passing on blind curves, or to find yourself at the back of a long line of cars stuck behind a slow-moving truck crawling up one of the steep hills.

Begin this route by taking the Interamerican Highway west out of San José and exiting just west of Alajuela near the town of Atenas. Follow any of the numerous signs to any hotel in Jacó or Manuel Antonio. The old highway meets the Costanera (Coastal) Highway a few kilometers west of Orotina. From here it's a straight and flat shot down the coast. You'll hit Playa Herradura first, and then Jacó. Playa Hermosa is about seven minutes beyond Jacó.

Alternatively, you can head out of San José on the highway to Escazú and Santa Ana. Continue on to the town of Ciudad Colón. From Ciudad Colón, follow signs to Puriscal and then Orotina. This route is scenic and winds through the mountains, with the same caveats as the old highway route. Though it is also slightly longer than the old highway route, I prefer it because it's less traveled and has almost no traffic.

Jaws of death: Looking for killer crocs

The Costanera Highway passes over the Tárcoles River, just outside the entrance to **Carara National Park,** about 14 miles south of Orotina. The river below this bridge is home to a hearty population of American crocodiles. This is a popular spot to pull over and gander at these gargantuan reptiles. Some can reach up to 4.5m (15 ft.) in length. Anywhere from 10 to 20 are easily visible, either swimming in the water or sunning on the banks.

You'll have to be careful on two counts. First, you'll be walking on a narrow sidewalk along the side of the bridge with cars and trucks speeding by. And, second, car break-ins are common here, although a new police post has somewhat reduced the risk. Still, don't leave your car or valuables unguarded for long, or better yet, leave someone at the car and take turns watching the crocs.

When you're in Jacó or any of the other nearby beach towns, you'll find several operators who run daily crocodile tours on the Tárcoles River. These are simple tours in open skiffs or Boston Whalers. Most of these companies bring along plenty of freshly killed chicken to attract the reptiles and pump up the adrenaline. Don't expect a highly trained naturalist guide or any semblance of respect for the natural world. Do expect to pay between $35 and $55 per person for the trip.

Finally, if you're coming from anywhere in northern Costa Rica, you'll need to take the Interamerican Highway and get off at the Puntarenas exit and follow signs to Caldera. From here, head south on the Costanera Highway. (*Note:* This section has been in horrible shape in recent years.)

By bus

Express buses (☎ 223-1109 in San José or 643-3135 in Jacó) leave San José for Jacó about five times daily from the Coca-Cola bus terminal at Calle 16 between avenidas 1 and 3. The trip takes between two and a half and three hours; the fare is $2.50. On weekends and holidays, extra buses are often added, so calling to check is a good idea.

No direct bus runs to Playa Herradura. The Jacó bus will drop you off at the crossroads. From here it's about 2km (1¼ miles) to the beach.

Grayline (☎ 220-2126; www.graylinecostarica.com) has a daily bus that leaves San José for Jacó at 8 a.m.; the fare is $21. **Interbus (☎ 283-5573;** www.costaricapass.com) has two daily buses that leave San José for Jacó at 9:30 a.m. and 2 p.m.; the fare is $17. Both companies will pick you up at most San José–area hotels.

Buses from San José to Quepos and Manuel Antonio also pass by Jacó. (They let passengers off on the highway about 1km/½ mile from town). However, during the busy months, some of these buses will refuse passengers getting off in Jacó or will accept them only if they pay the full fare to Quepos or Manuel Antonio.

The Jacó bus station is at the north end of town, at a small mall across from the Jacó Fiesta Hotel. Buses returning to San José from Quepos pass periodically and pick up passengers on the highway. Because schedules can change, asking at your hotel about current departure times is wise.

Orienting yourself in and around Jacó and Playa Herradurra

Both of these beaches are located about 1km (½ mile) off the Costanera Highway. Aside from the large Marriott Los Sueños resort, marina, and condominium project, which dominates the northern section of the beach here, very little has been developed in Playa Herradura.

Playa de Jacó is much more developed. Still, one main road runs parallel to the beach, with a host of arteries heading toward the water. You'll find most of the hotels, restaurants, and shops on or just off the main road.

Villa Caletas is located down a private road off the Costanera Highway, on the hillsides above Playa Herradura.

Jacó doesn't have an official tourist information office, although several tour-booking agencies masquerade as such. Most hotels have a knowledgeable front-desk staff, concierge, or in-house tour desk that can answer any questions. Also, keep an eye out for *Jaco Guide,* a free, glossy, monthly local tourist magazine packed with information, articles, and advertisements; it's available at most souvenir shops, restaurants, and hotel lobbies around town.

Getting around

Almost everything is within walking distance in Jacó, but you can rent a bicycle or scooter from several shops on the main street. A bike rental should run you around $8 to $12 per day, and a scooter should cost between $30 and $45 per day.

Taxis are plentiful and inexpensive in this area. If you can't flag one down on the street, have your hotel call for you, or dial **Jacó Taxi** (☎ 643-3030).

For longer excursions, you can rent a car from **Budget** (☎ 643-2265), **Economy** (☎ 643-1098), **National** (☎ 643-2881), **Payless** (☎ 643-3224), or **Zuma** (☎ 643-3207). Expect to pay approximately $50 for a one-day rental. You may also consider hiring a local taxi driver, who would probably take you wherever you wanted to go for the same $50 per day, thus saving you some hassle and headache.

Central Pacific Playas

ACCOMMODATIONS ◼
Arenal Pacífico **6**
Club del Mar Condominiums
& Resort **6**
Hotel Fuego del Sol **7**
Hotel Mar de Luz **6**
Marriott Los Sueños Ocean
& Golf Resort **5**
Pochote Grande **6**
Villa Caletas **4**
Villa Lapas **2**

DINING ◆
Caliche's Wishbone **6**
El Hicaco **6**
El Nuevo Latino **5**
Pacific Bistro **6**
Rioasis **6**

ATTRACTIONS ●
Biajagual Waterfalls **3**
Carara National Park **1**
Pura Vida Botanical
Gardens **3**

NIGHTLIFE ★
Beatle Bar **6**
Disco La Central **6**
El Zarpe **6**
Hotel Copacabana **6**
Hotel Poseidon **6**
Jazz Casino **6**

Onyx Bar **6**
Stelaris Casino **5**

SHOPPING ◼
Guacamole **6**
La Galería Heliconia **6**

Spending the night

Arenal Pacífico
$$ Jacó

This is the best midrange option in Jacó, and it's right on the beach, to boot. The rooms are nothing special — and almost none offers an ocean view — but they are clean and cool, and most are pretty spacious. The three superior rooms come with an unstocked minifridge, a microwave, and a coffeemaker. The grounds are lush. You even have to cross a shady bridge over a little stream to get from the parking lot and reception to the rooms and restaurant. A small pool, with a little waterfall filling it, and a separate unheated Jacuzzi rest outside. Beside the pool, a few hammocks are hung in the shade. The restaurant serves standard Tico and international fare, but it is set right up against the sand and just steps from the sea.

See map p. ###. Playa de Jacó. ☎ *253-5080 or 643-3419. Fax: 253-5016.* www.arenal pacifico.com. *Rack rates: $90–$110 double. Rates include continental breakfast. Rates lower in the off season. AE, MC, V.*

Club del Mar Condominiums & Resort
$$$–$$$$ Jacó

This has long been the top hotel right in Jacó. A major expansion and remodeling has only made it an even better option. Club del Mar is at the far southern end of the beach, where the rocky hills meet the sand. Most of the rooms are actually one- or two-bedroom condo units, with full kitchens. All are spacious and feature private balconies or porches. You'll find eight rooms on the second floor of the large main building, as well as two huge and luxurious penthouse suites up on the third floor. All units come with an ocean view, although some are more open and expansive than others. The grounds are lush and chock-full of flowering heliconia and ginger. A midsize, multiuse pool and a good open-air restaurant, as well as some modest spa facilities, are also available. Over the years, this place has prided itself on being a family resort. The full kitchens in the condo units just make it all that much better in this regard.

See map p. ###. Playa de Jacó. ☎ *643-3194. Fax: 643-3550.* www.clubdelmar costarica.com. *Rack rates: $132 double; $192–$275 condo; $550 penthouse. Rates lower in the off season; higher during peak weeks. AE, DC, MC, V.*

Hotel Fuego del Sol
$–$$ Playa Hermosa

This place is located right on the beach and offers good value for someone looking for a clean, cool, and comfortable room, as well as easy access to waves. Most of the rooms are housed in a long, two-story block set perpendicular to the beach. Each comes with a queen-size and a twin bed and a private balcony overlooking the free-form pool. Rooms closest to the water will also give you a glimpse of the sea. About half the rooms have televisions. The suites come with king-size beds, a separate sitting room, and a fully stocked kitchenette, and everything is well-maintained. Although the food is pretty standard fare, you get a nice view of the beach from the restaurant here.

See map p. ###. Playa Hermosa. ☎ *289-6060 reservations in San José, or 643-3737 at the hotel.* www.fuegodelsolhotel.com. *Rack rates: $75 double; $120–$135 suite. Rates include breakfast. Lower rates in the off season. AE, MC, V.*

Hotel Mar de Luz
$ Jacó

This is one of Playa de Jacó's best deals and a comfortable alternative to the typical string of cut-rate *cabinas* (cabins) you'll see all over this popular beach town. All the rooms are immaculate and comfortable. Some feature stone walls, small sitting areas, and one or two double beds placed

Playa Jacó

ACCOMMODATIONS ■
Arenal Pacífico **15**
Club del Mar Condominiums
& Resort **16**
Hotel Mar de Luz **6**
Pochote Grande **1**

DINING ◆
Caliche's Wishbone **8**
El Hicaco **13**
Pacific Bistro **5**
Rioasis **10**

NIGHTLIFE ★
Beatle Bar **4**
Disco La Central **11**
El Zarpe **2**
Hotel Copacabana **3**
Hotel Poseidon **7**
Jazz Casino **14**

SHOPPING ▮
Guacamole **12**
La Galería Heliconia **9**

on a raised sleeping nook. My only complaint is that the windows are too small and mostly sealed, so you're forced to use the air-conditioning. In the gardens just off the pools, a couple of grills are available for guest use. You'll also find a comfortable common sitting area, with a selection of magazines and books in several languages.

See map p. ###. Jacó. ☎/*fax 643-3259.* www.mardeluz.com. *Rack rates: $56 double. Rates lower in the off season; higher during peak weeks. AE, MC, V.*

Marriott Los Sueños Ocean & Golf Resort
$$$$–$$$$$ Playa Herradura

This is the closest large-scale resort to San José and is one of the most luxurious places to stay in the country. The hotel is a massive, four-story, horseshoe-shaped building facing the beach. The whole thing is decorated in Spanish colonial style, with stucco walls, heavy wooden doors, and red-clay roof tiles. The rooms are all spacious and tastefully done. They come with one king-size or two queen-size beds, a large armoire, a desk, and a sitting chair with an ottoman. The bathrooms are large and have plenty of counter space. Every room has a balcony, but all are not created equal. Most have only small Juliet-style balconies. Those facing the ocean are clearly superior, and a few of the ocean-facing rooms even have large, comfortable balconies with chaise lounges and tables and chairs.

The pool is a vast, intricate maze built to imitate the canals of Venice, with private nooks and grottos. Kids love exploring it. The beach here is calm and good for swimming, although it's one of the least attractive beaches on this coast, with a mix of rocks and hard-packed, dark-brown sand. The Ted Robinson–designed 18-hole golf course winds through some of the neighboring forest and is an excellent, if not particularly challenging, resort course. The resort's Stellaris casino is the largest and most comfortable I've found at a beach resort in Costa Rica.

See map p. ###. Playa Herradura. ☎ *888-236-2427 in the United States, 298-0844 toll-free in Costa Rica, or 630-9000 from Costa Rica. Fax: 630-9090.* www.marriott.com. *Rack rates: $205–$295 double; $600–$950 suite; $1,500–$1,800 presidential suite. Rates lower in the off season. AE, MC, V.*

Pochote Grande
$ Jacó

Named for a huge old pochote tree on the grounds, this well-kept and attractive hotel is located right on the beach at the far north end of Jacó. The grounds are shady and lush and boast a refreshing little pool. All the rooms are quite large, although sparsely furnished, and have white-tile floors, one queen-size and one single bed, a small fridge, and a balcony or patio. I prefer the second-floor rooms, which are blessed with high ceilings. The modest restaurant and snack bar serve a mixture of Tico, German, and American cuisines.

See map p. ###. Jacó. ☎ *643-3236. Fax: 220-4979.* www.hotelpochotegrande. net. *Rack rates $60 double. Add $10 for a room with A/C. Rates lower in the off season; higher during peak weeks. AE, MC, V.*

Villa Caletas
$$$–$$$$ Above Playa Herradura

This is easily one of the top luxury hotels in Costa Rica. It's certainly hard to find one with a more spectacular setting. Perched 350m (1,148 ft.) above the sea, Villa Caletas enjoys commanding views of the Pacific over forested hillsides. The regular rooms are all elegantly appointed and spacious, but you'll definitely want to stay in a villa or suite here. Each individual villa is situated on a patch of hillside facing the sea or forests. Inside you'll find a main bedroom with a queen-size bed and a comfortable sitting room with couches that convert into two single beds. The villas feature white-tile floors, modern bathrooms, and a private terrace for soaking up the views. The junior suites are even larger and come with their own outdoor Jacuzzi. The suites and master suites are larger still — and even come with their own private swimming pools. Some of the villas and suites are located a vigorous hike downhill from the main hotel building and restaurants.

Although most guests are happy to lounge around and swim in the free-form "infinity" pool that seems to blend into the sea below and beyond, Villa Caletas offers hourly shuttle service to its own little private beach, as well as a host of tour options. You'll also find a Greek-style amphitheater that hosts periodic concerts of jazz or classical music.

See map p. ###. Cuesta Caletas. ☎ *637-0606. Fax: 637-0404.* www.hotelvilla caletas.com. *Rack rates: $150–$165 double; $190 villa; $255–$380 suite. Rates slightly lower in the off season. Extra person $35. AE, MC, V.*

Villa Lapas
$$ Tarcoles

Villa Lapas is a good choice if you're looking to combine a bit of ecoad-venture and bird-watching with some beach time. The rooms here are spacious, with two double beds, cool red-clay tile floors, air-conditioning, ceiling fans, and a shady veranda with wooden benches for taking in the scenery. The hotel's best feature is its massive, open-air restaurant and deck overlooking the river, where buffet-style meals are served. Villa Lapas has 217 hectares (536 acres) of land with excellent trails, a series of sus-pended bridges crossing the river, and its own canopy tour. The newest addition here is a small re-creation of a typical Costa Rican rural village of times gone by. This riverside attraction features three massive gift shops, a large open-air restaurant, an atmospheric old-style Costa Rican bar, and a small chapel. Located on a lush piece of property along the Río Tarcolitos and bordering Carara National Park, the hotel is about 15 to 20 minutes north of Jacó. You'll see the signs for Villa Lapas on the left, just after pass-ing Carara National Park.

See map p. ###. Tárcoles. ☎ *637-0232. Fax: 637-0227.* www.villalapas.com. *Rack rates: $97 double. Rates lower in the off season; higher during peak weeks. AE, MC, V.*

Dining locally

Caliche's Wishbone
$–$$ Jacó   SEAFOOD/MEXICAN

This casual spot is a bit of an anomaly. It is popular with surfers who come here to carb-load on Tex-Mex standards and homemade pizzas as well as hearty stuffed potatoes and a variety of sandwiches served in homemade pita bread. However, they also serve excellent fresh fish and perfectly pre-pared seafood dishes. No matter what you order, the portions are huge. Caliche's almost always has delicious fresh tuna lightly seared and served with a soy-wasabi dressing. The nicest tables are street-side on a covered veranda. Inside, you'll find more tables, as well as a bar with television sets showing surf videos.

See map p. ###. On the main road in Jacó. ☎ *643-3406. Main courses: $4–$16. V. Open: Thurs–Tues 11:30 a.m.–3 p.m. and 5:30–10 p.m.*

El Hicaco
$$ Jacó SEAFOOD/COSTA RICAN

This is the best of the bunch, in terms of the many basic Costa Rican seafood joints in Jacó. The food is good but not outstanding — but the setting is simply wonderful: right on the edge of the beach, with the majority of the tables outdoors under the stars, tall palm trees, and some interesting lighting. They've gussied up the joint and raised prices some in recent years, but this is still a great choice. Stick with the freshly caught grilled seafood or lobster, although plenty of meat and chicken selections are on the menu as well.

See map p. ###. On the beach in downtown Jacó. ☎ *643-3226. Reservations recommended during high season. Main courses: $5–$21. V. Open: Daily 11 a.m.–11 p.m.*

El Nuevo Latino
$$$–$$$$ Playa Herradura LATIN FUSION

This restaurant offers creative and modern takes on local and regional dishes. The dozen or so tables are set in a narrow room that features a glass wall running its length, fronting a gorgeous pool fed by a series of spouts from a story-high aqueduct. The service and setting are semiformal, but the restaurant doesn't have a dress code — they realize that you're at the beach and on vacation here. Standout dishes include the plantain-crusted red snapper and the guava-glazed baby-back ribs. Be sure to start things off with the lamb empanadas (small Argentine pastries stuffed with minced lamb and served with several tasty sauces) or the lobster-and-shrimp croquettes, which come with a roasted-corn and pepper salsa.

See map p. ###. At the Marriott Los Sueños resort, Playa Herradura. ☎ *630-9000. Reservations recommended. Main courses: $18–$40. AE, MC, V. Open: Daily 6– 11 p.m. Closed Mon during the off season.*

Pacific Bistro
$$–$$$ Jacó PACIFIC-RIM FUSION

Chef Kent Green changes the menu here almost nightly, but fresh seafood and top-quality cuts of meat are always the building blocks for his inventive Asian-influenced creations. You'll usually find some fresh tuna, mahimahi, and jumbo shrimp on the menu, but on any given night the sauces will range from a homemade teriyaki to a spicy Thai sauce to coconut curry. Portions are large, but it's worth saving some room for dessert. Set just off the sidewalk on the main drag in town, the restaurant has only six or so tables, so reservations are often essential.

See map p. ###. On the main road in Jacó. ☎ *643-3771. Reservations recommended. Main courses: $8–$18. MC, V. Open: Wed–Sun 6–10 p.m.*

Rioasis
$–$$ Jacó   **PIZZA/MEXICAN**

Rioasis serves hearty burritos, simple pasta dishes, and a wide array of freshly baked wood-oven pizzas. My favorite dish is the Greek pizza, with olives, feta cheese, and anchovies, but the barbecue chicken pizza is also delicious. Both indoor and terrace seating is offered, as well as a bar area, complete with a pool table, dartboards, and a couple of TVs for sports events and surf videos. This place gets crowded and raucous most nights throughout the high season and on weekend nights year-round.

See map p. ###. On the main road in Jacó. ☎ *643-3354. Main courses: $4–$14. V. Open: Wed–Mon noon to midnight.*

Exploring Jacó and Playa Herradurra

The attractions listed in this section can easily be combined in a one-day trip. All the hotels in this area can arrange tours to these attractions, or you can book and visit them yourself with the numbers and information provided.

The top attractions

Bijagual Waterfalls

A series of spectacular stepped jungle waterfalls rests near the remote village of Bijagual. The highest waterfall here is 180m (590 ft). Excellent swimming holes can be found near the bottom of this impressive waterfall.

You can choose from one of several ways to visit these falls. Various companies run tours from Jacó or from entrances both at the top and bottom of the falls. Try either **Grayline Tours** (☎ **643-3231**), which operates out of the Best Western Jacó Beach Hotel, or **Explorica** (☎ **643-3586**). Alternatively, you can drive yourself or take a cab (see "Getting around," earlier in this chapter, for cab information).

Near the top, a local family runs the **Complejo Ecológico La Catarata** (☎ **661-8263**), which features a basic restaurant and a campground. They run horseback tours down to the falls for around $35. Alternatively, you can hike in from an entrance lower down. The hike takes about 45 minutes each way, and the entrance is $10 per person. Either way, you'll end up at the base of the tallest fall.

While you're up this way, you can also stop in at the **Pura Vida Botanical Gardens** (☎ **200-5040**). Entrance to the gardens is a bit steep, at $15, but the grounds and gardens are beautiful.

See map p. ###. To get here, turn off the Costanera Highway at the signs for Hotel Villa Lapas. From here, it's about 5km (3 miles) to the lower entrance, and 8km (5 miles) up to the top entrance to the falls. ☎ *661-8263. Admission: $10 for hiking; $35 for horseback tour. Open: Daily 8 a.m.–4 p.m.*

Watching the sun set

Perched on a high hillside overlooking the Pacific Ocean, **Villa Caletas** (see listing earlier in this chapter) is a perfect place to enjoy sunsets. What's more, the Greek-style amphitheater here is set facing the nightly solar sayonara. Even if you're not staying here, you can come for a cocktail and to watch the sun sink into the sea.

However, the word has gotten out, and during the high season, hoards of other tourists come here for the same pleasure. When it's crowded, getting a good seat can be difficult and service can be a little slow.

Carara National Park

A little more than 15km (9⅓ miles) north of Jacó is Carara National Park, a world-renowned nesting ground for **scarlet macaws.** It has a few kilometers of trails open to visitors. A loop trail here takes about an hour, and another trail is only open to tour groups. The forests here are lush transitional forests, loaded with wildlife.

The macaws migrate daily, spending their days in the park and their nights among the coastal mangroves. It's best to view them in the early morning when they arrive, or around sunset when they head back to the coast for the evening, but a good guide can usually find them for you during the day. Whether or not you see them, you should hear their loud squawks. Among the other wildlife that you might see here are caimans, coatimundis, armadillos, pacas, peccaries, river otters, kinkajous, and, of course, hundreds of species of birds.

 Be sure to bring along insect repellent, or, better yet, wear light cotton long sleeves and pants. (I was once foolish enough to attempt a quick hike in beach clothes and flip-flops — not a good idea.)

You can hike the trails of Carara independently, but my advice is to take the guided tour; you'll learn a lot more about your surroundings. Several companies offer tours to Carara National Park for around $30 to $40. Check at your hotel.

If you're looking for a more personalized tour, check out Lisa Robertson, a knowledgeable and amiable guide who runs **Happy Trails** (☎ 643-1894).

See map p. ###. Located just off the Costanera Highway, a little more than 15km (9⅓ miles) north of Jacó. ☎ *383-9953. Admission: $8. Open: Daily 8 a.m.–4 p.m.*

More cool things to see and do

Although this area has few major attractions, there's plenty to keep you busy. Your choices run from just hanging out on the beach, to taking a zip-line canopy tour, to trying your hand at some deep-sea sportfishing.

Enjoying the beaches in and around Jacó and Playa Herradura

All of these beaches are easily reached by car, moped, or bicycle — if you have a lot of energy. There are road signs at the entrance/access roads to each of the beaches, so you'll have no trouble finding them.

- Unfortunately, **Playa de Jacó** has a reputation for dangerous riptides — as do most of the beaches along Costa Rica's Pacific coast. Even strong swimmers have been known to have trouble with the power rips here. In general, the far southern end of the beach is the calmest and safest.

- The same waves that often make Playa de Jacó dangerous for swimmers make it one of the most popular beaches in the country with surfers. Those who want to challenge the waves can rent surfboards for around $3 an hour or $10 to $15 per day, and boogie boards for $2 an hour, from any one of the numerous surf shops along the main road. If you want to learn how to surf, check in at the **Surfing Academy of Costa Rica** (☎ 643-1948; acasurf45@hotmail.com).

- If you're looking for a calmer beach, head to **Playa Herradura.** This is a hard-packed, brown-sand-and-rock beach ringed by lush hillsides. Despite the presence of the Marriott Los Sueños resort complex, Playa Herradura still feels a lot more isolated and deserted than Jacó.

- Experienced surfers will want to head to **Playa Hermosa,** 10km (6¼ miles) southeast of Jacó. This long, black-sand beach has the most consistent surf along this coast. From July to December, sea turtles nest along Playa Hermosa most nights.

- Finally, for a sense of solitude, check out **Playa Esterillos,** 22km (14 miles) southeast of Jacó. This beach is long and wide and almost always nearly deserted.

Heading to sea in search of a trophy catch

- If you're interested in doing some sportfishing, I recommend that you head on over to the 250-slip marina next to the Marriott Los Sueños resort (see listing earlier in this chapter). Two dependable operators that have already set up here are **Bobcat & Spanish Fly Sportfishing** (☎ 866-888-6426 in the United States, or 637-8824 in Costa Rica; www.spanishflysportfishing.com) and **Costa Rica Fishing Charters** (☎ 800-215-0276 in the United States, or 643-2906 in Costa Rica). A half-day fishing trip for four people costs around $250 to $500, and a full day costs between $600 and $1,400.

Paddling around

- **Kayak Jacó** (☎ 643-1233; www.kayakjaco.com) runs a couple of different trips. Tours range from gentle paddles and floats on the Tulin River to a combination ocean-kayaking and snorkel trip on Herradura Bay, to full-on kayak surfing at one of the local beach breaks. You can also do some moderate white-water kayaking in easy-to-use inflatable kayaks or try your hand in the ocean on one of the eight-person outrigger canoes. Most options run around four hours and include transportation to and from the start of the tour, as well as fresh fruit and soft drinks during the trip. The tours cost between $50 and $80 per person, depending on the particular trip and group size.

Rough riding

✔ Several operators take folks out on ATV tours through the surrounding countryside. Expect to ford rivers and ride over some rough terrain. Tours range in length from two to six hours and cost between $65 and $125 per person. **Paraiso Adventures** (☎ 643-2724) and **Ricaventura** (☎ 818-6973) are two dependable companies offering this type of tour.

Saddling up

✔ Horseback-riding tours give you a chance to get away from all the development in Jacó and see a bit of nature. Contact **Happy Trails** (☎ 643-1894) or **Hermanos Salazar** (☎ 643-3203) to make a reservation. Down in Playa Hermosa, check in with **Diana's Trail Rides** (☎ 643-3808). Over in Playa Herradura, you can try the **Jacó Equestrian Center** (☎ 643-1569).

Seeing the sights from on high

✔ You have several ways to enter the forest canopy in this area: The gentlest approach is to take the **Rain Forest Aerial Tram Pacific** (☎ 257-5961; www.rainforestram.com). A sister project to the original Rain Forest Aerial Tram, this attraction features modified ski-lift-type gondolas that take you through and above the transitional forests here bordering Carara National Park. The $55 entrance fee includes the guided 40-minute tram ride, as well as a guided 45-minute hike on a network of trails. You can also hike the company's trails at your leisure for as long as you like. The Aerial Tram is located a few kilometers inland from an exit just north of the first entrance into Jacó.

✔ A few zip-line and harness-style canopy tours are also available if you want more adventure. **Chiclets Tree Tour** (☎/fax 643-1879) offers up a canopy adventure ($60 per person) just outside Jacó in nearby Playa Hermosa. This is an adventurous tour, with 13 platforms set in transitional forest, and some sweeping views of the Pacific.

✔ **Villa Lapas** (see listing earlier in this chapter) has two different tours through the treetops outside of Jacó. The better option, for my money, is a guided hike on its network of trails and five suspended bridges ($20 per person). The operator also has a relatively low-adrenaline zip-line canopy tour ($35 per person), with seven platforms connected by six cables.

Pampering yourself

Serenity Spa (☎ 643-1624) offers massage, as well as mud packs, face and body treatments, and manicures and pedicures. The spa's Jacó branch is located on the first floor, among a tiny little cul-de-sac of shops next to Zuma Rent-A-Car. These folks also have operations at the Marriott Los Sueños resort, Villa Caletas, and Club del Mar Condominiums & Resort.

Shopping for local treasures

If you try to do any shopping in this area, you'll be overrun with shops selling T-shirts, cut-rate souvenirs, and handmade jewelry and trinkets. The two notable exceptions are **Guacamole** (☎ 643-1120), a small clothing store that produces its own line of batik beachwear and **La Galería Heliconia** (☎ 643-3613), a high-end gift shop that carries a good selection of artworks and pottery. Both of these shops are located on the main road in Jacó.

Living it up after dark in Jacó and Playa Herradura

Playa de Jacó is the Central Pacific's party town, with tons of bars and several discos. The **Disco La Central** (☎ 643-3076) is packed every night of the high season and every weekend during the off season. La Central is right on the beach near the south end of town. A huge open-air hall features the requisite 1970s flashing lights and suspended mirrored ball, as well as a garden bar in a thatch-roofed building that's a slightly quieter place to have a drink. The disco charges a nominal cover charge.

For a more casual atmosphere, head to either the **Beatle Bar** or **Onyx Bar** (☎ 643-3911). Both are located right on the main drag in town. However, be forewarned, a fair amount of prostitution goes on in Jacó. It's not uncommon to find working women at any of the abovementioned places, as well as cruising other bars around town.

Sports freaks can catch the latest games at **Hotel Copacabana** (☎ 643-1005), **Hotel Poseidon** (☎ 643-1642), or **El Zarpe** (☎ 643-3473). El Zarpe serves up good, reasonably priced burritos, burgers, and other assorted bar food.

The **Jazz Casino** (☎ 643-2316), located at the Hotel Amapola, is a modest casino, but if you're into gaming, you should head to the **Stelaris Casino** (☎ 630-9000) at the Marriott Los Sueños resort.

Fast Facts: Jacó and Playa Herradura

Ambulance

Call ☎ 128.

ATMs

You'll find several ATMs around Jacó and at the Marriott Los Sueños Resort in Playa Herradura.

Country Code and City Code

The country code for Costa Rica is **506**. Costa Rica doesn't have city or area codes. To call from the United States, dial 011-506 plus the seven-digit number. From within Costa Rica, you simply dial the seven-digit number.

Currency Exchange

Most hotels will exchange money for you at decent rates. To get official rates, head to the Banco Nacional (☎ 643-3072) or the Banco de Costa Rica (☎ 643-3695). Both have branches in town on the main road and are open Monday through Friday from 8:30 a.m. to 3 p.m.

Fire

Call ☎ 118.

Hospitals

The closest hospitals are located in Quepos and Puntarenas. A decent medical center (☎ 643-3667) is located at the Municipal Center, toward the southern end of Jacó.

Information

No official information offices are located in Jacó or Playa Herradura. Most hotels have a tour desk, concierge, or helpful front desk where you can ask questions.

Internet Access

Several Internet cafes are located in Jacó, as well as one at the Marriott Los Sueños Resort in Playa Herradura. Many hotels also have their own in-house Internet cafes or wireless service. Rates run between $1 and $3 per hour.

Newspapers

Several gift shops around town and various hotels can get you current or day-late editions of the *Miami Herald, New York Times,* or *USA Today,* as well as all the local papers, including the *Tico Times.* Also, keep an eye out for *Jaco's Guide,* a free monthly tourist magazine that has a wealth of information and local advertising.

Pharmacies

Jacó has several well-stocked pharmacies. Farmacia Fischel (☎ 643-2683) in the El Galeone shopping center and the Farmacia Jacó (☎ 643-3205) are both on the main road through town.

Police

Call ☎ **911** or 643-3011.

Post Office

A post office is located in downtown Jacó (☎ 643-2175), toward the southern end of town, in the Municipal Center. Alternatively, most hotels can mail your letters and postcards for you.

Taxis

Taxis are plentiful in Jacó, and to a much lesser extent in Playa Herradura and Playa Hermosa. If you can't flag one down on the street, have your hotel call for you or dial Jacó Taxi (☎ 643-3030).

Dominical and the Beaches South of Dominical

Although no longer the best-kept secret in Costa Rica, **Dominical** and the coastline just south of it remain excellent places to find isolated beaches, spectacular views, remote jungle waterfalls, and excellent and affordable lodgings.

The beach at Dominical itself has both right and left beach breaks, which means plenty of surfers are usually in town. In fact, even though the beach at Dominical does get broad, flat, and beautiful at low tide, it's primary appealing to surfers and is often too rough for casual bathers. However, you'll find excellent beaches for swimming, sunbathing, and strolling just a little farther south.

From Dominical south, the coastline is dotted with tide pools, tiny coves, cliff-side vistas, and some of Costa Rica's most unexplored beaches. Among the beaches you'll find are **Playa Ballena, Playa Uvita, Playa Piñuela, Playa Ventanas,** and **Playa Tortuga.**

Getting there

Whether you're coming from San José, or from Quepos and Manuel Antonio, driving is your best option for reaching this area because bus service is infrequent. However, if you want or need to travel by bus, the details are listed in the following sections.

By car

From San José, head south, toward Cartago, on the Interamerican Highway. Continue on this road all the way to San Isidro de El General, where you'll see an exit for Dominical.

The long and winding stretch of the Interamerican Highway between San José and San Isidro is one of the most difficult sections of road in the country. Not only are the usual car-eating potholes and periodic land-slides present, but you must also contend with driving over the 3,300m (10,824-ft.) **Cerro de la Muerte (Mountain of Death).** This aptly named mountain pass is legendary for its dense afternoon fogs, blinding torren-tial downpours, steep drop-offs, severe switchbacks, and unexpectedly breathtaking views. Drive with extreme care, and bring a sweater or sweatshirt — it's cold up at the top.

Pay attention as you approach San Isidro. The exit for Dominical is marked, but it's a simple right-hand turn onto a busy city street that passes through the center of San Isidro. After passing through the city, continue on this same street until it turns into the winding two-lane road to Dominical and the coast. The entire drive takes about four hours.

You can also drive here from Manuel Antonio and Quepos. Just take the road out of Quepos toward the hospital and airport. Follow the signs for Dominical. It's a straight, albeit bumpy, shot. However, the road has been slated to be paved for a few years now, and if that happens, it should no longer take more than an hour to cover the mere 40km (25 miles).

By bus

To reach Dominical by bus, you must first head to San Isidro de El General or Quepos. Plenty of daily buses will take you to San Isidro. **Musoc** (☎ 222-2422 in San José, or 771-3829 in San Isidro) buses leave from their modern terminal at Calle Central and Avenida 22 roughly hourly between 5:30 a.m. and 6:30 p.m. **Tuasur** (☎ 222-9763 or 771-0419) runs express buses between San José and San Isidro that leave roughly every hour between 5 a.m. and 5 p.m. from Calle 16 between avenidas 1 and 3. Whichever company you choose, the trip takes a little over three hours, and the fare is roughly $2.75. Leave no later than 9 a.m. if you want to be sure to catch the 1:30 p.m. bus to Dominical.

From San Isidro de El General, buses (☎ 257-4121 in San José, or 771-4744 in San Isidro) leave for Dominical at 7 and 9 a.m. and 1:30 and 4 p.m. The bus station for Dominical is 1 block south of the main bus station and 2 blocks west of the church. The trip takes one and a half hours and the fare is $1.50.

Buses leave Quepos for Dominical daily at 5 and 9:30 a.m. and 1:30 and 7 p.m. The trip duration is two hours; the fare is $3.

When you're ready to leave, buses depart Dominical for San Isidro at 6:45 and 7:15 a.m., and 2:30 and 3:30 p.m. If you want to get to San José the same day, you should catch the morning bus. Buses to Quepos leave Dominical at approximately 5:45 and 8 a.m., and 1 and 2:30 p.m.

Orienting yourself in and around Dominical

Dominical is a small town on the banks of Río Barú. The dirt road into and through town is to the right after you cross the bridge. It runs parallel to and a bit inland from the beach. As you first come into town, you'll see a soccer field and the San Clemente Bar & Grill, which has a couple of public telephones. As you continue on the dirt road, you'll come to a small side street that cuts through and joins the beachfront access road.

On the Costanera Highway heading south, just beyond the turnoff into Dominical is a little strip mall, **Plaza Pacífica,** with a couple of restaurants, gift shops, and the town's main grocery store.

Heading south from Dominical, the Costanera Highway is paved and in beautiful shape all the way to Ojochal and beyond.

You won't find any official tourist-information offices in this area. However, most hotels have a helpful and knowledgeable front-desk staff, or in-house tour desk. The tour office at San Clemente Bar & Grill (see "Dining locally," later in this chapter) is also a good bet.

Getting around

Taxis congregate around the soccer field in the center of Dominical. Alternatively, you can have your hotel call you one. The actual town/ village of Dominical is very compact and can easily be navigated on foot. If you're heading farther afield, taxis are the best option. There are no car-rental agencies in Dominical and bus service (to the beaches south, to Quepos, and to San Isidro and San José) is infrequent, and not really an option for getting around the area.

Spending the night

Cabinas San Clemente
$ Dominical

In addition to running the town's most popular restaurant and serving as the social hub for the surfers, beach bums, and expatriates passing through, this place offers basic, but clean, budget rooms just steps from the beach. Some of the newer second-floor rooms have wood floors and wraparound verandas and are a real steal in this price range. The grounds are shady, and you can relax in one of several hammocks strung between coconut palms. The least expensive rooms are housed in a bunk-bed hostel-style affair in a separate building dubbed the **Dominical Backpacker's Hostel.** All rooms here come with access to a communal kitchen.

Dominical. ☎ *787-0026 or 787-0055. Fax: 787-0158. Rack rates: $10 per person with shared bathroom; $25–$65 double with private bathroom. AE, MC, V.*

Hotel Diuwak
$ Dominical

This hotel offers the most modern and comfortable accommodations close to Dominical's principal surf break. However, it's not right on the beach — it is located about 50m (164 ft.) inland. The rooms are clean, bright, and fairly spacious. About half the rooms come with air-conditioning, and a few bigger suites and bungalows are available for larger groups and families. Most have some sort of private or semiprivate veranda facing lush gardens. At the center of the complex, you'll find a refreshing pool, and in the adjacent shopping center there's a coffee shop, an Internet cafe, and a minimarket. This place is the best option for surfers seeking a little extra comfort just steps away from the waves.

Dominical. ☎ *787-0087. Fax: 787-0089.* www.diuwak.com. *Rack rates: $50–$70 double. Rates lower in the off season; higher during peak weeks. MC, V.*

Hotel Roca Verde
$ Dominical

This popular hotel offers the best beachfront accommodations in Dominical. The setting is superb — on a protected little cove with rocks and tide pools. The rooms are located in a two-story building beside the swimming pool. Each room comes with one queen-size and one single bed and a small patio or balcony. The large open-air restaurant boasts a popular bar that keeps folks dancing most weekend nights. The rooms are a bit close to the bar, so it can sometimes be hard to get an early night's sleep, especially on weekends during the high season.

1km (½ mile) south of Dominical, just off the coastal highway. ☎ *787-0036. Fax: 787-0013.* www.rocaverde.net. *Rack rates: $75 double. Rates lower in the off season; higher during peak weeks. MC, V.*

La Cusinga Lodge
$$–$$$ Bahia Ballena

This should be a top choice for bird-watchers and those looking for a comfortable room that also feels entirely in touch with the natural surroundings. The individual and duplex cabins here all feature lots of varnished woodwork and large screened windows on all sides for cross-ventilation. Most have interesting stone and tile work in their bathrooms. The whole small complex is set on a hill overlooking Ballena National Park and Playa Uvita. Heavy stone paths connect the main lodge to the various individual cabins. With high ceilings, lots of light through large picture windows, and sparkling varnished wood floors and walls, the two dorm rooms here may just be the nicest dorm rooms I've ever seen.

Bahia Ballena. ☎ */fax 770-2549.* www.lacusingalodge.com. *Rack rates: $80 per person including all meals, nonalcoholic beverages, and guided hikes. MC, V.*

Pacific Edge
$ Dominical

This place isn't that close to the beach, but the views from each individual bungalow are so breathtaking that you might not mind. Spread along a lushly planted ridge on the hillside over Dominical, these comfortable cabins have wood floors, solar-heated water, and solar reading lights. Their best feature is surely the private porch with a comfortable hammock in which to laze about and enjoy the view. A wide range of tours and activities can be arranged here, and a refreshing swimming pool awaits you if you're too tired or lazy to head down to the beach. Pacific Edge is 4km (2½ miles) south of Dominical and then another 1.2km (¾ mile) up a steep and rocky road; four-wheel-drive vehicles are highly recommended — I'd say required.

Dominical. ☎ */fax 787-8010.* www.pacificedge.info. *Rack rates: $50–$75 double. AE, MC, V (7 percent surcharge).*

Renting a luxurious hillside villa

In addition to the places listed throughout this section, you'll find that a host of beautiful private homes built on the hillsides above Dominical are regularly rented out. Most come with several bedrooms and full kitchens, and quite a few have private pools. The setting and views you'll find here are spectacular.

If you're here for an extended stay and have a four-wheel-drive vehicle (a must for most of these), check in with **Paradise Costa Rica** (☎ 388-0155; www.paradise costarica.com) or with the folks at **Cabinas San Clemente** or **Hotel Roca Verde** (see listing earlier in this chapter).

Dining locally

El Balcon de Uvita
$$ Uvita   THAI/INDONESIAN

It's a rugged and steep drive up here, but the view and food are worth it. Seven simple wooden tables are set around an open-air porch. The menu changes regularly but always includes a savory mix of Thai and Indonesian specialties. The best plan often is to order the rijsttafel, a traditional Indonesian seven-course tasting menu. Although this is a great place for dinner, I actually prefer it for lunch or around sunset, when you can really enjoy the spectacular view.

1km (½ mile) north (uphill) from the gas station in Uvita. ☎ *743-8034. Reservations recommended. Main courses $5–$9. MC, V. Open: Thurs–Sun noon to 9 p.m.*

Exotica
$$–$$$ Ojochal   FRENCH

This little place is tucked away deep along the dirt road that runs through Ojochal. With polished concrete floors, roll-up bamboo screens for walls, and only a few tree-trunk slab tables and plastic lawn chairs for furniture, it is, nonetheless, one of the most popular restaurants in the area. The chalkboard menu changes regularly but might feature shrimp in a coconut curry sauce or duck breast à l'orange. The Chicken Exotica is chicken stuffed with bacon, prunes, and cheese, topped with a red-pepper sauce. The lunch menu is much more reduced, with a small selection of fresh salads and a few more-filling mains.

1km (½ mile) inland from the turnoff for Ojochal. No phone. Lunch $2.50–$5. Main courses: $6–$19. No credit cards. Open: Mon–Sat 11 a.m.–9:30 p.m.

La Parcela
$$ Dominical SEAFOOD/INTERNATIONAL

This open-air restaurant has a lovely setting on a rocky bluff overlooking the ocean. Try to get one of the tables by the railing and you'll be able to watch the waves crashing on the rocks below. The menu features fresh seafood, meat, and poultry dishes, as well as a selection of pastas. The sauces and presentation are all interesting. Start things off with a tuna tartar tower, and then try either their fresh mahimahi with a mango relish or the filet mignon in a porcini mushroom sauce.

At Cabinas Punto Dominical. ☎ *787-0166. Reservations recommended. Main courses: $7–$19. V. Open: Daily 7:30 a.m.–9 p.m.*

San Clemente Bar & Grill
$–$$ Dominical SEAFOOD/MEXICAN

The social center of Dominical, this place specializes in massive breakfasts, an extensive menu of hefty sandwiches and tasty Mexican-American food, and nightly specials. The fresh fish, done blackened or simply grilled, is delicious. One unique (and sobering) décor touch here is the ceiling full of broken surfboards. If you break a board out on the waves, bring it in, and they'll hang it and even buy you a bucket of beer.

Downtown Dominical. ☎ *787-0055. Reservations not necessary. Main courses: $4.50–$15. MC, V. Open: Daily 7:30 a.m.–10 p.m.Exploring Dominical and the beaches south of Dominical*

All the hotels in the area can arrange tours and visits to the following attractions. You can also book and visit them on your own with the information provided, or contact **Southern Expeditions** (☎ **787-0100**; www. southernexpeditionscr.com), the largest tour operator in the area.

The top attractions

Ballena Marine National Park

Ballena Marine National Park protects a coral reef that stretches from Uvita south to Playa Piñuela and includes the little Isla Ballena, just offshore. Although the park is predominantly offshore, it does include **Playa Uvita,** an expansive and beautiful beach. Playa Uvita is well protected and good for swimming. At low tide, an exposed sandbar allows you to walk about and explore another tiny island.

This park is named for the whales that are sometimes sighted close to shore in the winter months. If you ever fly over this area, you'll also notice that this little island and the spit of land that's formed at low tide compose the perfect outline of a whale's tail.

You'll find a park's office at the entrance. These folks administer the park and even run a small turtle-hatching shelter and program. Camping is allowed here for around $2 per person per day, with access to a public bathroom and shower.

Located about 16km (10 miles) south of Dominical, the main entrance to the National Park is at Playa Uvita. To get here, drive south on the Costanera Highway until the village of Bahia. Turn right here and drive another 3km (1¾ miles) east along a rough dirt road until you hit the beach. ☎ 743-8236. Admission: $1. Open: Daily 8 a.m.–4 p.m.

Hacienda Barú

Hacienda Barú is a private wildlife refuge and tourism project located just north of Dominical, on the other side of the Barú River. These folks offer a variety of hikes and tours, including a walk through mangroves and along the riverbank (for some good bird-watching), a rain-forest hike through virgin jungle, an all-day trek from beach to mangrove to jungle that includes a visit to some Indian petroglyphs, an overnight camping trip, and a combination horseback-and-hiking tour.

They even have tree-climbing tours and a small canopy platform 30m (98 ft.) above the ground. If you're traveling with a group, you'll be charged a lower per-person rate, depending on the number of people in your group.

Hacienda Barú is located 1.5km (1 mile) north of Dominical on the road to Quepos and Manuel Antonio. ☎ 787-0003. Fax: 787-0004. www.haciendabaru.com. Tour prices range from $20 (for the mangrove hike) to $60 (for the jungle overnight).

Nauyaca Waterfall

The Nauyaca waterfall is a two-tiered jungle waterfall with an excellent swimming hole. This waterfall is also called Santo Cristo, and sometimes even Don Lulo's waterfall. The latter name belongs to a local man who pioneered and continues to lead many of the tours here. Most include a mix of hiking, horseback riding, and hanging out at the falls.

All the hotels in town can arrange a visit to Nauyaca Waterfall, or you can call **Don Lulo** himself at ☎ 787-0198. A full-day tour, with both breakfast and lunch, should cost around $45 per person. This site has become so popular that Don Lulo has set up a little welcome center at the entrance (just off the road into Dominical from San Isidro) and even allows camping here. Round-trip car transportation can be arranged for a nominal charge.

The main entrance to these falls is located 10km (6¼ miles) outside of Dominical, on the road to San Isidro. ☎ 787-8013. Admission: $45 for a full-day tour, with both breakfast and lunch. Round-trip transportation can be arranged for a nominal charge. Open: Daily 8 a.m.–4 p.m.

Parque Reptilandia

Located a few miles outside of Dominical, on the road to San Isidro, this place features over 50 terrariums and open-air exhibits of snakes, frogs, turtles, and lizards, as well as crocodiles and caimans. Although I'm generally disappointed in this type of attraction, the display enclosures here are the best I've seen in Costa Rica. Be sure to check out the brilliantly colored mottled eyelash viper.

Located 7km (4⅓ miles) outside of Dominical, on the road to San Isidro. ☎ *787-8007. Admission: $10. Open: Daily 9 a.m.–4:30 p.m.*

More cool things to see and do

The Dominical area offers visitors a host of adventurous and educational options:

- ✔ **Diving:** If you want to take a scuba-diving trip out to the rocky sites off of Ballena National Park, or all the way out to Caño Island, call **Mystic Dive Center** (☎ 788-8636; www.mysticdivecenter.com), which has its main office in a small roadside strip mall down toward Playa Tortuga and Ojochal.

- ✔ **Flying:** If you're looking for a bird's-eye view of the area, **Skyline Ultralights** (☎ 743-8037; www.flyultralight.com) offers a variety of airborne tours. Located near the beach in Uvita, these folks offer options ranging from a 20-minute introductory flight for $65, to a circuit exploring the Ballena Marine National Park and neighboring mangrove forests, lasting a bit over 45 minutes for $120.

- ✔ **Learning Spanish:** If you're looking to learn or bone up on your Spanish, **Adventure Education Center** (☎ 787-0100; www.adventurespanishschool.com) is located right in the heart of Dominical and offers a variety of immersion-style language programs.

Getting wet in Dominical and at the beaches south of Dominical

Dominical is a major surf destination, and the long and varied beach break here is justifiably popular. In general, the beach boasts powerful waves, best suited for experienced surfers. However, when the waves aren't too big, this is a good place to learn how to surf. Beginners should check in with the folks at the **Green Iguana Surf Camp** (☎ 787-0157; www.greeniguanasurfcamp.com), who offer hourly lessons and comprehensive "surf camps."

Because the beach in Dominical itself is unprotected, it's often too rough for swimming; however, you can go for a swim in the calm waters at the mouth of the **Río Barú,** or head down the beach a few kilometers to the little sheltered cove at **Roca Verde.**

If you have a car, you should continue driving south, exploring beaches as you go. You'll first come to **Dominicalito,** a small beach and cove that shelters the local fishing fleet and can be a decent place to swim. But I recommend you continue on a bit. You'll soon hit **Playa Hermosa,** a long stretch of desolate beach with fine sand. As in Dominical, this is unprotected and can be rough, but it's a nicer place to sunbathe and swim than Dominical.

Among the beaches you'll find further south are **Playa Ballena, Playa Uvita, Playa Piñuela, Playa Ventanas,** and **Playa Tortuga.** Of these, Playa Ballena and Playa Uvita (see "The Top Attractions" earlier in this section), are the best for swimming. Playa Piñuela is made up predominantly of large, smooth stones, especially near the high tide line. All of these beaches have an isolated and undiscovered feel to them.

Several of the beaches mentioned here are considered part of **Bahia Marine National Park** and charge an entrance fee of around $1 per person. If you're visiting several of these beaches in one day, save your ticket, it's good at all of them.

Shopping for local treasures

Aside from your standard souvenir shops, no notable shopping options stand out in this area.

Living it up after dark in Dominical

Nightlife options are extremely limited in Dominical, and virtually nonexistent south of Dominical. However, the young surfers who fill up this beach town do like to party, so the available bars are put to good use.

Most nights of the week, the **San Clemente Bar & Grill** (☎ 787-0055; located beside the soccer field, in the center of Dominical village) is the main meeting place and jumping-off point in town, while **Tortilla Flats** (no phone) serves the same purpose down on the beach.

Thrusters (☎ 787-0127; on the main road through the village, about 3 blocks south of the soccer field) is a popular surfer bar with pool tables and dartboards, located on the dirt road heading from the center of Dominical towards the beach. Further south, the bar and restaurant at **Hotel Roca Verde** (☎ 787-0036; 1km south of Dominical, just off the coastal highway) is one of the livelier places in town, with occasional live music.

Fast Facts: Dominical and the Beaches South of Dominical

Ambulance

Call ☎ 128.

ATMs

You'll only find one ATM in Dominical, located at the little shopping plaza adjacent to the San Clemente Bar & Grill (see earlier in this chapter).

Country Code and City Code

The country code for Costa Rica is **506.** Costa Rica doesn't use city or area codes. To call from the United States, dial 011-506 plus the seven-digit number. From within Costa Rica, simply dial the seven-digit number.

Currency Exchange

Dominical doesn't have any banks or money-exchange houses. Most hotels and restaurants will exchange money for you at decent rates.

Fire

Call ☎ 118.

Hospitals

The closest hospitals are Hospital Quepos (☎ 777-0922) and Hospital San Isidro (☎ 771-3122).

Information

Dominical doesn't have any official information offices, nor will you find any at the beaches south of Dominical. Most hotels have a tour desk, concierge, or helpful front desk.

Internet Access

Several Internet cafes are located in Dominical, as well as one in Bahia and another in Ojochal.

Newspapers

The hotels and shops in this area only carry the local papers, however this includes the

Tico Times. Also, keep an eye out for *Dominical Days,* a free monthly tourist publication that has a wealth of information and local advertising; it's available at a host of hotel lobbies, restaurants, and stores.

Pharmacies

Farmacia Dominical (☎ 787-0197) is a reasonably well-stocked pharmacy in the Pueblo del Río shopping center.

Police

Call ☎ 911 or 787-0011.

Post Office

No official post office is located in Dominical. However, a window at the San Clemente Bar & Grill (see "ATMs," earlier in this section) functions as one. In addition, most hotels can mail your letters and postcards for you.

Taxis

Taxis congregate around the soccer field in the center of Dominical. One reliable operator is Eric Marin (☎ 828-0786).

Part VI
Monteverde and Environs

"We're entering the Raincoat Forest. The Cloud Forest should be just ahead."

In this part . . .

Costa Rica offers much more than its coastal beaches. Much of the country's natural beauty can be found inland, in the Monteverde area. You'll find everything from active volcanoes and mystical cloud forests, to large inland lakes and pristine rivers and jungle waterfalls here. This is also the place to come for high-octane adventure, including mountain biking, canyoning, and riding zip-line canopy tours.

Monteverde, and the cloud forests around it, boast a distinct and unique beauty. The misty cloud forests here are home to the resplendent quetzal, one of the most stunning and revered birds of Mesoamerica. And Arenal volcano is one of Costa Rica's most mesmerizing sights. This active volcano regularly spews molten lava from its perfectly conical crater. At the foot of the volcano sits Lake Arenal, a mecca for windsurfers, kiteboarders, and bass fishermen alike.

Chapter 17

Visiting the Cloud Forests of Monteverde

*I*f you're looking for cool mountain air, a taste of rural Costa Rica, and the chance to visit a cloud forest, Monteverde is the place for you. *Monteverde* translates as "green mountain," and that's exactly what you'll find at the end of the steep and windy dirt road that leads here. Perched on a high mountain ridge, this small, scattered village and its surrounding cloud forests are well known among both scientific researchers and ecotravelers.

Monteverde was settled in 1951 by Quakers from the United States who wanted to leave behind the fear of war, as well as an obligation to support continued militarism through paying U.S. taxes. They chose Costa Rica, a country that had abolished its army just a few years earlier, in 1948.

Although Monteverde's founders came here primarily to farm the land, they wisely recognized the need to preserve the rare cloud forests that covered the mountain slopes above their fields, and to that end they dedicated the largest adjacent tract of cloud forest as the Monteverde Cloud Forest Reserve.

Cloud forests are a unique phenomenon. If you think about it, the name says it all. Rain forests get their name from the fact that they receive copious amounts of rainfall, often heavy at times. Cloud forests get their moisture — and their moniker — from being nearly constantly enveloped in a combination of mist and clouds. Cloud forests are formed when moist, warm air sweeping in off the ocean cools as it reaches the cooler temperatures of higher elevation, thus forming clouds.

This constant level of moisture has given rise to an incredible diversity of innovative life forms and a forest in which nearly every square inch of space has some sort of plant growth. Within the cloud forest, the branches of huge trees are draped with epiphytic plants: orchids, ferns, and bromeliads. This intense botanic competition has created an almost equally diverse population of insects, birds, and other wildlife.

Monteverde Cloud Forest Reserve covers 10,400 hectares (25,688 acres) of forest, including several different life zones that are characterized by different types of plants and animals. Within this small area are more than 2,500 species of plants, including 400 types of orchids, 400 species of birds, and 100 species of mammals. It's no wonder that the reserve has been the site of constant scientific investigations since its founding in 1972.

For many, the primary goal of a visit to Monteverde is a chance to glimpse the rare and elusive resplendent quetzal, a bird once revered by the pre-Columbian peoples of the Americas. This beautiful bird is a sight to see, with a bright red breast, iridescent blue-green back feathers, and, in the case of the males, tail feathers that can reach some 2 feet in length.

Getting There

There are no airstrips in or around Monteverde, so you have to arrive by some sort of vehicle. Given the lay of the land here, and the fact that various attractions and activities are spread out, I recommend driving your own rental car. However, bus service to Monteverde is available, and after you're there, taxis are available for getting around. These various options are described in more detail in the following sections.

By car

Take the Interamerican Highway north towards Nicaragua. About 20km (12 miles) past the turnoff for Puntarenas there will be a marked turnoff for Sardinal, Santa Elena, and Monteverde. From this turnoff, the road is paved almost as far as the tiny town of Guacimal. From here it's another 20km (12 miles) to Santa Elena. It should take you a little over two hours to reach the turnoff and another one and a half hours or so from there.

An alternative route is to continue on the Interamerican Highway until just before the Río Lagarto Bridge. This turnoff isn't always well marked. From the Río Lagarto turnoff, it's 38km (24 miles) to Santa Elena and Monteverde.

Whichever route you take, the final going is slow because the roads into Santa Elena are rough, unpaved dirt-and-gravel affairs. Many people are told that these roads are not passable without four-wheel-drive, but I've been driving them in regular cars for years, albeit in the dry season. Don't try it in the rainy season (mid-Apr–Nov) unless you have four-wheel-drive.

Taking a horse, boat, and taxi to La Fortuna, or vice versa

You can travel between Monteverde and La Fortuna by boat and taxi, or on a combination boat, horseback, and taxi trip. A 10- to 20-minute boat ride across Lake Arenal cuts over an hour or more of rough driving off the route circling it. It's about a one-and-a-half-hour four-wheel-drive taxi ride between Santa Elena and the Río Chiquito dock on the shores of Lake Arenal. It's just a 20-minute taxi ride from the dock on the other side and the city of La Fortuna. These trips can be arranged in either direction for between $20 and $35 per person, all-inclusive.

You can also add on a horseback ride on the Santa Elena/Monteverde side of the lake. Several routes and rides are offered. This is most commonly done in the direction of La Fortuna to Monteverde. The steepest route heads up the mountains and through the forest to the town of San Gerardo, which is only a 30-minute car ride from Santa Elena. Other routes throw in mellower and shorter sections of horseback riding along the lakeside lowlands. With the horseback ride, this trip runs around $55 to $65 per person.

The riding is sometimes rainy, muddy, and steep. Many find it much more arduous than awe-inspiring. Moreover, I've received numerous complaints about the condition of the trails and the treatment of the horses, so be very careful and demanding before signing on for this trip. Find out what route you will be taking, as well as the condition of the horses, if possible. **Desafío Expeditions** (☎ **645-5874** in Monteverde, or 479-9464 in La Fortuna; www.desafiocostarica.com) is one of the more reputable operators. They will even drive your car around for you while you take the scenic (and sore) route.

Just before you enter the town of Santa Elena, you'll be stopped at a little tollbooth collecting 200 colones. The money is ostensibly going to maintain the road, which is sort of ironic. Appropriately, the payment is optional.

By bus

Express buses (☎ **222-3854** in San José, or 645-5159 in Santa Elena) leave San José daily at 6:30 a.m. and 2:30 p.m. from Calle 12 between avenidas 7 and 9. The trip takes around four hours; the fare is $6. Buses arrive at and depart from Santa Elena; if you're staying at one of the hotels or lodges closer to the reserve, you'll want to arrange pickup if possible, or you'll have to take a taxi or local bus.

Grayline (☎ **220-2126**; www.graylinecostarica.com) and **Interbus** (☎ **283-5573**; www.costaricapass.com) both have regular service to Monteverde. The fare with Grayline is $38; with Interbus it is just $30. Another option is to take a **Costa Rica Expeditions** van (☎ **257-0766**; www.costaricaexpeditions.com) from San José; the fare is $40. Any of these companies will pick you up and drop you off at most

San José- and Monteverde-area hotels. Both **Grayline** and **Interbus** offer routes with connections to most major destinations in Costa Rica.

There is a daily bus from Tilarán (Lake Arenal) at 12:30 p.m. The trip duration, believe it or not, is two hours (for a 40km/25-mile trip); the fare is $2.

The express bus departs for San José daily at 6:30 a.m. and 2:30 p.m. Buses from Santa Elena to Puntarenas leave daily at 4:15 a.m. and 6 a.m. If you are heading to Jacó, Playa Herradura, or Manuel Antonio, take one of the Santa Elena/Puntarenas buses and transfer in Puntarenas for a bus down the coast to any of these destinations.

To reach Liberia, take any bus down the mountain and get off when you hit the Interamerican Highway. You can then flag down a bus bound for Liberia (almost any bus heading north). The Santa Elena–Tilarán bus leaves daily at 7 a.m.

Orienting Yourself in Monteverde

As you near the top of the local mountain, you'll approach the small village of **Santa Elena.** Take the right fork in the road if you're heading directly to Monteverde or the reserve.

If you continue straight, you'll hit the center of Santa Elena, which is centered around a block-long triangle of rugged streets. Here you'll find the bus stop, a health clinic, a bank, a small supermarket, a laundromat, and a few simple restaurants, budget hotels, souvenir shops, and tour offices.

A marked road heads out of Santa Elena toward the Monteverde Cloud Forest Reserve — where the road ends.

Monteverde is not a village in the traditional sense of the word. There's no center of town — only dirt lanes leading off from the main road to various farms, hotels, and attractions. This main road has signs for all the hotels and restaurants mentioned here.

You won't find any official tourist information offices in Santa Elena or Monteverde, although several tour-booking agencies masquerade as such. Most hotels have a knowledgeable front-desk staff, concierge, or in-house tour desk that can answer any questions. Also, keep an eye out for *Good Times,* a free local tourist paper that is loaded with information, articles, and advertisements.

Getting Around

There are two buses daily between the town of Santa Elena and the Monteverde Cloud Forest Reserve. The buses leave Santa Elena for the reserve at 6:15 a.m. and 1 p.m., returning at noon and 4 p.m. The fare is $1.50.

Monteverde

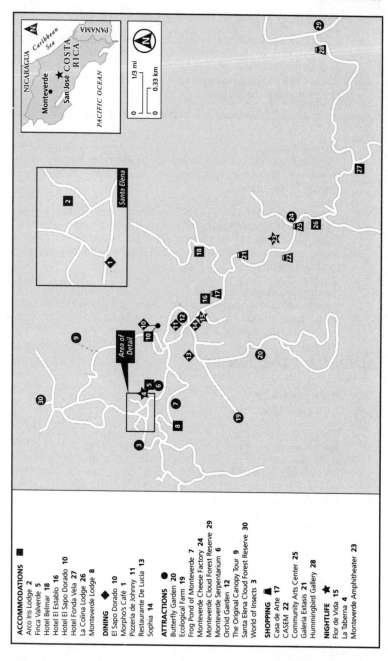

ACCOMMODATIONS ■
Arco Iris Lodge **2**
Finca Valverde **5**
Hotel Belmar **18**
Hotel El Establo **16**
Hotel El Sapo Dorado **10**
Hotel Fonda Vela **27**
La Colina Lodge **26**
Monteverde Lodge **8**

DINING ◆
El Sapo Dorado **10**
Morpho's Café **1**
Pizzeria de Johnny **11**
Restaurante De Lucia **13**
Sophia **14**

ATTRACTIONS ●
Butterfly Garden **20**
Ecological Farm **19**
Frog Pond of Monteverde **7**
Monteverde Cheese Factory **24**
Monteverde Cloud Forest Reserve **29**
Monteverde Serpentarium **6**
Orchid Garden **12**
The Original Canopy Tour **9**
Santa Elena Cloud Forest Reserve **30**
World of Insects **3**

SHOPPING ▲
Casa de Arte **17**
CASEM **22**
Community Arts Center **25**
Galeria Extasis **21**
Hummingbird Gallery **28**

NIGHTLIFE ★
Flor de Vida **15**
La Taberna **4**
Monteverde Amphitheater **23**

Reading up on the early Quaker settlers

If you want an in-depth look into the lives and history of the local Quaker community, try to pick up a copy of the *Monteverde Jubilee Family Album*. Published in 2001 by the Monteverde Association of Friends, this collection of oral histories and photographs is 260 pages of local lore and memoirs. Although it's very simply bound and printed, it's well worth the $20 price.

There's also periodic van transportation between the town of Santa Elena and the Santa Elena Cloud Forest Reserve. Ask around town, and you should be able to find the current schedule and book a ride for around $2 per person.

A taxi (☎ **645-6969** or 645-5148 for private operators) between Santa Elena and either the Monteverde Cloud Forest Reserve or the Santa Elena Cloud Forest Reserve costs around $8 for up to four people. Count on paying between $4 and $8 for the ride from Santa Elena to your lodge in Monteverde.

Finally, several places around town rent all-terrain vehicles (ATVs), for around $45 to $55 per day. Hourly rates and guided tours are also available. These vehicles are particularly well-suited to the roads up here.

Spending the Night

Arco Iris Lodge
$ Santa Elena

This is the nicest hotel right in Santa Elena, and it is a great value. The rooms are spread out in eight separate buildings (so, in effect, most are individual cabins). All have wood or tile floors and plenty of wood accents. My favorite is the "honeymoon cabin," which has its own private balcony with a forest view and good bird-watching. Budget travelers can stay in one of the two rooms here equipped with bunk beds (for $25 single, $32 double). The management here is helpful and can arrange a wide variety of tours. Although they don't serve lunch or dinner, there's a breakfast buffet for $6.50; beer, wine, and other refreshments are available throughout the day and evening.

See map p. 237. Santa Elena. ☎ *645-5067. Fax: 645-5022.* www.arcoirislodge. com. *Rack rates: $46–$63 double. AE, MC, V.*

Finca Valverde
$–$$ Just outside Santa Elena

This place is located right on the outskirts of Santa Elena, yet, when you head uphill to the rooms you'll feel far from the hustle and bustle of the tiny burg. The standard rooms are set behind the main lodge and restaurant and are reached via a small suspension bridge over a small forest creek. Most have one queen-size and two twin beds. All share a broad common veranda. The junior suites and cabins are larger, more private, and feature bathtubs. The junior suites are the highest up the hill and also have televisions, small refrigerators, and coffeemakers. The grounds are lush and well-tended. A buffet breakfast and all other meals are served in a large restaurant just off the lobby.

See map p. 237. Monteverde. ☎ *645-5157. Fax: 645-5216.* www.monteverde.co. cr. *Rack rates: $70–$85 double. Rates lower in the off season. MC, V.*

Hotel Belmar
$–$$ On the road to the Monteverde Cloud Forest Reserve

Set on the top of a grassy hill, the Belmar has stunning views of the Nicoya Gulf and the Pacific. Afternoons in the dining room or lounge are idyllic, with bright sunlight streaming in through a west-facing glass wall. Sunsets are spectacular. Most of the guest rooms are fitted with wood paneling, French doors, and little balconies that open onto splendid views. There are actually two buildings here. My favorite rooms are in the main building; those in the Swiss chalet–style building are a bit smaller. The restaurant serves a mix of well-prepared Tico and international cuisine. The Belmar is up a dirt road that passes to the left of the gas station as you come into the village of Monteverde.

See map p. 237. Monteverde. ☎ *645-5201. Fax: 645-5135.* www.hotelbelmar.net. *Rack rates: $70–$80 double. Rates lower in the off season. V.*

Hotel El Establo
$–$$$ On the road to the Monteverde Cloud Forest Reserve

From a working stable with a few budget rooms, this hotel has morphed into what could prove to be the most luxurious and comfortable hotel in Monteverde. The original budget rooms still stand down by the road, while a massive block of newer suites is located a couple hundred meters inland and up a steep hill, giving them all great views. Each of these rooms is quite large and has a private balcony or patio, a tub, and a separate shower. The large and luxurious honeymoon suite has a fabulous view and private Jacuzzi. All rooms come with cable television, a rarity in Monteverde. Up by the new wing, you'll find a pretty good-sized heated swimming pool and sauna.

See map p. 237. Monteverde. ☎ *645-5110. Fax: 645-5041.* www.hotelelestablo. com. *Rack rates: $70 standard double; $126–$181 suite; $210 honeymoon suite. Rates include breakfast. AE, MC, V.*

Hotel El Sapo Dorado
$$ Just outside of Santa Elena

Located on a steep hill between Santa Elena and the reserve, El Sapo Dorado offers some of the most charming and comfortable accommodations in Monteverde. The spacious cabins are built of hardwoods both inside and out and are surrounded by a grassy lawn. Big windows let in lots of light, and high ceilings keep the rooms cool during the day. Some of the older cabins have fireplaces, which are a welcome feature on chilly nights and during the peak parts of the rainy season. My favorite rooms are the sunset suites, which have private terraces with views of the Nicoya Gulf and wonderful sunsets.

Not only does El Sapo Dorado own and manage the nearby **Reserva Sendero Tranquilo** (see later in this chapter), but it also has a network of well-maintained trails into primary forest on-site. To find the hotel and restaurant, watch for the sign on the left-hand side of the main road to the reserve, a few hundred yards outside of the town of Santa Elena.

See map p. 237. Monteverde. ☎ *645-5010. Fax: 645-5180.* www.sapodorado.com. *Rack rates: $89–$99 double. MC, V.*

Hotel Fonda Vela
$$ Monteverde, close to the reserve entrance

This is one of the closer lodges to the Cloud Forest Reserve, an easy 15-minute walk away. And, although it's one of the older hotels here, Fonda Vela is still one of the best choices in Monteverde. Guest rooms are housed in various buildings scattered among the forests and pastures of this former farm. Most have views of the Nicoya Gulf. The newer junior suites, some of which have excellent views, are the best rooms in the house, and I prefer them to the older and larger junior suites. All junior suites come with cable television. The dining room has great sunset views, and it sometimes even features live music. Throughout the hotel, you'll see paintings by co-owner Paul Smith, who also handcrafts violins and cellos and is a musician himself.

See map p. 237. Monteverde. ☎ *257-1413 or 645-5125. Fax: 257-1416.* www.fondavela.com. *Rack rates: $94 double; $112 junior suite. AE, MC, V.*

La Colina Lodge
$ Monteverde, close to the reserve entrance

Formerly the Flor Mar Pension, this is another of the older lodges in Monteverde. It has changed hands a couple of times in recent years and gotten some much-needed attention and renovation. The rooms are housed in two separate buildings. Everything is very basic here but quite clean and comfortable. The general ambience and individual rooms are more appealing than those found in most other budget options. Most rooms have one double and one single bed, although a couple still have bunk beds.

Staying at the reserve

If you don't mind roughing it, you can stay in a simple dormitory room right at the **Monteverde Biological Cloud Forest Reserve** (☎ 645-5122; www.cct.or.cr). This is a good way to meet any visiting scientists and get friendly with the local guides and workers. A bunk bed and three meals per day here run $24 per person. Admission to the reserve is still extra.

The restaurant area is warm and cozy, with a big fireplace, and there's a separate common lounge area with satellite television. Service is friendly and attentive, and they even allow camping here, with access to the shared bathrooms. The lodge is pretty close to the reserve, which is a plus for budget travelers without a car.

See map p. 237. Monteverde. ☎ *645-5009. Fax: 645-5580.* www.lacolina lodge.com. *Rack rates: $38 double with shared bathroom; $45 double with private bathroom; $5 per person camping. Rates include full breakfast except for campers. V.*

Monteverde Lodge
$$ Just outside of Santa Elena

The Monteverde Lodge was one of the first true ecolodges to open in Monteverde, and it remains one of the best. Guest rooms are large and comfortable and thanks to a recent remodeling are some of the most modern in town. Most feature angled walls of glass with chairs and a table placed so that avid bird-watchers can do a bit of birding without leaving their rooms.

The gardens and secondary forest surrounding the lodge have some gentle groomed trails and are also home to quite a few species of birds. Perhaps the lodge's most popular attraction is the large hot tub in a big atrium garden just off the lobby. After hiking all day, you can soak your bones under the stars.

The hotel's dining room offers great views, good food, and excellent formal service provided by bow-tied waiters. The adjacent bar is a popular gathering spot and is the setting for regular evening slide shows focusing on the cloud forest. The excellent guides who work for the owner, Costa Rica Expeditions, have lots of experience with family groups.

See map p. 237. Monteverde. ☎ *257-0766 reservations in San José, or 645-5057 at the lodge. Fax: 257-1665.* www.costaricaexpeditions.com. *Rack rates: $109 double. Rates slightly lower in the off season. AE, MC, V.*

Dining Locally

El Sapo Dorado
$$ Just outside of Santa Elena   INTERNATIONAL

Located high on a hill above the main road, El Sapo Dorado offers up great sunsets and delicious food. The regularly changing menu might include grilled corvina in heart-of-palm sauce, shrimp in a Sambucca mushroom sauce, or filet mignon in pepper-cream sauce. The emphasis is on fresh ingredients and healthy preparation, and vegetarian and vegan options are always available to choose from. If you come for lunch or a sunset dinner, definitely grab a table in the large, covered dining room, which has full walls of picture windows for taking in the views, or, weather permitting, on their outdoor terrace.

See map p. 237. On the left as you go from Santa Elena toward the reserve. ☎ *645-5010. Reservations recommended during high season. Main courses: $9–$20. AE, MC, V. Open: Daily 7–10 a.m., noon to 3 p.m., and 6–9 p.m.*

Morpho's Café
$ Downtown Santa Elena   COSTA RICAN/INTERNATIONAL

Easily the most popular restaurant in the town of Santa Elena, this simple second-floor affair serves up hearty and economical meals. You'll find soups, sandwiches, and *casados* (plates of the day) for lunch and dinner, and delicious fresh fruit juices, ice-cream shakes, and home-baked desserts throughout the day. The tables and chairs are made from rough-hewn lumber and whole branches and trunks, and the place brims with a light convivial atmosphere. This place is a very popular hangout for backpackers and budget travelers.

See map p. 237. In downtown Santa Elena, across from the supermarket. ☎ *645-5607. Main courses: $3–$9. MC, V. Open: Daily 11 a.m.–10 p.m.*

Pizzería de Johnny
$$ Just outside of Santa Elena   ITALIAN/PIZZA

This perennially popular pizza joint has grown from a little hole-in-the-wall to a downright institution here in Monteverde. The thin-crust wood-oven pizzas are delicious, and there's a large menu of meat, chicken, and pasta dishes as well. You can start things off with a bruschetta or mussels Parmesan. The signature pizza Traviesa comes with artichoke hearts, onions, mushrooms, garlic, and marinated tomatoes. There's a little gift shop and a quiet bar off the large open dining room. The nicest tables are on the covered veranda out back.

See map p. 237. On the road to the reserve, on your right, just beyond El Sapo Dorado. ☎ *645-5066. Reservations recommended during high season. Small pizzas $4–$7, medium pies $8–$14, large pies $14–$22; other main courses $5–$14. MC, V. Open: Daily 11 a.m.–10 p.m.*

Taking a coffee break

Monteverde and Santa Elena sit in the heart of some prime coffee-growing lands. The area boasts several local coffeehouses where you can sit and enjoy a cup of some locally grown and roasted beans. Moreover, the frequently wet and misty climate here makes this an even more atttractive option.

In Santa Elena, **Rain Forest Café** (☎ 645-5841) is a delightlful spot with organic and fair-trade coffee for sale and served up in a variety of forms. Along the road to the reserve, **Flor de Vida** (☎ 645-6081) is a cheery little joint, with a variety of fresh baked goods.

Restaurante De Lucía
$$ **Monteverde   COSTA RICAN/INTERNATIONAL**

There's really not much of a menu here. But after you sit down, your waiter will bring out a platter with the nightly selection of meats and fresh fish, which are then grilled to order. One of the more interesting dishes is the chicken in orange sauce. All meals come with fresh homemade tortillas and a full accompaniment of side orders and vegetables. The sweet *plátanos* prepared on the open grill are delicious. Service is informal and friendly. Heavy wood tables and chairs are spread comfortably around the large dining room.

See map p. 237. On the road down to the Butterfly Farm, on your right. ☎ *645-5337. Reservations recommended during high season. Main courses: $8–$14. AE, MC, V. Open: Daily 7 a.m.–9 p.m.*

Sophia
$$ **Monteverde   COSTA RICAN/FUSION**

This new-in-2004 restaurant is the most exciting and eclectic dining option in the Monteverde area. Start everything off with a mango-ginger mojito and then try one of their colorful and abundant salads. Main courses range from seafood chimichangas to chicken breast served in a guava reduction. The tenderloin comes with a chipotle butter sauce over a bed of mashed sweet potato. Everything is very well prepared and reasonably priced. You'll find two good-sized dining rooms here, both with heavy wood furniture. The best seats are close to the large arched picture windows overlooking the neighboring forest and gardens.

See map p. 237. Cerro Plano, just past the turnoff to the Butterfly Farm, on your left. ☎ *645-7017. Reservations recommended during high season. Main courses: $7.50–$10. MC, V. Open: Daily 11:30 a.m.–9 p.m.*

Exploring Monteverde

Monteverde has an abundance of attractions and activities. All the hotels and lodges in this area offer or can book all the tours and activities listed in this section. If you have your own vehicle, you can also visit all these attractions on your own.

The top attractions

Monteverde Cloud Forest Reserve

The Monteverde Cloud Forest Reserve is one of the most developed and well-maintained natural attractions in Costa Rica. The trails are clearly marked, regularly traveled, and generally gentle in terms of ascents and descents.

The cloud forest here is lush and largely untouched. Still, keep in mind that most of the birds and mammals you've been reading about are rare, elusive, and nocturnal. Moreover, to all but the most trained of eyes, those thousands of exotic ferns, orchids, and bromeliads tend to blend into one large mass of indistinguishable green.

Perhaps the most famous resident of the cloud forests of Costa Rica is the resplendent quetzal, a robin-size bird with iridescent green wings and a ruby-red breast. The male quetzal also has two long tail feathers that can reach nearly 0.6m (2 ft.) in length, making it one of the most spectacular birds on earth. The best time to see quetzals is early morning to mid-morning, and the best months are February through April, when the birds are mating.

After the quetzal, Monteverde's most famous resident was the golden toad (*sapo dorado*), a rare native species. However, the golden toad has recently disappeared from the forest and is feared extinct. Competing theories of the toad's demise include adverse effects of a natural drought cycle, the disappearing ozone layer, pesticides, and acid rain.

Other animals that have been seen in Monteverde, although sightings are extremely rare, include jaguars, ocelots, and tapirs. However, you do have a good chance of seeing one of several different monkey species and an almost innumerable number of bird species.

I highly recommend taking one of the reserve's official guided two- to three-hour hikes; you can see and learn far more than you could on your own. At $15 per person, the reserve's tours may seem like a splurge, especially after you pay the entrance fee, but unless you have a lot of experience in the Neotropical forests, it will be money well spent.

Before venturing off on your tour or self-guided hike, have a look around the information center. Several guidebooks are available here, as well as posters and postcards of some of the reserve's more famous animal inhabitants.

Because only 120 people are allowed into the reserve at any one time, you may be forced to wait for a while before entering. Most hotels can reserve a guided walk and entrance to the reserve for the following day for you, or you can get tickets in advance directly at the reserve entrance.

Some of the trails here can be very muddy, depending on the season, so ask about current conditions. If the mud is heavy, you can rent rubber boots at the reserve entrance for $2 per day. They may make your hike much more pleasant.

Night tours of the reserve leave every evening at 7:15 p.m. The cost is $13 per person, including admission to the reserve, a two-hour hike, and, most important, a guide with a high-powered searchlight. For an extra $2, they'll throw in round-trip transportation to and from your area hotel.

See map p. 237. Located at the end of the dirt road 6km (3¾ miles) from Santa Elena. ☎ *645-5122.* www.cct.or.cr. *Admission: $12 adults, $6 students and children; $15 per person for a guided tour; $13 for night tour. Open: Daily 7 a.m.–4 p.m. and 7:15–9 p.m.*

Santa Elena Cloud Forest Reserve

Although the Monteverde Cloud Forest Reserve is the area's most famous and popular attraction, plenty of other areas of cloud forest lie in this region. The **Santa Elena Cloud Forest Reserve** is a 360-hectare (889-acre) reserve located 5km (3 miles) north of the village of Santa Elena. This reserve has a maximum elevation of 1,680m (5,510 ft.), which makes it the highest cloud forest in the Monteverde area.

You'll find 13km (8 miles) of hiking trails, as well as an information center here. Because it borders the Monteverde Reserve, you can find a similar richness of flora and fauna, although quetzal sightings are not nearly as common. The $8 entry fee at this reserve goes directly to support local schools.

See map p. 237. Located 5km (3 miles) northeast of Santa Elena. ☎ *645-5390. Admission: $8; $15 additional for a three-hour guided tour. Open: 7 a.m.–4 p.m., with night tours starting at 7 p.m.*

Getting the most out of a visit to the reserve

Because the entrance fee to the Monteverde Cloud Forest Reserve is valid for a full day, I recommend taking an early-morning tour with a guide and then heading off on your own either directly after that hike or after lunch. A guide will point out and explain a lot, and you're almost assured of seeing more wildlife with a guide. But there's also much to be said for walking quietly through the forest on your own or in very small groups. This will also allow you to stray from the more popular paths in the park.

Other attractions in Monteverde

The **Butterfly Garden** (☎ 645-5512) displays many of Costa Rica's most beautiful butterfly species. Besides the hundreds of preserved and mounted butterflies, you'll find a garden and a greenhouse where you can watch live butterflies, as well as an informative guided tour that takes you through the life cycle of this fascinating insect. The garden is located near the end of the Cerro Plano road and is open daily from 9:30 a.m. to 4 p.m. Admission is $8 for adults and $6 for students and children, including a guided tour. The best time to visit is between 9:30 a.m. and 1 p.m., when the butterflies are most active.

If your taste runs toward the slithery, you can check out the **Monteverde Serpentarium** (☎ 645-5238; www.snaketour.com), on the road to the reserve. This place features a broad selection of reptiles, including many species of venomous and nonvenomous snakes. It's open daily from 9 a.m. to 8 p.m. and charges $7 for admission.

The **Frog Pond of Monteverde** (☎ 645-6320; www.ranario.com), located a couple of hundred meters north of the Monteverde Lodge, is probably a better bet. The $8 entrance gets you a 45-minute tour, and your ticket is good for two days. A variety of species populate a series of glass terrariums. This place is open daily from 8 a.m. to 8 p.m. If you visit first during the daytime, I recommend that you stop by at least once after dark, when the various tree frogs are active.

Another entry in this field is the **World of Insects** (☎ 645-6859), which features a couple dozen terrariums filled with some of the area's more interesting creepy crawlers. My favorites are the giant horned beetles. This place is located 300m (984 ft.) west of the supermarket in Santa Elena. It's open daily from 8 a.m. to 9 p.m.; admission is $7.

If you've had your fill of birds, snakes, frogs, bugs, and butterflies, you may want to stop at the **Orchid Garden** (☎ 645-5510), on the main road toward the reserve. This small botanical garden boasts more than 400 species of orchids. Admission is $5 for adults and $3 for students. It's open daily from 8 a.m. to 5 p.m.

Finally, it's also worth stopping by the **Monteverde Cheese Factory** (no phone) to savor some homemade ice cream and to pick up some of the best cheese in Costa Rica. From the little store here, you can watch the process in action. The cheese factory is located right on the main road about midway between Santa Elena and the Reserve. It's open Monday through Saturday from 7:30 a.m. to 4 p.m., and Sunday from 7:30 a.m. to noon.

Canopy tours, suspended bridges, and canyoning

You have several zip-line canopy tour options to choose from in this area. I list them here in my order of preference. The final listing is for a canyoning adventure, which is a much different, more adventurous experience.

Anybody in average physical condition can do any of the adventure tours in Monteverde, but they're not for the faint-hearted or acrophobic. Try to book directly with the companies listed here or through your hotel. Beware of agents working the streets of Monteverde, who make a small commission and frequently try to steer tourists to the operator paying the highest percentage.

One of the oldest and best canopy tours in the country is run by **The Original Canopy Tour** (☎ 645-5243; www.canopytour.com), which has an office right in the center of Santa Elena. This is one of the more interesting canopy tours in Costa Rica because you'll climb up the hollowed-out interior of a giant strangler fig during your initial ascent. This tour also has 11 platforms and 2 rappels, making it the most adventurous canopy tour in Monteverde. The three-hour tours run three times daily and cost $45 for adults, $35 for students, and $25 for children under 12.

One of the newest additions to the canopy-tour field is **Selvatura Park** (☎ 645-5929; www.selvatura.com). The extensive canopy tour here features 15 cables connecting 18 platforms. The canopy tour costs $35; the walkways and bridges cost $15. A number of other attractions are also here, so various packages are available; see "Visiting the best one-stop adventure and activity spot," later in this chapter, for information.

The sister projects of **Sky Walk** and **Sky Trek** (☎ 645-5238; www.skytrek.com) combine a traditional canopy-tour attraction with a network of forest trails and suspension bridges. **Sky Trek** is one of the more extensive canopy tours in the country, with two very long cables to cross. The longest of these is some 770m (2,525 ft.) long, high above the forest floor. There are no rappel descents here, and you brake using the pulley system for friction. This tour costs $40.

Visiting the best one-stop adventure and activity spot

Selvatura Park (☎ 645-5929; www.selvatura.com) is the best one-stop shop for various adventures and attractions in the area. In addition to its extensive canopy tour, they also have a network of trails and suspended bridges, as well as a huge butterfly garden, hummingbird garden, and wonderful insect display and museum. Prices vary depending upon how much you want to see and do. Individually, the canopy tour costs $35; the walkways and bridges, $15; the butterfly garden, $10; and the insect museum, $10. Various packages are available. It's open daily 8 a.m. to 4 p.m.

Enjoying the sounds of music

Each year, throughout much of the high season, the **Monteverde Institute** (☎ **645-5053;** www.mvinstitute.org) hosts the annual **Monteverde Music Festival.** There's a different concert every Thursday, Friday, and Saturday evening. Featuring mostly Costa Rican groups, the repertoire ranges from folk to jazz to classical. Admission is $10 for adults and $5 for students.

Sky Walk features a loop trail through primary and secondary forest, with a series of bridges spanning large canyons and ravines. The bridges reach 39m (128 ft.) above the ground at their highest point. The Sky Walk is open daily from 7 a.m. to 4 p.m. Admission is $15 and no reservation is necessary. For an extra $10, a knowledgeable guide will point out the diverse flora and fauna on the walk.

For $45 per person, you can do the Sky Trek canopy tour and then walk the trails and bridges of the Sky Walk. Reservations are recommended for the Sky Trek part of the excursion.

Sky Walk and Sky Trek are located about 3.5km (2¼ miles) outside of the town of Santa Elena, on the road to the Santa Elena Cloud Forest Reserve. These folks will provide round-trip transportation from Santa Elena for just $2 per person.

Finally, your most adventurous option is to take a **canyoning** tour with the folks at **Desafío Adventures** (☎ **645-5874;** www.monteverdetours. com). This half-day tour ($55) is a mix of hiking down a mountain gorge and rappelling down the faces of a series of waterfalls. The largest of these waterfalls are around 18m (60 ft.) in height. Be prepared to get wet on this tour.

More cool things to see and do

✔ **Hiking:** In addition to hiking in cloud forests, you can hike the trails and grounds of the **Ecological Farm** (☎ **645-5554;** www. fincaecologicamonteverde.com), a family-run wildlife refuge and private reserve located down the Cerro Plano road. This place has four main trails, which run through a variety of ecosystems. Because some of the farm is secondary forest and some is cleared land, the wildlife viewing is often quite good here. In fact, the wildlife viewing is often better than that in Monteverde Cloud Forest Reserve and Santa Elena Cloud Forest Reserve. There are a couple of pretty waterfalls off the trails, and night tours are also offered. The Ecological Farm is open daily from 7 a.m. to 5 p.m.; admission is $7.

The **Bajo del Tigre Trail** (☎ 645-5003; www.acmcr.org) is a 3.5km (2¼-mile) trail that's home to several different bird species not usually found within the reserve. You can take several different loops, lasting anywhere from one hour to several hours. The trail starts a little past the CASEM artisans' shop and is open daily from 8 a.m. to 5 p.m. Admission is $5 adults and $2 for students and children.

You can also go on guided three-hour hikes at the **Reserva Sendero Tranquilo** (☎ 645-5010), which has 80 hectares (198 acres) of land, two-thirds of which is in virgin forest. This reserve is located up the hill from the cheese factory. It charges $20 for its tours and is open daily from 7 a.m. to 3 p.m. seasonally.

✔ **Horseback riding:** The rugged dirt roads, untouched forests, and pasturelands surrounding the protected reserves here provide excellent opportunities for getting in the saddle. **Meg's Riding Stables** (☎ 645-5560), **La Estrella Stables** (☎ 645-5075), **Palomina Horse Tours** (☎ 645-5479), and **Sabine's Smiling Horses** (☎ 645-5051; www.horseback-riding-tour.com) are the most established operators, offering guided rides for around $10 per hour.

Another option is to set up a day tour and sauna at **El Sol** (☎ 645-5838; www.elsolnuestro.com). Located about a ten-minute car ride down the mountain from Santa Elena, these folks take you on a roughly three-hour ride either to San Luis or to an isolated little waterfall with an excellent swimming hole. After the ride back, you'll find the wood-burning traditional Swedish sauna all fired up, with a refreshing and beautiful little pool beside it. The tour costs around $50 per person, including lunch. These folks also have two very rustically luxurious private cabins ($60–$80 double), with excellent views.

✔ **Learning Spanish:** The **Centro Panamericano de Idiomas** (☎ 645-5441; www.spanishlanguageschool.com) offers immersion language classes in a wonderful setting. A one-week program, with four hours of class per day and a home-stay with a Costa Rican family, costs $365.

Shopping for Local Treasures

Monteverde may just be one of the best tourist destinations in Costa Rica for shopping. Several good art galleries and gift shops rest in the area, and even the locally produced crafts are of a higher quality than in most of the rest of the country.

Perhaps the best-stocked gift shop in Monteverde is the **Hummingbird Gallery** (☎ 645-5030). You'll find the gallery just outside the reserve entrance. Hanging from trees around it are a series of hummingbird feeders that attract more than seven distinct species of these hyperactive little birds. At any given moment, there might be several dozen hummingbirds buzzing and chattering around the building and your head. Inside you will, of course, find a lot of beautiful color prints of hummingbirds and other local flora and fauna, as well as a wide range of craft items, T-shirts, and other gifts.

Another good option is **CASEM** (☎ 645-5190). This craft cooperative sells embroidered clothing, T-shirts, posters, and postcards with photos of the local flora and fauna, Boruca weavings, locally grown and roasted coffee, and many other items to remind you of your visit to Monteverde. CASEM is located about halfway along the road between Santa Elena and the reserve.

Over the years, Monteverde has developed a thriving little community of artists. Around town, you'll see paintings by local artists such as Paul Smith and Meg Wallace, among others. You may also check out **Galería Extasis** (☎ 645-5548), which sells the intriguing wooden sculptures of artist Marco Tulio Brenes, or the new **Casa de Arte** (☎ 645-5275), which has a mix of arts and crafts in many media. Casa de Arte is located on the road between Santa Elena and the reserve, while Galería Extasis is a short ride down a dirt driveway just off this road. You'll see their sign pointing out at the turnoff.

Another good place to visit is the **Community Arts Center** (☎ 645-6121). In addition to studio space, where classes and workshops are regularly held, there's a well-stocked gallery and gift shop here selling the work of local artists and artisans. You'll find this place just across from the Monteverde Cheese Factory.

Living It Up After Dark in Monteverde

The most popular after-dark activities in Monteverde are night hikes in one of the reserves and a natural-history slide show (see recommendations earlier in this chapter).

If you want a taste of the local party scene, head to **La Taberna** (☎ 645-5157), which is just outside of downtown Santa Elena before the Serpentarium. This place attracts a mix of locals and tourists, cranks its music loud, and often gets people dancing.

You'll certainly want to check whether any live music or another performance is on offer at the new **Monteverde Amphitheater** (☎ 645-6270), a beautiful open-air performance space, located up a steep driveway across from CASEM. However, be forewarned, the concrete seats here are uncomfortable; try to bring something soft to sit on. Alternatively, the **Flor de Vida** restaurant (☎ 645-6081) sometimes features live music or open-mic jam sessions.

Fast Facts: Monteverde

Ambulance

Call ☎ **128** or 645-6128.

ATMs

You'll find an ATM at the Banco Nacional in Santa Elena (☎ 645-5610).

Country Code and City Code

The country code for Costa Rica is **506**. There are no city or area codes within Costa Rica. To call from the United States, dial 011-506 plus the seven-digit number. From within Costa Rica, simply dial the seven-digit number.

Currency Exchange

Most hotels will exchange money for you at decent rates. To get official rates, head to the Banco Nacional in Santa Elena (☎ 645-5610).

Fire

Call ☎ 118.

Hospitals

Neither Santa Elena nor Monteverde has a hospital, although you will find a small medical clinic, Clinica Santa Elena, (☎ 645-5076), that can handle most emergencies.

Information

No official information offices are located in Santa Elena or Monteverde. Most hotels have a tour desk, concierge, or helpful front desk.

Internet Access

You'll find several Internet cafes in Santa Elena, as well as a few strung along the road to the Santa Elena Cloud Forest Reserve. Many hotels also have their own in-house Internet cafes or wireless service. Rates run between $1 and $3 per hour.

Newspapers

Several gift shops around town and various hotels can get you current or day-late editions of the *Miami Herald, New York Times,* or *USA Today,* as well as all the local papers, including the *Tico Times.* Also, keep an eye out for *Good Times,* a small tourist paper with some good information and local advertising.

Pharmacies

The Farmacia Monteverde (☎ 645-7110) is located in downtown Santa Elena and is fairly well-stocked.

Police

Call ☎ **911** or 645-5127.

Post Office

You'll find a post office in Santa Elena (☎ 645-5042). Alternatively, most hotels can mail your letters and postcards for you.

Taxis

Taxis are usually available in Santa Elena and around Monteverde. If you don't feel like flagging one down on the street, have your hotel call for you or dial ☎ 645-6969 or 645-5148 for two reliable, private operators.

Chapter 18

La Fortuna and the Arenal Area

• •

In This Chapter

▶ Getting to and around La Fortuna and the Arenal volcano
▶ Deciding where to stay and dine near the Arenal volcano
▶ Enjoying the volcano viewing, hot springs, and other attractions of this area
▶ Having fun and adventures on the shores of Lake Arenal
▶ Buying arts and crafts at a couple of excellent lakeside shops

• •

*A*nchoring the north-central zone of Costa Rica, Arenal volcano and Lake Arenal are two of the country's most striking natural attractions. In fact, the entire area is a naturalist's dream come true. In addition to the volcano and lake, you'll find rain forests, jungle rivers and waterfalls, smaller mountain lakes, hot springs, and an unbelievable wealth of birds and other wildlife. Small, classy, isolated lodges abound, and the sheer diversity of terrain, flora, and fauna is astounding.

If just enjoying the natural beauty and wonders of this area isn't enough, you'll also find ample opportunities to engage in a wealth of exciting adventure sports and tours.

La Fortuna and the Arenal Volcano

If you've never experienced them firsthand, the sights and sounds of an active volcano erupting are awesome. **Arenal volcano** is one of the world's most regularly active volcanoes. Frequent powerful explosions send cascades of red-hot lava rocks tumbling down the western slope, and the lava flows steam and rumble. Although this is all very impressive during the day, at night the volcano puts on its most mesmerizing show. If you're lucky enough to be here on a clear and active night, you'll see the night sky turned red by lava spewing from Arenal's crater and watch the glowing lava flows stream down its flanks.

Rising in a near perfect cone, the 1,607m (5,271-ft.) Arenal volcano lay dormant for hundreds of years until July 1968, when a sudden eruption leveled the former town of Tabacón and killed almost 80 of its inhabitants.

Lying at the eastern foot of Arenal volcano is the small rural community of **La Fortuna.** This town has become a magnet for volcano watchers from around the world. You'll find a host of hotels and restaurants in and near La Fortuna, and from here you can arrange night tours to the best volcano-viewing spots, which are 17km (11 miles) away on the western slope, on the road to and beyond Tabacón Hot Springs.

Getting there

This area is best visited in a four-wheel-drive rental car. Although bus transportation to the area is available, the freedom of having your own car really pays dividends. However, the easiest and quickest way to visit the area is to take a commuter plane to La Fortuna and then rent a car after you're in town. You'll find details on all these options in the following sections.

By plane

Nature Air (☎ 800-235-9272 in the United States and Canada, or 299-6000 in Costa Rica; www.natureair.com) flies to Arenal/La Fortuna daily at 11:40 a.m. from Tobías Bolaños International Airport in Pavas. Return flights depart for San José at 12:20 p.m. The flight duration is 30 minutes; the fare is $65 each way.

By car

You can take several routes to La Fortuna from San José. The most popular is to head west on the Interamerican Highway and then turn north at Naranjo, continuing north through Zarcero to Ciudad Quesada. From Ciudad Quesada, one route goes through Jabillos, while the other goes through Muelle. The former route is better marked, more popular, slightly shorter, and generally better maintained, but the severe weather and heavy traffic quickly take their toll, and the roads up here can be notoriously bad for long stretches. This route offers wonderful views of the San Carlos Valley as you come down from Ciudad Quesada, and Zarcero, with its topiary gardens and quaint church, makes a good place to stop, stretch your legs, and snap a few photos.

You can also stay on the Interamerican Highway until San Ramón (west of Naranjo) and then head north through La Tigra. This route is also very scenic and passes the hotels Villablanca and Valle Escondido.

The travel time on any of these routes is between three and four hours.

Finally, if you're combining your visit here with a stop at the Poás volcano and La Paz waterfall, or a stay at Peace Lodge (see later in this chapter), you can go first to Alajuela or Heredia and then head north to Varablanca before continuing on to San Miguel, where you turn west toward Río Cuarto and Aguas Zarcas. From Aguas Zarcas, continue west through Muelle to the turnoff for La Fortuna. This is the longest route, and it's only really worthwhile if you combine it with visits to the attractions listed in the preceding paragraphs.

By bus

If the timing is right, you'll want to take a bus going straight on through to La Fortuna. Direct buses (☎ 255-4318) leave San José for La Fortuna roughly every two hours between 6 a.m. and 5:30 p.m. from the **Atlántico del Norte** bus station at Avenida 9 and Calle 12. The trip takes four and a half hours. The fare is $3.

Some of the direct buses to La Fortuna will be labeled "Tilarán" buses; others will be labeled just "La Fortuna." All of these buses leave from the same terminal. There are two routes to Tilarán: one via Ciudad Quesada and La Fortuna, the other via the Interamerican Highway and Cañas. If you take a bus labeled "Tilarán," be sure to ask the driver beforehand if it passes through Ciudad Quesada. If it doesn't, you'll end up in Tilarán via the Interamerican Highway, a long way from La Fortuna.

However, if there's a long wait until the next direct bus, taking a bus first to Ciudad Quesada and then transferring will get you to La Fortuna quicker. These buses depart roughly every hour between 5 a.m. and 7:30 p.m. The fare for the two-and-a-half-hour trip is $2.50. Local buses between Ciudad Quesada and La Fortuna run regularly through the day, although the schedule changes frequently, depending on demand. The trip lasts one hour; the fare is $1.50.

A bus departs **Monteverde** and **Santa Elena** for Tilarán every day at 7 a.m. This is a journey of only 35km (22 miles), but the trip lasts two and a half hours because the road is in such horrendous condition. People with bad backs should think twice about making this trip, especially by bus. The return bus from Tilarán to Santa Elena leaves at 12:30 p.m. The fare is $2.

Buses from Tilarán to La Fortuna depart daily at 7 a.m. and 12:30 p.m. (hence, a person coming from Monteverde would have to wait for the 12:30 p.m. bus) and make the return trip at 8 a.m. and 2:30 p.m. The trip is three to four hours. The fare is $2.50.

Buses depart La Fortuna for San José roughly every two hours between 5 a.m. and 5:30 p.m. In some instances, you may have to transfer in Ciudad Quesada; from there, you can catch one of the frequent buses to San José.

Grayline (☎ 220-2126; www.graylinecostarica.com) has a daily bus that leaves San José for La Fortuna at 8 a.m.; the fare is $25. **Interbus** (☎ 283-5573; www.costaricapass.com) has two buses daily leaving San José for La Fortuna at 8 a.m. and 1 p.m., also for $25. Both companies will pick you up at most San José–area hotels, and they also run routes from La Fortuna with connections to most other major destinations in Costa Rica.

For information on taxi, boat, and horseback transfers between La Fortuna and Monteverde, see Chapter 17.

Orienting yourself in La Fortuna and around the volcano

As you enter La Fortuna, you'll see the massive volcano directly in front of you. La Fortuna is only a few streets wide, with almost all the hotels, restaurants, and shops clustered along the main road that leads out of town toward Tabacón and the volcano. You'll find several tour-booking offices, and Internet cafés, as well as a Laundromat, on the streets that surround the small central park that fronts the Catholic church, La Iglesia de La Fortuna.

From the center of La Fortuna, a road heads toward Lake Arenal. This road passes first through Tabacón and then by the entrance to Arenal National Park, before crossing the dam over Lake Arenal and continuing on around the lake to Nuevo Arenal and Tilarán.

 Many of the hotels with the best views of the Arenal volcano are located along the section of this road between La Fortuna and the Tabacón Hot Springs.

Getting around

Tons of taxis can be found in La Fortuna (you can flag one down practically anywhere), and there is always a line of them ready and waiting along the main road beside the central park. A taxi between La Fortuna and Tabacón should cost around $5. Call Arenal Taxi at ☎ **479-8522** or **479-9605.**

Another alternative is to rent a car when you get here. **Alamo** (☎ **479-9090;** www.alamo.com) and **Poás** (☎ **479-9400;** www.carentals.com) both have offices in La Fortuna.

You'll also find several places to rent scooters around town. As long as it's not raining too heavily, this is a good way to get around. Rates run around $35 to $45 per day.

 If you don't have a car, you'll need to either take a cab or go on an organized tour if you want to visit the hot springs or view the volcano's eruptions.

No official information offices are in this area, although many of the local gift shops and tour agencies advertise themselves as such. Your hotel tour desk, concierge, or front desk will probably be your best source of information (besides this book, of course).

Spending the night

Arenal Lodge
$$ Near Lake Arenal

Located high on a hillside above Lake Arenal, this lodge has a direct view of Arenal volcano over a forested valley. Although it's not as close to the volcano as some of the other lodges mentioned in this section, the view is still stunning. The standard rooms, while attractively decorated, have no views at all. The best rooms here are the junior suites, which have two queen-size beds, balconies, large picture windows, and lots of space. The matrimonial suite comes with its own private Jacuzzi. Five separate buildings on a hill behind the main building house the ten chalet rooms; these rooms all have plenty of space, small kitchenettes, and good views from their balconies or patios, although they feel too spartan for my taste.

Common areas here include a well-stocked library, where there's a huge stone fireplace and a pool table. A separate lounge has a TV and VCR — there are no televisions in the rooms. There's also a large outdoor Jacuzzi.

See map p. 257. Just over the dam on Lake Arenal. ☎ 253-5080 in San José, or 460-1881 at the lodge. Fax: 253-5016. www.arenallodge.com. *Rack rates: $71 double; $119–$149 suites and chalet rooms. Rates include buffet breakfast and mountain-bike tour. AE, MC, V.*

Arenal Observatory Lodge
$–$$ On the flanks of Arenal volcano

This hotel is built on a high ridge with a spectacular view of the volcano's cone. Rooms come in a variety of shapes and sizes, and in a variety of locations around the lodge's expansive grounds. The best rooms here are the five junior suites built below the restaurant and main lodge, as well as the four rooms in the Observatory Block, and the new White Hawk villa. The "Smithsonian" rooms feature massive picture windows, with a direct view of the volcano. The standard rooms are simple and rustic affairs with no volcano views, and the most basic rooms are housed in the original *casona* (big house) and are located about 500m (1,640 ft.) from the main lodge.

This is one of the better nature lodges for travelers with disabilities, with five rooms truly equipped for wheelchair access and a paved path extending almost a kilometer (½ mile) into the rain forest. When you're not hiking or touring the region, you can hang by the volcano-view swimming pool and Jacuzzi. The only downside here is that, due to the shifting of vents and a major blowout on the side of the main crater, you now get better views of lava flows from the Tabacón side of the volcano.

To get here, head to the national park entrance, stay on the dirt road past the entrance, and follow the signs to the Observatory Lodge. A four-wheel-drive vehicle used to be required for the 9km (5½-mile) dirt road up to the lodge, but two bridges now eliminate the need to ford any major rivers, and a traditional sedan will usually make it even in the rainy season — although you'll always be better off with the clearance afforded by a four-wheel-drive vehicle.

See map p. 257. On the flanks of Arenal volcano. ☎ 290-7011 in San José, or 695-5033 at the lodge. Fax: 290-8427. www.arenal-observatory.co.cr. *Rack rates: $64–$86 standard double; $116 Smithsonian; $133 junior suite. Rates include breakfast buffet. Rates lower in the off season. AE, MC, V.*

La Fortuna and the Arenal Volcano

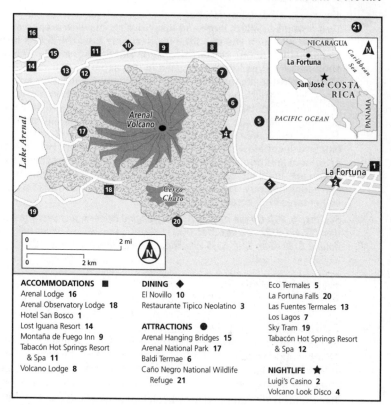

ACCOMMODATIONS ■
Arenal Lodge **16**
Arenal Observatory Lodge **18**
Hotel San Bosco **1**
Lost Iguana Resort **14**
Montaña de Fuego Inn **9**
Tabacón Hot Springs Resort
  & Spa **11**
Volcano Lodge **8**

DINING ◆
El Novillo **10**
Restaurante Tipico Neolatino **3**

ATTRACTIONS ●
Arenal Hanging Bridges **15**
Arenal National Park **17**
Baldi Termae **6**
Caño Negro National Wildlife
  Refuge **21**

Eco Termales **5**
La Fortuna Falls **20**
Las Fuentes Termales **13**
Los Lagos **7**
Sky Tram **19**
Tabacón Hot Springs Resort
  & Spa **12**

NIGHTLIFE ★
Luigi's Casino **2**
Volcano Look Disco **4**

Hotel San Bosco
$ **La Fortuna**

Located a block off La Fortuna's main street, the San Bosco offers the best rooms to be found right in town. The hotel actually has two styles of rooms. The older units are all well maintained and feature tile floors and fans. However, these are standard budget hotel affairs. The more expensive rooms are much more attractive and have stone walls, tile floors, reading lights, televisions, and benches on the veranda in front. You'll find an observation deck for volcano viewing on the top floor of the hotel, as well as a helpful front-desk staff.

See map above. La Fortuna, San Carlos (200m/656 ft. north of the central park). ☎ *479-9050. Fax: 479-9109.* www.arenal-volcano.com. *34 units. $38–$46 double. Rates lower in the off season. AE, MC, V.*

Lost Iguana Resort

$$$–$$$$ Near Lake Arenal

This new place offers large and luxurious rooms with great views of the volcano, although you're a little farther away from the action here than you are at the hotels closer to Tabacón Hot Springs and La Fortuna. Most of the rooms here are housed in two separate two-story buildings set on a hillside facing the volcano. The rooms themselves are quite spacious, with either one king or two twin beds on bamboo frames and attractive handmade wooden furniture. All feature a wall of glass letting out on a private balcony or porch, which in itself lets out onto the view. The suites are even larger and come with a Jacuzzi tub on the porch or balcony. Just below the open-air restaurant is a pretty two-tiered swimming pool and poolside bar. You can also stay in one of several villas, which are, in effect, two-bedroom suites, with a full kitchenette, and extra-long balcony. The hotel has a small network of trails on its own 40 hectares (100 acres) of land.

See map p. 257. On the road to Arenal Hanging Bridges, just over the Lake Arenal dam. ☎ *461-0122. Fax: 461-0121.* www.lostiguanaresort.com. *Rack rates: $130 double; $180 suite; $210–$395 villa. Rates include breakfast. AE, MC, V.*

Montaña de Fuego Inn

$$ On the road to Tabacón

Most of the rooms here have amazing volcano views from a spacious glass-enclosed porch. The hotel is a mix of individual cabins and a few two-story buildings built on stilts over a small artificial lake, housing the new suites. All are wooden affairs, with plenty of varnished wood, yet sparse appointments inside. The junior suites all have air-conditioning and minifridges, and some even have back balconies overlooking a forested ravine, in addition to the volcano-facing front porch. Behind the hotel are some rolling hills that lead down to a small river surrounded by patches of gallery forest, where they conduct an adventurous horseback, hiking, rappel, and kayak loop tour.

See map p. 257. 8km (5 miles) outside La Fortuna on the road to Tabacón. ☎ *460-1220. Fax: 460-1455.* www.montanadefuego.com. *Rack rates: $93–$112 double; $143 suite. Rates include buffet breakfast. MC, V.*

Tabacón Hot Springs Resort & Spa

$$$–$$$$ Between La Fortuna and Lake Arenal

This is by far the most upscale and popular place in the Arenal area. However, its popularity is threatening to spoil its charm. Many rooms here have excellent, direct views of the volcano. Rooms on the upper floors of the 300-block building have the best vistas. Still, quite a few of the rooms have obstructed, or no, views. Book a "standard superior" which will come with a view — it's definitely worth the slight splurge over the straight "standard."

All rooms are spacious, with nice wooden furniture; each has a private terrace or balcony with a table and a couple of chairs. Nine of the rooms here are truly designed to be accessible to travelers with disabilities, and 11 are suites, with separate sitting rooms and many with a private volcano-view Jacuzzi. Guests here enjoy privileges at the spectacular hot springs complex and spa across the street, including slightly extended hours. The hotel boasts a large hot spring–fed pool and separate Jacuzzi as well.

See map p. 257. On the main road between La Fortuna and Lake Arenal, Tabacón. ☎ *877-277-8291 in the United States and Canada; 519-1900 in Costa Rica. Fax: 221-3075.* www.tabacon.com. *Rack rates: $159–$184 double; $229–$264 suite. Rates include buffet breakfast. AE, DC, MC, V.*

Villablanca Hotel
$$$ Outside of San Ramón

This venerable old hotel has received a major facelift and is now part of a new group of "green hotels" that includes Sí Como No in Manuel Antonio. The lodge consists of a series of Tico-style casitas surrounded by 800 hectares (1,976 acres) of farm and forest. All have been completely remodeled. Each casita is built of adobe and has tile floors, open-beamed ceilings, and whitewashed walls. Inside, you'll find a fireplace in one corner, comfortable hardwood chairs, and either one queen or two twin beds covered with colorful bedspreads. The deluxe units and suites have a separate sitting area with a fold-out couch and whirlpool bathtubs and separate showers. In many rooms, the bathroom tubs look out through a wall of windows onto lush gardens. Some have private patios.

Four of the old casitas were converted into a new branch of **Serenity Spa**. Adjacent to the lodge are 11km (6¾ miles) of trails through the **Los Angeles Cloud Forest Reserve.** You can also rent horses or take an adventurous swing through the canopy on a canopy tour here. Villablanca is actually over an hour from La Fortuna, but it's on the way and makes a good overnight stop en route.

San Ramón, Alajuela. ☎ *461-0300. Fax: 461-0302.* www.villablanca-costarica.com. *Rack rates: $155 double; $175 deluxe; $195 suite. Rates include buffet breakfast. AE, DC, MC, V.*

Volcano Lodge
$$ Between La Fortuna and Lake Arenal

This lodge is located directly across the road from and facing the volcano. All the rooms come with two double beds, a private bathroom, two wicker chairs inside, and a small terrace with a couple of wooden rocking chairs for volcano viewing outside. The appointments are simple, but the rooms are spacious and get plenty of light through big picture windows. Rooms 1 through 12 have the best views. Like many places in this area, heavy demand has allowed this lodge to raise its prices precipitously in just a few short years. I personally don't think the rooms and level of service are worth these rates. Still, the view of the volcano here is top notch, and a wide range of tours is available.

See map p. 257. On the main road between La Fortuna and Lake Arenal. ☎ *460-6080 or 460-6022. Fax: 460-6020.* www.volcanolodge.com. *Rack rates: $93 double. Rates include continental breakfast. Rates lower in the off season. AE, MC, V.*

Dining locally

El Novillo

$ Between La Fortuna and Lake Arenal   STEAKHOUSE/COSTA RICAN

This place is the definition of "nothing fancy." In fact, it's just some plastic lawn furniture set on a concrete slab underneath a high, open zinc roof. Still, it has garnered a well-deserved reputation as the best steakhouse in the area. The steaks are big and tender and well prepared. The chicken and fish dishes are huge as well and also nicely done. Meals come with garlic bread, fries, and some slaw. If you want a real local treat, order some fried yuca as a side. If the night is clear, you can get a great view of any volcanic activity from the parking lot here.

See map p. 257. On the road to Tabacón, 10km (6¼ miles) outside of La Fortuna. ☎ *460-6433. Main courses: $5–$9. No credit cards. Open: Daily 10 a.m. to midnight.*

Restaurante Típico Neolatino

$$ Just outside of La Fortuna   COSTA RICAN/NUEVO LATINO

A significant step above most "typical" Costa Rican restaurants, this cozy joint sits on the site of the former Vaca Muca. The menu covers all the traditional bases, with some Nuevo Latino touches. The fresh tilapia in papaya and tamarind sauce is a good bet, as is the Peruvian ceviche. The steaks are hearty and well-prepared, and the menu boasts some excellent desserts. A popular bar lies off the main dining room, and behind the restaurant is a butterfly and orchid garden.

See map p. 257. On the road to Tabacón, 2km (1¼ miles) outside of La Fortuna. ☎ *479-9186. Main courses: $5–$16. MC, V. Open: Daily 11:30 a.m.–11 p.m.*

Exploring La Fortuna and the Arenal volcano area

While the La Fortuna waterfall and various hot springs are easy to visit on your own, the other attractions and activities listed here are best experienced as part of an organized tour or outing.

The top attractions

Arenal Volcano and Arenal National Park

Arenal volcano is an impressive site. It is Costa Rica's most active volcano, regularly spewing lava from its near perfect cone. Still, the first thing you should know is that Arenal volcano borders a region of cloud and rain forests, and the volcano's cone is often socked in by fog. Many people come to Arenal and never get to see the exposed cone. Moreover, the volcano does go through periods when it's relatively quiet.

The second thing you should know is that you can't climb Arenal volcano; it's not safe due to the constant activity. Several foolish people who have ignored this warning have lost their lives, and others have been severely injured. The most recent fatalities occurred in August 2000.

Still, waiting for and watching Arenal's regular eruptions is the main activity in La Fortuna and is best done at night, when the orange lava glows against the starry sky. Although you can simply look up from the middle of town and see Arenal erupting, the view is best from the north and west sides of the volcano along the road to Tabacón and toward the national-park entrance. If you have a car, you can drive along this road, but if you've arrived by bus, you'll need to take a taxi or tour.

Arenal National Park constitutes an area of more than 2,880 hectares (7,114 acres), which includes the viewing and parking areas closest to the volcano. The trails inside the park are gorgeous and fun, running through forest and over old lava flows. However, at night, the view from inside the park is no better than on the roads just outside it.

If you don't have a car and you're staying in La Fortuna, every hotel in town and several tour offices offer night tours to the volcano. The tours usually don't actually enter the park; they stop on the road that runs between the park entrance and the Arenal Observatory Lodge. These tours cost between $7 and $15 per person. Often these volcano-viewing tours include a stop at one of the local hot springs, and the price goes up accordingly.

Although it's counterintuitive, the rainy season is often a better time to see the exposed cone of Arenal volcano, especially at night. I don't know why this is, but I've had excellent volcano-viewing sessions at various points during the rainy season, whereas during the dry season, the volcano can often be socked in solid for days at a time. The bottom line is that catching a glimpse of the volcano's cone is never a sure thing.

See map p. 257. 17km (11 miles) west of La Fortuna. Admission: $6 per person. Open: Daily 8 a.m.–10 p.m.

Caño Negro National Wildlife Refuge

Caño Negro National Wildlife Refuge is a vast network of marshes and rivers, best known for its amazing abundance of bird life, including roseate spoonbills, jabiru storks, herons, and egrets, but you can also see caimans and crocodiles. Bird-watchers should not miss this refuge, although keep in mind that the main lake dries up in the dry season (mid-Apr to Nov), which reduces the number of wading birds.

All the hotel tour desks and tour agencies in this area offer tours to Caño Negro. Full-day tours average between $40 and $60 per person. However, most of the trips run out of the La Fortuna area that are billed as Caño Negro tours never really enter the refuge but instead ply sections of the nearby Río Frio, featuring similar wildlife and ecosystems.

See map p. 257. About 100km (62 miles) north of La Fortuna near the town of Los Chiles. Admission: $6 per person. Open: Daily 7 a.m.–4 p.m.

Soaking your weary bones

Arenal volcano has bestowed a terrific fringe benefit on the area around it: several naturally heated thermal springs. **Tabacón Hot Springs Resort & Spa** (☎ 519-1900; www.tabacon.com) is the most extensive and luxurious spot where you can soak your tired bones. A series of variously sized pools, fed by natural springs, are spread among lush gardens. At the center is a large, warm, spring-fed swimming pool with a slide, a swim-up bar, and a perfect view of the volcano. One of the stronger streams flows over a sculpted waterfall, with a rock ledge underneath that provides a great spot to sit and receive a free hydraulic shoulder massage. The resort also has a spa on the grounds offering professional massages, mud masks, and other treatments at reasonable prices.

In addition to the poolside swim-up bar, you'll find a restaurant and separate snack bar and grill here. You can sign a credit card voucher when you enter and charge your food and drinks throughout your stay. This sure beats pulling soggy bills from your bathing suit.

Entrance fees are $29 for adults and $17 for children under 9. The hot springs are open daily from noon to 10 p.m. Spa treatments can be scheduled as early as 8 a.m., and guests at the hotel here can enter at 10 a.m. There's a slight discount for entering after 7 p.m. The management sometimes enforces its policy of limiting the number of visitors at any one time, so reservations are recommended during the high season.

Across the street from the resort and down a gravel driveway is **Las Fuentes Termales,** another bathing spot fed by the same springs and run by the same folks. You'll find several large pools here, but far more basic facilities and no view. Admission is $8 weekdays, $10 weekends. There are changing rooms and showers, but you won't find the Disneyland atmosphere, pampering spa treatments, or magnificent gardens that prevail at the Tabacón resort.

Baldi Termae (☎ 479-9652), next to the Volcano Look Disco, are the first hot springs you'll come to as you drive from La Fortuna toward Tabacón; however, I'd avoid this place. The pools and grounds are far less appealing than any of the other options listed here. The main draw seems to be the swim-up bar set in the center of a circular concrete pool. Admission is $17.

Just across the street from Baldi Termae is the unmarked entrance of a new hot spring option, **Eco Termales** (☎ 479-8484). Smaller and more intimate than Tabacón, this series of pools set amid lush forest and gardens is almost as picturesque and luxurious, although the spa services are much less extensive and there is no view of the volcano. Reservations are absolutely necessary here. Admission is $15.

La Fortuna Falls

The La Fortuna waterfall is an impressive jungle torrent plunging in a strong plume from dense rain forest into a perfectly round pool far below. There's a sign in town to indicate the road that leads out to the falls. You can drive or hike to just within viewing distance. It's another 15- to 20-minute hike down a steep and often muddy path to the pool formed by the waterfall. The hike back up will take slightly longer. You can swim, but stay away from the turbulent water at the base of the falls — several people have drowned here. Instead, check out and enjoy the calm pool just around the bend, or join the locals at the popular swimming hole under the bridge on the paved road, just after the turnoff for the road up to the falls. You can hike or drive, or sign up for one of the many horseback or mountain-bike tours out here.

See map p. 257. 5.5km (3½ miles) outside of La Fortuna. ☎ _479-8360. Admission: $6 for view of falls. Open: Daily 8 a.m.–4 p.m._

Los Lagos

Families with kids may want to head to **Jungla y Senderos Los Lagos.** Children and the young at heart seem to love the pool, fountain, and water slide here. I come here more for the network of trails and small lakes that are also on the property. You'll also find a small crocodile hatchery and tilapia farm, a canopy tour, and some basic hot springs here.

See map p. 257. On the road to Tabacón, a few kilometers out of La Fortuna. ☎ _461-1818._ www.hotelloslagos.com. _Admission: $10 for daily use of facilities. Open: Daily 8 a.m.–4 p.m._

More cool things to see and do

✔ **Fishing:** Lake Arenal is the largest body of fresh water in Costa Rica, and fishing is a popular activity here. The big action on Lake Arenal is _guapote,_ a Central American species of rainbow bass. However, you can also book fishing trips to Caño Negro, where snook, tarpon, and other game fish can be stalked. Most hotels and adventure-tour companies can arrange fishing excursions. Costs run around $100 to $200 for a half day, and $200 to $400 for a full day.

✔ **Canopy tours, hanging bridges, and canyoning:** The **Original Canopy Tour** company (☎ 257-5149; www.canopytour.com) has an operation set up right at the Tabacón Hot Springs Resort & Spa. The two-hour tour ($45 per person) leaves right from the hot springs and includes the entrance to the **Las Fuentes Termales** pools. You strap on a climbing harness, ascend more than 30m (98 ft.) to a treetop platform, and careen from tree to tree while hanging from a pulley on a skinny cable.

For a mellower means of getting into the forest canopy, you can hike the trails and bridges of **Arenal Hanging Bridges** (☎ 253-5080; www.hangingbridges.com). Located just over the Lake Arenal dam, this attraction is a complex of gentle trails and suspension bridges through a beautiful tract of primary forest. It's open daily from 7 a.m. to 4 p.m.; admission is $20. Guided tours and night tours are also available here.

If you'd like a bigger rush than the canopy tours offer, you should go "canyoning" with **Pure Trek Canyoning** (☎ 479-9940; www. puretrek.com). This new adventure sport is a mix of hiking through and alongside a jungle river, punctuated with periodic rappels through and alongside the faces of four waterfalls. The largest rappel is 50m (164 ft.). The tour is wet and adventurous, and costs $85 per person, including lunch. Tours leave twice daily, at 7a.m. and noon.

The newest entry in this field is **Sky Tram** (☎ 479-9944; www.sky tram.net), an open gondola-style ride that begins near the shores of Lake Arenal and rises up, providing excellent views of the lake and volcano. From here you can hike their series of trails and suspended bridges. In the end, you can either hike down, take the gondola, or strap on a harness and ride their cable canopy tour down to the bottom. The cost is $60, and Sky Tram is open daily from 8 a.m. to 4 p.m.

✔ **Horseback riding:** Horseback riding is a popular activity in this area, and you'll find scores of good rides on dirt back roads and through open fields and dense rain forest. Volcano and lake views come with the terrain on most rides. Horseback trips to the Río Fortuna waterfall are perhaps the most popular tours sold, but remember, the horse will get you only to the entrance; from there, you'll have to hike a bit. A horseback ride to the falls should cost between $25 and $30, including the entrance fee.

✔ **Mountain biking:** This region is very well suited for mountain biking. Rides range in difficulty from moderate to extremely challenging. You can combine a day on a mountain bike with a visit to one or more of the more popular attractions here. **Bike Arenal** (☎ 479-9454; www.bikearenal.com) is the only dedicated operator in the field, with an excellent collection of top-notch bikes and equipment, as well as a wide range of tour possibilities.

✔ **Water-skiing and wakeboarding:** If you're a dedicated wakeboarder (wakeboarding is a lot like water-skiing but on a single, wide board) or water-skier, or just a beginner, the folks at **Aqua Ski** (☎ 388-1771; www.aquaski.com) will take you out on their glassy 3,500-foot-long manmade lake. Rates start at around $50 per skier for a two-hour outing with a group of friends. Multiday packages and lesson rates are also available.

✔ **White-water rafting: Desafío Expeditions** (☎ 479-9464; www. desafiocostarica.com) offers daily raft rides of Class I to II, III, and IV to V on different sections of the Toro, Peñas Blancas, and Sarapiquí rivers. A half-day trip on the Peñas Blancas, leaving from La Fortuna, costs around $45 to $55 per person; a full day of rafting costs $60 to $70 per person, depending on what section of what river you ride. Both of these companies also offer mountain biking and most of the standard local guided trips. Desafío has recently begun taking inflatable kayaks, or *duckies,* down the pristine Arenal River, ending up at their new Endless Wave river center and restaurant.

Shopping for local treasures

Aside from your run-of-the-mill souvenir and gift shops, you won't find any notable shopping options in this area. Your options get much better as you drive around the lake. See "Along the Shores of Lake Arenal" later in this chapter for two good craft and gift shops found on the road that circles Lake Arenal.

Living it up after dark in La Fortuna and around the Arenal volcano

Waiting and watching for a volcanic eruption is the most popular after-dark activity in this neck of the woods. Taking a soak in one of the local hot springs runs a close second.

The **Volcano Look Disco** (☎ 479-9616) is located just out of town on the road to Tabacón. This place is very popular with locals and really gets going on Friday and Saturday nights. There's also a small casino in downtown La Fortuna, Luigi's Casino (☎ 479-9636), although it feels out of place in this rural town and is seldom crowded.

Fast Facts: La Fortuna and the Arenal Volcano

Ambulance

Call ☎ 128.

ATMs

You'll find ATMs at the Banco Nacional and Banco de Costa Rica in La Fortuna.

Country Code and City Code

The country code for Costa Rica is **506**. There are no city or area codes within Costa Rica. To call from the United States, dial 011-506 plus the seven-digit number. From within Costa Rica, you simply dial the seven-digit number.

Currency Exchange

Most hotels will exchange money for you at decent rates. To get official rates, head to either the Banco Nacional or Banco de Costa Rica in La Fortuna.

Fire

Call ☎ 118.

Hospitals

The closest hospital is Ciudad Quesada hospital (☎ 401-1200), although there are several doctors and a local clinic (☎ 479-9798) in La Fortuna.

Information

There are no official information offices in La Fortuna. Most hotels have a tour desk, concierge, or helpful front desk.

Internet Access

Several Internet cafes are located in La Fortuna, as well as a few strung along the road to the national park. Many hotels also have their own in-house Internet cafes or wireless service. Rates run between $1 and $3 per hour.

Newspapers

Several gift shops around town carry all the local papers, including the *Tico Times*.

Pharmacies

La Fortuna's best pharmacy, Farmacia Catedral (☎ 479-9518), is on the main street just off the small park in downtown La Fortuna.

Police

Call ☎ **911** or 479-9689.

Post Office

There is a post office in La Fortuna (☎ 479-8070). Alternatively, most hotels can mail your letters and postcards for you.

Taxis

Taxis are plentiful in La Fortuna, and they frequently ply the road between La Fortuna and Tabacón Hot Springs. If you can't flag one down on the street, have your hotel call for you or dial Arenal Taxi at ☎ 479-8522 or 479-9605.

Along the Shores of Lake Arenal

The area surrounding Lake Arenal is beautiful and peaceful. A visit here gives you a taste of rural Costa Rica. Rolling hills and virgin forest flank Lake Arenal, the largest lake in Costa Rica. The perfect cone of Arenal volcano lies just beyond the eastern end of the lake, while the small rural towns of Tilarán and Nuevo Arenal anchor the western end. The volcano's barren slopes are a stunning sight from here, especially when reflected in the waters of the lake.

From December through April, strong and steady winds buffet the western end of the lake. Locals used to curse these winds. Today they draw hoards of avid sailboarders and kitesurfers. Lake Arenal's combination of warm, fresh water, steady blows, and spectacular scenery, have made this spot a mecca for practitioners of these water sports.

Although the towns of Tilarán and Nuevo Arenal are little more than quiet rural communities, hotels have sprung up all along the shores of the lake. If you prefer to visit during less windy months, you may enjoy simply hanging out by the lake, hiking in the nearby forests, and catching glimpses of Arenal volcano.

Getting there

This is a region best visited in a rental car. There are no local airstrips, and bus service is infrequent. The drive around Lake Arenal is one of the prettiest in the country, although the road is in horrendous shape in places, so a four-wheel-drive vehicle is a virtual necessity.

By car

From San José, take the Interamerican Highway west toward Puntarenas, and then continue north on this road to Cañas. In Cañas, turn east toward Tilarán. The drive takes four hours. If you're continuing on to Nuevo Arenal, follow the signs in town, which will put you on the road that skirts the shore of the lake. Nuevo Arenal is about a half-hour drive from

Tilarán. You can also drive here from La Fortuna, along a scenic road that winds around the lake. From La Fortuna, it's approximately one hour to Nuevo Arenal and one and a half hours to Tilarán.

By bus

Express buses (☎ **222-3854**) leave San José for Tilarán several times a day from Calle 12 between avenidas 7 and 9. The trip lasts from four to five and a half hours, depending on road conditions; the fare is $3.

A bus leaves from **Santa Elena** and **Monteverde** daily at 7 a.m. The fare for the three-hour trip is $2. Buses from **La Fortuna** leave for Tilarán daily at 8 a.m. and 2:30 p.m., returning at 7 a.m. and 12:30 p.m. The trip is three to four hours; the fare is $2.50.

From Tilarán, the bus to Santa Elena and Monteverde leaves daily at 12:30 p.m. Buses also leave regularly for Cañas, where you can catch buses north or south along the Interamerican Highway.

Orienting yourself along the shores of Lake Arenal

Nuevo Arenal is about 50km (31 miles) east of La Fortuna. Tilarán is another 35km (22 miles) beyond Nuevo Arenal. If you're coming from the Interamerican Highway, Tilarán is 24km (15 miles) northeast of Cañas.

Both Tilarán and Nuevo Arenal are small rural towns of just a few blocks in any direction. Both have a Catholic church and central plaza at the heart of town.

Getting around

Having a rental car is a good idea in this area. The road around Lake Arenal, particularly between Nuevo Arenal and La Fortuna, has historically been very rough and poorly maintained. Despite many promises to the contrary, the situation has remained the same. A four-wheel-drive vehicle is recommended, mostly for the added clearance.

If you need a taxi to get to a lodge on Lake Arenal, call ☎ **695-5324** in Tilarán, or ☎ **817-6375** in Nuevo Arenal.

Spending the night

Chalet Nicholas
$ **Nuevo Arenal**

This friendly bed-and-breakfast sits on a hill and features great views of the lake from its garden. All three rooms have a view of Arenal volcano in the distance. The upstairs loft room is the largest and comes with its own private deck. Chalet Nicholas is set on 6 hectares (15 acres) and has beautiful flower gardens, an organic vegetable garden, and an orchid garden. Behind the property are acres of forest through which you can hike in search of birds, orchids, butterflies, and other tropical treasures. No smoking is allowed in the house or on the grounds. Owners John and Catherine Nicholas go out of their way to make their guests feel at home, although their four Great Danes may intimidate you when you first drive up.

2.5km (1½ miles) west of Nuevo Arenal. ☎ *694-4041.* www.chaletnicholas.com. *Rack rates: $69 double. Rates include full breakfast. No credit cards.*

Hotel Tilawa
$–$$ Between Tilarán and Nuevo Arenal

Built to resemble the Palace of Knossos on the island of Crete, the Hotel Tilawa sits high on the slopes above the lake and has a sweeping vista down to the water. It's primarily a windsurfers' and kiteboarders' hangout. Unusual colors and antique paint effects give the hotel a weathered look; inside there are wall murals and other artistic paint treatments throughout. Rooms have dyed cement floors, Guatemalan bedspreads, and big windows. Some have kitchenettes. Tilawa can arrange windsurfing, kiteboarding, mountain biking, horseback riding, and fishing trips. The hotel even boasts a small skate park for radical skateboarders and BMX freestyle bikers, which makes this a good place to bring teenagers. The newest addition here is a small spa and one of the few micro-brew operations in Costa Rica.

On the road between Tilarán and Nuevo Arenal. ☎ *695-5050.* Fax: 695-5766. www.hotel-tilawa.com. *Rack rates: $48–$65 double; $65–$82 suite. Rates lower in the off season, higher during peak periods. MC, V.*

Mystica
$ Between Tilarán and Nuevo Arenal

Set on a high hill above Lake Arenal, this Italian-run joint has simple but spacious and cheery rooms. The painted cement floors are kept immaculate, and the rooms get good ventilation from their large windows. All rooms open onto a long and broad shared veranda with a great view of the lake. The owners can help you book a wide range of adventures and tours. Perhaps the star attraction here is the hotel's excellent Italian restaurant and pizzeria by the same name (see later in this chapter).

On the road between Tilarán and Nuevo Arenal. ☎ *692-1001.* Fax: 692-1002. www.mysticalodge.com. *Rack rates: $60 double. Rates include continental breakfast. V.*

Rock River Lodge
$ Between Tilarán and Nuevo Arenal

This small lodge is *the* joint for serious windsurfers. The rooms are housed in a long, low lodge set on stilts. Walls and floors are made of hardwood, and there are bamboo railings along the veranda, where you'll find sling chairs to relax in after a day of windsurfing and wind chimes that let you know when the breezes are kicking up. The rooms themselves are midsize; each has one double bed and a bunk bed, as well as a small tiled bathroom. The independent bungalows, which are farther up the hill, offer more privacy

Along the Shores of Lake Arenal

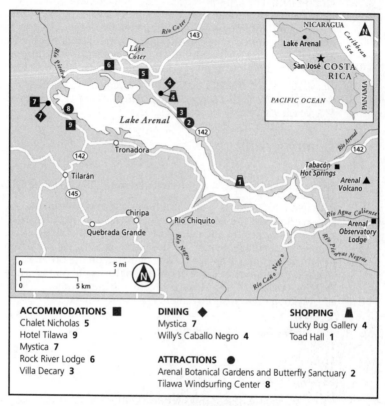

ACCOMMODATIONS ■
Chalet Nicholas **5**
Hotel Tilawa **9**
Mystica **7**
Rock River Lodge **6**
Villa Decary **3**

DINING ◆
Mystica **7**
Willy's Caballo Negro **4**

ATTRACTIONS ●
Arenal Botanical Gardens and Butterfly Sanctuary **2**
Tilawa Windsurfing Center **8**

SHOPPING ▲
Lucky Bug Gallery **4**
Toad Hall **1**

and space and have small sculpted bathtubs in larger bathrooms. It's a long walk down to the lake (not to mention the walk back up), so a car is recommended. Although windsurfing is the main activity here, the lodge also offers mountain-biking trips and horseback and hiking adventures around the region.

On the road between Tilarán and Nuevo Arenal. ☎ *293-8537 reservations office in San José, or* ☎ */fax 692-1180 at lodge.* www.rockriverlodge.com. *Rack rates: $63 double; $78 bungalow. Rates include full breakfast. AE, MC, V.*

Villa Decary
$$ Nuevo Arenal

Named after a French explorer, and the rare palm species that he discovered and named, this small bed-and-breakfast is nestled on a hill above Lake Arenal, just outside the town of Nuevo Arenal. Each room comes with one queen-size and one twin bed, large picture windows, and a spacious private balcony with an excellent lake view. The rooms get plenty of light, and the bright Guatemalan bedspreads and white-tile floors create a vibrant look. The separate casitas have full kitchens, more room, and even better views of the lake from their slightly higher perches. Breakfasts are extravagant and memorable, with a steady stream of fresh fruits; fresh juice; strong coffee; homemade pancakes, waffles, or muffins; and usually an excellent omelet or soufflé. There's great bird-watching on the hotel grounds, and howler monkeys are common guests here as well.

Nuevo Arenal. ☎ *383-3012, or* ☎ */fax 694-4330.* www.villadecary.com. *Rack rates: $89 double; $109–$129 casita for 2. Rates include full breakfast. Extra person $15. No credit cards.*

Dining locally

Mystica
$–$$ Between Tilarán and Nuevo Arenal ITALIAN/PIZZERIA

The restaurant at this Italian-run hotel has a wonderful setting high on a hill overlooking the lake. The large dining room features rustic wooden chairs and tables, varnished wood floors, colorful tablecloths, and abundant flower arrangements. The most striking features, aside from the view, are the large open fireplace on one end and, on the other, café large brick oven, in the shape of a small cottage, that turns out pizzas. The pastas and delicious main dishes are authentically northern Italian. Whenever possible, Mystica uses fresh ingredients from its own garden.

On the road between Tilarán and Nuevo Arenal. ☎ *692-1001. Main courses: $3–$10. MC, V. Open: Daily 7:30 a.m.–9:30 a.m. and 11:30 a.m.–9 p.m.*

Willy's Caballo Negro
$$ Nuevo Arenal GERMAN

The German owners of this attractive little roadside cafe serve up three different types of schnitzel, both chicken and veal cordon bleu, and a host of other old-world meat dishes. Try the Zigeuner Schnitzel, a tender veal cutlet in a slightly spicy sauce of onions and bell peppers, served with spätzle. Despite the emphasis on meats and sausages, vegetarians will find several tasty and filling options here, including stuffed potatoes and eggplant Parmesan. Wooden tables are set around the edges of the round dining room, with a high peaked roof. Candles and creative lighting give the place a cozy and warm feel.

Nuevo Arenal (about 3km/1¾ miles out of town on the road to Tilarán). ☎ *694-4515. Main courses: $4–$14. MC, V. Open: Daily 8 a.m.–8 p.m.*

Exploring along the shores of Lake Arenal

The only true "attraction" in this region is the Arenal Botanical Gardens and Butterfly Sanctuary. However, if you have your own car, the scenic drive around the lake could be considered an attraction in and of itself.

Combine a visit to the botanical gardens with a leisurely drive, and stops at the two unique gift shops listed below in "Shopping for local treasures."

The top attractions

Arenal Botanical Gardens and Butterfly Sanctuary

This private garden and butterfly sanctuary was only started in 1991, but it's already quite beautiful and extensive. Winding paths bring you past seemingly innumerable species of tropical plants and flowers. The butterfly garden also is quite large and well stocked. The many flowers attract a large number of bird species, over 400 in fact, and you'll usually spot scores of hummingbirds buzzing around the gardens here.

See map p. 269. Located 4km (2½ miles) outside of Nuevo Arenal, on the road to La Fortuna. ☎ *694-4305. Open: Nov–May daily 9 a.m.–5 p.m. Admission: $8, including a guide.*

Tilawa Windsurfing Center

From early December through April, strong and steady winds kick across the western end of Lake Arenal providing windsurfers and kiteboarders with the primary attraction and activity offered up by this region.

Kiteboarding is an adventure sport, similar to windsurfing, except you're tethered by a harness to a large kite, which you can steer via some control lines. The sport is known for the long and high jumps achieved by experienced practitioners.

If you want to try your hand at either windsurfing or kiteboarding, you can rent equipment from **Tilawa Windsurfing Center,** which has its facilities on one of the lake's few accessible beaches. Boards rent for around $50 to $60 per day, and lessons are also available.

Tico Wind (☎ 692-2002; www.ticowind.com) is also popular with serious sailboarders. It sets up shop on the shores of the lake each year from December 1 to the end of April, which is when the winds here blow most fiercely. Rates run around $65 per day, including lunch, with multiday packages available.

Located on the lake shore 8km (5 miles) from Tilarán. ☎ *695-5050.* www.windsurf costarica.com. *Open: Daily 7:30 a.m.–5 p.m. Admission: Variable rates for equipment rental and lessons.*

More cool things to see and do

✔ **Fishing:** Ask at your hotel if you want to try your hand at fishing for *guapote.* These large members of the cichlid family are known locally as rainbow-bass. Their sharp teeth and fighting nature make them a real challenge. A half-day fishing trip should cost around $150 per boat, and a full day goes for around $250. The boats used will usually accommodate up to three people fishing.

✔ **Horseback riding and mountain biking:** The hills, fields, and forests of this area are perfect for exploring on horseback or riding a mountain bike. Any of the hotels in the area can hook you up with a horseback-riding tour for around $10 to $15 per hour. **Rock River Lodge** (☎ 692-1180) has some high-end mountain bikes, which will run you around $35 per day. You can also rent bikes from the **Hotel Tilawa** (see earlier in this chapter).

Shopping for local treasures

If you're in the area, don't miss **Toad Hall** (☎ 692-8020). Located 9km (5½ miles) outside of Nuevo Arenal, toward La Fortuna, this roadside gallery and cafe has one of the best collection of high-end arts and crafts you'll find in the country. You'll find the works of Lil Mena, Cecilia Figueres, Patricia Erickson, and Barry Biesanz, among others, as well as a good selection of craftworks. They also serve up excellent breakfasts, light lunches, and a wide range of coffee drinks and desserts.

Just outside Nuevo Arenal, you'll find **The Lucky Bug Gallery,** (☎ 604-4515) another excellent little roadside arts-and-crafts and souvenir shop, attached to Willy's Caballo Negro restaurant (see earlier in this chapter). Many of the works here are produced by the owner's triplet daughters.

Fast Facts: Lake Arenal

Ambulance

Call ☎ **128** or 695-5256 in Tilarán.

ATMs

The Banco Nacional branches in both Tilarán and Nuevo Arenal have ATM machines.

Country Code and City Code

The country code for Costa Rica is **506.** There are no city or area codes within Costa Rica. To call from the United States, dial 011-506 plus the seven-digit number. From within Costa Rica, you simply dial the seven-digit number.

Currency Exchange

Most hotels will exchange money for you at decent rates. To get official rates, head to one of the banks in Tilarán or Nuevo Arenal.

Fire

Call ☎ **118.**

Hospitals

The closest hospital is Hospital Enrique Baltodano (☎ **666-0011**) in downtown Liberia. There are also small health clinics in both Tilarán (☎ 695-5299) and Nuevo Arenal (☎ 694-4163).

Information

There are no official information offices in either Tilarán or Nuevo Arenal. Most hotels have a tour desk, concierge, or helpful front desk.

Internet Access

You'll find several Internet cafes in both Tilarán and Nuevo Arenal. Many hotels also offer Internet access. Rates run between $1 and $3 per hour.

Pharmacies

There's a pharmacy at the small health clinic in Tilarán (☎ 695-5299) which is located in the center of town.

There's a pharmacy at the small health clinic in Nuevo Arenal (☎ 694-4163), located on the main street in the center of town.

Police

Call ☎ **911** or 695-5011 in Tilarán.

Post Office

There are post offices in both Tilarán (☎ 695-5387) and Nuevo Arenal (☎ 694-4310). Alternatively, most hotels can mail your letters and postcards for you.

Taxis

Taxis are plentiful in both Tilarán and Nuevo Arenal. If you don't feel like flagging one down on the street, have your hotel call for you or dial Taxi Tilarán at ☎ 695-5324 in Tilarán, or a private operator at ☎ 817-6375 in Nuevo Arenal.

Part VII
Touring the Rest of Costa Rica

The 5th Wave   By Rich Tennant

COSTA RICA'S ESCALATOR FALLS

In this part . . .

T his part is the place to turn if you're looking to explore Costa Rica's less traveled roads and destinations. In this part, you'll find out all about the beautiful intimate beach resorts and secret getaway spots of the southern Nicoya Peninsula. Nature lovers will want to read up on the remote, and often luxurious, rain-forest lodges of the rich southern zone. Finally, Costa Rica's Caribbean coast, which often gets short shrift, is explained in detail from the jungle canals and rainforests of Tortuguero, to the sleepy beach towns of Cahuita and Puerto Viejo.

Chapter 19

Seeking Solitude in Southern Nicoya

* *

In This Chapter

▶ Landing a great room in Montezuma

▶ Bathing in the pool of a beautiful jungle waterfall

▶ Enjoying Malpaís before the adoring throngs discover it

▶ Opting for a romantic and luxurious getaway at Punta Islita

* *

*T*he beaches and resorts of the southern Nicoya peninsula are more isolated, less developed, and in general a bit wilder than those found to the north on Guanacaste's Gold Coast. This is a place to come if you really want to get away from it all.

The two main beach destinations in this area are Montezuma and Malpaís (which is a general term for a string of isolated beaches stretching north from Malpaís itself). Both offer miles of uncrowded beaches and lush forests all around. Montezuma features a couple of gorgeous waterfalls to visit, while Malpaís is becoming one of the country's top surf destinations.

On the northern stretch of the Nicoyan coastline sits Punta Islita, one of the most exclusive and luxurious little resorts in the country.

Montezuma

Montezuma enjoys near-legendary status among backpackers, UFO seekers, hippie expatriates, and European budget travelers. Although it still maintains its alternative vibe, Montezuma is a great destination for all manner of travelers looking for a quiet beach retreat surrounded by some stunning scenery. Today the town has a well-tended, somewhat booming feel to it, and there are lodgings of value and quality in all price ranges. After all, the natural beauty, miles of almost abandoned beaches, rich wildlife, and jungle waterfalls first made Montezuma famous, and they continue to make this one of my favorite beach towns in Costa Rica.

Getting there

Flying to Tambor and taking a taxi to Montezuma is the fastest and easiest way to travel out here. Taking a car or bus, however, includes a pretty and relaxing ferry ride.

By air

The nearest airport is in Tambor, 17km (11 miles) away. **Sansa** (☎ 221-9414; www.flysansa.com) and **Nature Air** (☎ 800-235-9272 in the United States and Canada, 299-6000 in Costa Rica; www.natureair.com) both have a couple of daily flights to Tambor. Flight duration is about 30 minutes, and fares run between $58 and $66 each way.

Some of the hotels listed later in this chapter may be willing to pick you up in Tambor for a reasonable fee. If not, you'll have to hire a taxi, which could cost anywhere from $15 to $25. Taxis are generally waiting to meet most regularly scheduled planes.

By car and ferry

The traditional route here is to take the Interamerican Highway from San José to Puntarenas and catch the ferry to Paquera. Montezuma is about 75 minutes south of Paquera.

Two companies, Naviera Tambor and Paquera Ferry, run a car ferry between Puntarenas and Paquera, and this has eased some of the load. However, you should still arrive early during the peak season and on weekends because lines can be quite long; if you miss the next ferry, you'll have to wait around two hours or more for the next one. **Ferries to Paquera** (Naviera Tambor: ☎ 661-2084; Paquera Ferry: ☎ 641-0515) leave roughly every two hours between 5 a.m. and 8:15 p.m. The trip takes one and a half hours. The fare is around $10 for a car and driver, $1.50 for additional adults, $1 for children; for first class, the fare is $4 for adults, $2 for children. The ferry schedule changes frequently, with extra ferries often added to meet demand. Checking in advance is always best.

The car ferry from Paquera to Puntarenas leaves roughly every two hours between 6 a.m. and 9 p.m.

By bus and ferry

If you're traveling from San José by public transportation, getting to Montezuma takes two buses and a ferry ride.

Express buses (☎ 222-0064) leave for Puntarenas from San José daily every 30 minutes between 6 a.m. and 9 p.m. from Calle 16 and Avenida 12. Trip duration is two and a half hours; the fare is $3.

From Puntarenas, you can take one of the car ferries mentioned in the preceding section or the passenger launch **Paquereña** (☎ 641-0515), which leaves from the pier behind the market at 6 and 11:30 a.m. and 3 p.m. The ferry-trip duration is one and a half hours; the fare is $2. The bus south to Montezuma will be waiting to meet the ferry when it arrives in Paquera. The bus ride takes one and a half hours; the fare is $3.

Be careful not to take the Naranjo ferry because it does not meet with regular onward bus transportation to Montezuma.

When you're ready to return, buses for Paquera leave Montezuma daily at regular intervals, timed to meet up with a departing ferry.

Orienting yourself in Montezuma

As the winding mountain road that descends into Montezuma bottoms out, you turn left onto a small dirt road that defines the village proper. On this 1-block road, you'll find El Sano Banano Village Cafe and, across from it, a small park with its own basketball court and children's playground. The bus stops at the end of this road. From here, hotels are scattered up and down the beach and around the village's few sand streets.

Buses these days are met by hordes of locals trying to corral you to one of the many budget hotels. *Remember:* They're getting a commission for every body they bring in, so their information is biased.

Getting around

The town itself is very compact, and you can easily walk from most hotels to the beach and nearby waterfall.

There aren't very many taxis in Montezuma, but you can usually flag one down around the small central downtown area. Taxis often park in front of the El Sano Banano Village Cafe. If you can't find one there, you can call Gilberto (☎ **642-0241**) or Ronald (☎ **822-0610**) for a cab.

Montezuma has no official tourist information offices, but several all-purpose tour agencies act as such. **Cocozuma Traveler** (☎ **642-0911**; www.cocozuma.com) and **Montezuma Travel Adventures** (☎ **642-0808**; www.montezumatraveladventures.com) can both arrange horseback riding; boat excursions; scuba-dive and snorkel tours; rafting trips; car and motorcycle rentals; airport transfers; international phone, fax, and Internet service; and currency exchange.

Spending the night

Amor de Mar
$–$$ Montezuma

It would be difficult to imagine a more idyllic spot in this — or *any* — price range. With its wide expanse of neatly trimmed grass sloping down to the sea, tide pools (one of which is as big as a small swimming pool), and hammocks slung from the mango trees, this is the perfect place for anyone who wants to do some serious relaxing. The rooms are all housed in a beautifully appointed two-story building, which abounds in varnished hardwoods.

Most of the rooms have plenty of space and receive lots of sunlight. The big porch on the second floor is a great place for reading or just gazing out to sea. Only breakfast and lunch are served here, but they're served on a beautiful open-air patio overlooking the sea. These folks also rent out a large fully equipped two-story, four-bedroom house right next to the hotel. *See map p. 281. Montezuma.* ☎/fax **642-0262.** www.amordemar.com. *Rack rates: $38–$48 double with shared bathroom; $53–$79 double with private bathroom; $105 house. Rates lower in the off season. V.*

El Sano Banano Village Bed & Breakfast
$ Downtown Montezuma

If you want a clean, comfortable, cool, and centrally located room in Montezuma, this is the place. Built above the popular restaurant of the same name, the rooms here are some of the most modern in town. All feature air-conditioning and satellite televisions, both rarities out here. Some are a bit small, so check out a few if you can before settling in. The downstairs restaurant is one of the most happening spots in town, but rarely will it cause you to lose any sleep. *See map p. 281. Montezuma.* ☎ **642-0638.** *Fax: 642-0631.* www.elbanano.com. *Rack rates: $65 double. Rates include full breakfast. Rates lower in the off season. AE, MC, V.*

Hotel La Aurora
$ Montezuma

It's hard to beat the value and laid-back vibe you'll find at this longstanding budget hotel. Located at the heart of the tiny village, the rooms are spread out over two neighboring buildings fronting Montezuma's small central park and playground. The rooms here are clean and well-kept. I prefer the older rooms, which are located in a spacious three-story wooden building. There's even a two-room apartment on the third floor here, with a private balcony and a bit of an ocean view through the treetops. The hotel also features a small lending library, some hammocks and comfortable chairs, a communal kitchen, and flowering vines growing up the walls. In fact, plants and vines are all over La Aurora, which keeps things cool and gives the place a very tropical feel. Fresh coffee, tea, and hearty breakfasts are served each morning. *See map p. 281. Montezuma.* ☎/fax **642-0051.** www.playamontezuma.net. *Rack rates: $21 double with shared bathroom; $30–$50 double with bathroom. Rates lower in the off season. AE, MC, V.*

Hotel Los Mangos
$ Montezuma

Situated across the road from the water a little bit before the waterfall on the road toward Cabo Blanco, this place takes its name from the many mango trees under which the bungalows are built. (If mango is your passion,

Montezuma

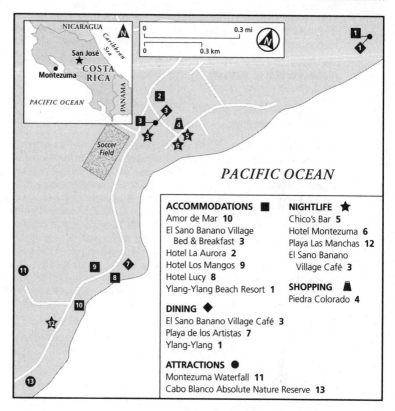

ACCOMMODATIONS ■

Amor de Mar **10**
El Sano Banano Village
Bed & Breakfast **3**
Hotel La Aurora **2**
Hotel Los Mangos **9**
Hotel Lucy **8**
Ylang-Ylang Beach Resort **1**

DINING ◆

El Sano Banano Village Café **3**
Playa de los Artistas **7**
Ylang-Ylang **1**

ATTRACTIONS ●

Montezuma Waterfall **11**
Cabo Blanco Absolute Nature Reserve **13**

NIGHTLIFE ★

Chico's Bar **5**
Hotel Montezuma **6**
Playa Las Manchas **12**
El Sano Banano
Village Café **3**

SHOPPING ▮

Piedra Colorado **4**

come in May, when it's in season.) The rooms are fairly basic, but they are a good value and you get access to the pool, to boot. The roomy thatch-roofed octagonal bungalows built of Costa Rican hardwoods are the better choice here. The swimming pool is built to resemble a natural pond — there's even an artificial waterfall flowing into it — and there's a separate Jacuzzi. The former restaurant here has been converted into a yoga studio, and daily yoga classes are offered.

See map above. Montezuma, Cóbano de Puntarenas. ☎ **642-0076.** *Fax: 642-0259.* www.hotellosmangos.com. *Rack rates: $35 double with shared bathroom; $70 double with private bathroom; $80 bungalow. Rates lower in the off season. V.*

Hotel Lucy

$ Montezuma

Situated on a pretty section of beach a bit south of town, in front of Los Mangos, this converted two-story home has the best location of any budget lodging in Montezuma. If you can snag a second-floor room with an ocean view, you'll be in budget heaven. When I last visited, they were in the middle of yet another remodeling and expansion. The beach here is a bit rough and rocky for swimming, but the sunbathing and sunset views are beautiful. There's a small restaurant serving Tico standards and fresh seafood at very reasonable prices all day long.

See map p. 281. Montezuma, Cóbano de Puntarenas. ☎ *642-0273. Rack rates: $15 double with shared bathroom; $20–$25 double with private bathroom. No credit cards.*

Ylang-Ylang Beach Resort
$$–$$$ **Montezuma**

This place is the sort of tropical retreat many travelers dream about finding. Set in a lush patch of forest just steps away from the sand, the hotel offers rooms that are about a 15-minute walk northeast of town along the beach. There is currently no road to the resort, but one may be in the works. For the foreseeable future, arrival and check-in will continue to be at the downtown El Sano Banano Village Café. Rooms and cabins come in a variety of shapes and sizes. Coco Joe's Rancho is the largest cabin and features a luscious wraparound balcony and a small sleeping loft. But I also like the smaller cabins, which are yellow ferroconcrete geodesic domes that look like igloos. Some of the showers are outdoor garden affairs, which match the surroundings perfectly. There's a beautiful little swimming pool with a sculpted waterfall, and the whole operation is set amid lush gardens planted with lots of banana, heliconia, and elephant-ear plants.

See map p. 281. Montezuma. ☎ *642-0636. Fax: 642-0068.* www.ylangylang resort.com. *Rack rates: $85 double room; $110–$160 bungalow or suite. Rates include full breakfast. Rates lower in the off season. AE, MC, V.*

Dining locally

El Sano Banano Village Café
$–$$ **Montezuma**   **VEGETARIAN/INTERNATIONAL**

Delicious vegetarian meals, including nightly specials, sandwiches, and salads, are the specialty of this perennially popular Montezuma restaurant. You'll also find a good selection of fresh fish and chicken dishes. Lunches feature hefty sandwiches on whole-wheat bread and filling fish and vegetarian *casados*. The yogurt fruit shakes are fabulous, but I like to get a little more decadent and have one of the mocha ice-cream shakes.

See map p. 281. On the main road into the village. ☎ *642-0638. Main courses: $5–$15. AE, MC, V. Open: Daily 7 a.m.–9:30 p.m.*

Playa de los Artistas
$$ **Montezuma**   **ITALIAN/MEDITERRANEAN**

This open-air restaurant is housed in an old house fronting the beach. There are only a few tables, so arrive early. If you don't get a seat and you feel hearty, try the low wooden table surrounded by tatami mats on the sand. Dishes are served in large, broad wooden bowls set on ceramic-ringed coasters or on fresh banana leaves laid over rough-hewn hunks of wood. The outdoor grill is great for grilled fish and seafood. Every meal comes with plenty of fresh bread for soaking up the sauces. The menu changes nightly but always features several fish dishes. The fresh grouper in a black-pepper sauce is phenomenal.

See map p. 281. Across from Hotel Los Mangos. ☎ *642-0920. Reservations recommended. Main courses: $7–$21. No credit cards. Open: Mon–Sat 5–10:30 p.m.*

Ylang-Ylang
$$ Montezuma FUSION

This newest restaurant in town is also one of the best. A pretty, open-air affair, Ylang-Ylang features a sculpted bar with indigenous and wildlife motifs. The menu is broad with a prominent Asian influence, ranging from fresh sushi to jumbo shrimp in a pineapple and coconut sauce to a vegetarian terriyaki stir-fry. There are also several crepe and pasta options and plenty of fresh seafood dishes. For lunch, you can have a bruschetta or some cool gazpacho and be just a few steps from the sand when you're done.

See map p. 281. At the Ylang-Ylang Beach Resort. ☎ *642-0920. Reservations recommended. Main courses: $6–$14. AE, MC, V. Open: Daily 7 a.m.–10 p.m.*

Exploring Montezuma
Both of the major attractions here are easily visited on your own. You can either drive yourself or take a taxi or shuttle to the **Cabo Blanco Absolute Nature Reserve,** while the trailhead for the Montezuma Waterfall is just a short walk from the center of town.

The top attractions

Cabo Blanco Absolute Nature Reserve
As beautiful as the beaches around Montezuma are, the beaches at **Cabo Blanco Absolute Nature Reserve** are even more stunning. Located at the southernmost tip of the Nicoya Peninsula, Cabo Blanco is a national park that preserves a nesting site for brown pelicans, magnificent frigate birds, and brown boobies. The main beach here is backed by lush tropical forest that is home to howler monkeys. You can hike through the preserve's lush forest right down to the deserted, pristine Playa Cabo Blanco, which is 4km (2½ miles) away. Or, you can take a shorter 2km (1¼-mile) loop trail through the primary forest here. This is Costa Rica's oldest official biore-serve and was set up thanks to the pioneering efforts of conservationists Karen Mogensen and Nicholas Wessberg.

The trails here are gentle and well-marked. However, if you want to see and learn about the local flora and fauna, you should hire one of the guides who hang out around the park office. A two-hour guided hike should cost around $25 for a group of up to four people.

Cabo Blanco Absolute Nature Reserve is located 11km (6¾ miles) south of the village, along a rough dirt road. Shuttle buses head from Montezuma to Cabo Blanco roughly every two hours beginning at 8 a.m., and then turn around and bring folks from Cabo Blanco to Montezuma; the last one leaves Cabo Blanco around 5 p.m. The fare is $2 each way. These shuttles often don't run during the off season. Alternatively, you can share a taxi: The fare is around $15 to $20 per taxi, which can hold four or five passengers.

See map p. 281. Cabo Blanco Absolute Nature Reserve is located 11km (6¾ miles) south of Montezuma, along the only road out of town. Admission: $6. Open: Wed–Sun 8 a.m.–5 p.m.

Montezuma Waterfall

Located a vigorous 20-minute hike into the rain forest, the Montezuma waterfall is a tropical fantasy, with a large torrent pouring down into a deep, cool pool. A couple of waterfalls are actually located up this stream, but the upper falls are by far the more spectacular. This is a popular spot and can get crowded during the high season and on weekends.

Be very careful when climbing close to the rushing water, and also if you plan on taking any dives into the pools below. The rocks are quite slippery, and several people each year get very scraped up, break bones and otherwise hurt themselves here.

You'll find the trail to the falls just over the bridge south of the village (on your right just past Las Cascadas restaurant). At the first major outcropping of rocks, the trail disappears and you have to scramble up the rocks and river for a bit. A trail occasionally reappears for short stretches. Just stick close to the stream, and you'll eventually hit the falls.

See map p. 281. 7km (4 ½ miles) southeast of Cóbano, 45km (28 miles) south of Paquera, 18km (11 miles) south of Tambor.

More cool things to see and do

✔ **Canopy tour:** The **Waterfall Canopy Tour** (☎ 823-6111 or 642-0808) is built right alongside Montezuma's famous falls. The tour, which features 9 cables connecting 11 platforms, includes a stop to swim at a large pool above the largest drop in the falls. This tour is run several times each day and costs $35 per person.

✔ **Chilling on the beach:** The ocean here is a gorgeous royal blue, and beautiful beaches stretch out along the coast on either side of town. Be careful, though: The waves can occasionally be too rough for casual swimming, and you need to be aware of stray rocks at your feet. Be sure you know where the rocks and tide are before doing any bodysurfing. The best places to swim are a couple hundred meters north of town in front of the basic campsite **El Rincón de los Monos,** or several kilometers farther north at Playa Grande.

If you're driving out to Cabo Blanco, you'll pass through the tiny village of **Cabuya.** You'll find a couple of hidden patches of beach to discover around here, if you poke around some of the deserted dirt roads.

In the center of the village, you'll find some rental shops where you can rent boogie boards and snorkeling equipment (although the water must be very calm for snorkeling).

✔ **Horseback riding:** Several people around the village will rent you horses for around $8 to $10 an hour, although most people choose to do a guided four-hour horseback tour for $30 to $40. The most popular ride is to a second waterfall 8km (5 miles) north of Montezuma. Dubbed **El Chorro,** this waterfall cascades down into a tide pool at the edge of the ocean. The pool here is a delightful mix of fresh water and seawater, and you can bathe while gazing out over the sea and rocky coastline. When the water is clear and calm, this is one of my favorite swimming holes in all of Costa Rica. However, a massive landslide in 2004 filled in much of this pool and also somewhat lessened the drama and beauty of the actual falls. Moreover, the pool here is dependent upon the tides — it disappears entirely at very high tide. Luis, whose rental place is down the road that leads from town out to the beach, is a reliable source for horses, as is "Roger the horse guy" — any local can direct you to him. However, you'll find the best-cared-for and -kept horses at **Finca Los Caballos** (☎ 642-0124), which is located up the hill on the road leading into Montezuma.

Shopping in Montezuma

Plenty of simple souvenir stores, as well as itinerant artisans selling their wares on the street, rest in Montezuma; most of the offerings are pretty standard fare. However, it's definitely worth stopping in at **Piedra Colorado** (☎ 841-5855) to check out their impressive silver, stone, and polished-shell creations. This place is located in the tiny strip mall in the center of Montezuma.

Living it up after dark in Montezuma

The local action is centered around a couple of bars in downtown Montezuma. Head to either **Chico's Bar** (no phone) or the bar at the **Hotel Montezuma** (☎ 642-0657). Both are located on the main strip in town facing the water. Alternatively, there's often something happening, either live music or a DJ at **Playa Las Manchas** (☎ 642-0415), located about a mile south of town on the road to Cabo Blanco. If your evening tastes are mellower, **El Sano Banano Village Cafe** (☎ 642-0638) doubles as the local movie house. Nightly DVD releases are projected on a large screen; the selection ranges from first-run to quite artsy, and there's a constantly growing library of more than 800 movies. The movies begin at 7:30 p.m. and require a minimum purchase of $5.

Fast Facts: Montezuma

Ambulance

Call ☎ 128.

ATMs

You'll find an ATM at the Banco Nacional in Cóbano.

Country Code and City Code

The country code for Costa Rica is **506**. There are no city or area codes within Costa Rica. To call from the United States, dial 011-506 plus the seven-digit number. From within Costa Rica, you simply dial the seven-digit number.

Currency Exchange

Most hotels will exchange money for you at decent rates. To get official rates, head to the Banco Nacional in Cóbano.

Fire

Call ☎ 118.

Hospitals

The closest hospital is Hospital Monseñor Sanabria in Puntarenas (☎ 663-0033), although there are several doctors and a local clinic (☎ 642-0118) in Cóbano.

Information

Montezuma has no official information offices. Most hotels have a tour desk, concierge, or helpful front desk.

Internet Access

Several Internet cafes are located in Montezuma; all are located in the small central downtown area.

Newspapers

Several gift shops around town carry all the local papers, including the *Tico Times.*

Pharmacies

There's no true pharmacy in Montezuma. You can get basic pharmaceutical products at the two minisupermarkets in town.

Police

Call ☎ 911.

Post Office

There is a post office in Cóbano (☎ 642-0047). Alternatively, most hotels can mail your letters and postcards for you.

Taxis

Only a limited number of taxis are in Montezuma. Most congregate in the tiny downtown area or park in front of El Sano Banano Village Café. Alternatively, you can call Gilberto (☎ 642-0241) or Ronald (☎ 822-0610) for a cab.

Malpaís and Santa Teresa

Malpaís translates as "badlands," and I can't decide whether this is an accurate description or a deliberate local ploy to keep this place private — if the latter, it has officially failed. The beach here is a long, wide expanse of light sand dotted with rocky outcroppings. Sure, it can get rough here, but the surfers love it. The road out here from Cóbano used to be even rougher than the surf, but it's gradually being tamed.

Punta Islita

On the northern stretch of coast making up the Nicoya Peninsula sits one of Costa Rica's premier small luxury resorts — **Hotel Punta Islita** (☎ **231-6122;** fax: 231-0715; www.hotelpuntaislita.com). Nothing else is around, but if you're looking for fabulous rooms, great views, an isolated beach, personalized service, and plenty of amenities and activities to choose from, this is a perfect spot.

Punta Islita is isolated on a high bluff between two mountain ridges that meet the sea. The rooms here are done up in a Santa Fe style, with red Mexican floor tiles, neo-Navajo-print bedspreads, and adobe-colored walls offset with sky-blue doors and trim. Each room has a king-size bed and a private patio with a hammock; a few of these also have a Jacuzzi. The suites come with a separate sitting room and a private two-person plunge pool or Jacuzzi; the villas have two or three bedrooms, their own private swimming pools, and full kitchens. The open-air poolside restaurant here serves excellent Continental cuisine with an emphasis on fresh local ingredients.

The beach below the hotel is a small crescent of gray-white sand with a calm, protected section at the northern end. It's about a ten-minute hike, but the hotel will shuttle you down and back if you don't feel like walking. You can take the hotel's small canopy tour, which leaves from just below the small gym and ends just steps from the beach. There's a rancho bar and grill down there for when you get hungry or thirsty, and a lap pool for when the waves are too rough. The hotel has an excellent little spa offering a full range of spa treatments and services, including regular classes and activities. Prices run from $198 to $275 for doubles, $330 to $385 for suites, and $450 to $700 for villa rooms. Room and suite rates include breakfast.

Although it's possible to drive here from San José or Liberia, I highly recommend flying. The flight takes about 55 minutes, and both **Nature Air** (☎ **800-235-9272** in the United States and Canada, 299-6000 in Costa Rica; www.natureair.com) and **Sansa** (☎ **221-9414;** www.flysansa.com) fly here, as well as several charter companies. Nature Air leaves out of the Pavas airport; Sansa leaves out of Juan Santamaría International. Charter companies work out of both. Because Punta Islita is such a luxury resort, with its own little airstrip, letting them book the travel and add it onto your bill is best. Rates run from $65 to $90 per person each way.

This place is one of Costa Rica's hottest new spots, and hotels and restaurants are opening up at a dizzying pace. Still, it will take some time before this area becomes overly crowded. What you'll find in Malpaís and Santa Teresa today is a scattering of beach hotels and simple restaurants, miles of nearly deserted beach, and easy access to some nice jungle and a host of adventure-tour options.

Getting there

Flying to Tambor and taking a taxi to Malpaís or Santa Teresa is the fastest and easiest way to travel out here. Taking a car or bus, however, includes a pretty and relaxing ferry ride across the Golfo de Nicoya.

By air

The nearest airport is in Tambor, 27km (17 miles) away. **Sansa** (☎ 221-9414; www.flysansa.com) and **Nature Air** (☎ 800-235-9272 in the United States and Canada, 299-6000 in Costa Rica; www.natureair.com) both have a couple of daily flights to Tambor. Flight duration is about 30 minutes, and fares run between $58 and $66 each way.

Some of the hotels listed here may be willing to pick you up in Tambor for a reasonable fee. If not, you'll have to hire a taxi, which could cost anywhere from $25 to $30. **Taxis** are generally waiting to meet most regularly scheduled planes, but if you can't find one, you can call Elber Chacón (☎ 640-0120).

By car and ferry

Follow the directions earlier in this chapter to Montezuma. At Cóbano, follow the signs to Malpaís and Playa Santa Teresa. It's another 12km (7½ miles) or so down a very rough dirt road that pretty much requires four-wheel-drive and is sometimes (although rarely) impassable during the rainy season.

By bus and ferry

Follow the directions earlier in this chapter for getting to Montezuma, but get off the Montezuma bus in Cóbano. From Cóbano, there are buses daily for Malpaís and Santa Teresa at 10:30 a.m. and 2:30 p.m.; the fare is $1.50. Buses return daily to Cóbano at 7 a.m. and noon.

 These bus schedules are subject to change according to demand, road conditions, and the whims of the bus company. Moreover, as the popularity of this destination grows, more buses are occasionally added, so checking with your hotel in advance is a good idea.

If you miss the bus connection, you can hire a cab in Cóbano for around $12.

Orienting yourself in Malpaís and Santa Teresa

Malpaís and Santa Teresa are two tiny beach villages. In fact, there are no real towns here — just a string of hotels, restaurants, and assorted shops spread along a rough coastal dirt road.

As you reach the ocean, the road forks; Malpaís is to your left, Playa Carmen is straight ahead, and Santa Teresa is to your right. If you continue beyond Santa Teresa, you'll come to the even more deserted beaches of Playa Hermosa and Manzanillo (not to be confused with beaches of the same names to be found elsewhere in the country).

Getting around

This is an area where it's a good idea to have a rental car. If not, a good option is to rent an ATV. Several hotels and a few shops in the area will

Malpaís and Santa Teresa

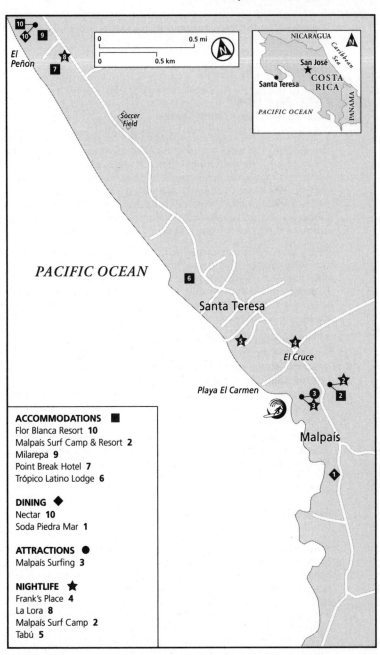

ACCOMMODATIONS ■
Flor Blanca Resort **10**
Malpaís Surf Camp & Resort **2**
Milarepa **9**
Point Break Hotel **7**
Trópico Latino Lodge **6**

DINING ◆
Nectar **10**
Soda Piedra Mar **1**

ATTRACTIONS ●
Malpaís Surfing **3**

NIGHTLIFE ★
Frank's Place **4**
La Lora **8**
Malpaís Surf Camp **2**
Tabú **5**

rent a rugged ATV for around $45 to $65 per day. If you need a taxi, call Elber Chacón (☎ **640-0120**).

Your best bet for information out this way will definitely be your hotel desk and staff.

Spending the night

Flor Blanca Resort
$$$$–$$$$$ Playa Santa Teresa

This intimate resort hotel is, hands down, the most luxurious option in this neck of the woods and one of the most luxurious boutique hotels in the country. The individual villas are huge, with a vast central living area opening onto a spacious veranda. The furnishings, decorations, and architecture boast a mix of Latin American and Asian influences, with some African adornments thrown in for good measure. Most overlook the lush gardens here, and about half have views through these to the sea. The top units here are beachfront villas.

Every villa features a large open-air bathroom with a garden shower and teardrop-shape tub set amid flowering tropical foliage. You can opt for either the one-bedroom villas with a four-poster king-size bed in the main bedroom or a two-bedroom, two-bathroom villa better suited to families, with two twin beds in a separate upstairs bedroom. You'll find several examples of the resort's namesake tree planted around the grounds.

The restaurant here features wonderfully prepared creative fusion cuisine (see the listing later in this chapter). There's a full-size and active dojo on grounds, where yoga, kickboxing, and cardio-workout classes are regularly offered. The beautiful free-form pool is on two levels, with a sculpted waterfall connecting them and a shady Indonesian-style gazebo off to one side for lounging around in. Flor Blanca is located toward the northern end of Playa Santa Teresa.

See map p. 289. Playa Santa Teresa. ☎ *640-0232. Fax: 640-0226.* www.florblanca. com. *Rack rates: $290–$340 double; $490–$540 2-bedroom villa for 4. Rates include full breakfast. Rates lower during the off season, higher during peak weeks. AE, DC, MC, V. No children under 6.*

Malpaís Surf Camp & Resort
$ Malpaís

Whether you're a wannabe or an experienced wave rider, this is the place to hang out when you're not hanging ten in Malpaís. You'll find a wide range of accommodations here, reflected in the equally wide range of prices. The most basic rooms are open-air ranchos with gravel floors, lathe-and-bamboo walls, bead curtains for a door, and shared bathrooms. From here, your options get progressively more comfortable, ranging from shared-bathroom bunk-bed rooms to new deluxe poolside villas, to private houses with all the amenities. You can also pitch a tent.

A refreshing free-form tile pool is in the center of the complex, and the large, open main lodge area serves as a combination restaurant, bar, lounge, and surfboard-storage area. There's satellite TV with surf videos playing most of the day, as well as pool, Ping-Pong, and foosball tables. The overall vibe here is loose and funky, as it should be. The restaurant serves filling, fresh, and, at times, quite creative cuisine, depending on how accomplished the itinerant surf-chef-of-the-month is. Surf rentals, lessons, and video sessions are all available.

See map p. 289. Malpaís, ☎ *640-0031. Fax: 640-0061.* www.malpaissurfcamp. com. *Rack rates: $20–$25 double with shared bathroom; $40–$70 double with private bathroom; $7 per person camping. AE, MC, V.*

Milarepa
$$ Playa Santa Teresa

Named after a Buddhist sage, this small collection of individual bungalows is spread around shady grounds fronting the beach, just next door to Flor Blanca. The bungalows are simple, roomy, and understated. All have wooden floors, a mix of teak and bamboo furniture, beds with mosquito netting, and a private porch. An overhead fan keeps things cool, and there are plenty of windows for cross-ventilation. The more expensive units are closest to the beach and have ocean views. There's a midsize pool here for when the surf is too rough, as well as an elegant little restaurant.

See map p. 289. Playa Santa Teresa. ☎ *640-0023. Fax: 640-0168.* www.milarepa hotel.com. *Rack rates: $105–$125 double. Rates include full breakfast. Rates lower during the off season, higher during peak weeks. AE, MC, V.*

Point Break Hotel
$ Playa Santa Teresa

Hard-core surfers will want to check out this place, opened in late 2004. The simple cabins here feature polished concrete floors, inset with cross-sections of tree trunks, two twin beds, and three walls comprised largely of screening. They also come with a refrigerator and a small patio area with a couple of chairs. None of the rooms has its own bathroom, but the shared bathrooms and showers are kept very clean. A large open-air lounge area is under a thatch roof strung with hammocks; it features a television. The greatest attraction here is the fact that this hotel sits just steps away from one of the best breaks along this stretch of coast — hence, the name and the steady stream of surfers who choose this simple place.

See map p. 289. Playa Santa Teresa. ☎ */fax* *640-0190. Rack rates: $40 double. AE, MC, V.*

Trópico Latino Lodge
$$ Playa Santa Teresa

One of the first hotels out here, this beachfront spread has aged well and is still a good choice. The nicest accommodations here are the new private bungalows, which have artistic tile work and décor touches, as well as views of the ocean. The original rooms here are housed in four duplex units. These are huge — the king-size bamboo bed barely makes a dent in the floor space. There's also a separate sofa bed, as well as a small desk, a wall unit of shelves, and closet space galore. Although none of the older rooms has any ocean view to speak of, each has a private patio with a hammock. The shady grounds are rich in the native *pochote* tree, which is known for its spiky trunk. The small restaurant here has excellent fresh fish and plenty of pasta dishes. When I last visited, there were plans to add some more bungalows, as well as a yoga studio.

See map p. 289. Playa Santa Teresa. ☎ *640-0062. Fax: 640-0117.* www.hotel tropicolatino.com. *Rack rates: $73–$116 double. Rates lower in the off season. No credit cards.*

Dining locally

Nectar
$$$ At Flor Blanca Resort   FUSION

The dimly lit open-air setting of this poolside and beachfront restaurant is elegant, yet casual. There's a Pacific Rim influence to the fusion cuisine served up here. On a recent visit, I started things off with a sashimi platter that mixed fresh tuna with thinly sliced beef carpaccio — it was exquisite. In addition to fresh seafood and several vegetarian entrees, you may also find lamb, rabbit, or duck on the regularly changing menu. The creativity, service, and presentation are some of the best you'll find in Costa Rica.

See map p. 289. At Flor Blanca Resort in Santa Teresa. ☎ *640-0232. Reservations recommended. Main courses: $8–$24. AE, MC, V. Open: Daily noon to 10 p.m.*

Soda Piedra Mar
$ Malpaís   SEAFOOD/COSTA RICAN

This simple open-air restaurant is set on a rocky outcropping just steps away from the sea. The place is little more than a zinc-roofed shack that seems as if a stiff breeze would quickly level it. There are only a few tables here under the low roof. Weather permitting, more tables are set in the sand under the sun or stars. The fare is simple, but the fish is guaranteed fresh, the portions are hearty, the lobster is very reasonably priced, and the setting and sunsets are wonderful.

See map p. 289. On the beach in Malpaís. ☎ *640-0069. Main courses: $3–$12. No credit cards. Open: Daily 7 a.m.–10 p.m.*

Exploring Malpaís and Santa Teresa

There are no major attractions in this area, but there are plenty of activities and adventures to be had. Join the surfer dudes and catch some waves, or take a hike or horseback ride on solid land. You'll find information and details about the area's most popular options below.

Top attraction

Malpaís surfing

Surfing is the main draw in this area. The long beaches of Malpaís, Playa Carmen, and Playa Santa Teresa offer up a steady stream of beach breaks, with enough peaks and points so that it's almost never crowded. If you want to rent a board or take a lesson, check out the Santa Teresa Surf School (☎ 640-0106; www.santateresasurfschool.com).

See map p. 289. There are rideable waves all along the length of the beaches here, but I like Malpaís best. Open: Daily 24 hours, but I don't recommend surfing at night.

More cool things to see and do

✔ **Canopy tour: Canopy del Pacífico** (☎ 640-0071) is located toward the southern end of Malpaís and inland. A two-hour tour over the nearly 1km (½ mile) of cables touches down on eight platforms, features two rappels, and offers good views of both the forest and the ocean below. The cost is $35.

✔ **Horseback riding and mountain biking:** The hills, fields, and forests of this area are perfect for exploring on horseback or riding a mountain bike. Any of the hotels in the area can hook you up with a horseback-riding tour for around $10 to $15 per hour.

✔ **Scuba diving:** If you want to go scuba diving, contact **Pacific Divers** (☎ 640-0187; www.pacificdivers-costarica.com), which offers daily boat dives into the rich waters off the Cabo Blanco reserve.

Living it up after dark in Malpaís and Santa Teresa

There's not much in the way of raging nightlife here. Some folks make the long and arduous journey over to Montezuma. The most popular bars are **Tabú** (☎ 640-0353), in Malpaís, and **La Lora** (☎ 640-0132), in Santa Teresa. Surfers and other travelers also tend to gather in the evenings at **Frank's Place** (☎ 640-0096) and the **Malpaís Surf Camp** (☎ 640-0031).

Fast Facts: Malpaís and Santa Teresa

Ambulance

Call ☎ 128.

ATMs

You'll find an ATM at the Banco Nacional in Cóbano.

Country Code and City Code

The country code for Costa Rica is **506**. There are no city or area codes within Costa Rica. To call from the United States, dial 011-506 plus the seven-digit number. From within Costa Rica, you simply dial the seven-digit number.

Currency Exchange

Most hotels will exchange money for you at decent rates. To get official rates, head to the Banco Nacional in Cóbano.

Fire

Call ☎ 118.

Hospitals

The closest hospital is in Puntarenas (☎ 663-0033), although there are several doctors and a local clinic (☎ 642-0118) in Cóbano.

Information

There are no official information offices in Malpaís or Santa Teresa. Most hotels have a tour desk, concierge, or helpful front desk.

Internet Access

You'll find several Internet cafes in Malpaís and Santa Teresa. One of the best is at Frank's Place (see earlier in this chapter).

Newspapers

Several gift shops around town carry all of the local papers, including the *Tico Times*.

Pharmacies

There's a small pharmacy in Malpaís. For a better selection, head to Cóbano. The Cóbano pharmacy (☎ 642-0685) is located at the main intersection for Montezuma.

Police

Call ☎ 911.

Post Office

There is a post office in Cóbano (☎ 642-0047). Alternatively, most hotels can mail your letters and postcards for you.

Taxis

You'll only find a limited number of taxis in Malpaís and Santa Teresa. The best place to find one is at the crossroads at the entrance to town, in front of Frank's Place. Alternatively, you can call Elber Chacón (☎ 640-0120) for a cab.

Chapter 20

Exploring Southern Costa Rica

. . . .

In This Chapter

▶ Getting to and around Costa Rica's remote southern zone
▶ Hiking and camping in Corcovado National Park
▶ Kayaking with dolphins on the Golfo Dulce
▶ Visiting a couple of bountiful botanical gardens

. . . .

osta Rica's southern zone is a place of rugged beauty, with vast expanses of virgin lowland rain forest and few cities or settlements. Lushly forested mountains tumble into the sea, streams run clear and clean, scarlet macaws squawk raucously in the treetops, and dolphins frolic in the Golfo Dulce.

This region is home to **Corcovado National Park,** the largest single expanse of lowland tropical rain forest in Central America, and its sister, **Piedras Blancas National Park.** Scattered around the edges of these national parks, on the Osa Peninsula and along the shores of the Golfo Dulce, are some of the country's finest nature lodges. These lodges, in general, offer comfortable to nearly luxurious accommodations, atten-tive service, knowledgeable guides, and a wide range of activities and tours, all close to the area's many natural wonders.

This area's beauty doesn't come easy. In many ways, this is Costa Rica's final frontier. The cities of Golfito and Puerto Jiménez are nearly as wild as the jungles that surround them. Moreover, the heat and humidity are more than many can stand. Some parts of the southern zone receive more than 635cm (250 in.) of rain per year. In addition to producing lush forests, this massive amount of rain produces more than a few disgrun-tled visitors.

Although most of the lodges listed in this chapter are quite cozy, and some are even spectacular, remember, none of these nature lodges have in-room televisions, telephones, or air-conditioning. Although this region is noted for its hot and steamy weather, most of these nature lodges are built with cool tile or wood floors and plenty of shade and ventilation. I never find it uncomfortable, and hoards of satisfied visitors seem to agree. However, if you are particularly sensitive to the heat, or particularly fond of air-conditioning, be sure to book a hotel with in-room A/C.

Drake Bay

Located on the northern end of the Osa Peninsula, Drake Bay is little more than a small and spread-out collection of isolated lodges catering to naturalists, anglers, scuba divers, and adventure travelers.

The remote bay is named after Sir Francis Drake, who is believed to have anchored here in 1579. Emptying into the bay is the tiny Agujitas River, which acts as a protected harbor for small boats and is a great place to do a bit of kayaking or swimming.

Stretching south from Drake Bay are miles of primary rain forest and deserted beaches. Adventurous explorers will find tide pools, spring-fed rivers, waterfalls, forest trails, and some of the best bird-watching in all of Costa Rica. If a paradise such as this appeals to you, Drake Bay makes a good base for exploring the southern zone.

Getting there

Flying directly into the small airstrip in Drake Bay is the preferred means of travel to this remote region. However, it is possible to get here via a combination of bus, taxi, and boat. I provide detailed information on both of these options in the following sections.

By air

Most visitors fly directly into the little airstrip at Drake Bay, although when demand is high, some are still routed through Palmar Sur. Most lodges in this area include transportation in their packages, so check with them before you book. **Sansa** (☎ **221-9414;** www.flysansa.com) and **Nature Air** (☎ **800-235-9272** in the United States and Canada, 299-6000 in Costa Rica; www.natureair.com) both have regular flights to Drake Bay and Palmar Sur.

If your travels take you to Drake Bay via Palmar Sur, you must then take a 15-minute bus or taxi ride over dirt roads to the small town of Sierpe. This bumpy ride takes you through several banana plantations and quickly past some important archaeological sites. In Sierpe, you board a small boat for a 40km (25-mile) ride to Drake Bay. The first half of this trip snakes through a maze of mangrove canals and rivers before heading out to sea for the final leg to the bay. Entering and exiting the Sierpe River mouth is often treacherous, and I've had several very white-knuckle moments here.

Whichever route you take, have your hotel or lodge arrange final transportation details from the airport to their site.

By bus, taxi, and boat

I recommend arranging your transportation in advance, but if you're really intrepid, you can get to Drake Bay on your own by bus, taxi, and boat.

Tracopa (☎ 222-2666) express buses leave San José daily for Palmar Norte roughly every two hours between 5 a.m. and 6 p.m. The ride takes six hours. You can also catch any Golfito-bound bus from this same station and get off in Palmar Norte. When you're in Palmar Norte, ask when the next bus goes out to Sierpe. If it doesn't leave for a while (buses aren't frequent), consider taking a taxi.

When you arrive at the Palmar Norte bus station, you'll need to take a taxi to the village of Sierpe. The fare should be around $15. When you get to Sierpe, head to the dock and try to find space on a boat. This should run you another $15 to $30. If you don't arrive early enough, you might have to hire an entire boat, which usually runs around $80 to $120 for a boat that can carry up to six passengers. Make sure that you feel confident about the boat and the skipper, and, if possible, try to find a spot on a boat from one of the established lodges in Drake Bay.

Getting around

Until 1997, there was no road into Drake Bay and no airstrip in town. Now that both exist, their effects are palpable. The town is growing and changing at a rapid pace. Legal and clandestine logging is taking place all along the road into Drake Bay and around — and even in — the national park.

Still, because of the bay's remoteness, major development is probably a long way off here. The tiny town itself still has just one dirt road running parallel to the beach along the crescent-shaped namesake bay. Only one lodge listed here is actually in the town of Drake Bay, the rest are across the Río Agujitas or farther south along the coast.

Spending the night

Cabinas Jinetes de Osa
$$$ Drake Bay

This former budget hotel in the village of Drake Bay has been spruced up, expanded, and turned into a very comfortable option for serious scuba divers and adventure tourists. Although it's now far from a budget lodging, it does offer a reasonable alternative to the more upscale options in the area. The wooden construction, attention to detail, and location directly above the beach give Jinetes an edge over other lodgings right in the village of Drake Bay. The nicest rooms here are quite plush and even have a view of the bay. The hotel is pretty close to the docks on the Río Agujitas, which is a plus for those traveling independently or with heavy bags. A wide range of tours and activities is available, as are dive packages, weekly packages, and Professional Association of Diving Instructors

(PADI) certification courses. At press time, they were building some newer, more luxurious rooms, as well as a swimming pool, up the steep hill behind the current lodge.

See map p. 299. Drake Bay. ☎ *800-317-0333 or 303-838-0969 in the United States and Canada, or 236-5637 in Costa Rica. Fax: 303-838-1914.* www.drakebayhotel.com. *Rack rates: $120–$200 double. Rates include 3 meals daily. DISC, MC, V.*

Casa Corcovado Jungle Lodge
$$$$–$$$$$ Osa Peninsula

This very isolated jungle lodge is the closest accommodation to Corcovado National Park from the Drake Bay side of the Osa Peninsula. The rooms are all private bungalows built on the grounds of an old cacao plantation on the jungle's edge. The bungalows are all quite spacious, with one or two double beds and a large tiled bathroom. Electricity and hot water are supplied by a combination solar and hydroelectric energy system.

Family-style meals are served in the main lodge, although most guests take lunch with them to the beach or on one of the various tours available. Late afternoons are usually enjoyed from a high point overlooking the sea and sunset, with your beverage of choice in hand.

Access is strictly by small boat here, and sometimes the beach landing can be a bit rough, so it's recommended that guests be in decent physical shape. When the sea is not too rough, the beach is great for swimming; when the sea *is* rough, the beach is a great place to grab a hammock in the shade and read a book. A wide range of tours and activities is available.

See map p. 299. Osa Peninsula. ☎ *888-896-6097 in the United States, or 256-3181 in Costa Rica. Fax: 256-7409.* www.casacorcovado.com. *Rack rates: $703–$803 per person for 3 days/2 nights with 1 tour; $863–$963 for 4 days/3 nights with 2 tours. Rates are based on double occupancy and include round-trip transportation from San José, all meals, park fees, and taxes. Rates slightly higher peak weeks, lower in the off season. AE, MC, V.*

Drake Bay Wilderness Resort
$$$–$$$$ Drake Bay

This is one of the best-located lodges at Drake Bay. It backs onto the Río Agujitas and fronts the Pacific. The rooms here are fairly simple, but they are clean and comfortable, with ceiling fans, small verandas, and good mattresses on the beds. A few of the rooms have actually been nicely upgraded in recent years, and they have added a deluxe honeymoon suite on a little hill toward the rear of the property, with a great view of the bay. The newest additions are five budget cabins that share bath and shower facilities. The family-style meals are filling, with an emphasis on fresh seafood and fresh fruits. My favorite treats here are the freshly baked chocolate-chip cookies frequently served for dessert.

Because it's on a rocky spit, there isn't a good swimming beach on-site (it's about a 15-minute walk away), but there's a saltwater swimming pool in

Osa Peninsula

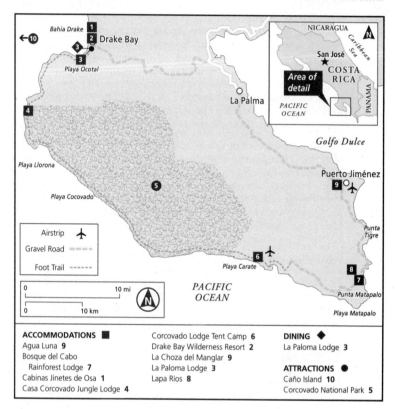

ACCOMMODATIONS ▪
Agua Luna **9**
Bosque del Cabo
  Rainforest Lodge **7**
Cabinas Jinetes de Osa **1**
Casa Corcovado Jungle Lodge **4**

Corcovado Lodge Tent Camp **6**
Drake Bay Wilderness Resort **2**
La Choza del Manglar **9**
La Paloma Lodge **3**
Lapa Ríos **8**

DINING ◆
La Paloma Lodge **3**

ATTRACTIONS ●
Caño Island **10**
Corcovado National Park **5**

front of the bay, and, depending on the tide, you can bathe in a beautiful
small tide pool formed by the rocks. The resort offers a wide range of tour
options. The lodge runs a small butterfly farm and iguana-breeding project
on some land inland from Drake Bay, and you can even spend the night
there, if you want.

See map above. Drake Bay. ☎ *770-8012 or 384-4107. Fax: 250-1145.* www.drake
bay.com. *Rack rates: $65 per person per day with shared bath, $95–$130 per person
per day standard and deluxe; rates include all meals and taxes. $530–$630 per person
for 4 days/3 nights with 2 tours, including all meals, and taxes. Rates lower in the off
season. AE, MC, V.*

La Paloma Lodge
$$$$–$$$$$ Drake Bay

Set on a steep hill overlooking the Pacific, with Caño Island in the distance,
the individual bungalows at La Paloma offer expansive ocean views that,

combined with the attentive and amiable service, make this my top choice in Drake Bay. All the cabins are spacious and private and are set among lush foliage facing the Pacific. All come with a large private balcony or veranda. The large two-story Sunset Ranchos are the choice rooms here: Sliding screen windows and doors keep you in touch with nature and let the ocean breezes blow through, and the views are to die for. The other cabins are a tad smaller but have been recently remodeled with updated and luxurious bathrooms and pretty good ocean views as well. The standard rooms, which are located in a row in one long building, are smaller and less private than the cabins, but they're still quite attractive and have good views from their verandas (which, like the cabins, have hammocks).

The main lodge building is a large, open-air structure with a long veranda that has a sitting area and swing chairs, where you can mingle with other guests. The beach is about a seven-minute hike down a winding jungle path, but the swimming pool is located close to all the action and, like everything else here, is set on the edge of the hillside, with great ocean and jungle views. There are single and double kayaks, as well as boogie boards and surfboards free for guests to use. The lodge also offers scuba certification courses.

See map p. 299. Drake Bay. ☎ *239-2801 or* ☎*/fax 239-0954.* www.lapaloma lodge.com. *Rack rates: $1,000–$1,210 per person for 4 days/3 nights with 2 tours; $1,130–$1,400 per person for 5 days/4 nights with 2 tours. Rates are based on double occupancy and include round-trip transportation from San José, all meals, park fees, indicated tours, and taxes. Rates slightly lower in the off season. AE, MC, V (5 percent surcharge).*

Dining locally

La Paloma Lodge
$$$$–$$$$$ Drake Bay   CONTINENTAL/COSTA RICAN

Drake Bay is an isolated region, and restaurants are hard to come by. Most resort restaurants tend to have good, tasty, hearty fare, however. The best can be found here at La Paloma. Hearty and delicious meals are served family-style, and the kitchen will accommodate vegetarians or those with special dietary needs with advance warning. Scrumptious freshly baked bread is served with almost every meal here.

See map p. 299. Drake Bay. ☎ *239-2801 or* ☎*/fax 239-0954.* www.lapaloma lodge.com. *Hotel rates include all meals. AE, MC, V. Open: Breakfast, lunch, and dinner daily.*

Exploring Drake Bay

Remember, this is a very remote region, with no cars. All of the major attractions here are reached and visited as part of an organized tour. All of the hotels in the area arrange tours to these attractions.

Those mysterious stone spheres

Although Costa Rica lacks the great cities, giant temples, and bas-relief carvings of the Maya, Aztec, and Olmec civilizations of northern Mesoamerica, its pre-Columbian residents did leave a unique legacy that continues to cause archaeologists and anthropologists to scratch their heads and wonder. Over a period of several centuries, hundreds of painstakingly carved and carefully positioned granite spheres were left by the peoples who lived throughout the Diquis Delta, in southern Costa Rica. The orbs, which range from grapefruit size to more than 2m (6½ ft.) in diameter, can weigh up to 15 tons, and many reach near-spherical perfection.

Archaeologists believe that the spheres were created during two defined cultural periods. The first, called the Aguas Buenas period, dates from around A.D. 100 to 500. Few spheres survive from this time. The second phase, during which spheres were created in apparently greater numbers, is called the Chiriquí period and lasted from approximately A.D. 800 to 1500. The "balls" believed to have been carved during this timeframe are widely dispersed along the entire length of the lower section of the Terraba River. To date, only one known quarry for the spheres has been discovered, in the mountains above the Diquis Delta, which points to a difficult and lengthy transportation process.

Some archaeologists believe that the spheres were hand-carved in a very time-consuming process, using stone tools, perhaps aided by some sort of firing process. However, another theory holds that granite blocks were placed at the bases of powerful waterfalls, and the hydraulic beating of the water eventually turned and carved the rock into these near-perfect spheres. And more than a few proponents have credited extraterrestrial intervention for the creation of the stone balls.

Most of the stone balls have been found at the archaeological remains of defined settlements and are associated with either central plazas or known burial sites. Their size and placement have been interpreted to have both social and celestial importance, although their exact significance remains a mystery. Unfortunately, many of the stone balls have been plundered and are currently used as lawn ornaments in the fancier neighborhoods of San José. Some have even been shipped out of the country. The **Museo Nacional de Costa Rica** (Chapter 12) has a nice collection, including one massive sphere in its center courtyard. It's a never-fail photo-op. You can also see the stone balls near the small **airports in Palmar Sur** and **Drake Bay,** and on **Caño Island** (which is located 19km/12 miles off the Pacific coast near Drake Bay).

The top attractions

Corcovado National Park

Corcovado National Park is a main attraction in this area. All the lodges in Drake Bay offer day trips and hikes into Corcovado National Park at the San Pedrillo entrance. The trails here are wonderful. One leads to a beautiful jungle waterfall, where you can take a refreshing dip.

If you want to spend a lot of time hiking and camping in Corcovado National Park, Puerto Jiménez is your best base and jumping-off point. See the Puerto Jiménez section later in this chapter for a much more detailed description of exploring Corcovado National Park.

See map p. 299. The San Pedrillo entrance to the park is located approximately 15km (9⅓ miles) south of Drake Bay. Admission: $8, usually included in the price of tour. Open: Daily 8 a.m.–4 p.m.

Caño Island

One of the most popular excursions from Drake Bay is a trip out to Caño Island and the **Caño Island Biological Reserve.** The island was once home to a pre-Columbian culture about which little is known. A trip to the island includes a short hike to an ancient cemetery, where you'll also be able to see some of the stone spheres that are commonly believed to have been carved by the people who once lived in this area (see "Those mysterious stone spheres," in this chapter). Few animals or birds live on the island, but the beach here is gorgeous, and the coral reefs just offshore teem with life. This is one of Costa Rica's prime scuba spots. Visibility is often quite good, and there's even easily accessible snorkeling right from the beach. It's about a 40-minute boat ride to the island. Trips here usually include a picnic lunch on the beach. All the lodges listed earlier in this chapter offer tours to Caño Island.

See map p. 299. 19km (12 miles) offshore from Drake Bay. Admission: $6 park entrance fee, usually included in the tour price. Open: Daily 8 a.m.–4 p.m.

More cool things to see and do

In addition to trips to Caño Island and Corcovado National Park, all the lodges in the area offer a host of half-day and full-day tours and activities, including horseback rides, scuba diving, and sportfishing. In some cases, tours are included in your room rate or package; in others, they must be bought à la carte. Other options include mountain biking and sea kayaking. Most of these tours run between $60 and $100, depending on the activity, with scuba diving ($100–$120 for a two-tank dive) and sportfishing ($450–$1,200, depending on the size of the boat and other amenities) costing a bit more.

  ✔ **Chilling on the beach:** Although the beach fronting Drake Bay itself is acceptable and calm for swimming, it's far from spectacular. The most popular swimming beach is a pretty small patch of sand about a seven-minute hike beyond and down from La Paloma Lodge. The nicest beaches around involve taking a day trip to either Caño Island or San Josesito, a beautiful beach farther south on the peninsula with excellent snorkeling possibilities.

  ✔ **Taking a canopy tour:** The folks from the **Original Canopy Tour** (☎ 257-5149; www.canopytour.com) have an operation in Drake

Bay in the forest behind the Cabinas Jinetes de Osa. This tour features nine platforms connected by six cables. The longest cable here is over 90m (300 ft.) in length. The two-and-a-half-hour tour costs $45 per person.

Living it up after dark in Drake Bay

Aside from one weekend disco in the center of town and the small bars at the individual lodges, there is virtually no nightlife in Drake Bay That is, unless you opt to take the two-hour **Night Tour** (www. thenighttour.com; $35 per person) offered by Tracie Stice. Tracie is affectionately known as "The Bug Lady." Equipped with flashlights and night-vision glasses, participants get a bug's-eye view of the forest at night (arachnophobes should stay away). You might see the reflection of some larger forest dweller, but most of the tour is a fascinating exploration of the nocturnal insect world. Consider yourself lucky if Tracie finds the burrow of a trap-door spider or large tarantula.

Puerto Jiménez and the Osa Peninsula

Despite its small size and languid pace, Puerto Jiménez is a bustling little burg, where rough jungle gold panners mix with wealthy ecotourists, budget backpackers, and a surprising number of celebrities seeking a small dose of anonymity and escape. Located on the southeastern tip of the Osa Peninsula, the town itself is just a couple of gravel streets with the ubiquitous soccer field, a block of general stores, some inexpensive *sodas* (diner-style restaurants), a butcher shop, and several bars. Scarlet macaws fly overhead, and mealy parrots provide wake-up calls.

Puerto Jiménez is Costa Rica's principal gateway to Corcovado National Park. The national park has its headquarters here, and this town makes an excellent base for exploring this vast wilderness. Although the in-town accommodations are decidedly budget-oriented, you'll find several far-more-luxurious places farther south on the Osa Peninsula.

Getting there

Flying into Puerto Jiménez is the best way to visit this remote region. However, you can get here by car or bus, although both are very long rides. You'll find more information on all these options in the following sections.

By air

Sansa (☎ 221-9414; www.flysansa.com) and **Nature Air** (☎ 800-235-9272 in the United States and Canada, 299-6000 in Costa Rica; www. natureair.com) both have a few daily flights to Puerto Jiménez from San José. On both airlines, picking up the flight in Quepos and Manuel Antonio, with advance notice, is also often possible.

Note that due to the remoteness of this area and the unpredictable flux of traffic, both Sansa and Nature Air frequently improvise on scheduling. Sometimes this means an unscheduled stop in Quepos or Golfito either on the way down from or back to San José, which can add some time to your flight. Less frequently, it might mean a change in departure time, so confirming the time is always best. Also, lodges down here sometimes run charters, so asking them is a good idea.

By car

Take the Interamerican Highway east out of San José (through San Pedro and Cartago) and continue south on this road. In about three hours, you'll reach San Isidro de El General. Although you can continue on the Interamerican Highway all the way south, it is currently faster, smoother, and safer to turn off in San Isidro and head to Dominical, picking up the Southern Highway or Costanera Sur in Dominical. From here, it's a fast and smooth shot down Palmar Norte, where you meet up again with the Interamerican Highway. Take the turnoff for La Palma, Rincón, and Puerto Jiménez. This road is paved at first, but at Rincón it turns to gravel. The last 35km (22 miles) are slow and rough, and, during the rainy season (mid-Apr to Nov), it's too muddy for anything but a four-wheel-drive vehicle.

By bus

Express buses (☎ 257-4121 in San José, ☎ 771-4744 in Puerto Jiménez) leave San José daily at 6 a.m. and noon from Calle 12 between avenidas 7 and 9. The trip takes eight hours; the fare is $5.50. Buses depart Puerto Jiménez for San José daily at 5 and 11 a.m.

Orienting yourself in Puerto Jiménez and the Osa Peninsula

Puerto Jiménez is a dirt-lane town on the southern coast of the Osa Peninsula. The public dock is over a bridge past the north end of the soccer field; the bus stop is 2 blocks east of the center of town. The airstrip runs north-south along the western edge of town.

From Puerto Jiménez, a rough dirt road runs out to Carate, where the road ends and Corcovado National Park begins. This road fords several rivers, which can sometimes be impassable for most vehicles during the rainy season.

Getting around

You can easily walk anywhere in Puerto Jiménez. Rugged four-wheel-drive taxis are available for trips out to Carate, Corcovado National Park, and the isolated lodges listed later in this chapter.

To travel out to Carate by "public transportation," pick up one of the collective taxis (actually, a four-wheel-drive pickup truck with a tarpaulin cover and slat seats in the back) that leave Puerto Jiménez daily at 6 a.m. and 1 p.m., returning at 8 a.m. and 4 p.m. *Remember:* These taxis are very informal and change their schedules regularly to meet demand or avoid bad weather, so always ask in town. The one-way fare is around $7. A small fleet of these pickups leaves from the main road in town, more or less in front of the Soda Carolina, and will stop to pick up anyone who flags them down along the way. Your other option is to hire a private taxi through **Taxi Puerto Jimenez** (☎ 735-5481), which will cost approximately $60 to $70 each way to Carate.

There is daily passenger launch service from Puerto Jiménez to Golfito from the public dock at 6 a.m. The trip takes one and a half hours; the fare is $3. The return trip departs at 11:30 a.m. from Golfito's municipal dock.

You can also charter a water taxi for the trip across the Golfo Dulce to Golfito. You'll have to pay between $40 and $60 for an entire launch, some of which can carry up to 12 people.

If you can't get to your next destination by boat, bus, taxi, commuter airline, or car, **Alfa Romeo Aero Taxi** (☎ 775-1515) runs airline charters to most of the nearby destinations, including Carate, Drake Bay, Sirena, and Golfito.

The Corcovado National Park office (☎ 735-5036) is in town here, across from the airstrip. This stop is necessary if you're thinking of camping in the park, and it's a good place to get general info on the park and area.

There are a couple of Internet cafes in town; the best of these is **Cafe Net El Sol** (☎ 735-5719; www.soldeosa.com), which is a great place to book tours and get information. The cafe is also a Wi-Fi hot spot.

Spending the night

Agua Luna
$ Puerto Jiménez

Agua Luna is located right at the foot of the town's public dock and backs up to a mangrove forest. The older rooms directly face the gulf across a fenced-in gravel parking area. The most surprising feature in each of these rooms is the bathroom, which includes both a shower and a tub facing a picture window that looks into the mangroves. There are two double beds in each room, and on the tiled veranda out front you'll find hammocks for lounging. The newer rooms are located a half-block away and are smaller and less attractive than those in the original building. The higher prices are for the larger rooms, which have tubs and minirefrigerators.

See map p. 307. In front of the public dock, Puerto Jiménez. ☎ *735-5034. Fax: 735-5393. Rack rates: $45–$65 double. V.*

Bosque del Cabo Rainforest Lodge
$$$$ Osa Peninsula

This secluded jungle lodge is a real charmer. The cabins are all spacious and attractively furnished, with wooden decks or verandas to catch the ocean views, and are set amid beautiful gardens. Bosque del Cabo is located 150m (492 ft.) above the water at the southern tip of the Osa Peninsula, where the Golfo Dulce meets the Pacific Ocean. The deluxe cabins come with king-size beds and slightly larger deck space. The Congo cabin is my choice for its spectacular view of the sunrise from your bed. All the cabins have indoor bathrooms, although most have tiled showers set outdoors amid flowering heliconia and ginger.

There's a trail down to a secluded beach that has some tide pools and ocean-carved caves. Another trail leads to a jungle waterfall, and several others wind through the rain forests of the lodge's 243 hectares (600-plus-acre) private reserve. The wildlife viewing here is excellent. If you're too lazy to hike down to the beach, there's a small pool by the main lodge. Surfing is a popular activity here, as are hiking and horseback riding. Attractions include a canopy platform 36m (118 ft.) up a Manu tree, reached along a 90m (295-ft.) zip line, as well as a bird- and wildlife-watching rancho set beside a little lake on the edge of their tropical gardens and surrounded by forest. Trips to the national park or fishing excursions can be arranged, as can guided hikes, sea kayaking, and a host of other activities and tours.

See map p. 299. Osa Peninsula. ☎/fax **735-5206** *or 381-4847.* www.bosquedel cabo.com. *Rack rates: $280–$310 double. Rates include 3 meals daily and taxes. $25 round-trip transportation from Puerto Jiménez. MC, V.*

Corcovado Lodge Tent Camp
$$ Osa Peninsula

If you're looking for a balanced blend of comfort and adventure, check out Corcovado Lodge Tent Camp, which is built on a low bluff right above the beach. Forested mountains rise up behind the tent camp, and just a few minutes' walk away is the entrance to the national park. Accommodations are in large tents pitched on wooden decks. Each tent has two twin beds, a table, a couple of plastic garden chairs on the front deck, and an ocean view. Toilets and showers are a short walk away, but there are enough that there's usually no waiting.

Meals are served family-style in a large open-air dining room furnished with picnic tables. A separate screen-walled building is furnished with hammocks, a small bar, a Ping-Pong table, and a few board games. Services at the lodge include guided walks and excursions, including hikes through the national park and horseback rides on the beach. The lodge has a canopy platform located 36m (118 ft.) up an ancient Guapinol tree. If you're truly adventurous, you can spend the night in a tent atop the platform. (Just don't wake up on the wrong side of the tent.)

Puerto Jiménez

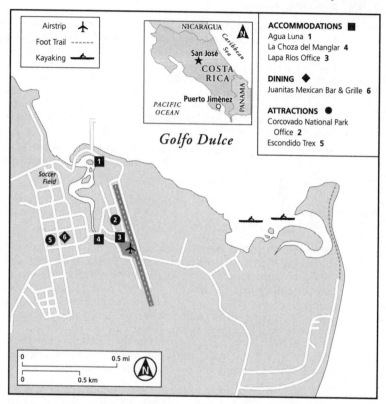

Just reaching this lodge is an adventure in itself. Most guests take a five-seat chartered plane to the gravel landing strip at Carate and then walk for around 30 minutes along the beach to the lodge. Don't worry: Your bags are hauled in on a mule-drawn cart. If you have a four-wheel-drive vehicle, you can get as far as Carate, arrange for safe parking, and then walk the remaining 1.6km (1 mile). Once you finally arrive, you'll be rewarded with a real sense of being very away from it all.

See map p. 299. Osa Peninsula. ☎ *257-0766. Fax: 257-1665.* www.costarica expeditions.com. *Rack rates: $138 double. Rates include 3 meals daily and all taxes. 3-day/2-night package $1,398 double, including air transportation (pickup and delivery from any San José hotel), 3 meals daily, 1 treetop/canopy tour, park entrance fee, and all taxes. Add $65 per person per day for extra days. Rates lower in the off season, slightly higher during peak periods. AE, MC, V.*

La Choza del Manglar
$ Puerto Jiménez

Located a short distance from the airstrip, this long-neglected hotel was restored and remodeled in late 2004. The rooms here are clean and comfortable, probably the most modern and tastefully decorated rooms you'll find in Puerto Jiménez proper. The hotel has several acres of mangroves and gardens, and the bird-watching and wildlife-viewing here are pretty good. The hotel's restaurant serves Costa Rican and international fare in a large, open-air space with colorful murals covering all the walls. Although this is a good in-town option, you're still several hundred meters or more from the water and from downtown Puerto Jimenez.

See map p. 307. 125m (135 yards) west of the airstrip, Puerto Jiménez. ☎ */fax 735-5002.* www.manglares.com. *Rack rates: $64–$79 double. Rates higher during peak weeks, lower in the off season. MC, V.*

Lapa Ríos
$$$$$ Osa Peninsula

This is Costa Rica's most famous ecolodge. The hotel consists of eight duplex buildings perched along a steep ridge. Each very large room is totally private and oriented toward the view. Walls have open screening, and the ceiling is a high-peaked thatched roof. Mosquito nets drape languidly over the two queen-size beds. A large deck and small tropical garden, complete with a hammock and outdoor shower, more than double the living space of each room. There's an indoor shower in the room, although this one features open screen walls letting out on the view, so it's not all that different from being outdoors. It's a bit of a hike back and forth from the main lodge to the rooms located farthest down the ridge.

The centerpiece of the lodge's large open-air dining room is a 15m (49-ft.) spiral staircase that leads to an observation deck tucked beneath the peak of the building's thatched roof. Lapa Ríos is surrounded by its own 400-hectare (988-acre) private rain-forest reserve, which is home to scarlet macaws, toucans, parrots, hummingbirds, monkeys, and myriad other wildlife. However, keep in mind that there are no TVs, no telephones, no air-conditioning, no discos, no shopping, no paved roads, and no crowds.

Moreover, the beach is a good 15-minute hike away, and it's not the best for swimming. In fact, other than a beautiful little pool, miles of hiking trails, an array of adventure tours and activities, and a quiet tropical bar, there is nothing around to distract your attention from the stupendous views of the rain forest all around and the ocean far below.

See map p. 309. Osa Peninsula. ☎ *735-5130. Fax: 735-5179.* www.laparios.com. *Rack rates: $440 double. Rates include 3 meals daily and taxes. Discounts for children under 11; rates lower in the off season, higher during peak periods. AE, MC, V.*

Southern Costa Rica

ACCOMMODATIONS ■
Agua Luna **6**
Bosque del Cabo
 Rainforest Lodge **5**
Cabinas Jinetes de Osa **11**
Cabinas Los Cocos **3**
Cabinas Sol y Mar **3**
Casa Corcovado Jungle
 Lodge **10**
Complejo Turístico Samoa
 del Sur **2**
Corcovado Lodge Tent
 Camp **8**
Drake Bay Wilderness
 Resort **11**
La Choza del Manglar **6**
La Paloma Lodge **11**
Lapa Ríos **5**
Oasis on the Beach **3**
Playa Nicuesa
 Rainforest Lodge **7**
Rainbow Adventures **7**
Tiskita Jungle Lodge **4**

DINING ◆
Bar & Restaurant La Cubana **2**
Bilge Bar, Restaurant, & Grill **2**

ATTRACTIONS ●
Banana Bay Marina **2**
Caño Island **12**
Casa Orquídeas **7**
Corcovado National Park **9**
Golfito Sportfishing **3**
King and Bartlett **2**
Roy's Zancudo Lodge **3**
Wilson Botanical Gardens **1**

Dining locally

Juanitas Mexican Bar & Grille
$–$$ Puerto Jiménez MEXICAN

This place offers good, hearty California-style Mexican food and fresh local seafood served up in a lively, convivial atmosphere. There are nightly specials and a popular happy hour. Movies are shown all day long on Tuesdays, and on Thursdays they have a raucous "crab race," with betting and prizes. You read it right, this place opens at 5 a.m., so if you're looking for an early start out to Corcovado, this is the joint to come to for a filling breakfast before heading out.

See map p. 307. Downtown Puerto Jiménez. ☎ 735-5056. Main courses: $3.50–$8. V. Open: Daily 5 a.m.–2 a.m.

Exploring Puerto Jiménez and the Osa Peninsula

The main attraction here is the massive and rugged Corcovado National Park. In this section you'll find detailed information on how to best visit and enjoy this park, as well as some suggestions for other activities and attractions around the region.

The top attractions

Corcovado National Park

Corcovado National Park is impressive. As I've said before, it is the single largest expanse of primary lowland tropical rain forest in Central America. It is home to an amazing amount of tropical flora and fauna and provides one of the few suitable habitats in Costa Rica for maintaining a healthy jaguar population.

Exploring Corcovado National Park is not something to be undertaken lightly, but neither is it the prohibitively arduous expedition that some people make it out to be. The weather is the biggest obstacle to overnight backpacking trips through the park. The heat and humidity are often quite formidable, and frequent rainstorms can make the trails pretty muddy. If you hike along the beach, you'll have to plan your hiking around the tides. Often, there is no beach at all at high tide, and some rivers are impassable at high tide.

Because of its size and remoteness, Corcovado National Park is best explored over several days; however, it is possible to enter and hike a bit of it on day trips. The best way to do this is to book a tour with your lodge.

There are four primary entrances to the park, which are really just ranger stations reached by rough dirt roads. When you've reached them, you'll have to strap on a backpack and hike. Perhaps the easiest one to reach from Puerto Jiménez is **La Leona ranger station,** near Carate, which is accessible by car, bus, taxi, or light aircraft. From Carate, it's a 3km (1¾-mile) hike to La Leona.

You can also travel to **El Tigre,** about 14km (8¾ miles) by dirt road from Puerto Jiménez, where there's another ranger station. But note that trails from El Tigre go only a short distance into the park.

The third entrance is in **Los Patos,** which is reached from the town of La Palma, northwest of Puerto Jiménez. From here, there's a 19km (12-mile) trail through the center of the park to **Sirena,** a ranger station and research facility.

The northern entrance to the park is **San Pedrillo,** which you can reach by hiking from Sirena or by taking a boat from Drake Bay or Sierpe. (See "Corcovado National Park" under "Drake Bay" earlier in this chapter). It's 14km (8¾ miles) from Drake Bay.

If you're not into hiking in the heat, you can charter a plane in Puerto Jiménez to take you to Carate or Sirena. A five-passenger plane should cost around $150 to $200 one-way, depending on your destination. Contact **Alfa Romeo Aero Taxi** (☎ **775-1515** or ☎/fax 735-5178) for details.

Sirena is the park's principal and most fascinating destination. As a research facility and ranger station, it's frequented almost constantly by scientists. One of the longest hikes, from San Pedrillo to Sirena, can be done only during the dry season. Between any two stations, the hiking is arduous and takes all day, so it's best to rest for a day or so between hikes, if possible.

Remember: This area is quite wild. Never hike alone, and take all the standard precautions for hiking in the rain forest. In addition, be especially careful about swimming in any isolated rivers or river mouths because most rivers in Corcovado are home to crocodiles.

Reservations are essential at the various ranger stations if you plan to eat or sleep inside the park. Make your reservations by contacting the Park Service in Puerto Jiménez (☎ **735-5036;** fax: 735-5276; www.corcovado. org). Its offices are adjacent to the airstrip. Only a limited number of people are allowed to camp at each ranger station, so make your reservations well in advance.

Sirena has a modern research facility with dormitory-style accommodations for 28 persons, as well as a campground, soda, and landing strip for charter flights. There is also camping at the **La Leona, Los Patos,** and **San Pedrillo** ranger stations. Every ranger station has potable water, but I recommend packing your own supply; whatever you do, don't drink stream water. Campsites in the park are $4 per person per night. A dorm bed at the Sirena station will run you $8 — you must bring your own sheets, and a mosquito net is highly recommended — and meals here are another $30 per day. Everything must be reserved in advance.

See map p. 309. 2.5km (1½ miles) north of Carate. ☎ *735-5036.* www.corcovado. org. *Admission: $8 per day. Camping: $4 per person per night. Dorm room: $8 per person per night. Open: Daily 24 hours.*

More cool things to see and do

✔ **Kayaking:** To arrange a kayaking trip around the estuary, up into the mangroves, or out into the gulf, contact **Escondido Trex** (☎ 735-5210; www.escondidotrex.com). These folks have an office in the Soda Carolina in the center of town. Escondido Trex runs daily paddles through the mangroves, as well as sunset trips out on the gulf, where you can sometimes see dolphins. These folks also do guided rain-forest hikes and can have you rappelling down the face of a jungle waterfall. More-adventurous multiday kayak and camping trips are also available, in price and comfort ranges from budget to luxury (staying at various lodges around the Golfo Dulce and Matapalo). They'll even take you gold panning (although there are no guarantees that your panning will pay for the trip).

✔ **Sportfishing:** If you're interested in doing some **billfishing** or **deep-sea fishing,** you'll probably want to stay at or fish with **Crocodile Bay Lodge** (☎ **800-733-1115** in the United States and Canada, or 735-5631 in Costa Rica; www.crocodilebay.com). This upscale fishing lodge is close to the Puerto Jiménez airstrip.

If you want a more budget-oriented fishing outing, check around the public dock for notices put up by people with charter boats, or call **Marco "Taboga" Loaiciga** (☎ **735-5265**). Rates can run between $250 and $1,200 for a full day, or between $100 and $600 for a half day, depending on the boat, tackle, number of anglers, and fishing grounds.

✔ **Surfing:** Although nearby Pavones gets all the international press and acclaim, three very dependable point breaks are located on the stretch of the Osa Peninsula between Puerto Jiménez and Carate. Matapalo, Pan Dulce, and Backwash are all well-formed right point breaks. These waves are excellent for learning on when they're small. And when the waves are large, they're long and clean.

Golfito and the Golfo Dulce

Golfito itself is not a very compelling destination for foreign travelers. Nevertheless, the city's setting is quite pretty, and it serves as the gateway to some truly beautiful isolated lodges located on the shores of the Golfo Dulce, or "Sweet Gulf."

Sportfishing cognoscenti know that Golfito's real draw is the marlin and sailfish just beyond its bay. Arguably one of the best fishing spots in Costa Rica, it provides pleasant, uncrowded surroundings in which die-hard sportfishers can indulge their greatest fantasies of landing the great one to end all great ones.

In its prime, Golfito was a major banana port, but United Fruit pulled out in 1985 following a few years of rising taxes, falling prices, and labor disputes. Now Ticos come here in droves on weekends and throughout

December to take advantage of cheap prices on name-brand goods and clothing sold at the duty-free zone, and sometimes all these shoppers make finding a room in town difficult.

In 1998, much of the rain forest bordering the Golfo Dulce was officially declared the **Piedras Blancas National Park,** which includes 12,000 hectares (29,640 acres) of primary forests, as well as newly protected secondary forests and pasturelands.

Along the southern shores of the Golfo Dulce, accessible either by boat or car from Golfito, are the two tiny beach towns of Playa Zancudo and Pavones. The former is a laid-back tropical getaway and sportfishing center, while the latter is one of the prime surf spots on the planet.

Getting there

Flying is the fastest and easiest way to get to Golfito and the Golfo Dulce region. You can drive or take a bus, although in each of these cases, it's a very long ride. You'll find more information on all these options in the following sections.

By air

Sansa (☎ 221-9414; www.flysansa.com) and **Nature Air** (☎ 220-3054; www.natureair.com) both fly to Golfito from San José. Taxis meet all incoming flights and can take you into downtown or to the boat docks for under $2.

By car

Take the Interamerican Highway east out of San José (through San Pedro and Cartago) and continue south on this road. In about three hours, you'll reach San Isidro de El General. Although you can continue on the Interamerican Highway all the way south, it is currently faster, smoother, and safer to turn off in San Isidro and head to Dominical, picking up the Southern Highway or Costanera Sur in Dominical. From here it's a fast and smooth shot down Palmar Norte, where you meet up again with the Interamerican Highway. When you get to Río Claro, you'll notice a couple of gas stations and quite a bit of activity. Turn right here and follow the signs to Golfito. If you end up at the Panama border, you've missed the turnoff by about 32km (20 miles). The drive takes about six hours.

If you're heading to either Playa Zancudo or Pavones, you'll see the turnoff at El Rodeo, about 4km (2½ miles) outside of Golfito, on the road in from the Interamerican Highway. About 20 minutes past the turnoff, you'll have to wait and take a small diesel-operated crank ferry. (Fare is $1 per vehicle.) The ferry generally operates from around 5 a.m. until 10 p.m. However, the hours can be erratic. Moreover, at very low tides, the ferry can't run, so sometimes you must wait a couple of hours. After the ferry, you should make a left at every major intersection; the road is fairly well marked. Follow the flow of traffic if there is any, or stick to the most well-worn route whenever in doubt, to reach either Playa Zancudo or Pavones. In each case, it takes about one hour when the road is in good condition and about two hours when it's not.

On most of the Interamerican Highway, you'll have to contend with potholes of sometimes gargantuan proportions. Just remember, if the road is suddenly smooth and in great shape, you can bet that around the next bend there will be a bottomless pothole that you can't swerve around. Take it easy.

By bus

Express buses leave San José daily at 7 a.m. and 3 p.m. from the Tracopa station at Avenida 5 and Calle 14 (☎ **222-2666**). The trip takes seven and a half hours; the fare is $6. Buses depart Golfito for San José daily at 5 a.m. and 1 p.m. from the bus station near the municipal dock.

Orienting yourself in Golfito and along the Golfo Dulce

Golfito is set on the north side of the Golfo Dulce, at the foot of lush green mountains. The gas station, or *bomba,* is the heart of Golfito, and just off this you'll find the municipal dock and compact downtown section.

Farther along the bay and slightly inland, you come to the old United Fruit Company housing, the Duty-Free Zone, and Golfito's small airstrip. In this area, you'll find well-maintained wooden houses painted bright colors and surrounded by neatly manicured gardens.

However, most of the hotels and lodges listed here are located along the shores of the Golfo Dulce, either north of Golfito where the only access is by boat, or down south in the beach towns of Playa Zancudo and Pavones.

This is an isolated and remote area; your best bet for information will invariably be the front desk at your hotel or lodge.

Getting around

With most of the lodges listed here, arranging transportation in advance is best. If you're staying at one of the lodges accessible only by boat and you miss your connection, you can always hire a boat at the Golfito public dock, or *muellecito.* Depending on which lodge you're going to, the cost could range from $35 to $70.

There are a couple of daily buses to Playa Zancudo and Pavones leaving from in front of the gas station in downtown Golfito. Alternatively, taxis can be hired for around $40 to $55. There's a steady supply of taxis constantly cruising the one main road through town. Or you can call **Taxi Golfito** (☎ **775-1170**).

If you can't get to your next destination by boat, bus, commuter airline, or car, **Alfa Romeo Aero Taxi** (☎ 775-1515) runs charters to most of the nearby destinations, including Carate, Drake Bay, Sirena, and Puerto Jiménez.

Spending the night

Cabinas Los Cocos
$ **Playa Zancudo**

If you've ever pondered throwing it all away and setting up shop in a simple house by the beach, these fully-equipped cabins might be a good place for a trial run. Set under the trees and only a few meters from the beach, the four cabins are quiet and semi-isolated from one another. Two of them served as banana-plantation housing in a former life until they were salvaged and moved here. These wood houses have big verandas and bedrooms and large eat-in kitchens. Bathrooms are down a few steps in back and have hot water. The two newer cabins also offer plenty of space, small kitchenettes, and a private veranda, as well as comfortable sleeping lofts. If you plan to stay in Zancudo for a while, this is a perennially good choice. The owners, Susan and Andrew Robertson, also run Zancudo Boat Tours, so if you want to do some exploring or need a ride into Golfito or Puerto Jiménez, they're the folks to see.

See map p. 309. Playa Zancudo. ☎ */fax* **776-0012.** www.loscocos.com. *4 units. $55–$60 double. Rates lower in the off season, and weekly discounts available. No credit cards.*

Cabinas Sol y Mar
$ **Playa Zancudo**

This friendly owner-run establishment is one of the most popular lodgings in Zancudo. All the accommodations were recently rebuilt from the ground up. There are two individual bungalows and two rooms in a duplex building with a shared veranda. I prefer the individual rooms for their privacy. The bathrooms in these have unusual showers that feature a tiled platform set amid smooth river rocks. There's also a small budget cabin that is quite a good deal, as well as a fully equipped house for longer stays. You can even camp here for a few bucks per night. All the options are just steps away from the sand. The hotel's open-air restaurant is one of the most popular places to eat in Zancudo.

See map p. 309. Playa Zancudo. ☎ **776-0014.** www.zancudo.com. *Rack rates: $25–$41 double. Rates lower in the off season. V (6.5 percent surcharge).*

Complejo Turístico Samoa del Sur
$ **Golfito**

If you have to spend the night in Golfito, this is a good choice. The hotel is well-located right on the waterfront near the center of town. The rooms are spacious and clean. Varnished wood headboards complement two firm and comfortable double beds. With red-tile floors, modern bathrooms, and carved-wood doors, the rooms all share a long, covered veranda that's set perpendicular to the gulf, so the views aren't great. If you want to watch the water, you're better off grabbing a table at the popular restaurant and bar here. The most recent additions here are a swimming pool and volleyball court, as well as a small marina. Future plans include more rooms and an expanded and improved marina. If you're driving down this way and heading to a lodge out on the Golfo Dulce, these folks will watch your car for around $10 per day.

See map p. 309. 1 block north of the public dock, Golfito. ☎ *775-0233. Fax: 775-0573.* www.samoadelsur.com. *Rack rates: $40–$50 double. AE, MC, V.*

Oasis on the Beach
$ Playa Zancudo

Located toward the southern end of Zancudo, this place was known for years as the Zancudo Beach Club. My favorite rooms here are the three individual bungalows. Although they're simple and lack the air-conditioning of the villa rooms, they are plenty spacious and I like their wood floors, private front porches, large bathrooms, and rustic, yet comfortable feel. The villa is a two-story building with rooms upstairs and down. These feature tile floors and air-conditioning. The upstairs unit has a high peaked ceiling and a great view over the Golfo Dulce to Cabo Matapalo from its private balcony. The restaurant here is quite good, with weekly pizza nights, featuring homemade pizzas made in a wood-fired brick oven.

See map p. 309. Playa Zancudo. ☎/*fax 776-0087.* www.oasisonthebeach.com. *Rack rates: $50–$65 double. Rates lower in the off season, and weekly discounts available. V.*

Playa Nicuesa Rainforest Lodge
$$$$ Golfo Dulce

Set on its own private bay, with a large stretch of black-sand beach, and accessible only by boat, this lodge is currently the most luxurious and impressive option on the Golfo Dulce. Although the four "Mango Manor" rooms are certainly very comfortable, you'll definitely want to snag one of the four individual cabins. These are all set amidst dense forest and are made almost entirely of wood, with large open air-showers, private verandas, and a true sense of being in touch with nature. The main lodge building is a huge, open-air affair with an abundance of varnished wood and a relaxed, inviting vibe that induces one to grab a book, play a board game, or chat with other guests. There's an excellent network of trails on the lodge's 165 acres (66 hectares), and a whole host of tours and activities are offered. Guests have unlimited use of the lodge's kayaks, windsurfers (also called sailboards), and snorkeling and fishing gear. Meals are served family style and are well-prepared and tasty. When I last visited, there was a 5-foot crocodile residing in the small river that runs through the lodge's property.

See map p. 309. Golfo Dulce. ☎ *866-348-7610 in the United States, or 735-5237 in Costa Rica. Fax: 735-5043 in Costa Rica.* www.nicuesalodge.com. *Rack rates: $300–$340 double. Rates include all meals, taxes, and transfers to and from either Golfito or Puerto Jiménez. MC, V.*

Rainbow Adventures
$$$$$ Golfo Dulce

The open architecture, varnished hardwoods, four-poster beds and scattered antiques, stained glass, and Oriental rugs make this one of the more unique jungle lodges in Costa Rica. The grounds immediately surrounding the lodge are beautifully manicured gardens planted with exotic fruit trees, flowering shrubs, and palms from around the world. The second-floor rooms in the main lodge are the smallest and least expensive. But for just a little more, you can have the penthouse, a large third-floor room with four open walls and treetop views of the gulf. The individual cabins, which are set off from the main building, have open living rooms and a large bedroom that can be divided into two small rooms, as well as one other separate bedroom.

A private, rocky beach provides protected swimming, and, when it's calm, there's some good snorkeling nearby. Boat charters and guided tours to neighboring attractions are available. The hotel has an air-conditioned library and reading room, with one of the most extensive collections of natural-history books I've ever seen. The hotel grounds also boast several well-maintained trails through primary rain forest, with jungle waterfalls and wonderful swimming holes.

See map p. 309. Playa Cativa. ☎ *800-565-0722 in the United States, or* ☎ */fax 735-5062 in Costa Rica.* www.rainbowcostarica.com. *Rack rates: $355–$395 double. Extra person $95. Rates include 3 meals daily, round-trip transportation between the lodge and Golfito, all nonalcoholic drinks, snacks, and taxes. MC, V.*

Tiskita Jungle Lodge
$$$ Pavones

This small ecolodge is nearly on the Panamanian border, with the beach on one side and rain-forest-clad hills behind. Originally an experimental fruit farm growing exotic tropical fruits from around the world, Tiskita has become a great place to get away from it all. The lodge itself is set on a hill a few hundred meters from the beach and commands a superb view of the ocean. There's a dark-sand swimming beach, tide pools, jungle waterfalls, a farm and forest to explore, and great bird-watching — 285 species have been sighted. Of the 160 hectares (395 acres) here, 100 hectares (247 acres) are in primary rain forest; the rest are in secondary forest, reforestation projects, orchards, and pastures.

Accommodations are in deluxe rustic cabins with screen walls and verandas. Constructed of local hardwoods, the cabins have a very tropical feel. If you're a bird-watcher, you can just sit on the veranda and add to your life list. My favorite cabin is no. 6, which has a great view and large deck space. Some of the cabins have two or three rooms, making them great for families. Most of the bathrooms are actually outdoors, although they are private and protected, allowing you to take in the sights and sounds as you shower and shave.

Meals are served family-style in the open-air main lodge. Although they're not fancy, they're certainly tasty and filling, and you'll be eating plenty of ingredients straight from the gardens.

The lodge is well over eight hours from San José by car, so most guests take advantage of the package tours, which include air transportation to Tiskita's private landing strip. If you've already driven all the way to Pavones, Tiskita is only 6km (3¾ miles) farther down the road.

See map p. 309. Pavones. ☎ *296-8125. Fax: 296-8133.* www.tiskita-lodge.co. cr. *Rack rates: $240 double. Rates include 3 meals and 1 guided walk daily, and all taxes. Packages with transportation to and from Golfito or Puerto Jiménez are available. AE, MC, V.*

Dining locally

Bar & Restaurant La Cubana
$ Golfito   COSTA RICAN

This small, open-air restaurant with a basic menu commands a good view of the gulf from its location on the bluff of a small hill. Despite the name, the food here is not Cuban. That's not a bad thing, though. Instead, you can get fresh seafood and filling local fare at rock-bottom prices. The bar is a quiet spot to have a drink in the evening.

See map p. 309. 150m (1½ blocks.) east of the gas station, on the upper road through downtown Golfito. No phone. Main courses: $3–$8. No credit cards. Open: Tues–Sun 6 a.m.–10 p.m.

Bilge Bar, Restaurant & Grill
$$–$$$ Golfito   INTERNATIONAL/SEAFOOD

This open-air restaurant attached to the Banana Bay Marina is easily the best restaurant in Golfito. The seafood is fresh and excellently prepared, but you can also get hearty steaks and great burgers. I personally recommend the fresh fish burger. Grab a table toward the water and watch the boats bob up and down while you enjoy your meal.

See map p. 309. At the Banana Bay Marina, on the waterfront in downtown Golfito. ☎ *775-0838. Main courses: $6–$15. AE, MC, V. Open: Daily 7 a.m.–9 p.m.*

Exploring Golfito and the Golfo Dulce

Most of the attractions and activities available in this region involve getting on or in the waters of the Golfo Dulce. The exception to this rule is Wilson Botanical Gardens, which is located about an hour's drive inland from Golfito. You'll find detailed information about all the various attractions and activities in this section.

The top attractions

Casa Orquídeas

Casa Orquídeas is a private botanical garden lovingly built and maintained by Ron and Trudy MacAllister. The gardens feature a broad array of tropical flowers and trees. During the tour, you'll sample a load of fresh fruits picked right off the trees.

Most hotels and lodges in the area offer trips here, including transportation and a two-hour tour of the gardens. If your hotel doesn't offer a tour, you can book a trip out of Golfito with the folks at **Land Sea Tours** (☎ 775-1614). The entrance and guided tour is only $5 per person, but it will cost you between $50 and $60 to hire a boat for the round-trip ride.

See map p. 309. 30 minutes by boat from Golfito, up along the Golfo Dulce.
☎ *775-1614. Admission: $5 per person. Tours: Sat–Thurs 8:30 a.m.*

Wilson Botanical Gardens

If you have a really serious interest in botanical gardens or bird-watching, consider an excursion to Wilson Botanical Gardens at the Las Cruces Biological Station.

The gardens are owned and maintained by the Organization for Tropical Studies and include more than 7,000 species of tropical plants from around the world. Among the plants grown here are many endangered species, which make the gardens of interest to botanical researchers. Despite the scientific aspects of the gardens, there are so many beautiful and unusual flowers amid the manicured grounds that even a neophyte can't help but be astounded. And all this luscious flora has also attracted at least 330 species of birds.

If you'd like to stay the night here, there are 12 well-appointed rooms on-site. Rates, which include one guided walk, three meals, and taxes, run around $70 per person; you definitely need to make reservations beforehand if you want to spend the night, and it's usually a good idea to make a reservation for a simple day visit and hike.

To get here from Golfito, drive back out to the Interamerican Highway and continue south toward Panama. In Ciudad Neily, turn north. A taxi from Golfito should cost around $40 each way.

See map p. 309. Located 65km (40 miles) northeast of Golfito, just outside the town of San Vito. ☎ *773-4004.* www.ots.ac.cr. *Admission: $10 for a half-day guided hike; $34 for a full-day guided hike, including lunch. Open: Daily 7:30 a.m.–5 p.m.*

More cool things to see and do

- ✔ **Sailboat charters:** There's no steady charter fleet here, but itinerant sailors often set up shop during the high season. If you're looking to charter a sailboat, you should check with Banana Bay Marina or King and Bartlett (see the following bullet for info on both of these).

✔ **Sportfishing:** The waters off Golfito also offer some of the best sportfishing in Costa Rica. If you'd like to try hooking into a possible world-record marlin or sailfish, contact **Banana Bay Marina** (☎ 775-0838; www.bananabaymarina.com) or **King and Bartlett** (☎ 775-1624; www.kingandbartlettsportfishing.com). Both of these operators have a full-service marina, a few waterside rooms for guests, and a fleet of sportfishing boats and captains. A full-day fishing trip costs between $800 and $1,600.

You can also try either **Golfito Sportfishing** (☎ 776-0007; www.costaricafishing.com) or **Roy's Zancudo Lodge** (☎ 776-0008; www.royszancudolodge.com). Both of these operations are based in Playa Zancudo.

✔ **Surfing:** Pavones is one of the world's top surfing destinations. When the swell is working, this point break is reputed to be the longest rideable break left in the world. Even if you don't surf, the seemingly endless rides this wave provides are impressive.

Fast Facts: Southern Costa Rica

Ambulance

Call ☎ 128.

ATMs

You'll find ATMs at Banco Nacional and Banco de Costa Rica locations in Puerto Jiménez and Golfito.

Country Code and City Code

The country code for Costa Rica is **506.** There are no city or area codes within Costa Rica. To call from the United States, dial 011-506 plus the seven-digit number. From within Costa Rica, you simply dial the seven-digit number.

Currency Exchange

Most hotels will exchange money for you at decent rates. To get official rates, you'll need to head to one of the banks in Puerto Jiménez or Golfito.

Fire

Call ☎ 118.

Hospitals

The closest hospital is Hospital Golfito (☎ 775-0011), although there are several doctors and a local clinic (☎ 735-5029) in Puerto Jiménez.

Information

There are no official information offices in southern Costa Rica. Most hotels have a tour desk, concierge, or helpful front desk.

Internet Access

There are Internet cafes in Puerto Jiménez and Golfito. Few of the isolated lodges down here provide Internet access for their guests.

Newspapers

This is a very isolated region, although most lodges here receive local newspapers, including the *Tico Times.*

Pharmacies

Farmacia Puerto Jiménez (☎ 735-5458) is located in the center of town, across from the Soda Carolina.

Farmacia Golfito (☎ 775-2442) and Farmacia Mendez (☎ 775-0416) are two well-stocked pharmacies in downtown Golfito.

Police

Call ☎ 911.

Post Office

There is a post office in Golfito (☎ 775-1911), and another in Puerto Jiménez (☎ 735-5045). Alternatively, most hotels can mail your letters and postcards for you.

Taxis

There are numerous taxis in Puerto Jiménez and Golfito. Try Taxi Puerto Jiménez ☎ 735-5481 or Taxi Golfito ☎ 775-1170.

Chapter 21

Chilling on Costa Rica's Caribbean Coast

*Y*ou'll feel as if you've entered another world, or at least another country, when you visit Costa Rica's Caribbean coast. Although this region was visited by Columbus in 1502, until recently it has remained historically and geographically isolated from the rest of the country.

So remote was the Caribbean coast from Costa Rica's population centers in the Central Valley that it has developed a culture all its own. The Guápiles Highway between San José and Limón was not completed until 1987. More than half of this coastline is still inaccessible except by boat or small plane.

The original inhabitants of the area included people of the Bribri, Cabécar, and Kéköldi tribes, and these groups maintain their cultures on indigenous reserves in the Talamanca Mountains. In fact, until the 1870s, few non-Indians resided in this area.

However, when Minor Keith built the railroad to San José and began planting bananas, he brought in black laborers from Jamaica and other Caribbean islands to lay the track and work the plantations. These workers and their descendants established fishing and farming communities up and down the coast. Today dreadlocked Rastafarians, reggae music, Creole cooking, and the English-based patois of this Afro-Caribbean culture give this region a quasi-Jamaican flavor.

Cahuita

Cahuita is a sleepy Caribbean beach village and the first "major" tourist destination you'll reach heading south out of Limón. Cahuita is one of the most laid-back villages in Costa Rica. The few dirt and gravel streets here are host to a languid parade of pedestrian traffic, parted occasionally by a bicycle, car, or bus. After a short time, you'll find yourself slipping into the heat-induced torpor that affects anyone who ends up here.

People come to Cahuita for its miles of pristine beaches, which stretch both north and south of town. The southern beaches, the forest behind them, and the coral reef offshore (one of just a handful in Costa Rica) are all part of **Cahuita National Park.**

The village traces its roots to Afro-Caribbean fishermen and laborers who settled in this region in the mid-1800s. Today, the population is still primarily English-speaking blacks whose culture and language set them apart from other Costa Ricans.

Getting there

There's no regular commuter air service to the Caribbean coast, so transportation options are limited to cars and buses. The drive here is quite beautiful, passing through the massive rain forest of Braulio Carillo National Park. Driving a rental car gives you independence and a certain level of convenience. However, if you want to leave the driving to others, several bus and minivan services are available. You'll find information on all these options in the following sections.

By car

The Guápiles Highway heads north out of San José on Calle 3 before turning east and passing close to Barva volcano and through the rain forests of Braulio Carrillo National Park, en route to Limón. The drive takes about two and a half hours and is spectacularly beautiful, especially when it's not raining or misty.

As you enter Limón, about 5 blocks from the busiest section of downtown, watch for a major intersection on your right, just before the railroad tracks. Take this road south to Cahuita, passing the airstrip and the beach on your left as you leave Limón. Alternatively, there's a turnoff with signs for Sixaola and La Bomba several miles before Limón. This winding shortcut skirts the city and puts you on the coastal road several miles south of town.

By bus

MEPE express buses (☎ 257-8129) leave San José every three or four hours from the Caribbean bus terminal (Gran Terminal del Caribe) on Calle Central, 1 block north of Avenida 11. The trip's duration is four hours; fare is $5. During peak periods, extra buses are often added. However, checking ahead of time is smart because this bus line is one of the most fickle.

Alternatively, you can catch one of the frequent buses to Limón from the same station and then transfer to a Cahuita- or Puerto Viejo–bound bus (☎ 758-0618) in Limón. These latter buses leave roughly every hour between 5 a.m. and 6 p.m. from Radio Casino, which is 1 block north of the municipal market.

Grayline (☎ 220-2126; www.graylinecostarica.com) and **Interbus** (☎ 283-5573; www.costaricapass.com) both have a daily bus to Cahuita from San José. The fare is $25. Both companies will pick you up and drop you off at most area hotels in both San José and Cahuita.

Orienting yourself in Cahuita

There are only about eight dirt streets in Cahuita. The highway runs parallel to the coast, with three main access roads running perpendicular. The northernmost of these bypasses town and brings you to the northern end of Playa Negra. It's marked with signs for the Magellan Inn and other hotels up on this end. The second road in brings you to the southern end of Playa Negra, a half-mile closer to town. Look for signs for Atlántida Lodge. The third road is the principal entrance into town. The village's main street in town, which runs parallel to the highway, dead ends at the entrance to the national park (a footbridge over a small stream).

Buses usually drop their passengers in front of Coco's Bar, across from the tiny public park. For all intents and purposes, this is the center of town. If you come in on the bus and are staying at a lodge on Playa Negra, head north out of town on the street that runs between Coco's Bar and the small park. This road curves to the left and continues a mile or so out to Playa Negra.

There are no official information offices in town, but several competing tour agencies all fill the bill. If your hotel can't provide the information or organize a tour for you, head to **Cahuita Tours and Adventure Center** (☎ 755-0232) or **Turística Cahuita Information Center** (☎/fax 755-0071), both on the village's main street.

Getting around

Downtown Cahuita is very compact and is easily navigable by foot. However, some of the hotels located out toward Playa Negra are a good kilometer or more away from the center. You'll usually spot a few taxis cruising around town. If you can't find one on the street, try calling **René** (☎ 755-0243), **Wayne** (☎ 755-0078), or **Dino** (☎ 755-0012).

Cahuita

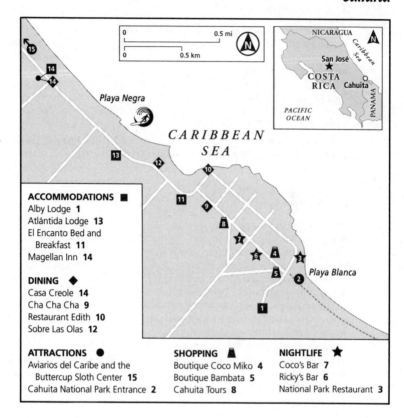

0.5 mi
0.5 km

Playa Negra

CARIBBEAN
SEA

NICARAGUA
San José
COSTA
RICA   Cahuita
PACIFIC
OCEAN
PANAMA
Caribbean Sea

Playa Blanca

ACCOMMODATIONS ■
Alby Lodge **1**
Atlántida Lodge **13**
El Encanto Bed and
  Breakfast **11**
Magellan Inn **14**

DINING ◆
Casa Creole **14**
Cha Cha Cha **9**
Restaurant Edith **10**
Sobre Las Olas **12**

ATTRACTIONS ●
Aviarios del Caribe and the
  Buttercup Sloth Center **15**
Cahuita National Park Entrance **2**

SHOPPING ▮
Boutique Coco Miko **4**
Boutique Bambata **5**
Cahuita Tours **8**

NIGHTLIFE ★
Coco's Bar **7**
Ricky's Bar **6**
National Park Restaurant **3**

Spending the night

Alby Lodge
$ Cahuita

With the feel of a small village, Alby Lodge is a fascinating little place hand-built by its German owners. Although the four small cabins are close to the center of the village, they're surrounded by a large lawn and feel secluded. The cabins are quintessentially tropical, with thatched roofs, mosquito nets, hardwood floors and beams, big shuttered windows, tile bathrooms, and a hammock slung on the front porch. There's no restaurant here, but there is a communal kitchen area if you want to cook your own meals. The turnoff for the lodge is on your right just before you reach the national-park entrance; the hotel is located about 136m (446 ft.) down a narrow, winding lane from here.

See map above. Cahuita. ☎*/fax* **755-0031.** www.albylodge.com. *Rack rates: $40 double. Children under 12 stay free in parent's room. No credit cards.*

Atlántida Lodge
$ **Playa Negra**

If you want to be just steps away from the beach, with a nice pool and a few basic amenities, this quiet oasis of a hotel is your best bet in Cahuita. The guest rooms have a rustic feel to them and some are a bit small, yet they are clean and comfortable, with pale-yellow stucco walls, red-tile floors, a ceiling fan, and plenty of bamboo trim. Each has a small patio with a bamboo screen divider for privacy, which opens onto the hotel's lush gardens. A host of different tours can be arranged here, from snorkeling to horseback riding to white-water rafting.

See map p. 325. Beside the soccer field on the road to Playa Negra, Cahuita. ☎ *755-0115. Fax: 755-0213. Rack rates: $55 double. Rates lower in the off season. AE, MC, V.*

El Encanto Bed and Breakfast
$ **Cahuita**

The individual bungalows at this little bed-and-breakfast are set in from the road, on spacious and well-kept grounds. The bungalows themselves are also spacious and have attractive touches that include wooden bed frames, arched windows, Mexican-tile floors, Guatemalan bedspreads, and framed Panamanian *molas* hanging on the walls. There is a separate two-story, three-bedroom, two-bathroom house with a full kitchen at the rear of the grounds, as well as a new deluxe room. Hearty breakfasts are served in the small open dining room surrounded by lush gardens. Recent additions here include a meditation hall, a covered garden gazebo, and an open-air massage room.

See map p. 325. Just outside of town on the road to Playa Negra, Cahuita. ☎ *755-0113. Fax: 755-0432.* www.elencantobedandbreakfast.com. *Rack rates: $59 double. Rates include full breakfast. Rates slightly lower in the off season, higher during peak weeks. MC, V.*

Magellan Inn
$–$$ **Playa Negra**

This small inn is the most sophisticated hotel in the area. The rooms are all carpeted and have French doors, vertical blinds, tiled bathrooms with hardwood counters, and two joined single beds. Although there's a ceiling fan over each bed, the rooms could use a bit more ventilation. Two of the units have wall-mounted air-conditioners. Each room has its own tiled veranda with a Persian rug and bamboo sitting chairs. The combination bar/lounge and dining room features even more Persian-style rugs and wicker furniture. Most memorable of all are the hotel's sunken pool and lush gardens, both of which are built into a crevice in the ancient coral reef that underlies this entire region — which leads to good bird-watching.

See map p. 325. At the far end of Playa Negra (about 2km/1¼ miles north of downtown), Cahuita. ☎*/fax 755-0035.* http://magellaninn.toposrealestate.org. *Rack rates: $69 double; $89 double with A/C. Rates include continental breakfast. AE, MC, V.*

Selva Bananito Lodge
$$$–$$$$ **Bananito**

This remote nature lodge is a welcome addition to the Caribbean coast, allowing you to combine some rain-forest adventuring with some serious beach time in Cahuita or Puerto Viejo. The individual raised-stilt cabins are all spacious and comfortable, with an abundance of varnished wood-work. Inside, you'll find two double beds, a desk and chair, and some fresh flowers, as well as a large private bathroom. Outside there's a wraparound veranda with a hammock and some chairs. It all adds up to what I call *rustic luxury.* Half the cabins have views of the Bananito River and a small valley; the other half have views of the Matama Mountains, part of the Talamanca mountain range.

There are no electric lights at Selva Bananito, but each evening as you dine by candlelight, your cabin's oil lamps are lit for you. Hot water is provided by solar panels. Tasty family-style meals are served in the large, open *rancho,* which is also a great spot for morning bird-watching. There's a wide range of tours and activities, including rain-forest hikes and horse-back rides in the jungle, tree climbing, self-guided trail hikes, and even the opportunity to rappel down the face of a jungle waterfall.

The owners are very involved in conservation efforts in this area, and approximately two-thirds of the 840 hectacres (2,100 acres) here are pri-mary forest managed as a private reserve. You'll need a four-wheel-drive vehicle to reach the lodge itself, although most folks leave their rental cars in Bananito and let the lodge drive them the final bit. You can also arrange to be picked up in San José.

Bananito. ☎ *253-8118. Fax: 280-0820.* www.selvabananito.com. *Rack rates: $220–$240 double. Rates include 3 meals daily and all taxes. Rates lower in the off season. No credit cards.*

Dining locally

Casa Creole
$$–$$$ **Playa Negra**   **FRENCH-CREOLE**

The rest of Cahuita might feel like a misplaced piece of Bob Marley's Jamaica, but this restaurant takes its inspiration from islands a little far-ther south in the Caribbean — and far more French. Tables in the open first-floor dining room are set with linen tablecloths and candles in glass lanterns. There's a sense of informal elegance about the whole affair. Start with a dish of the pâté *maison* or a shrimp, coconut, and pineapple cock-tail. The spiced shrimp *martiniquaise* and the jumbo coconut shrimp soup are both excellent, as is the fresh fish, seasoned and baked inside a banana leaf. The emphasis here is on seafood, but the ample menu includes meat, chicken, and pasta dishes. Top it off with some fresh raspberry coulis, homemade profiteroles, or exquisite homemade fresh-fruit sherbet.

See map p. 325. At the Magellan Inn, Playa Negra Rd., 2.5km (1½ miles) north of Cahuita. ☎ *755-0035. Reservations recommended during the high season. Main courses: $7–$20. AE, MC, V. Open: Mon–Sat 6–9 p.m.*

Cha Cha Cha
$$–$$$ Cahuita   SEAFOOD-INTERNATIONAL

Fresh seafood and grilled meats, simply and expertly prepared. What more could you ask from a casual, open-air restaurant in a funky beach town? In addition to the fresh catch of the day and filet mignon, the menu here is an eclectic mix, including everything from jerk chicken and Thai shrimp salad to pasta primavera and fajitas. The grilled squid salad with a citrus dressing is one of the house specialties and a great light bite. The restaurant occupies the ground floor of an old wooden building. Everything is painted pure white, with some blue trim and accents. There are only a half-dozen or so tables, so the place fills up fast.

See map p. 325. On the main road in town, 3 blocks north of Coco's Bar. ☎ *394-4153 or 755-0191. Reservations recommended during the high season. Main courses: $6–$20. MC, V. Open: Tues–Sun 2–10 p.m.*

Restaurant Edith
$–$$ Cahuita   CREOLE-SEAFOOD

This place is a local landmark, and deservedly so. Quite some years ago, Miss Edith decided to start serving home-cooked meals to all the hungry visitors hanging around. If you want a taste of the local cuisine in a homey, sit-down environment, this is the place. While one of Miss Edith's daughters take the orders, Mom cooks up a storm out back. The menu, when you can get hold of it, is long, with lots of local seafood dishes and Creole combinations such as *yuca* in coconut milk with meat or vegetables. The sauces here have spice and zest and are a welcome change from the typically bland fare served up throughout the rest of Costa Rica. After you've ordered, it's usually no more than 45 minutes until your meal arrives. It's often crowded here, so don't be bashful about sitting down with total strangers at any of the big tables.

See map p. 325. By the police station, Cahuita. ☎ *755-0248. Main courses: $3.50–$12. No credit cards. Open: Mon–Sat 11 a.m.–10 p.m., Sun 4–9 p.m. Opening hours vary.*

Sobre Las Olas
$$ Cahuita   ITALIAN-SEAFOOD

Set on a slight rise of rocks above a coral cove and breaking waves, this place has by far the best location in Cahuita. The funky wooden building housing the restaurant features full walls of large picture windows letting out onto the sea view. The Italian owners serve a mix of local and Italian fare. They serve excellent fresh squid or shrimp in a tangy local coconut milk sauce, as well as a host of pasta dishes. The fresh grilled snapper is also always a good way to go.

See map p. 325. Just north of town on the road to Playa Negra. ☎ *755-0109. Main courses: $5–$16. MC, V. Open: Daily noon to 10 p.m.*

That rundown feeling

Don't be put off by signs advertising "rundown" soup or stew. It's not roadkill. Rundown (or *rondon*) soup is a spicy coconut-milk stew made with anything the cook can run down. Ingredients usually include some fresh seafood, as well as a mix of local tubers, roots, and vegetables. Be sure to try this authentic taste of the Caribbean.

Exploring Cahuita

The main attraction in this area is Cahuita National Park, which is located right where the main street in town ends. The other major attraction, **Aviarios del Caribe and the Buttercup Sloth Rescue Center,** is located a few miles north of town. You'll find detailed information about visiting and enjoying both of these places in this section.

Top attractions

Aviarios del Caribe and the Buttercup Sloth Rescue Center

This place has morphed from a small bed-and-breakfast offering unique canoe-based bird-watching trips into one of the world's foremost research and rescue centers for two- and three-toed sloths. They no longer rent out rooms. Instead, a visit here will feature a tour of their new natural history center, as well as their sloth rehabilitation facilities. They still offer canoe tours through the surrounding estuary, where more than 325 species of birds have been spotted. And you can hike their compact series of rain-forest and island trails.

*See map p. 325. Located 9km (5½ miles) north of Cahuita. ☎/fax **750-0775**. www. slothrescue.org. Admission: $20 for 1¼-hour canoe tour combination that includes a visit to the sloth rehabilitation center and self-guided hike on its trails; $30 for a 3½-hour canoe tour. Open: Daily 6 a.m.–4 p.m.*

Cahuita National Park

Cahuita National Park stretches south from the edge of town. The park features a long, beautiful curve of white sand backed by dense lowland rain forest. Although the soft white sand, lush coastal forest, and picture-perfect palm lines are a tremendous draw, the park was actually created to preserve the 240-hectare (787-acre) **coral reef** just offshore. The reef contains 35 species of coral and provides a haven for hundreds of brightly colored tropical fish.

The trail behind the beach stretches a little more than 6.4km (4 miles) to the southern end of the park at **Puerto Vargas,** where you'll find another beautiful white-sand beach, the park headquarters, and a basic campground with showers and outhouses. It's a nice, flat walk, but a rewarding one because there's good wildlife viewing and access to the beach. The loud grunting sounds you hear off in the distance are the calls of howler monkeys, which can be heard from more than a kilometer away. Nearer at hand, you're likely to hear crabs scuttling amid the dry leaves on the forest floor — there are half a dozen or so species of land crabs living in this region.

The main **in-town park entrance** to the park is just over a footbridge at the end of the village's main street. It has bathroom facilities, changing rooms, and storage lockers. This is the best place to enter if you're just interested in spending the day on the beach and maybe taking a little hike in the bordering forest. The official park entrance is at the southern end of the park in **Puerto Vargas.** This is where you should come if you plan to camp at the park or if you don't feel up to hiking a couple of hours to reach the good snorkeling spots. The road to Puerto Vargas is approximately 5km (3 miles) south of Cahuita on the left.

There is an extra $2-per-person charge for **camping.** The 50 campsites at Puerto Vargas stretch along for several kilometers and are either right on or just a few steps from the beach. My favorite campsites are those farthest from the entrance. There are basic shower and bathroom facilities at a small ranger station, but these can be a bit far from some of the campsites.

See map p. 325. Located south of Cahuita village. The primary public entrance to the park is at the southern edge of the village. The official park entrance and campsites are at Puerto Vargas 7km (4⅓ miles) south of Cahuita. ☎ 755-0060. Admission: $6 per day at the Puerto Vargas entrance; voluntary donation at the town entrance. Open: Daily 6 a.m.–5:30 p.m.

More cool things to see and do

- ✔ **Horseback riding: Brigitte** (☎ 755-0053; www.brigittecahuita.com) rents horses for $10 per hour (you must have experience) and offers guided horseback tours for $35 to $40. She also rents mountain bikes for $8 per day or $25 per week.

- ✔ **Snorkeling:** Although there's snorkeling right from the beach at Puerto Vargas inside Cahuita National Park, the nicest coral heads are located several hundred meters offshore, and it's best to have a boat take you out. A three-hour **snorkel trip** should cost between $15 and $25 per person with equipment. These can be arranged by your hotel or with **Cahuita Tours and Adventure Center** (☎ 755-0232).

Shopping for local treasures in Cahuita

For a wide selection of beachwear, local crafts, cheesy souvenirs, and batik clothing, try **Boutique Coco Miko** or **Boutique Bambata,** which are both on the main road near the entrance to the park. The latter is also a good place to have your hair wrapped in colorful threads and strung with beads. Out toward Playa Negra, similar wares are offered at the gift shop at **Cahuita Tours.** Handmade jewelry and crafts are sold by local and itinerant artisans in makeshift stands near the park entrance.

Ask around town, and you may be able to pick up a copy of Paula Palmer's *What Happen: A Folk-History of Costa Rica's Talamanca Coast*. The book is a history of the region, based on interviews with many of the area's oldest residents. Much of it is in the traditional Creole language, from which the title is taken. It makes fun and interesting reading, and you just might bump into someone mentioned in the book.

If you're interested in the local music scene, you should definitely pick up a disc by Walter "Gavitt" Ferguson. The local 86-year-old calypso singer and songwriter is a living legend and has recently released two separate CDs of his original songs, *Babylon* and *Dr. Bombodee*. Ask around town, and you should be able to find a copy. If you're lucky, you may even bump into Walter, as well.

Living it up after dark in Cahuita

Coco's Bar (no phone), a classic Caribbean watering hole located at the main crossroads in town, has traditionally been the place to spend your nights (or days, for that matter) if you like cold beer and very loud reggae and soca music. **Ricky's Bar** (☎ 755-0228), located just across the street, is giving Coco's a run for its money. Check them both out; on any given night, you may be more drawn to one or the other. There are usually local women hanging out on the front porches of each establishment selling fresh *paty* (meat turnovers) or bowls of local stew.

Located at the park entrance at the southern end of the town's main street, the **National Park Restaurant** (☎ 382-0139) has a popular bar and disco on most nights during the high season and on weekends during the low season.

Puerto Viejo and the Southernmost Beaches

Although Puerto Viejo is farther down the road from Cahuita, it's more popular and has a livelier atmosphere, due in part to the many surfers who come here from around the country (and around the world) to ride the village's famous Salsa Brava wave.

As you head still farther south, you'll come to the most beautiful beaches on this coast, with white sand and turquoise seas. When it's calm (Aug–Oct), the waters down here are some of the clearest anywhere in the country, with good snorkeling among the nearby coral reefs. The recent paving of the road, all the way to Manzanillo, has made these beaches much more accessible, and there's been a slew of small moderately priced and budget hotels built along this stretch of coast.

This is the end of the line along Costa Rica's Caribbean coast. After the tiny town of Manzanillo, some 15km (9⅓ miles) south of Puerto Viejo, a national wildlife reserve stretches a few final kilometers to the Panamanian border.

Getting there

As with Cahuita, driving a rental car in Puerto Viejo gives you independence and the ability to explore the region on your own. However, if you want to leave the driving to others, bus and minivan services are available. You'll find information on all these options in the following sections.

By car

To reach Puerto Viejo, continue south from Cahuita for another 16km (10 miles). Watch for a prominent fork in the highway. The right-hand fork continues on to Bribri and Sixaola. The left-hand fork (it actually appears to be a straight shot) takes you into Puerto Viejo on 5km (3 miles) of paved road.

By bus

MEPE express buses (☎ 257-8129 in San José, or 750-0023 in Puerto Viejo) to Puerto Viejo leave San José several times a day from the Caribbean bus terminal (Gran Terminal del Caribe) on Calle Central, 1 block north of Avenida 11. The trip's duration is four and a half to five hours; fare is $5.70. During peak periods, extra buses are sometimes added. Always ask whether the bus is going into Puerto Viejo (you don't want to end up getting dropped off at the turnoff for Sixaola) and whether it's continuing on to **Manzanillo** (especially helpful if you're staying in a hotel south of town). Regardless, don't be surprised if it doesn't do exactly what you were told.

Alternatively, you can catch one of the frequent buses to Limón from the same station and then transfer to a Puerto Viejo–bound bus in Limón. These latter buses (☎ 758-0618) leave roughly every hour between 5 a.m. and 6 p.m. from Radio Casino, which is 1 block north of the municipal market. Buses from Limón to Manzanillo also stop in Puerto Viejo and leave daily at 6 a.m. and 2:30 p.m.

If you arrive by bus, be leery of hucksters offering you hotel rooms. In most cases, they just work on a small commission from whatever hotel or *cabina* is hiring, and, in some cases, they'll steer you away from one of my recommended hotels or falsely claim that it's full.

Grayline (☎ 220-2126; www.graylinecostarica.com) and **Interbus** (☎ 283-5573; www.costaricapass.com) both have daily bus service between San José and Puerto Viejo. The fare for either service is $25. Both companies will pick you up and drop you off at most hotels, both in San José and in Puerto Viejo.

Orienting yourself in Puerto Viejo and the southernmost beaches

The road in from the highway runs parallel to Playa Negra, or Black Sand Beach, for a couple hundred meters before entering the village of Puerto

Viejo, which has all of about ten dirt streets. The sea will be on your left and forested hills on your right as you come into town. It's another 15km (9⅓ miles) south to Manzanillo. Along this road you'll pass the beaches of Playa Cocles, Playa Chiquita, and Punta Uva. Aside from some short sections of gravel, this road is paved all the way to Manzanillo.

The **Asociación Talamanqueña de Ecoturismo y Conservación (ATEC),** across the street from the Soda Tamara (☎ **750-0398** or ☎/fax 750-0191; www.greencoast.com), is concerned with preserving both the environment and the cultural heritage of this area and promoting ecologically sound development. In addition to functioning as the local **information center,** Internet cafe, and traveler's hub, ATEC runs a little shop that sells T-shirts, maps, posters, and books. If you're looking to stay in Puerto Viejo for an extended period of time and would like to contribute to the community, you can ask here about volunteering.

Getting around

You can rent bicycles at almost every hotel or corner around Puerto Viejo, and they make an excellent means of getting around.

The town's main **taxi** driver is named **Bull** (☎ **750-0112** or 836-8219). You might find him hanging around the *parquecito* (little park), or you can ask a local to point you to his house. If Bull's not around or he's busy, you could try **Delroy** (☎ **750-0132**).

Spending the night

Almonds & Corals Tent Camp
$$$ **Manzanillo**

This isn't camping in any traditional sense, so don't expect to be roughing it. You'll find large raised platforms, big enough so that within the stretched-tarp roof and screened walls there's another large standing-room tent, providing double protection against rain and mosquitoes. This second tent takes up about half of the platform's screened-in floor space and still leaves room for a hammock, a table, chairs, and a bathroom area with a cold-water shower and toilet. Inside the tent you'll find either two single beds or one double bed, a small table, two oil lamps, and a small closet. The tents are in dense secondary forest, with nothing but screen and cloth for walls, so you'll feel very close to nature. There are wooden walkways connecting the tents to the main lodge and dining area. Perhaps the best part of the whole setup is the fact that Manzanillo Beach is just about 180m (590 ft.) away through the jungle. Snorkel equipment, sea kayaks, and a variety of tours are also available, and there's a zip-line canopy tour through the forest here that ends right at the beach.

See map p. 339. Manzanillo. ☎ 272-2024, or 759-9057 at the lodge. Fax: 272-2220. www.almondsandcorals.com. Rack rates: $150 double. Rates include breakfast, dinner, and taxes. Rates slightly lower in the off season. AE, MC, V.

Azania Bungalows
$ Playa Cocles

This collection of individual bungalows is an excellent option for those seeking a quiet, romantic tropical getaway. The spacious bungalows are set apart from each other amid the hotel's high flowering gardens, giving each a sense of seclusion. All come with one queen-size bed and one double bed downstairs and another double bed in the small loft. The thatch roofs are high-pitched and, combined with large, screened windows, allow for good cross-ventilation. The lounge area features a television with DirecTV, a small lending library, and a collection of board games. The newest additions here include a small, refreshing swimming pool and open-air thatch-roofed poolside restaurant.

See map p. 339. Playa Cocles. ☎ *750-0540. Fax: 750-0371.* www.azania-costa rica.com. *Rack rates: $75 double. Rates include full breakfast. Rates lower in the off season, higher during peak weeks. AE, DC, MC, V.*

Cabinas Casa Verde
$ Puerto Viejo

This little hotel is located on a side street on the south side of town and is my favorite hotel right in Puerto Viejo, regardless of price. A quiet sense of tropical tranquility pervades this place. The rooms with shared bathrooms are housed in a raised building with a wide, covered breezeway between the rooms. The front and back porches of this building are hung with hammocks and surrounded by lush gardens, where you'll find the showers and toilets. The rest of the rooms are spread around the small complex. Most are larger, with high ceilings, tile floors, private bathrooms, and a private veranda. There's also a small separate bungalow with a kitchenette. Everything is very well maintained, and even the shared bathrooms are kept immaculate. There's also a small but well-stocked gift shop, a coffee shop, and even a poison dart frog garden. Even though it's an in-town choice, there's great bird-watching all around the grounds here.

See map p. 339. Puerto Viejo. ☎ *750-0015. Fax: 750-0047.* www.cabinascasa verde.com. *Rack rates: $26–$31 double with shared bathroom; $44 double with private bathroom. Rates slightly higher during peak weeks, lower in the off season. AE, MC, V.*

Cariblue Bungalows
$$ Playa Cocles

This Italian-run miniresort is a wonderful choice. The rooms are spread around the well-tended and lush grounds. My favorites are the individual raised-stilt wood bungalows. The beds are covered with mosquito nets, and there's a small veranda with a hammock. The nicest features here are the bathrooms, with their intricate mosaic tile designs. The standard rooms are in a couple of concrete-block buildings with high-pitched thatch roofs. They're spacious and comfortable but not quite as private or charming as the bungalows. There's also a two-bedroom house with a full kitchen, for families or for longer stays. The resort has a midsize free-form swimming pool with swim-up bar, and plans to add an open-air yoga studio and exercise room. Cariblue is located about 90m (295 ft.) or so inland from the southern end of Playa Cocles.

See map p. 339. Playa Cocles. ☎ *750-0035 or* ☎ */fax 750-0057.* www.cariblue. com. *Rack rates: $75–$90 double; $180 house. Rates include breakfast buffet. Rates slightly lower in the off-season. AE, MC, V.*

La Costa de Papito
$ Playa Cocles

This small collection of individual and duplex cabins offers some of the same feel and character as Shawandha and Cariblue, with fewer amenities and less luxury — but at lower rates. La Costa de Papito is located just across from Cocles Beach, about 1.6km (1 mile) south of Puerto Viejo. The wooden bungalows come with one or two double beds, artfully tiled bathrooms, and an inviting private porch with a table and chairs and either a hammock or a swing chair. Only breakfast, snacks, and drinks are served here, but there are several restaurant options nearby, both in Puerto Viejo and farther down the coast.

See map p. 339. Playa Cocles. ☎ */fax 750-0080.* www.lacostadepapito.com. *Rack rates: $59 double. Rates lower in the off season. AE, MC, V.*

Playa Chiquita Lodge
$ Playa Chiquita

Set amid the shade of large old trees several kilometers south of Puerto Viejo toward Punta Uva (watch for the sign), the lodge consists of several wooden buildings set on stilts and connected by a garden walkway. There are wide verandas with built-in seating and rocking chairs. The spacious rooms are painted in bright colors. A short trail on the grounds leads down to a semi-private little swimming beach with tide pools and beautiful turquoise water. This stretch of beach is the site of a daily 4 p.m. volleyball game.

The owners have three children, ranging from a toddler to a teenager, and travelers with kids often feel like part of the family. The owners also rent out fully equipped houses for those interested in longer stays or more privacy and independence.

See map p. 339. Playa Chiquita. ☎ *750-0062 or* ☎ */fax 750-0408.* www.playa chiquitalodge.com. *Rack rates: $46 double. Rates lower in the off season. Rates include breakfast. AE, MC, V.*

Shawandha Lodge
$$ Playa Chiquita

If you're looking for an isolated and romantic getaway, in a style best described as rustic luxury, this small collection of individual bungalows is a great choice. Set in a lush patch of forest about 180m (590 ft.) or so inland from Playa Chiquita, Shawandha has the feel of a small village. Artistic flourishes abound. The thatch-roofed, raised bungalows feature painted exterior murals, high-pitched ceilings, varnished wood floors, and either one king-size bed or a mix of queen-size and single beds.

The bathrooms are practically works of art, each with original, intricate mosaics of hand-cut tile highlighting a large, open shower. Each bungalow has its own spacious balcony, with both a hammock and a couch, where you can lie and look out on the lush, flowering gardens. The beach is easily accessed by a private path, and a host of activities and tours can be arranged.

There's a large open-air restaurant and lounge where meals and drinks are served. The menu is an eclectic mix, featuring fresh fish and meats in a variety of French, Caribbean, and Polynesian sauces.

See map p. 339. Playa Chiquita. ☎ *750-0018. Fax: 750-0037.* www.shawandha lodge.com. *Rack rates: $90 double. Rates higher during peak weeks, lower in the off season. Rates include full breakfast. AE, MC, V.*

Dining locally

El Loco Natural
$$ Puerto Viejo INTERNATIONAL

A funky, hippy vibe pervades this second-floor open-air restaurant. Seating is at heavy wooden tables, and if the few smaller, more private tables are all taken, you can take any empty seat at one of the larger communal tables. The short menu features several vegetarian items, as well as fresh fish and some chicken and meat dishes, prepared in curry, Thai, and Mexican sauces. There's often live music here, running the gamut from reggae to jazz, to Latin American folk.

See map p. 339. On the main road. ☎ *750-0263. Main courses: $4–$10. AE, MC, V. Open: Thurs–Sun 6–10 p.m.*

La Pecora Nera
$$$ Playa Cocles ITALIAN

This open-air joint on the jungle's edge has quickly earned its reputation as the finest Italian restaurant in the region, if not the country. Owner Ilario Giannoni is a whirlwind of enthusiasm and activity, switching hats all night long from maître d' to chef to waiter to busboy and back in an entertaining blur. Sure, he's got some help, including his grandmother making gnocchi, but it seems like he's doing it single-handedly. The menu has a broad selection of pizzas and pastas, but your best bet is to just ask Ilario what's fresh and special for that day and to trust his instincts and inventions. I've had fabulous fresh pasta dishes and top-notch appetizers every time I've visited. A recent expansion and remodeling has only served to make this an even better and more enjoyable option.

See map p. 339. 50m (164 ft.) inland from a well-marked turnoff on the main road south just beyond the soccer field in Cocles. ☎ *750-0490. Reservations recommended. Main courses: $7–$26. AE, MC, V. Open: Tues–Sun noon to 10 p.m.*

Salsa Brava
$$–$$$ Puerto Viejo   SPANISH/MEDITERRANEAN

Fresh grilled seafood and meats are the specialty here, and everything is simply yet expertly prepared. The new owners have broadened the menu and improved greatly in the area of service and consistency. There's usually a wide range of fresh-caught fish available, grilled either whole or in fillets, plus grilled calamari, shrimp, or filet mignon. There are even several hearty vegetarian options. Wash down whatever you choose with the homemade sangria. The dozen or so wooden tables are painted bright primary colors and are set on a gravel floor under an open-air thatched roof. This is a great place for lunch, especially if you can snag one of the oceanfront tables with a picture-perfect view of the restaurant's namesake wave — Salsa Brava.

See map p. 339. On the southern outskirts of town. ☎ *750-0241. Main courses: $8–$15. MC, V. Open: Tues–Sun noon to 10 p.m.*

Soda Tamara
$–$$ Puerto Viejo   COSTA RICAN/CREOLE

This little open-air restaurant has long been popular with budget-conscious travelers and has an attractive setting for such an economical place. The painted picket fence in front gives the restaurant a homey feel. The menu features standard fish, chicken, and meat entrees, served with a hefty help-ing of Caribbean-style rice and beans. You can also get *patacones* (fried chips made out of plantains) and a wide selection of fresh-fruit juices. At the counter inside, you'll find homemade cocoa candies and unsweetened cocoa biscuits made by several women in town. They're definitely worth a try. Soda Tamara also has a second-floor open-air bar that's open nightly from 6 p.m. until the last straggler calls it quits.

See map p. 339. On the main road. ☎ *750-0148. Main courses: $3.50–$15. AE, MC, V. Open: Daily 7 a.m.–9:30 p.m.*

Exploring Puerto Viejo and the southernmost beaches

Miles of often deserted beaches backed by thick rain forest are the main attraction of this region, and in this section I tell you how to best enjoy them.

The top attractions

The Beaches South of Puerto Viejo

The beaches south of Puerto Viejo are arguably some of the best in the country. Here, thick rain forests and coastal coconut palms come right down to the shore, meeting soft white-sand beaches that front clear, blue Caribbean seas.

The first beach you reach as you head south out of town is **Playa Cocles.** This long, white-sand beach is popular with surfers, especially those not up to the challenge of the massive and treacherous Salsa Brava reef break.

Beyond Playa Cocles lies **Playa Chiquita.** This stretch is characterized by small protected patches of swim-able beach and tide pools punctuating a wavy coastline of exposed and shallow reefs. This is a good place to come and search out a little private cove or tide pool.

Perhaps the most popular beach down here is **Punta Uva,** or "Grape Point," a beautiful and protected curve of soft sand lying in the lee of a small forested hillside and outcropping. There's a short loop trail through the forest and over the rocks of this gorgeous outcropping.

At the end of the road lies **Manzanillo,** a tiny village with only a few basic *cabinas* and funky *sodas*. The town is the gateway to the Manzanillo-Gandoca Wildlife Refuge (see listing later in this section). The beaches just off the town, as well as those inside the refuge, are stellar. The whole area off the town and much of the refuge is protected by coral reef, making these some of the most beautiful beaches on the coastline, as well as some of the best for swimming.

If you have a rental car, you can explore the various beaches down here at your whim and leisure. However, don't fret if you are carless. To reach any of these beaches, you can catch the 7:30 a.m. bus from Puerto Viejo down to Manzanillo. There are a couple more buses throughout the day as well. The last bus back leaves Manzanillo at 5 p.m. It's always wise to check with **Asociación Talamanqueña de Ecoturismo y Conservación** (ATEC) about current local bus schedules. Call ☎ **750-0398** or ☎/fax 750-0191; also visit www.greencoast.com. You could also hire a cab for around $6 to Punta Uva or $9 to Manzanillo. Call **Bull** (☎ **750-0112** or 836-8219) or **Delroy** (☎ **750-0132**).

Alternatively, it should take you less than an hour each way by bicycle, with only two relatively small hills to contend with; except for a couple of short washed-out patches, the road is paved all the way to Manzanillo. It's even possible to walk along the beach all the way from Puerto Viejo to Manzanillo, with just a couple of short and well-worn detours inland around rocky points.

*See map p. 339. **Playa Cocles** is 2km (1¼ miles) south of Puerto Viejo, **Playa Chiquita** is 5km (3 miles) from town, **Punta Uva** is 8km (5 miles) away, and **Manzanillo** is about 15km (9⅓ miles) south of town.*

Finca La Isla Botanical Gardens

One of the nicest ways to spend a day in Puerto Viejo is to visit the Finca La Isla Botanical Gardens. Host Peter Kring, and his late wife Lindy, poured much time and love into the creation of this meandering collection of native and imported tropical flora. There are medicinal, commercial, and just plain wild flowering plants, fruits, herbs, trees, and bushes here. Visitors get to gorge on whatever is ripe at the moment. You're almost guaranteed to see some poison dart frogs here. There is also a rigorous rain-forest loop trail leaving from the grounds.

See map p. 339. A couple hundred meters inland from the Black Sand Beach on the road that leads into town. ☎ ***750-0046.*** jardbot@racsa.co.cr. *Admission: $5*

Puerto Viejo

ACCOMMODATIONS ■
Almonds & Corals Tent Camp **22**
Azania Bungalows **16**
Cabinas Casa Verde **10**
Cariblue Bungalows **15**
La Costa de Papito **17**
Playa Chiquita Lodge **19**
Shawandha Lodge **20**

DINING ◆
El Loco Natural **2**
La Pecora Nera **18**
Salsa Brava **13**
Soda Tamara **7**

SHOPPING ▌
Color Caribe **8**
Jewelry Factory **3**
Luluberlu **9**

ATTRACTIONS ●
Asociación Talamanqueña de Ecoturismo y
     Conservación (ATEC) **4**
Finca La Isla Botanical Gardens **1**
Manzanillo **22**
Manzanillo-Gandoca Wildlife Refuge **23**
Punta Uva Butterfly Garden **21**

NIGHTLIFE ★
El Bambu **12**
El Tesoro **14**
Hot Rocks **5**
Johnny's Place/Mike's Playground **6**
Stanford's **11**

*per person for the garden or loop trail, or $10 per person with the guided tour. Open:
Fri–Mon 10 a.m.–4 p.m., but visits can sometimes be arranged for other days with
advance notice.*

Manzanillo-Gandoca Wildlife Refuge

The Manzanillo-Gandoca Wildlife Refuge encompasses the small village of
Manzanillo and extends all the way to the Panamanian border. Manatees,
crocodiles, and more than 350 species of birds live within the boundaries
of the reserve. The reserve also includes the coral reef offshore — when
the seas are calm, this is the best snorkeling and diving spot on this entire
coast. Four species of sea turtles nest on one 8.9km (5½-mile) stretch of
beach within the reserve between March and July. Three species of dolphin
also inhabit and frolic in the waters just off Manzanillo. Many local tour
guides and operators offer boat trips out to spot them. If you're looking for
a more in-depth experience, including research internships, contact the
Talamanca Dolphin Foundation (☎ **759-9115;** www.dolphinlink.org).

If you want to explore the refuge, you can easily find the single, well-maintained trail by walking along the beach just south of town until you have to wade across a small river. On the other side, you'll pick up the trail head. Otherwise, you can ask around the village for local guides or check out **Aquamor** (☎ 759-9012), a kayak and dive operation located on the one main road in Manzanillo. These folks rent kayaks for $6 per hour and offer a variety of guided excursions for between $15 and $55 per person. Depending on tides and sea conditions, this is a great way to explore the mangroves and estuaries, visit several nearby beaches, and even snorkel or dive the nearby coral reef.

See map p. 339. 10km (6 miles) southeast of Puerto Viejo. ☎ *750-0398. Open: Daily 7 a.m.–4 p.m.*

More cool things to see and do

- ✔ **Getting to know the local culture:** The **Asociación Talamanqueña de Ecoturismo y Conservación (ATEC;** ☎ 750-0398 or ☎/fax 750-0191; www.greencoast.com) offers half-day and full-day tours that focus on nature and either the local Afro-Caribbean culture or the indigenous Bribri culture. These tours pass through farms and forests, and along the way you'll learn about local history, customs, medicinal plants, and mythology. You'll also have an opportunity to see sloths, monkeys, iguanas, keel-billed toucans, and other wildlife.

  You'll find a range of different tours through the nearby Bribri Indians' Kékóldi Reserve, as well as more strenuous hikes through the primary rain forest. Bird walks and night walks will help you spot more of the area wildlife; there are even overnight camping treks. The local guides who lead these tours have a wealth of information and make a hike through the forest a truly educational experience. Half-day walks (and night walks) are $15, and a full day costs between $25 and $40. ATEC can arrange snorkeling trips to the nearby coral reefs, as well as snorkeling and fishing trips in dugout canoes. A half-day of snorkeling or fishing costs around $20 to $40 per person.

- ✔ **Scuba diving and snorkeling:** Scuba divers can check in with **Aquamor** (☎ 759-9012) or **Reef Runners Dive Shop** (☎ 750-0480). Between them, these two operations frequent about ten different dive sites between Punta Uva and Manzanillo. When the seas are calm and visibility is good, this beach offers some good snorkeling and diving.

- ✔ **Surfing:** Just offshore from Puerto Viejo's tiny village park is a shallow reef where powerful storm-generated waves sometimes reach 6m (20 ft.). **Salsa Brava,** as it's known, is the prime surf break on the Caribbean coast. Even when the waves are small, this spot is recommended only for very experienced surfers because of the danger of the reef. Less experienced riders should head for the beach break at Playa Cocles. You can rent surfboards and boogie boards from several makeshift roadside stands around town.

✔ **Taking a yoga class or getting a massage:** If either of these options sounds interesting, check in with **Samasati** (☎ 750-0315; www. samasati.com), a lovely jungle yoga retreat with spectacular hillside views of the Caribbean Sea and surrounding forests. You can come up for yoga classes ($12), meditations ($5), or private massages ($60–$110) with advance notice. Samasati is located a couple of kilometers before Puerto Viejo (near the turnoff for Bribri) and roughly 1.6km (1 mile) up into the jungle.

✔ **Visiting a butterfly garden:** Just outside of Punta Uva, you'll find the **Punta Uva Butterfly Garden** (☎ 750-0086). This small yet well-run facility is the only butterfly-breeding and production facility along the coast and is open daily from 8 a.m. to 4 p.m. Admission is $5 for adults; children enter free.

Shopping for local treasures

Puerto Viejo attracts a lot of local and international bohemians, who seem to survive solely on the sale of handmade jewelry, painted ceramic trinkets (mainly pipes and cigarette-lighter holders), and imported Indonesian textiles. You'll find them at makeshift stands set up by the town's *parquecito* (little park), in a line of wooden kiosks fronting the sea between Soda Tamara and Stanford's.

If you venture away from the makeshift artisan stands, **Luluberlu,** located inland across from Cabinas Guaraná, features locally produced craftwork, including shell mobiles and mirrors with mosaic-inlaid frames, as well as imports from Thailand and India. **The Jewelry Factory** and **Color Caribe,** both on the main road into town, sell a wide range of jewelry, crafts, and gift items, as well as Costa Rican hammocks.

Living it up after dark in Puerto Viejo

Puerto Viejo has one of the best nightlife scenes in the country. There are two main discos/bars in town. **Johnny's Place** (☎ 750-0623), also known as **Mike's Playground,** is near the Rural Guard station, about a block or so north of the ATEC office. You'll find **Stanford's** (☎ 750-0608) overlooking the water out near Salsa Brava just as the main road heads

South Caribbean Music Festival

Each year, the folks at Playa Chiquita Lodge (see earlier in this chapter) organize a month-long festival of concerts and workshops featuring local and national musical groups and solo artists. The dates vary, but the festival tends to fall somewhere during the months of March and April and always ends the week before Easter. Concerts are held on Fridays and weekends at Playa Chiquita Lodge and other venues around the area.

south of town. Both have small dance floors with ground-shaking reggae and rap rhythms blaring. The action usually spills out from the dance floor at both joints on most nights. I like the atmosphere better at Johnny's, where they have tables and candles set out on the sand, near the water's edge.

Another place I like is **El Bambú** (no phone), just beyond Stanford's on the road toward Punta Uva. It's smaller and more intimate than either of the other bars, yet it still packs them in and gets them dancing on Monday or Friday reggae nights.

The newest, largest, and loudest place in town is **Hot Rocks** (☎ 750-0525), a large dirt lot with some canvas catering tents over its bar and some of its table area. This place, which is located right where the main road hits the water, also has a huge screen upon which late-run movies are projected each night.

Finally, just south of town, at the start of Cocles Beach, **El Tesoro** (☎ 750-0128) hosts open jam sessions every Wednesday night.

Tortuguero

Tortuguero comes from the Spanish name for the giant sea turtles *(tortugas)* that nest on the beaches of this region every year from early March to mid-October. The chance to see this nesting attracts many people to this remote region, but just as many come to explore the intricate network of jungle canals that serve as the region's main transportation arteries. This stretch of coast is connected to Limón, the Caribbean coast's only port city, by a series of rivers and canals that parallel the sea, often running only about 90m (295 ft.) from the beach. This aquatic highway is lined for most of its length with a dense rain forest that is home to howler and spider monkeys, three-toed sloths, toucans, and great green macaws. A trip up the canals is a bit like cruising the Amazon, but on a much smaller scale.

Getting there

Independent travel is not the norm in this area, although it's possible. Most folks rely on their lodge for boat transportation through the canals and into town. At most of the lodges around Tortuguero, almost every-thing (bus rides to and from, boat trips through the canals, and even family-style meals) is done in groups. Depending on a variety of factors, this group feeling can be intimate and rewarding, or overwhelming and impersonal.

By air

Nature Air (☎ 800-235-9272 in the United States and Canada, 299-6000 in Costa Rica; www.natureair.com) and **Sansa** (☎ 221-9414; www.flysansa.com) both have regular daily flights to the small airstrip in

Tortuguero. In addition, many lodges in this area operate charter flights as part of their package trips. Flights take between 35 and 45 minutes and cost $58 each way on Sansa, $66 each way on Nature Air.

 It always pays to check with both Sansa and Nature Air. Additional flights are often added during the high season, and departure times can vary according to weather or the whims of the airline.

By land and water

You can't drive to Tortuguero. If you have a car, your best bet is to leave it in San José and take an organized tour or drive it to Limón or Moín, find a secure hotel or public parking lot, and then follow my directions for arriving by boat. You can also leave your car at the lot at Caño Blanco Marina (☎ 256-9444), but you should try to arrange your boat transportation and lodging in advance. (There is actually a road sign declaring TORTUGUERO at the turnoff for Caño Blanco Marina.) There is also secure parking in La Pavona, which meets the boats plying the Cariari and La Pavona route outlined here.

Flying to Tortuguero is convenient if you don't have much time, but a boat trip through the canals and rivers of this region is often the highlight of any visit to Tortuguero. However, although this trip can be stunning and exciting, it can also be tiring and uncomfortable. You'll first have to ride by car, bus, or minivan from San José to Moín, Caño Blanco, or one of the other embarkation points; then it's two to three hours on a boat, usually with hard wooden benches or plastic seats.

All of the more expensive lodges listed later in this chapter offer their own bus and boat transportation packages, which include the boat ride through the canals. However, if you're coming here independently, you'll have to arrange your own transportation. In this case, you have a few options.

The most traditional option is to get yourself first to Limón and then to the docks in Moín, just north of Limón, and try to find a boat on your own. Buses leave roughly every half-hour throughout the day for Limón from **Gran Terminal del Caribe,** on Calle Central, 1 block north of Avenida 11 (☎ 222-0610). If you're coming by car, make sure you drive all the way to Limón or Moín unless you have prior arrangements out of Cariari or Caño Blanco Marina.

From Limón, you can catch one of the periodic local buses to Moín right from the main bus terminal or hire a taxi for around $5. There are always plenty of taxis hanging around the bus terminal and cruising the streets of Limón. **Taxi Limón** is the main cab company (☎ 758-1539).

At the docks, you should be able to negotiate a fare of between $50 and $70, depending on how many people you can round up to go with you. These boats tend to depart between 8 and 10 a.m. every morning. Usually, the fare you pay covers the return trip as well, and you can arrange with the captain to take you back when you're ready to leave. The trip from Moín to Tortuguero takes between three and four hours.

It is also possible to get to Tortuguero by bus and boat from Cariari. This is the cheapest and most adventurous means of reaching Tortuguero from San José, but it's also more work — and if you miss a connection or the boats aren't running, you could get stuck in a backwater banana village. To take this route, begin by catching the 9 a.m. direct bus to Cariari from the **Gran Terminal del Caribe,** on Calle Central, 1 block north of Avenida 11 (☎ **222-0610**). This bus will actually drop you off in a new terminal in Cariari, from which you'll have to walk 5 blocks north to catch the noon bus to La Pavona. A boat will be waiting to meet the bus at the dock at the edge of the river at around 1:30 p.m. The fare to Tortuguero should be between $7 and $10 each way. Return boats leave Tortuguero for Cariari every morning at 6 and 11:30 a.m., making return bus connections.

Be careful if you decide to take this latter route. I've received reports of unscrupulous operators providing misinformation to tourists. Be especially careful if the folks selling you boat transportation aggressively steer you to a specific hotel option, claim that your first choice is full, or insist that you must buy a package with them that includes the transportation, lodging, and guide services. If you have doubts or want to check on the current state of this route, contact Daryl Loth in Tortuguero (☎ **833-0827;** safari@racsa.co.cr).

Orienting yourself in Tortuguero

Tortuguero is one of the most remote locations in Costa Rica. There are no roads into this area and no cars in the village, so all transportation is by boat or foot. Most of the lodges are spread out over several kilometers to the north of the village of Tortuguero on either side of the main canal; the small airstrip is at the north end of the beachside spit of land.

Tortuguero Village is a tiny collection of houses connected by footpaths. The village is spread out on a thin spit of land, bordered on one side by the Caribbean Sea and on the other by the main canal. At most points, it's less than 300m (984 ft.) wide. In the center of the village you'll find a small children's playground and a soccer field, as well as a kiosk that has information on the cultural and natural history of this area.

There is a private **information center** (☎ **833-0827**) in front of the Catholic church in the center of town. This is a good place for independent travelers looking to arrange local tours and onward travel.

Getting around

Transportation in and around Tortuguero is either by foot or small boat. If you stay at a hotel on the ocean side of the canal, you'll be able to walk into and explore the village at your leisure; if you're across the canal, you'll be dependent on the lodge's boat transportation.

Tortuguero

ACCOMMODATIONS ■
Casa Marbella **2**
Laguna Lodge **6**
Mawamba Lodge **5**
Tortuga Lodge **7**

DINING ◆
Miss Junie's Restaurant **3**

ATTRACTIONS ●
Tortuguero National Park **1**
Caribbean Conservation Corporation's
  Visitors' Center and Museum **4**

There are no banks, ATMs, or currency-exchange houses in Tortuguero, be sure to bring sufficient cash in colones to cover any expenses and incidental charges. The local hotels and shops generally charge a bit of a commission to exchange dollars.

Spending the night

Casa Marbella
$ Tortuguero Village

This in-town house is a great choice for budget travelers looking for a bit more comfort and care than that offered at most of the more inexpensive in-town options. The four rooms here all have high ceilings, tile floors, firm mattresses, and white walls with varnished wood trim. Owner Daryl Loth is a longtime resident and well-respected naturalist guide. Breakfast is served on a little patio facing the main Tortuguero canal in back of the house. A wide range of tours and onward travels can be arranged. They're planning to add a library, lounge, and small Internet cafe.

See map p. 345. Tortuguero. ☎ *709-8011, 709-8094, or 833-0827. Fax: 709-8011 or 709-8094.* http://casamarbella.tripod.com. *Rack rates: $48 double. Rates include breakfast. Rates lower in the off season. No credit cards.*

Laguna Lodge
$$$ Tortuguero

This comfortable lodge is located 2km (1¼ miles) north of Tortuguero Village, on the ocean side of the main canal (which allows you to walk along the beach and into town, at your leisure). The rooms are all spacious and attractive. Most have wood walls, waxed hardwood floors, and tiled bathrooms with screened upper walls to let in air and light. Each room also has a little shared veranda overlooking flowering gardens.

The large dining room, where basic buffet-style meals are served, is located on a free-form deck that extends out over the Tortuguero Canal. Another covered deck, also over the water, is strung with hammocks for lazing away the afternoons. Several covered *palapa* huts strung with hammocks have also been built among the flowering ginger and hibiscus. There's a large and inviting pool, with a poolside bar and grill. All the standard Tortuguero tours are available.

See map p. 345. Tortuguero. ☎ *225-3740 for reservations, or 709-8082 at the lodge. Fax: 283-8031.* www.lagunatortuguero.com. *Rack rates: $398 double for 2 days/ 1 night; $498 double for 3 days/2 nights. Rates include round-trip transportation from San José, tours, taxes, and 3 meals daily. AE, DC, MC, V.*

Mawamba Lodge
$$$ Tortuguero

Mawamba is quite similar to Laguna Lodge (see preceding listing). In fact, they're owned by brothers. Also located on the ocean side of the canal, Mawamba is even closer to the village. Rooms have varnished wood floors, twin beds, hot-water showers, ceiling fans, and verandas with rocking chairs. A recent remodeling has spruced things up, and the walls are now painted in bright Caribbean colors. The gardens are lush and overgrown with flowering ginger, heliconia, and hibiscus. There are plenty of hammocks around for anyone who wants to kick back and a beach volleyball court for those who don't.

The family-style meals here are above average for Tortuguero. Rates include a four-hour boat ride through the canals and a guided forest hike. These folks have an extensive menu of kayaking tours and excursions, including one package in which you actually kayak part of the way into Tortuguero. There's a small gift shop on the premises, a small butterfly garden, and nightly lectures and slide shows that focus on the natural history of this area.

See map p. 345. Tortuguero. ☎ *293-8181 or 709-8100. Fax: 239-7657.* www.grupo mawamba.com. *Rack rates: $418 double for 2 days/1 night; $524 double for 3 days/ 2 nights. Rates include round-trip transportation from San José, 3 meals daily, taxes, and some tours. Rates lower in the off season. AE, MC, V.*

Tortuga Lodge
$$$$ Tortuguero

This is one of the oldest hotels in Tortuguero, but thanks to steady renovations, maintenance, and additions, it has not only aged well but has improved over time. The nicest feature here is the long multilevel deck located off the main dining room, where you can sit and dine, sip a cool tropical drink, or just take in the view as the water laps against the docks at your feet.

There's also a lovely little pool built by the water's edge and designed to create the illusion that it blends into Tortuguero's main canal. Most of the rooms have new furniture, tropical décor, and loads of freshly varnished hardwood. They come with either one double and one twin bed or one king-size bed; each room has a ceiling fan and a comfortable private bathroom. If possible, I'd opt for the second-floor rooms, which feature varnished wood walls and floors and come with a small, covered veranda. There's also a new two-bedroom, two-bath, second-floor penthouse suite, great for families or those wanting more space.

Run by Costa Rica Expeditions, service here is top-notch, as are the family-style meals. There are several acres of forest behind the lodge, and a few kilometers of trails wind their way through the trees. This is a great place to look for howler monkeys and colorful poison-arrow frogs.

See map p. 345. Tortuguero. ☎ *257-0766 in San José, or 710-8016 at the lodge. Fax: 257-1665.* www.costaricaexpeditions.com. *Rack rates: $578 double for 2 days/1 night; $758 double for 3 days/2 nights. Rates include round-trip transportation (bus and boat one-way, charter flight the other) from San José, tours, taxes, and 3 meals daily. Rates lower in the off season, slightly higher during peak periods. AE, MC, V.*

Dining locally

Miss Junie's Restaurant
$ Tortuguero Village   CARIBBEAN/COSTA RICAN

There's little in the way of style or flare at this simple, screened-in restaurant with concrete floors and spartan décor. But the food is hearty and well-prepared, and Miss Junie is a delightful host. Have the local rice and beans cooked in coconut milk along with some fresh fish or lobster.

See map p. 345. Tortuguero Village. ☎ *709-8102. Main courses: $3–$8. No credit cards. Open: Daily 6 a.m.–10 p.m.*

Exploring Tortuguero

This is a very remote region, with no cars. All travel around the region is by boat. Most of the hotels include visits to the various attractions here as part of their package prices. If not, they will certainly offer them as added-on tour options.

The top attractions

Caribbean Conservation Corporation's Visitors' Center and Museum

Aside from the national park, the only other real attraction in town is the small Caribbean Conservation Corporation's Visitors' Center and Museum. The museum has information and exhibits on a whole range of native flora and fauna, but its primary focus is on the life and natural history of sea turtles. Most visits to the museum include a short, informative video on these turtles. There's a small gift shop here, and all the proceeds go toward conservation and turtle protection.

See map p. 345. ☎ *709-8091.* www.cccturtle.org. *Admission: $1. Open: Mon–Sat 10 a.m. to noon and 2–5:30 p.m., Sun 2–5 p.m.*

Tortugero National Park

Tortuguero National Park exists primarily to protect a major nesting site for several species of sea turtles. According to existing records, sea turtles have frequented the beaches here since at least 1592, largely due to its extreme isolation. Over the years, turtles were captured and their eggs were harvested by local settlers; by the 1950s, this practice became so widespread that the turtles faced extinction. Regulations controlling this mini-industry were passed in 1963, and in 1970, Tortuguero National Park was established.

Today four different species of sea turtles nest here: the green turtle, the hawksbill, the loggerhead, and the giant leatherback. The prime nesting period is from **July to mid-October** (with Aug–Sept being the peak months). The nestings take place at night, and if you're lucky you'll be able to watch one of these mammoth maritime reptiles laboriously dig a deep hole and then deposit scores of eggs into it. (Once the nesting is completed, the turtle covers up the hole and heads back to sea.)

When the turtles are nesting, you'll have to arrange a night tour in advance with either your hotel or one of the private guides working in town. These guided tours generally run between $10 and $15. Flashlights and flash cameras are not permitted on the beach at night because the lights discourage the turtles from nesting.

You can also explore the park's rain forest, either by foot or by boat, and look for some of the incredible varieties of wildlife that live here: jaguars,

---

Turtle tour tips

Visitors to the beach at night must be accompanied by a licensed guide. Tours generally last between two and four hours.

Sometimes you must walk quite a bit to encounter a nesting turtle. Wear sneakers or walking shoes rather than sandals. The beach is very dark at night, and you can easily trip or step on driftwood or other detritus.

Wear dark clothes. White T-shirts are not permitted.

Flashlights, flash cameras, and lighted video cameras are prohibited on turtle tours.

Smoking is prohibited on the beach at night.

---

anteaters, howler monkeys, collared and white-lipped peccaries, some 350 species of birds, and countless butterflies, among others. Boat tours are far and away the most popular way to visit this park, although one frequently very muddy trail here starts at the park entrance and runs for about 2km (1¼ miles) through the coastal rain forest and along the beach.

 Most people visit Tortuguero as part of a package tour. Be sure to confirm whether the park entrance is included in the price. Moreover, only certain canals and trails leaving from the park station are actually within the park. Many hotels and private guides take their tours to a series of canals that border the park and are very similar in terms of flora and fauna but don't require a park entrance.

See map p. 345. Located at the southern edge of Tortuguero Village. The Tortuguero National Park entrance and ranger station are at the south end of Tortuguero Village. ☎ *710-2929. Admission: $7 per day, or $10 for a 3-day pass. Open: Daily 8 a.m.–4 p.m.*

More cool things to see and do

- ✔ **Canoeing or kayaking on your own:** In the village, you can rent dugout canoes, known in Costa Rica as *cayucos* or *pangas*. Be careful before renting and taking off in one of these; they tend to be heavy, slow, and hard to maneuver, and you may be getting more than you bargained for. **Miss Junie** (☎ 709-8102) rents more-modern, lighter fiberglass canoes for around $10 for a half-day.

- ✔ **Enjoying the beach:** Although Tortuguero's beaches are excellent places to watch sea turtles nest, they are not particularly well suited for swimming. The surf is usually very rough, and the river mouths have a nasty habit of attracting sharks that feed on the turtle hatchlings and many fish that live here.

Fast Facts: The Caribbean Coast

Ambulance

Call ☎ 128.

ATMs

You'll find several ATMs in the port city of Limón and one in Puerto Viejo. There are no ATMs in Cahuita or Tortuguero.

Country Code and City Code

The country code for Costa Rica is **506**. There are no city or area codes within Costa Rica. To call from the United States, dial 011-506 plus the seven-digit number. From within Costa Rica, you simply dial the seven-digit number.

Currency Exchange

Most hotels will exchange money, although they often either charge a commission or give below the official rate. To get official rates, you'll need to head to one of the banks in Limón or the Banco de San José in Puerto Viejo.

Fire

Call ☎ 118.

Hospitals

The closest hospital is Hospital Tony Facio in Limón (☎ 758-2222), although there are either local doctors or a small clinic in each of the major destinations here — Tortuguero, Cahuita, and Puerto Viejo.

Information

There are few official information offices in southern Costa Rica. Most hotels have a tour desk, concierge, or helpful front desk.

Internet Access

There are Internet cafes in the general "downtown" areas of Cahuita and Puerto Viejo. A few of the isolated lodges in Tortuguero provide Internet access for their guests.

Newspapers

This is a very isolated region, although most lodges here receive local newspapers, including the *Tico Times*.

Pharmacies

There are pharmacies in Cahuita and Puerto Viejo but none in Tortuguero. The Cahuita pharmacy (☎ 755-0466) is located in the health clinic on the principal access road into town, about a block before you hit the main crossroad at the center of the village. Farmacia Amiga (☎ 750-0698) in Puerto Viejo is located in the small shopping center smack dab in the center of the village.

Police

Call ☎ 911.

Post Office

There is no post office in Tortuguero, but most hotels can mail your letters and postcards for you. There is a post office in Cahuita (☎ 755-0096), and another in Puerto Viejo (☎ 750-0404). Alternatively, most hotels can mail your letters and postcards for you.

Taxis

There are numerous taxis in Cahuita and Puerto Viejo. Try calling René (☎ 755-0243), Wayne (☎ 755-0078), or Dino (☎ 755-0012) in Cahuita. Taxi Limón is the main cab company in Puerto Viejo (☎ 758-1539). In Tortuguero, you'll either have to walk or tour around by boat.

Part VIII
The Part of Tens

"In Costa Rica everything's served with rice and beans. Just pay the man for your dry cleaning and let's go."

In this part . . .

*I*n this part, I dispel the top ten myths and misconceptions many folks have about Costa Rica. I then point you toward my list of the top ten moments and experiences available to travelers here. Finally, I give you ten interesting options to take advantage of any time you find yourself stranded in the rain in Costa Rica.

Chapter 22

Ten Myths about Costa Rica

Despite its current popularity, many misconceptions exist concerning Costa Rica. This chapter should help dispel a few.

Costa Rica Is Just for the Adventurous

Although this may have been true in the past, it's certainly no longer the case. You can rough it if you want, but you can also choose from a host of very luxurious options, which run the gamut from ultra-exclusive boutique hotels to large luxury resorts run by the Four Seasons and Marriott chains.

Costa Rica Isn't for Families

You won't find many amusement parks or video arcades here, but Costa Rica has a ton of fun and interesting stuff for the whole family. Options that will thrill all ages range from educational hikes in the rain forest, to rafting trips, to zip-line canopy tours, to butterfly gardens. In addition, Costa Rican hotels are increasingly gearing up to meet the needs of families. Children's programs and reliable babysitting are becoming more and more common.

Bugs Are Bad

You'll probably encounter far fewer biting bugs in Costa Rica than you'd expect. Moreover, the insect world is one of the most diverse, fascinating, and vitally important elements of all tropical ecosystems. Learn to love the shimmering beetles, long-legged stick bugs, and industrious leaf-cutter ants, and your visit to Costa Rica will be much more enjoyable. Of course, some insect repellent and light, long-sleeved clothing are always good when mosquitoes or sand flies are present.

Costa Rica Is an Ecological Eden

Although this is partially true, Costa Rica nevertheless faces serious challenges and threats from legal and illegal logging, as well as animal hunting and poaching and general development.

You Can't Drink the Water

Some travelers will get a bit sick or queasy with any change to their intestinal flora, but in general, the water is safe to drink in most major tourist hotels and destinations in Costa Rica. That said, if you're at all of a tender tummy, do rely on bottled water and drinks.

The Caribbean Coast Is Dangerous

This myth is quite prevalent in Costa Rica, and I blame a few high-profile crimes and basic racism in equal measure. The fact is that the Caribbean coast is no more or less dangerous than any other major tourist destination in Costa Rica.

It's Okay to Feed the Monkeys

Don't listen to any guide or hotel owner who tells you this. *Remember:* It is *not* cool to feed monkeys or any other wild animal. Wild animals are just that: wild. Close contact with humans — especially humans offering food — alters their behavior and survival mechanisms.

It's Always Raining in the Rain Forest

Sure, it rains a lot in the rain forest — over 508cm (200 in.) per year in many cases. However, these rains are often hard and intense for short durations. Apart from the period between early September and mid-November, it's rare for a visit to a rain-forest lodge to be characterized by constant rainfall. Mornings are often clear and sunny. During the months when the rain forests are, well, rainy, the Caribbean coast is generally bathed in sunshine and calm weather, so you're better off staying there. If you do get caught in the rain, remember, this is what makes the rain forest so vibrant and verdant.

Everybody Speaks English

Although most hotel, restaurant, and tour-agency workers have a working knowledge of English, most rural Costa Ricans do not. Knowing a few important Spanish words and phrases can go a long way toward improving your interactions and relationships with Costa Ricans. See Chapter 2 for more information.

Costa Rican Coffee Is the Best

Costa Rica does produce some of the world's finest coffee, but most of the best beans are destined for export. Moreover, Costa Ricans themselves seem to prefer a weak and very sweet brew. Still, you can get good coffee at most of the better restaurants and hotels, as well as in establishments catering to foreigners. If you're buying coffee to bring home, make sure you get whole beans, and shoot for a reputable brand like Cafe Britt, or one of the high-end roasters, like Cafe Milagro or Cafe Monteverde.

Chapter 23

Top Ten Costa Rican Moments

The activities, adventures, and attractions listed here range from the classic to the obscure, and from calm and mellow to wet and wild. Many more are outlined in the various destination chapters of this book. But be sure to try to fit a few of these into your trip to Costa Rica.

Pouring Salsa Lizano on Your Gallo Pinto

Salsa Lizano, a tart but mild sauce made with vinegar, and *gallo pinto* (rice and beans) are both ubiquitous staples of Costa Rican cuisine. So, order up some *gallo pinto* and pour on some tangy *Salsa Lizano.* If you want to really sound like a local, simply ask for some *"Lizano para mi pinto."* See Chapter 2 for more information on Costa Rican cuisine.

Waking Up to the Sound of Howler Monkeys

You can leave the alarm clock at home. At many jungle lodges, the first sound you'll hear is the deep guttural roar of a howler monkey. First reactions can range from fear to awe to laughter. If they start going off around 4 a.m., you might simply be annoyed. . . .

Catching Your First Wave

Costa Rica's miles of coastline are loaded with wonderful surf spots. Many of these are excellent waves for beginners. Sign up for a class and you could be hanging ten before you know it.

Zipping between Treetops on a Canopy Tour

Canopy tours are the rage in Costa Rica. If you're reasonably fit and not particularly *acrophobic* (afraid of heights), there's no reason not to strap on a climbing harness, hook on your pulley system, and glide off into the void.

Dancing All Night at El Bambú

Monday and Friday nights are the time to boogie at **El Bambú,** in Puerto Viejo. The dance floor is tiny, but there's plenty of space on the sand, where plastic chairs are set just steps away from the Caribbean Sea. The whole place is lit by the stars and moon and scores of candles. See Chapter 21 for more information.

Enjoying a Pacific Ocean Sunset

Villa Caletas (☎ **637-0606;** www.hotelvillacaletas.com) offers up perhaps the most popular sunset spectacle. But you can enjoy the beauty of a sunset over the Pacific Ocean from almost any beach in Guanacaste, as well as from most hotels and lodges in Manuel Antonio, Drake Bay, and along the Osa Peninsula. See Chapter 16 for more information on Villa Caletas.

Marvelling at the City Lights at a Mirador

If you're spending a night in San José, grab a cab and head for the hills. A *mirador* is the local name for a restaurant with a view. **Mirador Ram Luna** (☎ **230-3060**) in the town of Asseri, and **Mirador Tiquicia** (☎ **289-5839**), above Escazú, are two good options. See Chapter 12 for more details.

Soaking in the Pool of a Jungle Waterfall

If you have to hike a little bit first, it makes the dip that much more refreshing. The waterfall at Montezuma is one of the popular places to take a plunge. But I prefer the lesser-known **La Cangrejo Falls** inside **Rincón de la Vieja National Park.** See Chapter 11 for more information.

The Glint of Sunlight off a Quetzal's Feathers

The iridescent feathers of a resplendent quetzal can range from blue to green to turquoise to deep indigo, with various shades in between, depending upon the angle of the light. This, combined with its bright red chest feathers and brilliant yellow beak, make the quetzal one of the most spectacular birds on the planet.

Watching Arenal Volcano Blow Its Top

It takes patience and luck, but if you get to catch a clear night with active eruptions, you're in for a treat. I recommend getting a room with a view at **Tabacón Hot Springs Resort and Spa** (☎ **877-277-8291** in the United States and Canada; www.tabacon.com), that way you can just roll over and watch whenever a loud blast wakes you. See Chapter 18 for more information.

Quick Concierge

Fast Facts

American Express

American Express Travel Services is represented in Costa Rica by ASV Olympia, Oficentro La Sabana, Sabana Sur, in San José (☎ 242-8585), which can issue traveler's checks and replacement cards, as well as provide other standard services. To report lost or stolen AMEX traveler's checks within Costa Rica, call ☎ 242-8585 or 257-0155.

ATMs

ATMs are quite common throughout Costa Rica, particularly in San José, and at most major tourist destinations around the country. You'll find them at almost all banks and most shopping centers. The two major networks, Cirrus (☎ 800-424-7787; www.mastercard.com) and PLUS (☎ 800-843-7587; www.visa.com) are both present in Costa Rica.

Credit Cards

Visa and MasterCard are the most widely accepted cards in Costa Rica, followed by American Express, and to a much lesser extent Diners Club. To report a lost or stolen American Express card from inside Costa Rica, you can call ☎ 0800-012-3211; for MasterCard, ☎ 0800-011-0184; for Visa, ☎ 0800-011-0130; and for Diners Club, call ☎ 295-9393.

Credomatic (☎ 295-9898) is the local representative of most major credit cards: American Express, Diners Club, MasterCard, and Visa. It has an office in San José across from the Banco de San José on Calle Central between avenidas 3 and 5. It's open Monday through Friday from 8 a.m. to 7 p.m., and Saturday from 9 a.m. to 1 p.m. You can also call ☎ 295-9898 to report all lost or stolen cards 24 hours a day.

Currency Exchange

You can change money at all banks in Costa Rica. Sometimes, especially at state-run banks, the service and process can be slow and tedious. Hotels will often exchange money as well. You won't have to wait in line, but they may shave a few colones off the exchange rate.

There's a Global Exchange currency exchange booth just outside the customs and immigration area of the Juan Santamaría International Airport in San José, but they give a rather anemic exchange rate.

Be very careful about exchanging money on the streets; it's extremely risky. In addition to forged bills and short counts, street money-changers frequently work in teams that can leave you holding neither colones nor dollars.

Customs

Visitors entering Costa Rica are officially entitled to bring in 500 grams of tobacco, 5 liters of liquor, and US$500 in merchandise. Cameras, computers, and electronic equipment for personal use are permitted duty-free. Customs officials in Costa Rica seldom check tourists' luggage.

For information on what returning U.S. citizens are allowed to bring back from Costa Rica, download the invaluable free pamphlet "Know Before You Go" online at www.cbp.gov, or contact the U.S. Customs & Border Protection (CBP), 1300 Pennsylvania Ave. NW, Washington, DC 20229 (☎ 877-287-8667) and request the pamphlet.

Canadian citizens can send for the booklet "I Declare," issued by the Canada Border Services Agency (☎ 800-461-9999 in Canada, or 204-983-3500 in Costa Rica; www.cbsa-asfc.gc.ca).

U.K. citizens should contact HM Customs & Excise at ☎ 0845-010-9000 (from outside the United Kingdom, 020-8929-0152), or consult their Web site at www.hmce.gov.uk.

Australian tourists can get "Know Before You Go," a helpful brochure available from Australian consulates or Customs offices, or by contacting the Australian Customs Service at ☎ 1300-363-263, or www.customs.gov.au.

New Zealanders can get the New Zealand Customs Guide for Travellers, Notice no. 4 from New Zealand Customs, The Customhouse, 17–21 Whitmore St., Box 2218, Wellington (☎ 04-473-6099 or 0800-428-786; www.customs.govt.nz).

Driving

Driving a car in Costa Rica is no idle proposition. The roads are riddled with potholes, most rural intersections are unmarked, and, for some reason, sitting behind the wheel of a car seems to turn peaceful Ticos into homicidal maniacs.

A current foreign driver's license is valid for the first three months you're in Costa Rica. Seat belts are required for the driver and front-seat passengers.

If you're involved in an accident, you should contact the National Insurance Institute (INS) at ☎ 800-800-8000. You should probably also call the Transit Police (☎ 222-9330 or 222-9245); if they have a unit close by, they'll send one. An official transit police report will greatly facilitate any insurance claim. If you can't get help from any of these, try to get written statements from any witnesses. Finally, you can also call ☎ 911, and they should be able to redirect your call to the appropriate agency.

Electricity

The standard in Costa Rica is the same as in the United States: 110 volts AC (60 cycles). However, three-pronged outlets can be scarce, so bringing along an adapter is helpful.

Embassies and Consulates

The following embassies and consulates are located in San José: United States Embassy, in front of Centro Commercial, on the road to Pavas (☎ 519-2000, or 220-3127 after hours in case of emergency); Canadian Consulate, Oficentro Ejecutivo La Sabana, Edificio 5 (☎ 242-4400); and British Embassy, Paseo Colón between calles 38 and 40 (☎ 258-2025). There are no Australian or New Zealand embassies in San José.

Emergencies

In case of any emergency, dial ☎ 911 (which should have an English-speaking operator); for an ambulance, call ☎ 128; and to report a fire, call ☎ 118. If 911 doesn't work, you can contact the police at ☎ 222-1365 or 221-5337, and they may be able to find someone who speaks English.

Information

See "Where to Get More Information," later in this chapter.

Internet Access and Cybercafes

Internet cafes can be found all over San José and at most major tourist destinations in Costa Rica. Rates run between $1 and $3 per hour. Many hotels either have their own Internet cafe or allow guests to send and receive e-mail. If your hotel doesn't provide the service and no Internet cafe is close by, you can buy prepaid cards in 5-, 10-, and 15-hour denominations for connecting your laptop to the Web via a local phone call. Some knowledge of configuring your computer's dial-up connection is necessary, and be sure to factor in the phone-call charge if calling from a hotel. These cards are sold at many supermarkets and drugstores around the country, or contact Racsa (☎ 287-0087; www.racsa.co.cr), the state Internet monopoly to find out where you can buy one.

Language

Spanish is the official language of Costa Rica. *Berlitz Latin American Spanish Phrasebook and Dictionary* is probably the best phrase book to bring with you. However, in most tourist areas, you'll be surprised by how well Costa Ricans speak English.

Liquor Laws

Alcoholic beverages are sold every day of the week throughout the year, with the exception of the two days before Easter and the two days before and after a presidential election. The legal drinking age is 18, although it's almost never enforced. Liquor, everything from beer to hard spirits, is sold in specific liquor stores, as well as at most supermarkets and even convenience stores.

Maps

The Costa Rican Tourist Board (☎ 800-343-6332; www.visitcostarica.com) can usually provide you with decent maps of both Costa Rica and San José. They have booths at the airport, as well as in downtown San José.

Other sources in San José for detailed maps include Seventh Street Books, Calle 7 between avenidas Central and 1 (☎ 256-8251) and Librería Universal, Avenida Central between calles Central and 1 (☎ 222-2222).

Police

In most cases, dial ☎ 911 for the police, and you should be able to get someone who speaks English on the line. Other numbers for the Judicial Police are ☎ 222-1365 and 221-5337. The numbers for the Traffic Police (Policía de Tránsito) are ☎ 222-9330 and 222-9245.

Post Office

A post office is called *correo* in Spanish. The main post office in San José is on Calle 2 between avenidas 1 and 3 (☎ 800-900-2000 toll-free in Costa Rica, or 202-2900; www.correos.go.cr).

Mailing a postcard or letter to the United States costs 120 colones (26¢); 140 colones (28¢) to Europe. Given the Costa Rican postal service's track record, I recommend paying an extra 430 colones (94¢) to have anything of any value certified.

For important documents or goods, you could use one of the international courier services. DHL, on Paseo Colón between calles 30 and 32 (☎ 209-6000; www.dhl.com); EMS Courier, with desks at most post offices (☎ 800-900-2000, or 202-2900); FedEx, which is based in Heredia but will arrange pickup anywhere in the metropolitan area (☎ 0800-052-1090; www.fedex.com); and UPS, in Pavas (☎ 290-2828; www.ups.com), all operate in Costa Rica.

Safety

Although most of Costa Rica is safe, crime has become much more common in recent years. San José is known for its pickpockets, so never carry a wallet in your back pocket. A woman should keep a tight grip on her purse. (Keep it tucked under your arm.) Thieves also target gold chains, cameras and video cameras, prominent jewelry, and nice sunglasses. Be sure not to leave valuables in your hotel room. Don't park a car on the street in Costa Rica, especially in San José; there are plenty of public parking lots around the city.

Rental cars generally stick out, and they're easily spotted by thieves, who know that such cars are likely to be full of expensive camera equipment, money, and other valuables. Don't ever leave anything of value in a car parked on the street, not even for a moment. Also be wary of solicitous strangers who stop to help you change a tire or bring you to a service station. Although most are truly good Samaritans, there have been reports of thieves preying on roadside breakdowns.

Public intercity buses are also frequent targets of stealthy thieves. Never check your bags into the hold of a bus if you can avoid it. If this can't be avoided, keep your eye on what leaves the hold. If you put your bags in an overhead rack, be sure you can see the bags at all times. Try not to fall asleep.

Smoking

Although smoking isn't as prevalent as in most of Europe, a large number of Costa Ricans smoke, and public smoking regulations and smoke-free zones have yet to take hold. Restaurants are required by law to have no-smoking areas, but enforcement is often lax, so separate rooms aren't always available, and air circulation may be poor. Bars, on the whole, are often very smoke-filled in Costa Rica.

Taxes

There is a 13 percent sales tax on most goods and services. Restaurants charge 13 percent tax and also add on a 10 percent service charge, for a total of 23 percent more on your bill. Hotels charge 16.9 percent in tax, which includes the 13 percent sales tax.

There is a $26 departure tax for all visitors leaving by air. At press time, there was talk of streamlining the process and including this tax in the ticket purchase price. Until that happens, the departure tax must be purchased at branches of the Banco Crédito Agrícola de Cartago (BCAC), which has an office in the main terminal at the airport (open daily 4 a.m.–8 p.m.). The tax can be paid in advance, and is sometimes recommended, because the line at the airport can be slow moving. BCAC has numerous branches around San José and in some of the major tourist towns. The principal office in San José is at Avenida 4, between Calle Central and Calle 2, on the west side of the Parque Central (☎ 212-7000; www.bancreditocr.com for other branch locations).

Telephone

Costa Rica has an excellent phone system, with a dial tone similar to that heard in the United States.

To call Costa Rica from another country, dial the international access code (011 in Canada and the United States; 0011 in Australia; 0170 in New Zealand; 00 in the United Kingdom) followed by the country code **506**, and the local seven-digit number.

To make a direct international call from within Costa Rica, dial the international access code 00, followed by the country code (1 for the United States and Canada; 61 for Australia; 64 for New Zealand; 44 for the United Kingdom), and finally the local number.

To make a call within Costa Rica, simply dial the seven-digit number. There are no area or long-distance codes.

A phone call within Costa Rica costs around 10 colones (3¢) per minute. Pay phones take either a calling card or 5-, 10-, or 20-colón coins. Calling cards are becoming more prominent, and coin-operated phones are getting harder to find. You can purchase calling cards in a host of gift shops and pharmacies. However, there are several competing calling-card companies, and certain cards work only with certain phones. CHIP calling cards work with a computer chip and just slide into specific phones, although these phones aren't widely available. A better bet are the 197 and 199 calling cards, which are sold in varying denominations. These have a scratch-off PIN and can be used from any phone in the country. In general terms, the 197 cards are sold in smaller denominations and are used for local calling, while the 199 cards are deemed international and are easier to find in larger denominations. Either card can be used to make any call, however, provided that the card can cover the costs. Another perk of the 199 cards is the fact that you can get the instructions in English. For local calls, calling from your hotel is often easiest, although you'll likely be charged around 150 to 300 colones (32¢–63¢) per call.

Numbers beginning with 0800 and 800 within Costa Rica are toll-free, but calling an 800 number in the States from Costa Rica is not toll-free. In fact, it costs the same as an overseas call.

Time Zone

Costa Rica is on Central Standard Time (same as Chicago and St. Louis), six hours behind Greenwich mean time. Costa Rica does not use daylight saving time, so the time difference is an additional hour April through October.

Water

Although the water in San José is generally safe to drink, water quality varies outside the city. Because many travelers have tender digestive tracts, I recommend playing it safe and sticking to bottled drinks as much as possible. If you're really susceptible, you may also want to avoid ice.

Toll-Free Numbers and Web Sites

Airlines

Air Canada
☎ 888-247-2262
www.aircanada.ca

American Airlines
☎ 800-433-7300 in U.S.
☎ 248-9010 in Costa Rica
www.aa.com

America West Airlines
☎ 800-235-9292
www.americawest.com

Continental Airlines
☎ 800-525-0280
www.continental.com

Delta Air Lines
☎ 800-221-1212
www.delta.com

Iberia
☎ 800-772-4642 in U.S.
☎ 902-400-500 in Spain
www.iberia.com

Mexicana
☎ 800-531-7921 in U.S.
☎ 01800-502-2000 in Mexico
www.mexicana.com

Nature Air
☎ 800-235-9272 in the U.S. and Canada
☎ 299-6000 in Costa Rica
www.natureair.com

Sansa
☎ 221-9414
www.flysansa.com

TACA
☎ 800-535-8780 in U.S.
☎ 503-267-8222 in El Salvador
www.taca.com

United Air Lines
☎ 800-241-6522
www.united.com

US Airways
☎ 800-428-4322
www.usairways.com

Car-rental agencies

Alamo
☎ 800-327-9633
www.goalamo.com

Avis
☎ 800-331-1212 in continental U.S.;
☎ 800-879-2847 in Canada
www.avis.com

Budget
☎ 800-527-0700
www.budget.com

Dollar
☎ 800-800-4000
www.dollar.com

Hertz
☎ 800-654-3131
www.hertz.com

National
☎ 800-227-7368
www.nationalcar.com

Payless
☎ 800-729-5377
www.paylesscarrental.com

Thrifty
☎ 800-367-2277
www.thrifty.com

Major hotel and motel chains

Best Western International
☎ 800-528-1234
www.bestwestern.com

Clarion Hotels
☎ 800-252-7466
www.clarionhotel.com

Comfort Inns
☎ 800-228-5150
www.hotelchoice.com

Courtyard by Marriott
☎ 800-321-2211
www.courtyard.com

Four Seasons
☎ 800-819-5053
www.fourseasons.com

Hampton Inn
☎ 800-426-7866
www.hampton-inn.com

Holiday Inn
☎ 800-465-4329
www.basshotels.com

Inter-Continental Hotels & Resorts
☎ 888-567-8725
www.interconti.com

Marriott Hotels
☎ 800-228-9290
www.marriott.com

Quality Inns
☎ 800-228-5151
www.hotelchoice.com

Radisson Hotels International
☎ 800-333-3333
www.radisson.com

Where to Get More Information

You can get a basic packet of information on Costa Rica by contacting the Costa Rican Tourist Board (ICT, or Instituto Costarricense de Turismo; ☎ 800-343-6332; www.visitcostarica.com). Travelers from the United Kingdom, Australia, and New Zealand will have to rely primarily on this Web site because the ICT does not have offices or a toll-free number in these countries.

In addition to this official site, you'll be able to find a wealth of Web-based information on Costa Rica with a few clicks of your mouse. In fact, you'll do better off surfing because the ICT site is rather limited and clunky.

Some good places to start include *The Tico Times* (www.ticotimes.net), which puts up the top story from its weekly print edition, as well as a daily update of news briefs, a business article, regional news, a fishing column, and travel reviews. There's also a link to current currency-exchange rates. The Latin America Network Information Center (www.lanic.utexas.edu/la/ca/cr) is hosted by the University of Texas Latin American Studies Department and houses a vast collection of diverse information about Costa Rica. This is hands down the best one-stop shop for Web browsing. There are helpful links to a wide range of tourism and general information sites. Finally, Maptak (www.maptak.com) is the best site I've found for online maps. The site is still expanding and improving, and there's a tiny bit of a learning curve here, but this is an excellent resource.

Index